Great American Schooner Yachts

Honoring the Last Remaining Classic Schooner Yachts, Their Owners, and Their Designers

Rudolph Arp

Schiffer Publishing Ltd
4880 Lower Valley Road • Atglen, PA 19310

Other Schiffer Books on Related Subjects:

Chesapeake Bay Schooners, 978-0-87033-508-2, $34.95
Chesapeake Bay Skipjacks, 978-0-87033-451-1, $29.95
Pacific Square-Riggers, 978-0-88740-106-0, $19.95

Unless indicated, all sail plans are by the author or the schooner owners.

Library of Congress Control Number: 2012937336

Designed by John P. Cheek
Cover design by Bruce Waters
Type set in Arrus BT/Minion Pro

ISBN: 978-0-7643-4089-5
Printed in Hong Kong

Schiffer Books are available at special discounts for bulk purchases for sales promotions or premiums. Special editions, including personalized covers, corporate imprints, and excerpts can be created in large quantities for special needs. For more information contact the publisher:

Published by Schiffer Publishing Ltd.
4880 Lower Valley Road
Atglen, PA 19310
Phone: (610) 593-1777; Fax: (610) 593-2002
E-mail: Info@schifferbooks.com

For the largest selection of fine reference books on this and related subjects,
please visit our website at **www.schifferbooks.com**
We are always looking for people to write books on new and related subjects.
If you have an idea for a book, please contact us at
proposals@schifferbooks.com

This book may be purchased from the publisher.
Please try your bookstore first.
You may write for a free catalog.

In Europe, Schiffer books are distributed by
Bushwood Books
6 Marksbury Ave.
Kew Gardens
Surrey TW9 4JF England
Phone: 44 (0) 20 8392 8585; Fax: 44 (0) 20 8392 9876
E-mail: info@bushwoodbooks.co.uk
Website: www.bushwoodbooks.co.uk

This book is dedicated to my father.
Over the course of his two circumnavigations,
he has shown me that the World is small and round.

Contents

Foreword

The very word schooner conjures up images of beautiful vessels with two masts. I love reading sea stories about courageous sailors racing along at high speed in gale force winds. The romance of the sea is brought to life by a schooner. It's with good reason that aspiring seamen of the past learned their trade on these magnificent, demanding sailing vessels. Rudolph Arp has carefully written a contemporary history of schooners and the people who created them. It is a beautiful tale.

Many of America's most successful yacht designers cut their teeth in schooners. These men were the giants of their day, including John G. Alden, William Starling Burgess, Bowdoin Bradlee Crowninshield, Nathanael Greene Herreshoff, and Olin Stephens II to name a few. Each designer was commissioned to build sturdy craft that were swift, reliable, and beautiful. These are boats that age well, and so do the stories behind these enduring masterpieces.

Happily, several classic schooners have been restored. But the boats are just part of the story. Through the tales in this volume we can appreciate the vision of the owners. These were people with bold ideas. They wanted their craft to be sturdy, swift, comfortable, and able to sail long distances. These aspiring mariners wanted to travel with their families in comfort and in style.

As one reads *Great American Schooner Yachts*, you begin to appreciate the diverse rigs and designs. These schooners were built by hand and eye. There were no computers to test hull shapes or calculate rig loads. Schooners were built on the experience of their designers.

My first sail on a schooner was as a Mug (freshman) at the New York Maritime College. The schooner *Mistress* was our sail training vessel in the 1960s. It was great fun adding clouds of canvas to the masts. The boat just seemed to go faster with every new sail. My favorite sail was the "fisherman" that was set high above the deck between the two masts. *Mistress* was designed by the brilliant tactician C. Sherman Hoyt who helped Harold "Mike" Vanderbilt successfully defend the America's Cup aboard *Rainbow* in 1930. She was 60' on deck and often sailed with 15 Cadets. *Mistress* is featured here in this volume.

A few years later I was hired as the sailing coach at the US Merchant Marine Academy. It was a lucky day when the replica of *America* was donated to the academy. I pretended I was sailing aboard *America* with John Cox Stevens and his bold crew that defeated England in that famous race around the Isle of Wight in 1851. *America* was purposeful in appearance and powerful under sail.

Twenty years later I saw a picture of a nifty schooner that was for sale in a brokerage advertisement. My long time friend Jack King and I had been talking about getting a cruising boat. We found the advertised vessel in Maine and bought her on first sight. She was named *Silver Heels*. The schooner was featured on the cover of the first issue of *Wooden Boat* magazine in 1974. She was a classic that was originally designed in 1929 by Murray Peterson. The stock market crash halted any chance of construction that year. In 1963 Howland Jones acquired the plans and had the boat built. Jack and I owned *Silver Heels* for five years. During that time I learned to appreciate the schooner rig. We drew cheers in every port. My three daughters loved to climb the rig, sit on the bow sprit, and, like me, set additional sails. And yes, *Silver Heels* had a fisherman sail.

It's rare to see schooners these days. The sloop rig is easier to handle and I suppose that modern boats are less expensive with only one rig. Watch when a schooner sails past and all hands on your vessel will stop what they are doing and stare admiringly. Schooners seem to make one statement and yet, there is always a lot to see. I first look at the mighty bow sprit aimed toward the horizon. Next, I like to see the water being broken by the bow. Then I note the sail plan and count the various sails that are flying. I inevitably wonder if they could add more sail? And, I study the crew. Everyone onboard seems to have jobs to do. Schooners require that the crew be engaged all the time. You can be sure the designers drew plans carefully so the schooners could sail efficiently.

I am always intrigued on how yachts are created. It always starts with a dream, and occasionally develops into an actual build. Great credit should be bestowed on the creators of these important craft. "Important" because these yachts carried people and cargo. "Important" because they connected the world. Goodwill was a new commodity to the people of distant lands. A schooner on the horizon must have generated considerable anticipation for the local inhabitants.

These boats are worth preserving. Schooners are part of America's maritime heritage. Thanks to Rudolph Arp we can appreciate the thinking behind the construction of these classics and what it was like to sail on them.

Gary Jobson
Annapolis, Maryland

Introduction

PRESERVING THE LAST REMAINING AMERICAN SCHOONER YACHTS

The schooner yacht has become a symbol of American yachting since the schooner *America*'s victory in the 1851 annual Royal Yacht Squadron race around the Isle of Wight, which later became the America's Cup race. Since then, schooner sailing has been an American tradition, while in Europe owners have preferred the ketch, yawl, or cutter rig. The "golden age" of the schooner yacht in the United States was between 1851 and 1945. After World War II, the seemingly easier-to-handle ketch, yawl, and sloop rigs received preference in coastal and offshore sailing. But before the war, hundreds of schooner yachts were built in the United States. These yachts came with all sorts of characteristics and in varying dimensions. The schooner was used on some very small boats of not even 30' length on deck, as well as on the largest yachts of the time. The transatlantic races and the Bermuda race contributed to boost the design and construction of fast and seaworthy schooners. The Gloucester fishing schooners, which were working the North Atlantic in the roughest conditions, inspired many schooner yacht designs. Their elegant lines, long overhangs, and large sail areas became a common feature on the American schooner yachts.

The schooner rig is known today as a specific fore-and-aft rig whereby a boat carries two or more masts, the tallest being the mainmast, with a smaller mast standing before the mainmast. The masts can carry different types of sails, as long as they are rigged fore-and-aft. If the masts carried square sails, for instance, the rig would not be a schooner, but instead a brig (two masts) or a full-rigged ship (three or more masts). Traditionally, schooners carried lugger or gaff sails on all masts, and eventually one or more fore-staysails. Later on, and specifically due to the development of American yacht design in the early twentieth century, schooners carried a Bermudian or Marconi main on the taller mainmast and a traditional gaff sail on the foremast (sometimes even called "schooner mast"). In the 1920s, the staysail schooner rig was invented. In that rig, the main carried a Marconi sail, and between the masts was set a staysail. The staysail was attached at approximately two-thirds of the height of the mainmast and went down to the base of the foremast. The challenge with this rig for yacht designers was how to fill in the space between the two masts left over from the staysail. Many attempts were made to find an appropriate solution to this challenge, the most popular being to set a fisherman above the staysail. The performance of such a rig was not optimal, however, and it was generally compensated with a very simple alternative: by hoisting a huge gollywobbler-sail that covered the entire space between main and foremast, and sometimes even overlapping the mainsail. Although such a sail enhanced the performance of staysail schooners, it required a large crew to handle the resulting cloud of sail. This made a staysail schooner less attractive for small crews when they wanted the boat to perform well.

More recently, other rig configurations for schooners have been developed, such as the French schooner designs that only set staysails from the top of each mast. Undoubtedly, these rigs are easy to handle, and a lightly built boat might perform reasonably well with them.

However, the origin of the schooner as a type of boat was not so much related to the rig as to the hull. The first schooner-rigged boats were built in Europe, as early as the seventeenth century, although they were not called schooners. The nautical term "schooner" developed in the United States. Originally, there was a two-mast vessel, identified as a "ketch" or "catch," which carried a square sail on one mast and a gaff sail on the other. Such a ketch might be the New World ancestor of the schooner, a theory favored by naval architect and historian Howard I. Chapelle. The actual transition from ketch to schooner is impossible to document. One can only guess that it may have occurred sometime in the 1720s when the term "ketch" disappeared from colonial port records, and "skooner" or "schooner" became a regular entry. This coincidence might suggest that people preferred the term gradually—as part of a new trend.

Further hindering an attempt to categorize early vessels was the fact that, until about 1800, ships were not identified by their rigs. Classification was related more to hull form or to the use to which ships were put, not to a particular sail combination. In fact, rig and hull form had little relationship before then. The same vessel often changed its rig over the course of a voyage to adapt to the prevailing circumstances in the regions where it was sailing. What stayed the same was the hull. Therefore, the hull categorized the boats. Not until the nineteenth century did builders begin to design the hulls of their vessels to carry particular rigs and to identify them by their rig.

This explains why many historians do not associate so much the early development of the schooner to the rig, but rather to the "beauty" of the entire ship, since *schoon* means "clear" or "nice" in Dutch. In other Germanic languages, similar words for beauty are used (*schön* in German, for instance). This "beauty" was necessary to produce fast boats, such as those needed as pilot boats in the narrow entrance to the Chesapeake Bay. There, private competition for piloting required shipwrights to build extreme boats with elegant hull lines that allowed them to promptly meet incoming merchant ships to put a pilot on board. These boats usually had very simple rigs, often with two identical masts from which gaff or lugger sails were hoisted. The gaff sails seldom had topsails, and the standing and running rigging were kept to a minimum.

This primitive (but already elegant) pilot schooner was further developed during the War of 1812 with England and the subsequent blockades. The Baltimore clippers emerged and quickly dominated any traffic—be it of passengers, slaves, or perishable goods—along the United States' east coast. In Europe, the schooner rig became popular in the North and South. In the Baltic Sea, the rig was much welcome due to the good windward capabilities in the narrow waters between the many islands in the region. In the Mediterranean, the American schooner was seen as the most appropriate substitute for the more labor-intensive, lateen-rigged vessels. In Spain, the preference for the American schooners went so far as to incorporate into Spanish the term "pilot-boats." To this day, schooners there are called *pailebotes*.

In yachting, the schooner showed its superiority in the 1851 race around the Isle of Wight. There, the schooner yacht *America* won over a fleet of 15 yachts, most of them cutter- or sloop-rigged. However, the schooner rig was not the only characteristic of the *America* that made her so special. Another decisive item was her large beam, which contrasted with the narrow shapes of the British yachts. In Europe, it was believed that a narrow boat performed better than a beamy one. Only many years later, with the development of the contemporary racing yacht, designers realized that a large beam is not necessarily a negative aspect of a high-performance yacht, and indeed racing yachts today tend to be beamy.

The schooner rig became very popular for all types of sailing yachts in the United States, large and small, including for the growing category of cruising yachts, which some Americans had built in a larger scale since the 1920s to explore the East Coast, sail down to the Caribbean, or sail even into the South Seas. While this type of cruising became popular, new hull forms were developed to comfortably accommodate the large crews of a sailing expedition. The rigs on these schooners became simple and easy to handle. While this development took place for the larger vessels, some designers tried to create ever-smaller boats that could be used as comfortable coastwise cruisers for shorter trips. Some of these boats were so successful that they were even built in series as early as the late 1920s. In general, the 1920s constituted the United States' building boom for yachts, which was only halted when the Great Depression ruined many businesses, specially of the middle class, which until that moment had commissioned hundreds of yachts of 40' to 70' of length on deck. These boats had been built mainly on the United States' East Coast, but some also at the first boatyards established on the West Coast.

Most of the yachts that were built in these years have ended up at graveyards. Wooden boats usually had a lifespan of 30 to 40 years. Given that these boats were built with iron or galvanized steel fasteners, an entirely new build seemed more advisable than a restoration. For this reason, many yacht owners decided to scrap their boats and to replace them with new ones, according to more "modern" sail and construction plans, often not schooner rigged. Only very few boats have survived to our present time, and each has her own story of abandonment and extensive restoration by a loving and caring owner. This type of story repeats over and over, although each story is individual and unique because each yacht has had its own circumstances, misfortunes, and good luck. However, all these yachts have one thing in common: The owners who decided to restore them have been very special people. It takes a resolute personality and strong perseverance to successfully complete such a complex project like restoring a classic yacht. This book is dedicated to these people.

On purpose, this book presents great American schooner yachts with many different specifications. Although restoring such large yachts as *Deva*, *Mariette*, or *Shenandoah* were very complex projects, both financially and from the point of view of the human resources involved, they required the same taste, dedication to detail, and knowledge as that required for a smaller but not less professional restoration, such as *Reveler*, *Rose of Sharon*, or *Santana*. In all cases, those performing the restoration need a broad knowledge about the construction materials, the design, and the finish of classic yachts. Unfortunately, this knowledge is dwindling at a fast pace, and only very few people receive the necessary education in boatbuilding to go beyond epoxy-pitching.

In addition to these great restorations, there are also cases of great schooner yachts that currently are abandoned or in disuse in some far-away harbor, waiting for somebody with the necessary energy to get them back in shape and prevent them from being lost forever. Among the greatest American schooner yachts ever built, the current situation of the Herreshoff schooner, *Vagrant*, deserves such attention. It is hard to believe that she has been sitting in Japan for more than 20 years without any attention or significant maintenance at all.

In addition to honoring the boats and their owners, this book is an homage to the exceptional yacht designers the United States produced in the early twentieth century. This book features 34 yachts from 23 different yacht designers or design firms that worked either on the East or West Coasts of the United States. Names such as Alden, Herreshoff, Crocker, and Paine figure in this list because their extraordinary talent for yacht design is widely known. Other designers were less famous, but the quality of their yachts more than justifies their inclusion among the list of the big names. However, these 23 designers by far were not all those who designed schooner yachts at the time. There are many others that would have been included in this selection if space had not been limited. This book is an attempt to at least offer a representative selection of those designs that were produced in the time. Other designers that should be mentioned here are A. Cary Smith, Georg Stadel, Howard I. Chapelle, and Murray Peterson. Also, William Garden was very influential in the United States' yacht market with his pronounced sheer lines, long bows, and richly decorated counter sterns. Finally, Philip Rhodes deserves a special mention. He worked at Cox & Stevens when the firm produced some of the finest schooner and tall-ship yachts. He surely had his masterful hand in many of them. However, he was not exclusively responsible for the design of a large number of schooner yachts, and those few he directly had built under his supervision do not exist any more or have been converted into other rigs.

In this book the reader will find a selection of one or two schooner yachts of each designer. The aim was to highlight a larger and a smaller yacht from each of them. I have opted for a wide range of types of boats, even running the risk of skipping some great schooners that many would have expected to find in such a book. My goal was to present each designer with at least one great and representative example of his designs.

Sailors will be fascinated by the diversity of rig configurations and hull forms of the schooners featured in this book. Such diversity introduces into an entire universe of possibilities to sail a schooner yacht. It is a demonstration of the richness of American yachting heritage. The reader will find rigs as diverse as the extreme solution opted for on Sherman Hoyt's designed *Mistress*, with a very small foremast and an impressive mainmast; one of the first staysail schooner rigs used on Burgess' *Niña*; the gunter rig tried out on Crocker's *Mahdee*; the particular staysail schooner rig on Paine's *Joan II* (now *Viveka*); the extremely large mainsail and narrow foresail typical of the earlier big schooners, such as Chasebrough's gigantic *Invader*; the well-balanced gaff-rig on Alden's *Puritan*; the handsome knockabout rig on Wayland's *Rejoice*; and the very simple and innovative rig used on Gielow's large *Black Douglas* (now *El Boughaz*). Each rig fulfils a specific function and has its place in the history of yacht design.

Some of the ideas applied to boatbuilding on these yachts from the early twentieth century have been lost over time, and there are good reasons why they should be remembered again today. The schooner *Mahdee* is a good example. In 1930, this vessel was already equipped with an electric drive system. At that time, the boat could only operate under fully charged batteries for about one hour, but an idea was born. This idea has recently been applied on some modern yachts with much improved technology, and its success points toward the future of yacht propulsion.

Some explanation should be given as to the reasons that inspired me to write this book. In 2003, I received a very unusual request from a prominent European yachtsman while sailing on his large wooden schooner. While heading off Ibiza in a calm and complaining about our vessel's bad performance, he said, "Let us buy a classic racing schooner!" I soon set out to search for an appropriate boat. However, although I knew most existing classic yachts, it was difficult to hone down on the appropriate boat. After more than four years' searching, I finally found the right one. It was a 90' Alden/Bugatti-designed vessel built in 1939. We knew she needed a total restoration, and so I took on the coordination of a vast multi-million Euro project. In 2008, the financial crisis ruined the owner, and with it the schooner project. The boat has since been scrapped. The guilt one feels when witnessing such a sad succession of events is difficult to overcome. Over the years, I had amassed such a rich collection of photos, construction plans (many of which I drew), and information about the history of the American schooner yachts that I thought that this material should be made available to a broader public. My aim is to communicate the fascination for these boats and the need to properly preserve the last remnants of a bygone era—an era that placed American yacht design and construction at the vanguard of the international sailing scene.

It would not have been possible to ultimately finish this book without the help of many people. Special recognition goes to all the schooner owners who greeted this project and supported the idea of bringing together all their schooners into a publication dedicated to them. I want to thank them for their interest and enthusiasm. In this context, also, the American Schooner Association should be mentioned. Their staff was useful in locating some owners, and some members have been particularly helpful in getting material for this book. I also want to thank the marine photographers involved in this project. They have helped in providing high-quality photographic material of yachts that are difficult to spot. Also special thanks go to the Mariner's Museum of Virginia. Their archivists and library personnel were very kind when they located some extraordinary early photographs of the featured yachts. The vast collections of books, magazines, and photographs at the Library of Congress were also extremely helpful for researching the history of the yachts and their designers. I am also glad that long-time sailor, America's Cup veteran, and former schooner owner Gary Jobson agreed to write a foreword to this book. Only he could offer the right mix of American-schooner-yacht experience to introduce this book. Finally, I should mention with gratitude my wife, Nancy, who systematically supports all the exotic adventures I get involved in.

Rudolph Arp
Washington, D.C., January 2012

John Gale Alden: Designing Sweet Shear-Lines

BIOGRAPHY OF JOHN GALE ALDEN

The first name that comes to mind when thinking about classic schooners is usually the name of John Gale Alden. His popularity is based on literally hundreds of schooner yacht designs of all lengths, which shared many common features: They looked and indeed were amazingly seaworthy, beautiful, graceful, and fast.

John G. Alden was born in Troy, New York, in 1884, and from early on he spent summers at his family's home in Sakonnet, Rhode Island. He was exposed to boats so much that when he was 6, he built his first boat—a row-boat for the pond. Then came a cat-boat on the open western end of Buzzards Bay. When the family moved to the Boston area in 1900, he started drawing sketches of the boats he found there. He soon became fascinated by the famous Gloucester fishing schooners. They generated a fascination in him that lasted for the rest of his life.

Alden was largely self-educated in naval architecture, although he did take some courses at Massachusetts Institute of Technology. He started his design career under Edward Burgess, and in 1902 moved to Crowninshield, who was already a leading designer at the time. At Crowninshield's he got involved in the design of some prominent Gloucester fishing schooners. During the first year, Alden worked without pay as an apprentice at Crowninshield's, and in 1903 he got on the payroll as a draftsman. He worked on the lines and other plans for the 130' sistership schooners, *Tarter* and *Fame*. The *Tarter* later was acknowledged as the fastest schooner in the fishing fleet and was "highliner" for several years.

John Alden founded his own Alden Design Office in 1909. He struggled financially for years, but gradually commissions for schooners, motoryachts, catboats, runabouts, yawls, ketches, and sloops began to flow into the office at the Boston Inner Harbor. His office also offered insurance and brokerage services. As time went by, Alden became known worldwide for producing fast and seaworthy offshore yachts, particularly the "Malabar" series of yachts, which won several Bermuda races in the 1920s and 1930s.

In the first ten boats—all schooners—he explored and refined the concept of the small racing schooner. He won first places in the revived Bermuda Race with *Malabar IV* in 1923; with *Malabar VII* in 1926; and then with *Malabar X* in 1932, when the first four places were all taken by Alden designs. *Malabar XI* was a yawl; *Malabar XII* and *XIII* were ketch rigged. In addition, Alden designed, but only sailed very shortly, a *Malabar XIV*, which was yawl rigged. In size, the Malabar series ranged from 41'3" for *Malabar I* to 58'3" for *Malabar X*. However, Alden did not design only offshore racing schooners, but also schooner yachts that were competitive in local races. The impressive lines of the racing schooner *Abaco*, built in 1921 and still sailing today, clearly demonstrate that.

Alden become very popular and famous all along the East Coast for his many small and medium size schooners. These schooners were masterpieces of simplicity and ease of handling, making them superb cruising boats. The larger schooners were magnificent yet seaworthy racing machines, allowing many possible sail combinations, while they were expected to be sailed efficiently by large crews. All the boats, large and small, could be sailed shorthanded, however, and all were perfectly beautiful.

Thanks to their particular seaworthiness and ease of handling, the Alden schooners greatly contributed to generate enthusiasm for offshore racing and cruising. Their strong, deep, short-ended hulls, which offered safety, easy motion, dry decks, and greater interior volume, stand in marked contrast to the coastwise racers and cruisers of the day and set a standard for healthy offshore boats that endured and evolved considerably for several decades.

Alden arranged construction of most of these schooners in small Maine boatyards, at least when he oversaw their construction. This setup allowed for the boats to be built at a lower price than if built closer to Boston or New York. Sometimes he had the boats built on speculation, but few waited very long for a buyer.

From 1925 to the 1950s, the Alden office produced more than 900 different yacht designs, as well as designs for fireboats, tugs, and trawlers. About 150 schooners between 37' and 131' were designed during these years. Besides the types of boats already mentioned, relevant examples of Alden's work were the widely admired (and still sailing) 65'6" *Lelanta* (*I*) and the 74' *Lelanta II* (now *Lelantina*), as well as the 103' *Puritan*. We will describe this last schooner more in detail in this chapter. Alden's largest schooner designed and built was the 124' *Starling*, built of steel, but which unfortunately has not survived until today.

Alden produced plans for 323 cutters, including several versions of the popular 31' *Malabar Junior*; the series-built 36' *Coastwise Cruiser*; the custom-designed 50' *Cock Robin* (now yawl rigged); and the 57' *Zaida*. Among the 216 yawls and ketches were the series of Off-Soundings yawls; the 53' *Malabar XIII*; the 71' *Royono* (ex- *Mandoo II*); and the 75' *Karenita*. Most of these boats are still sailing today. In addition to this, Alden also designed many successful racing boats.

During World War II, Alden worked in partnership with the nearby office of Eldrige-McInnis, stocking up their firm with 90 employees. During the Korean War the Alden office expanded even further to more than 100 people and designed a number of vessels for the United States government. After the war, the primary handicapping rule in the United States was the CCA Rule, which encouraged more aerodynamically efficient Marconi-rigged sloops and yawls with mostly inboard rigs. This led the racing scene to lose interest in the classic schooner-rigged sailboat for which Alden had become so famous during the inter-war years. He tried to adapt to the new times and offered more modern designed ketches, yawls, and sloops, some of which went into fiberglass mass-production in the 1960s and later years. To a certain extent, however, even these boats preserved Alden's sturdy seaworthy charm with the typical Alden lines. When comparing the classic lines of an old Alden fiberglass boat with any newer production boat, Alden's boats stand out even today.

Probably no other design office of the time has produced as many successful designers as the large Alden office in Boston. All the young designers who learned with Alden later became famous in their own right and branded a very particular type of "American" yacht design. At one time or another, the following men worked in the Alden office: Carl Alberg, Sam Crocker, Clifford Swaine, William McNary, Charles MacGregor, Dwight S. Simpson, Winthrop L. Warner, Howard I. Chapelle, K. Aage Nielsen, Ralph Winslow, Fenwick Williams, Murray Peterson, Al Mason, Charles W. Witholz, Charles Schock, and Phil Ross.

John Alden retired from his office in 1955, selling the business to his associates. He died at the age of 78 in Winter Park, Florida.

THE ALDEN #309 AND #270 SCHOONERS: AMONG THE FIRST SERIAL SAILING CRUISING YACHTS

Until the use of fiberglass made the construction of sailing yachts easier and allowed for mass-production of hulls, only very few large stock boats were built. Although the establishment of the sailing rules for competition purposes favored the building of very similar boats, cruising yachts were usually not built as stock boats. Every owner had his boat custom built according to his or her own individual requirements regarding length on deck, interior layout, and rig configuration. Due to the individualized building method with wood, this was reasonable also from a cost perspective.

John Alden, however, was among the first to introduce the serial construction of cruising boats in the late 1920s, thus reducing the price for an individual sailing boat. In addition, he turned to several well-regarded and established ship builders in Maine who had the necessary skills and labor force to turn out these larger vessels economically. This in turn allowed access to cruising for people who until that time had been prevented from owning a sailing boat.

As a further development of his own *Malabar I*, *II*, and *III* designs, John Alden developed cruising versions of these boats for owners who demanded a sturdy cruising vessel to take the whole family with them for weekend cruises along the shallow New England coast. These boats were the *Heart's Desire* (design No. 253), which is still sailing, and the *Golden Hind* (design No. 266), which led to the popular 43', 270 designs. These schooners of design No. 270 were 43' long on deck and had a long keel with iron ballast. To our knowledge, only three of the sixteen schooners built to the 270 design remain today. *Revenge* is currently being restored in California, *Golden Hind* was restored in Warwick, Rhode Island, and *Vanda* is in a poor state of maintenance located in Hawaii.

The 270 schooners were 43'2" long on deck and 32'6" long at the waterline. With 11'6" they were not so beamy as the centerboarders, and instead they had a draft of 6'4" with a fixed keel. They displaced 13.56 tons All sixteen of these boats were schooner rigged.

Lady Jane II was the first 309 schooner built. She carried the original Aage Nielson sail plan, with a somewhat larger main sail than later versions of this boat built in series at Gaudy & Stevens (*Rosenfeld*).

Another photo of *Lady Jane II*, sailing a fresh breeze. Her rig is powerful, as if done for a larger boat (*Rosenfeld*).

The schooner *Allegro* is another very well-kept 309 Alden schooner. She sails out of Chicago (*Matt Howard*).

Another view of *Allegro* displays the original sail plan of the 309J, drawn by Aage Nielson. This sail plan features a larger mainsail and a more reduced fore gaff sail. The boomkin is a later addition to avoid having a running backstay (*Matt Howard*).

Design No.	Year Built	Original Name	First Owner	Shipyard	Later Names
270A	1926	*Twilight*	C.P. Cottrell, Jr., Westerly, RI	Harvey Gamage, So. Bristol, ME	*Jean, Purwana, Tethys, Sulu*
270B	1926	*Katinka*	O. E. Schoenwerk, Philadelphia, PA	Britt Bros, West Lynn, MA	*Vanda*
270C	1926	*Half Moon*	F. C. Nobel, New York, NY	Harvey Gamage, So. Bristol, ME	*Golden Hind*
270D	1926	*Hilaria*	A. E. Bibber, Philadelphia, PA	Harvey Gamage, So. Bristol, ME	*Trojan, Rubaiyat, Auf Wiedersehen, Sea Witch*
270E	1926	*Melodie*	R.A. Bell, Detroit, MI	Harvey Gamage, So. Bristol, ME	*Ptarmigan IV*
270F	1926	*Sea Lady*	Pearcy Mack	Harvey Gamage, So. Bristol, ME	*Shagwong*
270G	1926	*Dolphin*	P. J. Woodward, Providence, RI	Harvey Gamage, So. Bristol, ME	
270H	1926	*Sea Breeze*	H.A. Jennings, Bridgeport, CT	Britt Bros., Lynn, MA	*Eleda, Sea Breeze, Irma, Ann V, Revenge*
270J	1927	*Discovery II*	R.W. Everest, Philadelphia, PA	Britt Bros., West Lynn, MA	*Nyala III, Beatrice, Sea Waif II*
270K	1927	*Lion's Whelp*	Shaw Sprague, Boston, MA	Harvey Gamage, So. Bristol, ME	*Caroline, Manako*
270L	1929	*Ethel May*	F. D. Rolfe, Quincy, MA	F. D. Rolfe & Sons, Quincy, MA	*Bassana*
270M	1927	*Vagabond*	Horace B. Merwin, Bridgeport, CT	Portland Yacht Yards, Inc., Portland, CT	*Yolu San, Black Douglas*
270N	1930	*Ptarmigan*	Nelson Cabot, Boston, MA	F.D. Rolfe, Quincy, MA	
270O	1930	*Spindrift*	J. J. Dyer, Hingham, MA	Harvey W. McFarland, So. Bristol, ME	
270P	1943		Donald D. Stuart, Detroit, MI		
270Q	1943		Eugene S. Kayner, Alto Deva, CO		

Note: The schooners that still exist have a grey background.

The experience gained with these yachts laid the foundation a year later for design No. 309, another schooner-design built in a series as a cruising vessel. This design can truly be considered one of the precursors of the modern production boat. While Alden was the naval architect responsible for the overall design, the original hull and lines, stock sail plans, construction plans, and the cabin plans were drawn by Aage Nielson. The 309 was the first of many successful designs completed by Aage Nielson for the Alden office, no doubt with the collaboration and cooperation of other top designers of Alden's office. It can thus be observed that being a development of the famous Malabar designs from some years earlier, the 309 schooner that resulted was an exceptional cruising yacht, with a layout and room below deck which was not attained until much later by the first mass-production boats, where the maximum of livability below deck was required for ever-smaller boats.

The 309 schooners had moderate dimensions, which allowed them to be maintained and sailed by their owners. While it was not uncommon for the owner to have a summer boy or captain on board as paid crew to help with maintenance and sailing of the vessel, the 309s are easily sailed by two people (note that the well-regarded yacht designer Ralph Stanley started out as cook and crew in 1947 on the 309 *Niliraga* for Mr. Dunn). The schooners had a length on deck of 43'3"; a waterline length of 33'3"; a beam of 12'6"; and a draft of 4'2" with the board up. While relatively small, the boats displace about 17 tons when they were wet and laden, while the design displacement was 14 tons. There were two stock sail plans available, a generous gaff on gaff plan with a double headsail, and a working sail area of 1,100 sq.ft. that also carried a main topsail and fisherman staysail (Plan B). The most popular sail plan (Plan A) was a very striking tall jib headed or Marconi main, with a gaff foresail and a single forestaysail (jib) on a fixed boom with a working sail area of 1,015 sq.ft exemplified by 309A, *Lady Jane II*. This sail plan also included a large spinnaker on a 20' spinnaker pole, a large genoa jib, a small and genoa fisherman staysail, and a gollywobbler. Sail plan A could also be had with a double headsail. The last 309 built (Q) had a custom sail plan by Carl Alberg that shortened and moved the mainmast aft to increase the size of the forestaysail resulting in a working sail area of 1,028 sq.ft. The 309s were also fitted out with a 50-hp gasoline engine that worked on one central shaft with a fixed propeller.

Sixteen schooners were built to this design, while a seventeenth construction was planned, the 309-R, rigged exceptionally as a ketch and without centerboard, but the order was subsequently cancelled.

The following table describes the essential information about each of the seventeen 309 schooners.

Design No.	Year Built	Original Name	First Owner	Later Names
309	1927	*Sartartia*	Benjamin Clayton	*Rubicon, Lady Jane II*
309B	1927	*Bimesa*	W.W. Knight	*Silhouette, Rogue's Moon, Pocahontas*
309C	1927	*Black Squall*	George A. Cutter, Dedham, MA	*Buccaneer*
309D	1927	*Blue Sea*	W. D. Scranton, New Haven, CT	*March Hare, Enchantress, Yankee Belle*
309E	1927	*Gamecock*	Robert L. Bacon, Glen Cove, IL	*Reejack, Norsquan, Fair Wind, Black Douglas, Baleen*
309F	1928	*Altair*	John Lee Merrill, Islesford, ME	
309G	1928	*Nooya*	T.H.P. Molson/C. P. Creighton, Canada	
309H	1928	*Niliraga*	Gano Dunn	
309J	1929	*Bald Eagle*	Robert M. Roloson	*Canigo II, Southern Cross II, Allegro*
309K	1930	*Beatrice B*	Dr. Fritz B. Talbot	*Araglin, Lanakai, Esperance, Marilyn, Splendid*
309L	1929	*Evanthia III*	Frederick M. Gardiner	*Topas, Sangrala, Antares, Nordlys, Fancy Free, Doubloon II, Amen Ra II*
309M	1930	*Emma Jean*	Frank B. Richmond, W. Warwick, RI	*Wilabil, Aegir, Ananda, Shadow Fox, Walter Mitty, Glory, True North*
309N	1930	*Pinafore*	Henry H. Laudon	*Wogg Too, Windrift, Orn Air II, Dingo Sweet, Black Jack, Qilak*
309O	1930	*Kia Ora*	Joseph H. Plumb	*Two Brothers, Stormy Petrel II, Tibby Dunbar*
309P	1930	*Bagheera*	George Squibb	
309Q	1930	*Blackbird*	Myron J. Arms	
309R			Frank Harris, Los Angeles, CA	

Note: The schooners that still exist have a grey background.

All these boats were built by Goudy & Stevens in East Boothbay, Maine, except the 309G *Nooya*, which was built in Canada at Oakville Yacht Building Co. in Oakville, Ontario. The construction of these boats consisted of carvel planking with 5/4' long leaf yellow pine on 1 7/8 by 2" steam-bent oak frames, long leaf yellow pine stringers, and carlins, oak timbers, painted white pine decks, mahogany covering boards, bulwarks, hatches, cap rail, cabin trunk, trim, and oval cockpit. The spars were made of Oregon pine, or Sitka spruce and the standing rigging and fasteners throughout were galvanized iron.

There existed three different stock accommodation plans for the owners to choose from, any of which could be further customized. The most popular cabin plan (Plan A), depicted and described in the 1929 advertisement was a galley forward arrangement with an enclosed owner's cabin to port forward of the main cabin, two upholstered transom seats in the main cabin that double as berths, and two quarter berths aft. This arrangement, which creates the illusion of a very large main cabin area, was modified in Plan B by eliminating the forward single stateroom, enlarging the galley area forward and creating an enclosed stateroom aft to port, with an additional fixed single berth forward in the foc's'le. Plan C was a galley aft arrangement with the galley to port, and storage to starboard, with a large double stateroom forward of the main cabin. The head to port amidships had doors leading to the main cabin and the stateroom. The last boat, 309Q, had a custom cabin plan to accommodate a hired captain and crew and consisted, from bow to stern, of a sail locker with a pipe berth and a crews head forward, then the galley forward, and then the enclosed owner's stateroom to port and an enclosed head to starboard. The main cabin had a sliding and hanging berth to port, upholstered transom seats and quarter berth to starboard, with a mahogany chest of drawers and hanging closet to port. All the cabin plans had four large hatches for ventilation, while Q had five, with an additional hatch (or two) for engine room access.

Alden's design No. 309 became one of the most popular stock boats in the late 1920s and early 1930s. These small schooners were easy to handle, handsome, and beamy, and allowed for much space below deck and comfortable accommodations. The schooner *Blackbird*, featured in this chapter, design number 309Q, was the last of this series of boats, and is the most original plank on frame 309 remaining.

Three other 309s are in sailing condition, though some have been moderately to significantly altered with respect to rig, hull, and interior layout. A well-preserved 309 schooner is the *True North*, which sails in New England waters. She has a modern cold-molded hull that was modeled from the exterior of the original boat but retains her original rig. Another one is the *Quilak*, which was refurbished in 1986 with a strip plank/cold-molded sheath over her original hull, and a new interior. *Quilak* is currently located in California. The final schooner is 309J *Allegro*, located in Chicago, a very original plank on frame example of the 309s. Like *Blackbird*, she has undergone extensive restoration over the years by her present owner. *Allegro* has had a third of her planks replaced and a new forefoot, new angelique keel timber, new frames, floor timbers, and stern post installed. Her centerboard trunk, now steel, is shorter, her rudder modified, and a boomkin added to provide for a fixed backstay.

BLACKBIRD

Type: centerboard, two-mast gaff-Marconi schooner
Designer: John G. Alden, design No. 309-Q
Length (sparred): 52'
Length on Deck: 43'3"
Length on Waterline: 33'3"
Beam: 12'6"
Draft: 4'2" (board up)
Year of Construction: 1930
Shipyard: Goudy & Stevens, East Boothbay, Maine
Construction: 1 1/4" thick long leaf yellow pine on white oak, galvanized iron/ silicon bronze replacement
Engine: Westerbeke 4-107 diesel
Owner: Sandy & Peter Thompson
Home Port: Freeport, Maine

Blackbird: A Proud Survivor of the Famous Alden 309 Schooners

Blackbird was built by the Goudy & Stevens yard in 1930, for the price of $10,000, commissioned and delivered "on or before July 4" (according to the terms of contract with Alden) in Marion, Massachusetts, for Myron Arms. Myron "Mike" Arms, grandson of the original owner, came to visit her in 2010 and relayed some of the family history. Charles Arms, son of Myron Arms, still remembers the day of her arrival with the Alden-provided Captain, Jesse Brewer, in full uniform and the cabin boy, Edgar ("Egge"), dressed in his sailors cap and middy. They stayed on board for the summer. *Blackbird* was christened by Mrs. Arms on the mooring just off Barden's Boatyard with a bottle of bootleg whiskey provided by Mr. Barden, the local bootlegger. The time of the vessel's building coincided with the Great Depression and Prohibition in the United States. Consequently, her liquor cabinet was fashioned as a hidden door in the head of the centerboard trunk. Myron Arms was not a sailor but purchased the schooner in the hopes of teaching his children to become yachtsmen. In this he succeeded. Both his son, Charles, and later his grandson, Mike Arms, became avid sailors, and have sailed extensively from the North Atlantic to the Mediterranean. The Arms family owned a steel mill in Youngstown, Ohio, and as the Great Depression worsened in 1930 and 1931, orders at the mill ceased; the family was forced to sell their newly acquired schooner the following year. As the decline of economic activity continued, *Blackbird*'s ownership changed quickly; after having been sold to Arthur Verseay of Haverhill, Massachusetts, in 1931 for $10,000, she was sold for an undisclosed amount to Hubert Toppin, the commodore of the Essex Yacht Club (EYC) in Connecticut in 1935. *Blackbird* was Toppin's pride and joy, sailing her to first place in EYC's 1937 regatta.

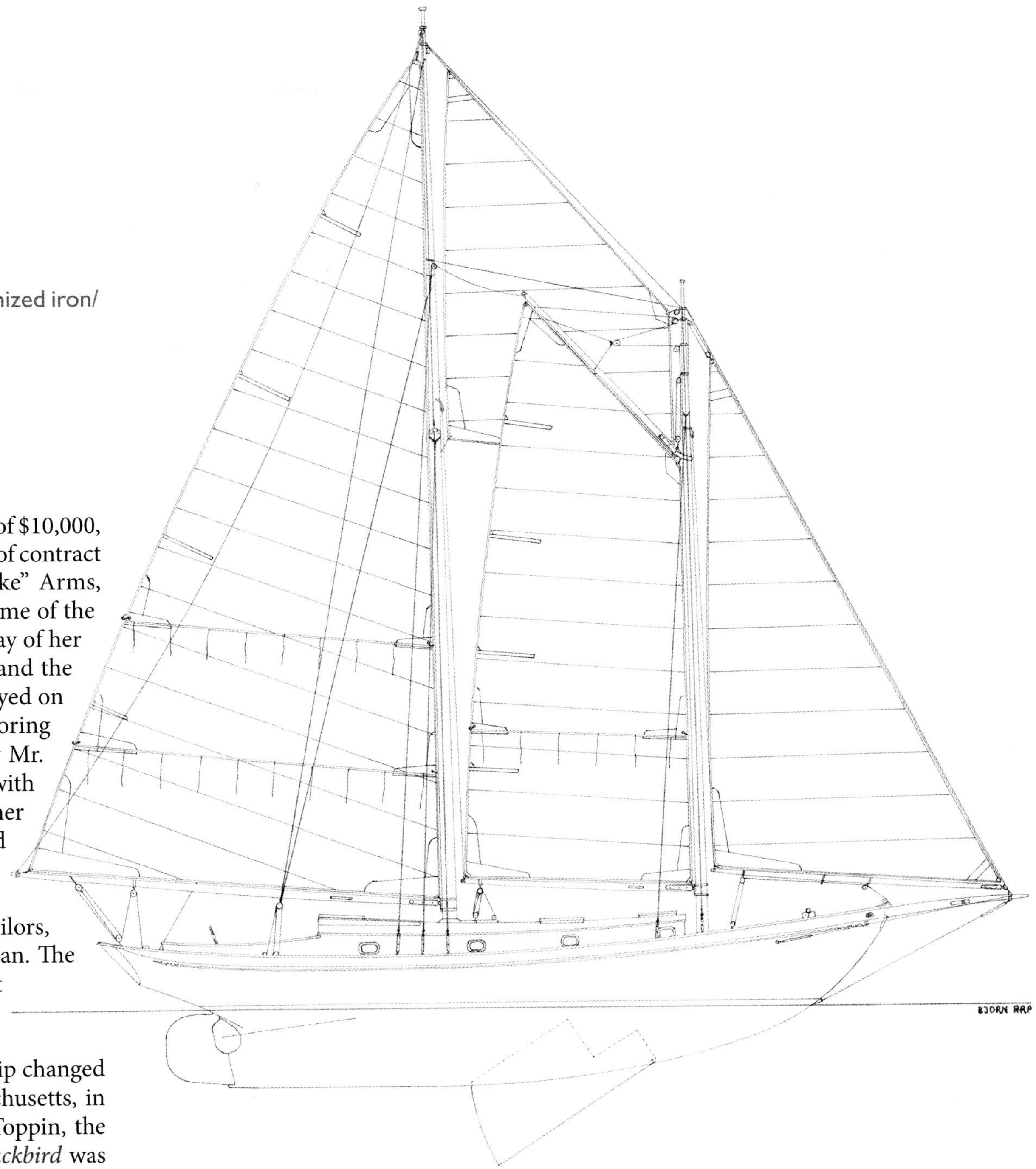

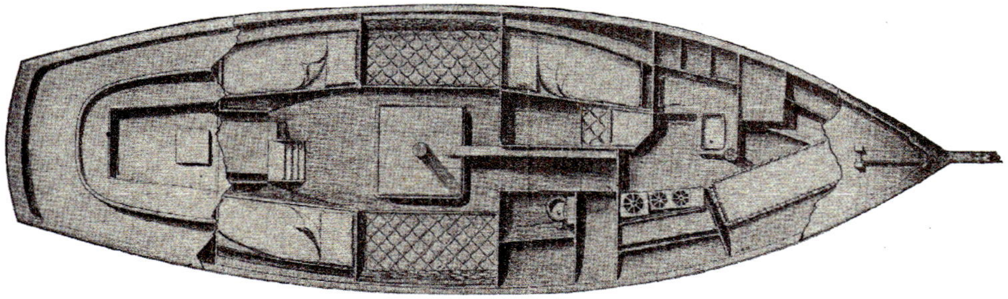

The original layout of most 309 schooners is shown in this original 1929 brochure drawing. As the drawing suggests, the saloon was very large, and the centerboard trunk was embedded in the bulkheads and the saloon table. This interior could be fitted into a 43' schooner because of the boat's considerable beam of 12'6".

September 21, 1938: *Blackbird*, Commodore Huber Toppin's 43-foot schooner, pounding against the pier of the Essex Yacht Club. The cutter *Typhoon* has sunk outside her. This photograph was taken at 3:45 P.M. by H. M. Baker (Yachting, *December 1938*).

Surviving the Great Hurricane of New England in 1938

In September of 1938, still under Toppin's care and ownership, she rode the 140-mph fury of the Great Hurricane of New England secured to the yacht club pier. As the tale goes, only one vessel remained floating at Essex when the hurricane had passed. That vessel was supposedly an Alden on charter, whose skipper remained on board all night shifting anchors. A photograph of the devastation, taken purportedly by the skipper of that vessel the next morning and handed down by H. Littlejohn, shows only *Blackbird*'s masts above the flood waters, flying a tattered burgee, over the tangled wreckage of two other yachts which were thrown clear onto the club lawn.

Commodore Toppin had his schooner refloated and repaired. Surprisingly, the damage was limited and only required replacement of a small section of the shear strake, and adjoining covering board, bulwark, and cap rail. Her lines still retain a slight lift in her shear along the port side at the location of the main chain plates, where she was battered against the piling at Essex. Several of what appear to be *Blackbird*'s original Egyptian cotton sails, bearing Toppin's name are still aboard and are still used, weather permitting. Toppin went on to sail his schooner another 12 years in Long Island Sound until 1950, when the boat was sold to Charles Phinney of Manchester by the Sea, Massachusetts.

Many Owners and Always the Same Dedicated Care

Since then she has changed owners six times, being purchased by Joshua Spaulding in 1960; Stephen Parsons in 1963; and Charles Hamblett of Kittery, Maine, in 1965. Hamblett purchased her for $13,500 and *Blackbird* became a well-known landmark at Kittery Point. Larry Wheeler purchased her in 1983 for $44,000, and removed the centerboard. Wheeler sold the boat to Collin Eggleton in 1989 for $42,000 and she was finally purchased by her present owners, Sandy and Peter Thompson, in 1993 for $32,000. They recovered the old centerboard from a barn in Cumberland, Maine, in 1997 to use as a pattern for a new one, relegating the old one to a life as a garden ornament.

Over the years, the repairs on *Blackbird* included replacement of the stem (late 1960s) and center fastening of a majority of planks. In the early 1970s, Charles Hamblett replaced her centerboard and somewhere along the line the trunk was resupported by cutting out the bottom corners of the floor timbers, sliding in rebar, and casting concrete around the base of the trunk and keel timber. While some may frown on such a repair, it did the trick for many years and provided much longitudinal strength to the vessel. During his ownership Hamblett corresponded with Mike Arms who sought an opportunity to repurchase the boat for his family. In the early 1980s Larry Wheeler removed the board and plugged the trunk. In the late 1980s, Collin Eggleton removed the iron ballast keel, rebolted the trunk area floor timbers through the keel timber, and reinstalled the ballast keel with galvanized steel keel bolts. *Blackbird*, at that point, had not spent a winter out of the water since at least the early 1960s.

Blackbird is known to a number of people up and down the New England Coast, and not surprisingly so. She always enjoyed her annual romp with Sandy at the helm, down the Maine coast to visit her former owners Charles and Eve Hamblett of Deer Isle, Maine. In 1995, *Blackbird* had the distinct pleasure of having Frank Eaton, Jr. aboard at the Bucks Harbor Yacht Club. Eaton's father once owned the 309L sistership, *Nordlys*, in the 1940s. Over the past years, *Blackbird* has introduced the current owners to many of her friends and acquaintances, which has been one of the great pleasures received in exchange for care given in maintaining and restoring this wonderful old cruising schooner.

Blackbird under Sandy and Peter Thompson's Committed Ownership

In her 82nd year, *Blackbird* is a humble testimony to the quality of the design, workmanship, and materials of her period. With good sensible care by many owners, she still retains all of her original planking (except her garboards), her original rig, blocks, compass, chronometer, lamps, interior, and most importantly, her name. Since the schooner was in a very good shape for her age when Sandy and Peter Thompson purchased her, they got married on her and continued sailing her out of Freeport, Maine, for eight years, until they decided to haul her out for a substantial restoration at the end of 2001.

The philosophy of this work has been to rebuild the vessel as closely as possible to her original construction at Goudy & Stevens. Thus, under her owner's dedicated ownership, *Blackbird* has had her horn timber, sternpost, and keel replaced, and her iron ballast, centerboard trunk and centerboard, frames, and floor timbers have been refastened and refurbished. Her deck and coach roof canvas still remain to be completed. In every sense of the word she has been fortunate enough to remain, faithfully in originality and appearance, one of the ruggedly built, 43' Alden cruising schooners.

When *Blackbird* returns soon to the water, she will have her original interior, and the cabin sole and ceilings will be replaced with materials identical to the original (except with the use of angelique in her keel structure and trunk). She will have original spars, cabin house, rails and bulwark, and original planking with exception of the garboards, and original iron ballast. Frames, fasteners, floors, keel bolts, keel timber, centerboard trunk, centerboard, false keel, rudder, and deck will be new. This work has benefited greatly from the generous advice of Niels Helleberg, the chief naval architect for Alden (now Niels Helleberg Yacht Designs); Ross Gannon of Gannon and Benjamin Marine Railway; Frank Luke of Paul E. Luke, her surveyor of record for the last 30 years; Cap Leonard; and able assistance from Jamie and Joe Lowell at Even Keel Marine.

Blackbird's profile showing Carl Alberg's sail plan. The main mast stands more aft, thus enlarging the foresail and reducing the mainsail for easier handling.

The owners, Sandy and Peter Thompson, get married on *Blackbird*, August 1993 (*Peter Thompson*).

Under sail in Casco Bay—a typical sailing breeze under full lowers in Casco Bay, Maine (*Peter Thompson*).

Down East—Sandy Thompson at the helm on *Blackbird's* annual romp downeast to visit old friends (*Peter Thompson*).

Waiting for visitors at anchor at Burnt Island, Muscongus Bay, Maine. This side-view shows again her handsome lines, with the appearance of a "large" yacht, although she measures only 43' on deck (*Peter Thompson*).

Under sail—a family sail off Sister's Island, Casco Bay, Maine. This photo shows the impressive beam of this centerboard schooner (*Peter Thompson*).

Sail handling—handling headsails while under wing and wing (*Peter Thompson*).

Restoration Progress

Blackbird's original construction was 1 1/4" carvel long leaf yellow pine planking on 1 7/8" x 2" steam-bent frames, fastened with galvanized "Swedish" nails. Clamps and carlins are also long leaf while the remaining timbers were oak, including the floor timbers, false keel, sternpost, deadwood, horn timber, forefoot, stem, rudder, centerboard, and centerboard trunk. The ceilings were 1/2" pine, and the floors vertical grain fir. Decks are sprung, painted vertical grain white pine, fastened with galvanized screws and nails. Covering board, bulwark, cap rail, cabin trunk, cockpit, and trim were mahogany.

Sections of the port covering boards and shear plank were replaced around the main chain plates when the vessel was refloated after the 1938 hurricane. A piece of original shear plank removed in that repair was found on a butt block behind the engine room ceiling when it was removed in 2001. The original paint on that piece of plank is still like new, gloss black with a yellow-gold cove stripe. In addition, a small children's toy, a choo-choo train, was found on a butt behind the ceiling in the owner's stateroom. From the red lead and blue enamel paint on the train, the Thompson's suspect it was made by someone at the Goudy and Steven yard at the time the boat was built and lost by some child playing with it along the top of the ceiling. This may demonstrate that *Blackbird* has been a real family cruising boat.

Coming home—*Blackbird* arrives at the Thompson's home in Freeport, 2001. The long restoration begins (*Peter Thompson*).

The Thompson's efforts started with maintenance and prioritized repair work determined by survey that could be accomplished in small areas when the boat was in the water or hauled in the spring. These efforts included replacing the forward port mast partner; installing a new pin rail around the foremast; reefing, caulking, and refastening portions of the fore deck; installing new house moldings; installing new foremast chain plates; refastening the garboard and adjacent planks; replacing the accessible frame ends in the engine room; installing new floor timbers and engine beds in the engine room; and removing the galley and head structures and installing new frames in those moisture-prone areas. In addition, some refastening was conducted in critical areas, and the boat was kept up with a thorough program of painting and varnishing. Their philosophy with the boat has been to resist taking so much apart at once that the time required to put it back together becomes overwhelming, to the detriment of the vessel. They continued with this approach until they took the vessel to their home on land.

Far too many boats have been lost because even the most well-intentioned owners run out of steam long before the job is done. It is not a sprint but a marathon. At the end of the 2000 sailing season, after sailing her since 1993, Peter Thompson decided to explore what would be required to reinstall the centerboard since, in addition to a loss of windward performance, the lack of a board was putting a lot of extra stress on the rudder shaft and strain on the aging stern post when sailing in rough conditions. Ultimately, it was determined that the sternpost had broken in half just forward of the rudder shaft.

The Thompsons started at the boatyard with a jack hammer to remove about 2,000 pounds of concrete, from around the keel and trunk to survey the trunk and keel timber. Given that the job would require replacement of a number of frames due to deteriorating frame heels, they decided to move her to their home and built a geo-synthetically reinforced boat pad next to their house. *Blackbird* was transported there in late August 2001. A metal pole shed was set up to protect the boat from sun and rain.

The next step in the work was to carefully remove the original interior joinery to permit it to be refurbished and reinstalled, and then cut away the ceiling planking and cabin sole, which was going to be replaced.

This was followed by removal of fastener bungs, cutting out every other oak frame from the inside and carefully driving the iron fasteners out through the planking. Minor repairs were made to refurbish the few fastener holes that did show minor iron sickness. The longleaf yellow pine planks appeared to be highly resistant to electrolysis due to the high pitch content of the wood. Only two small sections of plank were replaced, not including the garboard.

Only a few frames showed extensional (tension) breaks, and were mostly damaged in their cores below the water line from iron sickening. The steam-bent frames were replaced from the bridge deck to the stem with laminated white oak frames glued with resorcinol. They were installed in-place without removing the bilge or shear clamps or the decks, covering board, bulwark or any planks. The frames were mechanically

Keel timber blank—chain-sawing the rough blank for the new keel timber (*Peter Thompson*).

Finished keel timber blank—comparison of the original and replacement keel timber. Note the deterioration that had taken place at the juncture with the old frame pockets (*Peter Thompson*).

Sternpost and horn timber—newly installed horn timber, sternpost, and keel timber (*Peter Thompson*).

fastened to produce paper-thin glue joints. The frames were then painted with red lead paint, and warmed with heat lamps to ensure attaining the 70-degree temperature required to properly cure the glue. Although this approach required more time, it allowed more of the original boat to be retained longer. It must be said that it would have been uneconomical if the owners had had a boatyard do this work.

Once the boat was reframed and fastened with silicon bronze screws, or largely so, a cradle was built under it to allow the wood blocking and iron ballast to be removed. When the cradle was in place, and prior to pulling the blocking, the keel bolts were driven out using a 50-lb lead sledge hammer. The four-and-a-half-ton iron ballast was then separated from the keel timber and lowered onto rollers and slid sideways, out of the way.

Then, following the removal of the garboard planks, the floor timber and keel timber drifts were cut, the old centerboard trunk removed, and the keel timber lowered and slid out the back of the boat. An angelique keel timber blank was purchased and chain sawed to rough dimensions prior to having it planed and finished by hand. As most of the damage to the old keel timber was associated with the frame pockets, the new frames are not pocketed into the new keel timber. The new keel timber was then fitted to the boat and the rabbet marked out and cut to accept the new garboard.

The full-width floor timbers under the mast step and aft under the companionway were installed prior to removal of the original keel timber to help locate the new keel timber relative to the waterline. Once positioned, a new sternpost and horn timber were made from angelique and bolted in place. Lastly, the frame ends were trimmed flush against the keel timber, and fastened in to the keel timber to hold the bottom shape of the hull while new floor timbers were laid out and fitted.

Next, the new centerboard trunk, also constructed from angelique, was installed. The trunk was fashioned in the identical manner as the original with splined sideboards. The original was drifted, but Thompson felt it prudent to bolt it through the entire trunk sides on one-foot centers. The bolts pass through, just grazing the outside edge of the splines. All components of the trunk (splines, joints, and bolts) were bedded in white lead. Following this, all remaining original floor timbers were removed and new white oak floor timbers cut and installed. Each is bolted (at an angle) through the keel timber to pull the joint in tight, and they are then fastened through the long leaf planks. Due to the long broad nature of the floor timbers, plank to floor timber fasteners run across the grain and additional frame-to-floor fastening should only be needed in the forward and aft ends, where end grain prohibits fastening the floors to the planking.

Thompson applies a generous layer of bedding compound on the ballast, ready for installation (*Peter Thompson*).

Newly installed centerboard trunk, floor timbers, and frames (*Peter Thompson*).

The iron ballast, including the slot, was chinked, ground down with angle grinders to bare metal on the outside, primed with acid etching zinc chromate, and painted with five coats of InterluxTM Interprotect 2000® to seal the metal. If that system is successful in keeping the iron ballast dryer, it will help protect against both corrosion and electrolysis. The original ballast was not flat, and the old ballast was ground flat to be fair with the new keel timber. The ballast was reinstalled in July 2011. To provide a superior long-lasting gasket between the ballast and the keel timber, 3MTM 5200® was selected over tar, or other more traditional bedding materials. So that the keel timber and ballast could be separated in the future, three coats of high-temperature mold-release wax were applied to both surfaces, and the keel bolts. All bolt holes were pre-drilled, the ballast and keel timber separated, the iron ballast coated with 5200, and repositioned and bolted. Keel bolts are 1 1/4 Aquamet 22 with bronze nuts, and a variety of backing plates ranging from ipe to angelique to 316 stainless steel, depending on location.

The original interior has been stripped, the new ceilings and deck materials cut, and the project has now moved to the final phase of removing the original deck to allow a new deck to be installed. The original painted white pine deck is still largely serviceable, even after 80 years; however, the cost of wood to replace it with locally grown old growth vertical grain white pine was so reasonable ($800), that simply replacing a few softening planks did not make sense. With a new deck on in the spring of 2012, the interior can be reinstalled over the winter and a new engine and garboards can wait until early spring 2012. With a little luck and hard work, *Blackbird* should end her long stint on the hard, and rejoice again in sailing the Maine Coast and beyond in 2012.

Ballast installed—newly installed iron ballast (*Peter Thompson*).

Ceilings removed—ceiling planking removed after removal of interior. The access to the frames from the interior allowed for renovation of several frames without the need to remove the planking, which was substantially sound on *Blackbird* (*Peter Thompson*).

While the work went on for years, Sandy and Peter Thompson never forgot their great days aboard *Blackbird* sailing in the 1990s. They will soon again be seen under full sail in Casco Bay (*Peter Thompson*).

Under sail reaching—leeward reaching leg of race in Portland, Maine, with reaching headsail and genoa fisherman set (*Peter Thompson*).

Owner Peter Thompson at the helm of his cherished schooner (*Peter Thompson*).

PURITAN

Type: centerboard two-mast gaff schooner
Designer: John G. Alden
Year of Construction: 1930-1931
Shipyard: Electric Boat Company, New London, Connecticut
Length on Deck: 102'9"
Length on Waterline: 74'8"
Beam: 22'10"
Draft: 9' (centerboard up), 14'8" (centerboard down)
Sail Area: 4,297 sq. ft.
Construction: steel
Engine: originally 150-hp Winton diesel, replaced with a Caterpillar diesel
Owner: Ferruzzi family
Home Port: Eolie, Italy

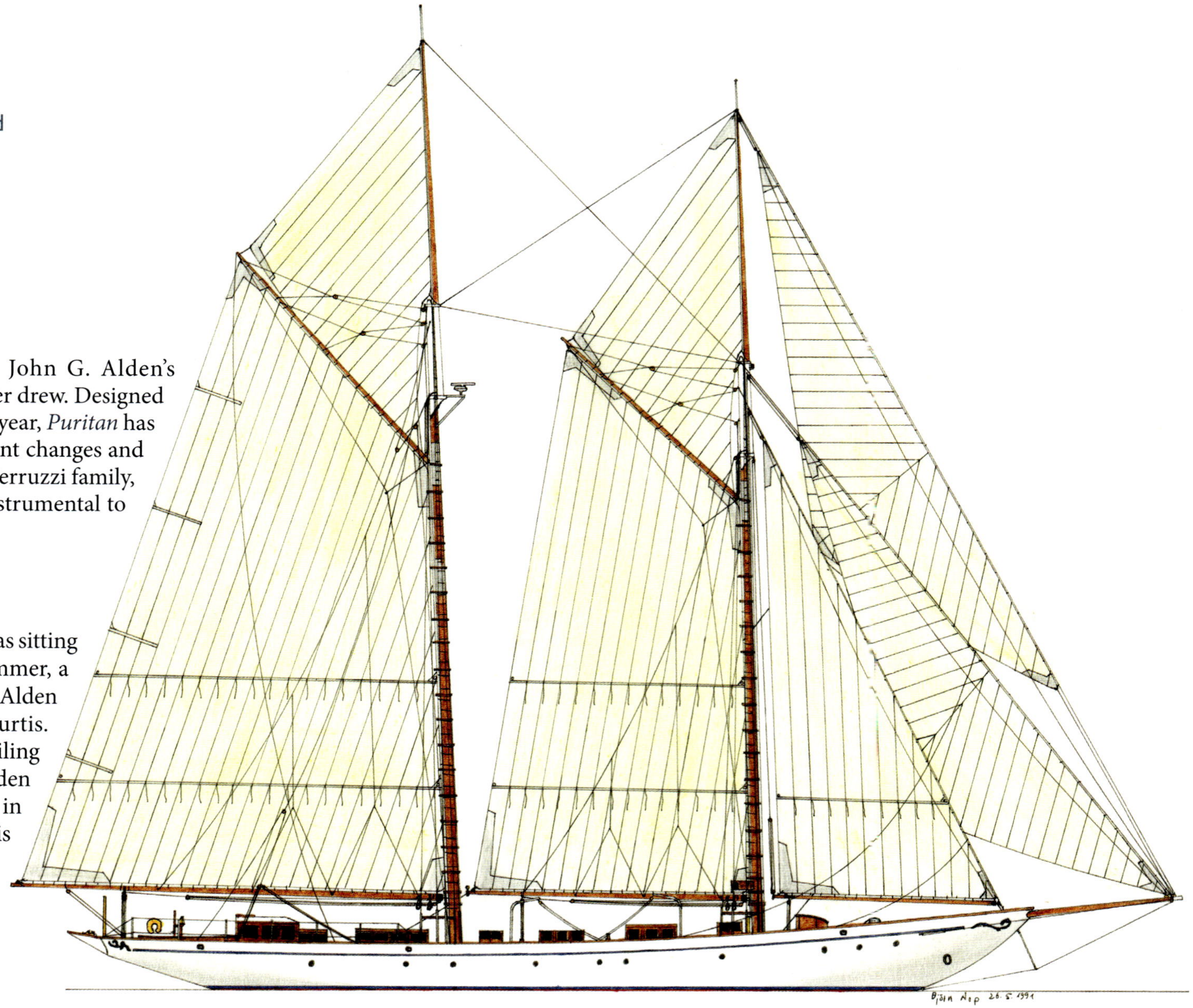

Most classic yacht lovers consider *Puritan* John G. Alden's masterpiece. It is also one of the largest yachts he ever drew. Designed in the turbulent year of 1929 and built the following year, *Puritan* has survived superbly maintained and without significant changes and visible aging. Her passionate owners, currently the Ferruzzi family, spare no expenses to keep her up and have been instrumental to the preservation of this nautical jewel.

Puritan's Wall Street Origins

It was Thursday, October 24, 1929: John Alden was sitting in his office at his drawing board. At the end of summer, a fresh breeze blew from Warren's Point across the bay. Alden reviewed his draft of a large schooner for H. J. Curtis. Outside the window he could see the dark clouds piling up. Suddenly, the telephone rang. It was Curtis. Alden thought: "What more does he now want to change in the design?" But the conversation ended quickly. Curtis was bankrupt, the Wall Street crash had left him little to live with, and it was impossible to think of building a new yacht. Therefore, Curtis retracted his order. Uneasily, Alden folded the plans together.

A few days later a small miracle happened: Edward M. Brown, also a member of the New York Yacht Club, assumed the order. But he also fell victim of the Great Depression, and he had to give up the yacht before her launch. Finally, the wealthy Californian, Henry J. Bauer, commissioned the schooner in mid-April of 1930 at the Electric Boat Company in New London, Connecticut, which was famous for building submarines. Thus, before her maiden voyage, *Puritan* had changed hands three times.

Puritan's Design

According to Richard Henderson's biography, *John G. Alden and His Yacht Designs*, plan No. 435-B, which became *Puritan*, was one of Alden's finest yachts. Others simply refer to her as Alden's masterpiece. *The Rudder* praised her as such when she was launched in February 1931. With a length of something over 90', *Puritan* was the third largest Alden ever built. Only the 124' *Starling* and the 103' *Seaward*, of Cecil B. de Mille, were larger. Alden had made plans for larger ships, as, for instance, the 152' long three-master *Priscilla Alden*, but they were never realized.

Like nearly all the large Alden yachts, *Puritan* was schooner-rigged. Also, characteristic of Alden was that her mainmast was well aft, giving a relatively small mainsail and large foresail, greatly adding to the ease of handling. This great balance of the rig—if comparing the two masts—was a special and positive feature of Alden's schooner designs. Otherwise, *Puritan's* rig was traditional with gaff fore and aft and fidded topmasts. For an Alden design, however, she was somewhat special in that she had a long bowsprit, a detail Alden usually tried to avoid, especially on smaller boats. But since *Puritan* was going to be sailed by a large professional crew, easy handling was not a priority. *Puritan* had a widely overhanging stern, a low freeboard and numerous very small hatches on deck, which were more discreet than on other yachts that resembled the New England fishing schooners. To further understand *Puritan's* design, it is useful to point to the 13 famous *Malabar* schooners and ketches that Alden had built for his own personal use between 1921 and 1945. The *Malabar X*, one of the greatest of Alden's private racing yachts, was built at the same time as the *Puritan*, and it was considered the highlight of U.S. yachting history, something comparable to L. Francis Herreshoff's *Ticonderoga* or Olin Stephens' *Dorade*. The *Puritan*, however, was not designed as a racing yacht. Her victories were all at traditional yacht races, for instance, the 1980 Classic Yacht Regatta in Newport, Rhode Island.

On deck, *Puritan* has remained unchanged over the years. Many more block-and-tackles are there than winches; and brass, copper and bronze, in addition to teak and mahogany, are the predominant materials. The sails are no longer made of cotton, however, but rather of synthetic fibers.

This yacht, always cared for by a permanent crew of five, is a joy to behold. The interior is in perfect condition. Parts of the interior are still original from 1930, and other parts have been faithfully reconstructed. Only some changes to the galley and engine room reflect modernity. For example, the 150-hp Winton engine was replaced with a Perkins, and most recently with a Caterpillar.

The entrance hatch, which resembles a staircase, is located in the aft deck area, leading to the cabins. The master cabin and three guest cabins are paneled in light Oregon pine. They are particularly inviting when the sunlight comes in through the large hatches. The saloon, which has an austere feeling, is decorated in the same style. On board this schooner the ambience is very different to that of the extravagances of, for instance, Barbara Hutton's *Sea Cloud*, since *Puritan* was designed primarily as a salty but stylish large sailing yacht, and was never intended to serve for sumptuous receptions.

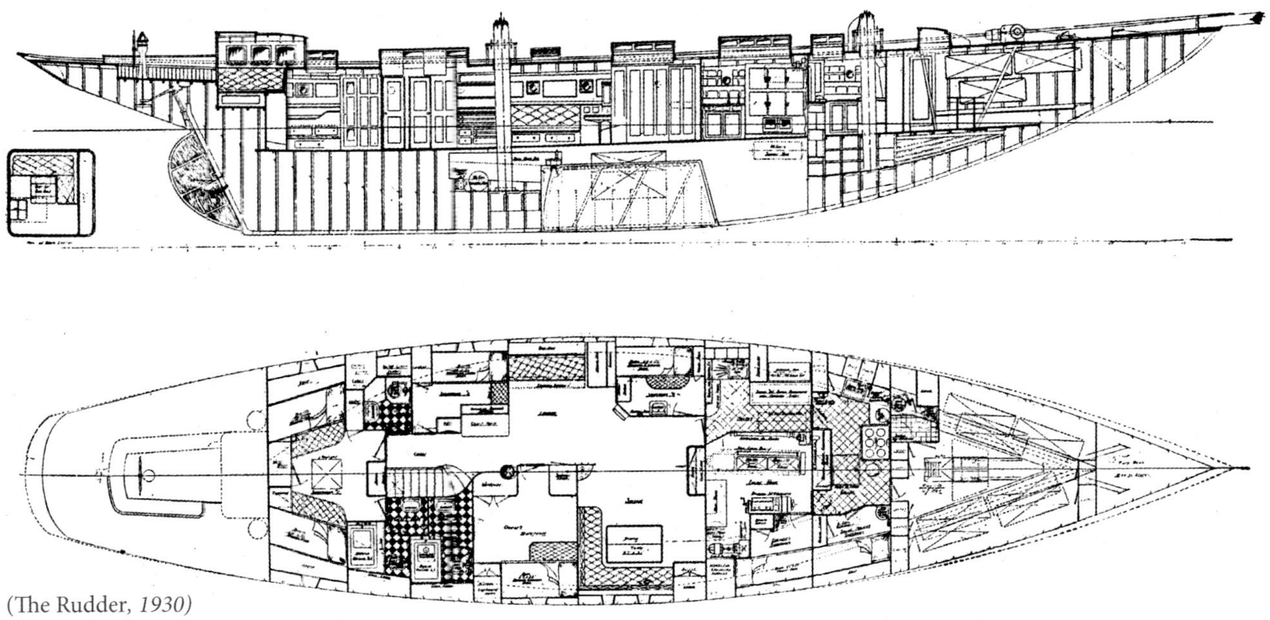

(The Rudder, *1930)*

Puritan's Owners

The first Californian owner was very manic with the care of the yacht. He had all paint and varnish renewed three times a year and kept deckhouses and hatches systematically covered and protected against sunlight. After his ownership, Mariano Prado Sosa, son of the Peruvian President Manuel Prado y Ugarteche, acquired the yacht. She was subsequently sold to the well-known restorer of classic yachts, William Bolling, from Fort Lauderdale, Florida, and in the late 1970s, the yacht was sold to the Austrian yacht specialist, Oscar H. Schmidt. The latter renovated the schooner in England. While registered in England, *Puritan* was primarily based out of Palma de Mallorca, from which she sailed all over the Mediterranean. She was a regular participant at the Veteran Boat Rally Porto Cervo and the Nioulargue in Saint-Tropez.

Since the early 1980s, *Puritan* has belonged to the Ferruzzi family from Italy, who keep her berthed at the island of Eolie in the Tyrrhenian Sea. After the main mast broke in a stormy Atlantic crossing in 1981, the Italian shipyard Dell Argentario replaced it. The family also restored the interior of the boat entirely according to the original plans. For this purpose, the Ferruzzis chased antique lamps, tables, chairs and paintings of the 1930s to recreate the "atmosphere" of the old times, which in some way had been lost during the long life of this magnificent vessel. Currently, *Puritan* looks better than ever and constitutes an iconic sight wherever she goes and at any port in the Mediterranean.

The beautiful Alden schooner *Puritan* is now sailing in the Western Mediterranean, where she is a familiar sight at classic yacht races and gatherings, such as in the case of this photo taken during the 2004 Les Voiles de Saint Tropez (*Patrick Débetencourt*).

Puritan combines elegant lines with the seaworthy appearance of any Alden schooner. There is something about his designs that make them very distinct from any other type of yacht (*Patrick Débetencourt*).

WENDAMEEN

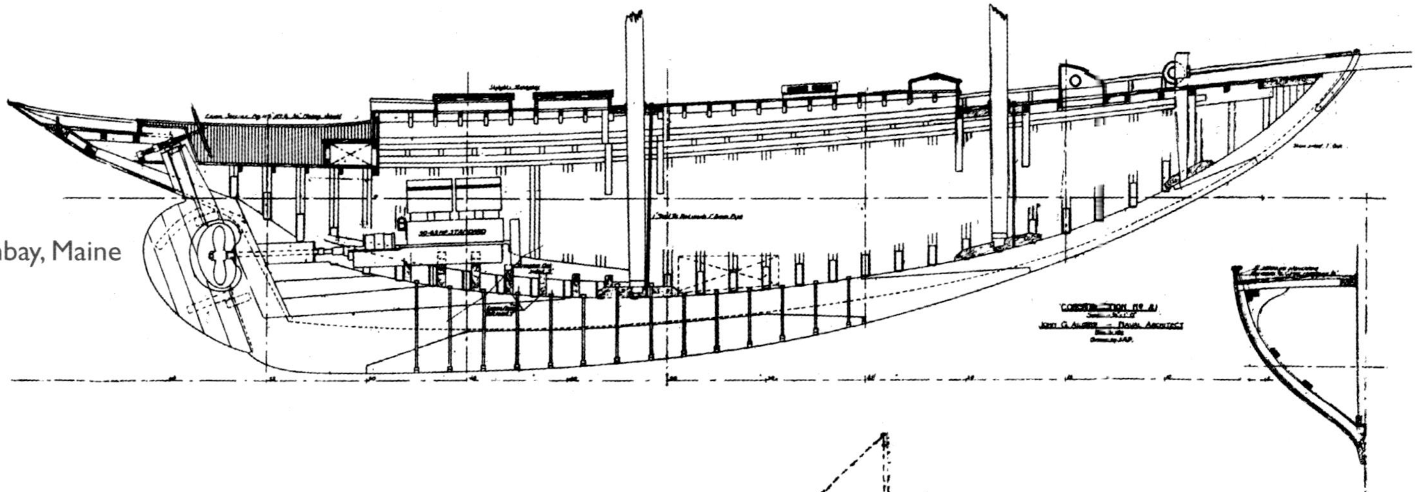

Type: two-mast gaff schooner
Designer: John G. Alden, Design no. 21
Year of Construction: 1912
Shipyard: Adams Shipbuilding, East Boothbay, Maine
Length (sparred): 88'
Length on Deck: 67'
Length on Waterline: 51'
Beam: 17'
Draft: 8'8"
Sail Area: 2,302 sq. ft.
Construction: wood
Owner: The Portland Schooner Company
Home Port: Portland, Maine

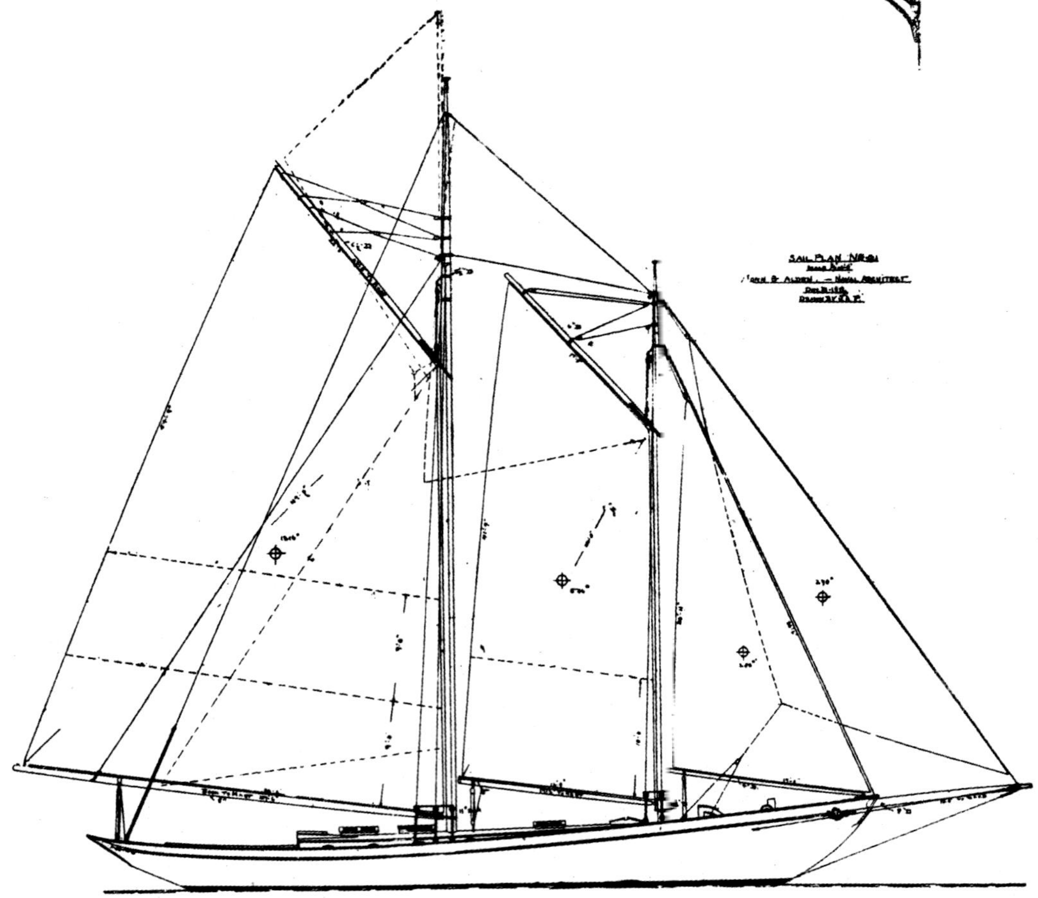

Built in 1912, *Wendameen* was an active cruising yacht until 1933, when she was laid up in New York. She stayed there until she had become a total wreck by 1987. Through brilliant planning, dogged perseverance, self-imposed poverty, and unbelievable economy, Neal Parker made the *Wendameen* sail again. He did it in record time, and for less money than anybody would have imagined. *Wendameen* is truly the most exhilarating Alden schooner afloat, because of her extraordinary lines as well as for her remarkable history.*

Wendameen's Design

John Alden's design No. 21 was the schooner *Wendameen*. He drew her lines in 1911 as his first large schooner yacht. When Alden developed this 67' schooner, he drew her relatively narrow with a sweeping sheer and long ends. Her construction was to be very heavy, appropriate for cruising. She was advertised at the time as a schooner yacht with characteristics of the Gloucester fishing schooners, which might be true with the exception of her comfortable accommodations below decks.

When built, *Wendameen* was finished in varnished mahogany, white trim paint, and nickel-plated bronze fixtures. The owner had a large stateroom with a private head. There were accommodations for three guests and a cabin for three crew members. The large saloon, with its tufted velvet cushions and electric lights, was ideal for entertaining. The schooner was equipped with an auxiliary engine with which she could reach up to 12 knots.

---

*The following text has been drawn from excerpts of historic research undertaken by her previous, very committed owner and restorer, Neal Parker. His research has been published in his book, Wendameen: *The Life of an American Schooner from 1912 to the Present* (Camden, Maine: Down East Books, 2002). This book is probably one of the best published accounts of an American schooner yacht's history.

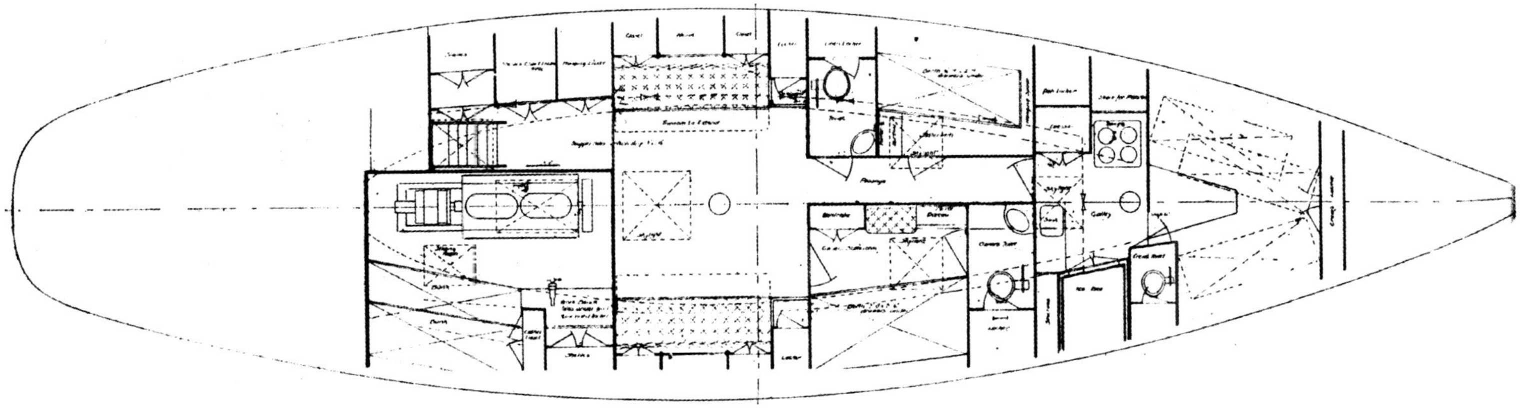

This schooner was one of the designs that launched Alden's career as a pioneer of comfortable cruising yachts, also suitable for ocean and long distance racing. The yard selected to build design No. 21 was the Frank Adams Shipyard in East Boothbay. They launched the vessel in spring 1912 and her first owner, Chester W. Bliss, of Springfield, Massachusetts, sailed her out of New London, Connecticut, during the first four seasons.

Climbing aloft is no easy task without ratlines, but this unknown guest managed to get himself up the 55-foot foremast with his bare hands and a good old-fashioned pair of sneakers (*Captain Neal Parker*).

John Alden in shirtsleeves supervises the last stages of construction aboard the *Wendameen* at the East Boothbay yard of Frank Adams. The carpenter at the right installs the steering gear (*Captain Neal Parker*).

The wind is light and the *Wendameen* sports a big *Yankee* jib, fisherman staysail, and main topsail. This photo, taken prior to 1915, was used by the brokerage firm of Gielow and Orr (*Captain Neal Parker*).

Subsequent Ownerships

In 1916, Bliss sold the *Wendameen* to the Uihlein family of Milwaukee, owners of the Schlitz breweries. But with the coming of Prohibition, they had to put her up for sale again. She was then moved to Chicago, where her new owner was a colorful lawyer named L'Amoreaux, who cruised with his family for ten years. Each year, L'Amoreaux entered the *Wendameen* in the Mackinac race, which took him close to Canada and gave him the opportunity to refill his liquor cabinets. L'Amoreaux brought the *Wendameen* back to Long Island Sound, intending to trade her for a powerboat that better suited his failing health, but he died before the transaction took place. The *Wendameen* became the property of yacht broker G. W. Ford of City Island, New York, who carefully labeled and stored all her gear when he hauled her for the winter at a local yard. The Depression interfered with the resale of the boat. Then came World War II. Ford chose to leave the *Wendameen* laid up rather than allow her to be requisitioned for submarine patrol. He had dreams of retiring onto her and did two major overhauls of the schooner (in 1936 and 1963) at a cost of a quarter of a million dollars. In 1984, when Ford was ninety-two years old, the shipyard where *Wendameen* had been stored was closed. Ford had neither retired nor ever sailed his schooner, but he abandoned his own hopes and launched her, offering her for sale. The *Wendameen* came adrift in a spring storm, suffering serious damage. Ford fixed these damages to keep her afloat and sell her; a purchaser attempted a restoration but gave up and left her stuck in a mud bank in western Connecticut.

Captain Neal Parker: Saving Alden's First Schooner

Captain Neal Parker found the hulk of the schooner still stuck in the mud bank in Connecticut in 1986. Most of her deck had collapsed from rot, and much of her topsides had fallen away. She had neither rudder, nor engine, only memories holding what once bronze, oak, and iron held fast.

Parker bought the *Wendameen* in the fall of 1986. In addition, he found her gear right where Ford had it stored in 1933. Parker used a great number of this gear in the restoration and was even able to utilize one original staysail during his first two seasons.

Hiring a small dragger, Parker tried to tow the empty hull to Maine, but after 90 miles, a strong easterly forced them to seek refuge in the Thames River. Just 100 yards from a New London dock the dragger lost steering. Wind and tide conspired, and set the *Wendameen* against the pier. Parker secured her lines and a small voice said, "Wait 'til spring." Shortly after, he discovered that the *Wendameen* had taken herself someplace familiar. She was berthed less than half a mile from her original mooring and her first owners' home! That was to be one of many coincidences, which eventually tied her new life to her past.

It was two years before Parker raised enough money to install the engine and rudder, which finally brought the *Wendameen* home to Maine. Parker lived on rice and frozen pizza, drove a car with no brakes, and heard hundreds of people say, "Give it up." But a few believed in him and the *Wendameen*. Much support came from descendants of the schooner's early owners. She had played such an important role in the lives of those she touched, that generations later, grandchildren and nephews still knew her story.

Under her new Chicago owners and painted yacht-white, *Wendameen* enjoys a cruise in the summer of 1924 (*Captain Neal Parker*).

Parker hauled the *Wendameen* at Rockland in the fall of 1988, just down the coast from the yard where she was launched decades before. He worked alone through the

The *Wendameen* ghosts along in light winds on a port tack. Crewmember Paul Pfeiffer changes a record on the gramophone as the ladies play cards in the cockpit. Mrs. L'Amoreaux stands in the main companionway (*Captain Neal Parker*).

Under a cover and ready for a long sleep (*Captain Neal Parker*).

The *Wendameen* in Long Island Sound in July 1933 (*Captain Neal Parker*).

winter, replacing most of her frames. Finally, a bank showed mercy and Parker was able to hire a shipwright. On July 1, 1990, they cast off and set the *Wendameen's* 2,400 sq. ft. of sail. The new *Wendameen* was underway! A guest pointed to a forgotten news clipping in the scrapbook, the date, "July 1, 1912." It read, "The new auxiliary schooner yacht *Wendameen* went into commission this morning, her owner and party aboard..."

Although a great deal of the boat had to be replaced, today she exudes much of her early history. The *Wendameen* looks distinguished with her white hull and varnished cockpit, skylight frames, and trim. Below, as when first launched, the appointments are airy, with white-painted panels and mahogany trim. Simple, green velvet cushions in the saloon evoke the charm of an older time.

Captain Parker has collected scrapbooks of pictures and stories about the *Wendameen* and her former owners. An old Victor gramophone was part of the equipment aboard; the George Gershwin recording of "Rhapsody in Blue" brought applause every time.

Parker continued successfully chartering *Wendameen* for the next 16 years, until he felt that he had to sell her. However, later on Parker realized that this sale was unfortunate, because *Wendameen*, being a very large classic yacht, needs special care and handling that only owners as dedicated as he could give her.

Wendameen Chartering out of Portland, Maine

The Portland Schooner Company, headed by Scott Reischmann and Twain Braden, bought the *Wendameen* in 2005. They wanted to create authentic experiences for passengers on large, storied yachts by sailing them through the waters of Casco Bay in Maine and beyond. Running partners Reischmann and Braden had gone to the Maine Boat Show in March 2002 looking for plans to build a dory for recreation in Casco Bay. At the show, Scott picked up a copy of *Wooden Boat* magazine, saw the 49-passenger classic Alden schooner *Bagheera* for sale in San Francisco, and an idea was born.

Two short trips across the country (*Bagheera*'s mast and hull made the cross-country trek from San Francisco to Maryland on two separate trips), and a sail up the coast from Maryland to Maine a few weeks later, and the Portland Schooner Company was open for business. *Bagheera* made her inaugural voyage on Memorial Day Weekend, 2002. Braden has since moved on to law school to pursue a law career, and Scott's wife Michelle left her job at MIT to run the business full-time with Scott in 2004. A few months later the time was ripe to purchase their second schooner, the *Wendameen*.

Since then, *Wendameen* sails in company with *Bagheera* out of Portland, Maine. *Wendameen* is Coast Guard certified for 14 overnight passengers, plus crew, or 49 day-sail passengers. However, chartering such a fine and distinctive schooner as *Wendameen* is no easy task. The crew aboard *Wendameen* had the opportunity to notice that in the 2011 season, when she grounded twice, in June and in August, in the Casco Bay with passengers on board. The Coast Guard had to come in rescue of the ship.

However, knowing *Wendameen's* firm determination to overcome any adverse circumstances, it seems almost sure that she will outlive many owners to come, sailing proudly as John G. Alden's first schooner. She is an irreplaceable monument to the American yachting history.

Wendameen was in this condition when Captain Neal Parker found her in 1987. She was only a shadow of her former glory. Missing deck, frames, and topside planks. The hull was actually damaged by recent repair attempts (*Captain Neal Parker*).

Under engine and with a testimonial auxiliary sail, *Wendameen* enters the choppy waters of the Race, a tide rip by the east end of Long Island Sound, on her long way up to Maine for restoration (*Captain Neal Parker*).

In the course of the restoration, and with the interior removed, Parker could finally conclude with certainty that the fore deck and beams were still intact. So he left them in temporarily to keep the weakened hull together. The long sweeping timbers are called bilge stringers. They add to the hull's longitudinal strength. Eventually they too had to be replaced (*Captain Neal Parker*).

It is 1 P.M. In a few minutes Parker's first guests would arrive. Several friends help get the mattresses below (*Captain Neal Parker*).

The schooner *Wendameen* shortly after her restoration. Parker decided to paint her white, after he had tried out dark blue. However he would paint her, *Wendameen* would always be a wonderful sight (*Captain Neal Parker*).

Captain Neal Parker, proud and happy after several years of hard work, when he finally could sit down on deck of his schooner (*Captain Neal Parker*).

Wendameen heeling in a breeze. After more than fifty years of storage, several attempts of restoration, and one total restoration at the end of the 1980s, she finally sails again like she had done until 1933 (*Captain Neal Parker*).

Wendameen chartering out of Portland, Maine (*Portland Schooner Company*).

Wendameen's wheel (*Portland Schooner Company*).

Wendameen sailing in a light breeze. Note her impressive lines and clear deck (*Portland Schooner Company*).

Wendameen sailing to windward (*Portland Schooner Company*).

Another image of *Wendameen* sailing to windward (*Portland Schooner Company*).

Wendameen's crew is waiting for wind (*Portland Schooner Company*).

Wm. Starling Burgess: Designing Efficient Beauty

BIOGRAPHY OF WM. STARLING BURGESS

William Starling Burgess was born in Boston on December 25, 1878, into a prominent and formerly wealthy New England family. His father was the successful yacht designer Edward Burgess, who in the 1880s had designed the three America's Cup contenders, *Puritan*, *Mayflower*, and *Volunteer*.

Edward Burgess died when his son Starling was twelve years old. Starling Burgess attended the prestigious Milton Academy and Harvard University. In 1902 he partnered with Alpheus Appleton Packard in Burgess & Packard. Three years later he established a shipyard on his own in Marblehead, designing and building yachts and small boats.

As it has happened with some other yacht designers at the time, in 1908 he became interested in aviation, and in 1909 he joined with airplane designer August Moore Herring, who had just left Glenn Curtiss, to form the Herring-Burgess Company. The Herring-Burgess Co. built the biplane *Flying Fish*, which flew over Plum Island on April 17, 1910. This was the second fully powered and controlled flight in New England. In 1911 Burgess built several planes licensed by the Wright Brothers. Norman Prince and his friends hired Burgess in 1912 to build a plane for them to race in the Gordon Bennett Cup Race.

Herring left in 1910, and Greely S. Curtis and Frank H. Russell joined Burgess to form the Burgess Company. In 1914, the Burgess Company built their first hydroplane from a John William Dunne design, and soon the company was selling the Burgess-Dunne hydroplanes to the U.S. Army and Navy, and even foreign armies. The company quickly grew to 800 employees, becoming the largest employer in Marblehead.

At some point in this same decade, Burgess designed what was most likely his most popular boat, the 14' *Brutal Beast*. Simple enough for inexpensive mass-production, the *Beasts* became the dominant instructional craft of Marblehead and other communities until late into the 1940s.

When the United States entered World War II, the Burgess Company was sold to John N. Willys, who then sold it to Curtiss Aeroplane and Motor Company. Burgess joined the Navy, became a Lieutenant Commander and designed planes for the Navy.

After the war, he returned to boat design and construction and later designed three successful J-Class yacht defenders of the America's Cup: *Enterprise* in 1930, *Rainbow* in 1934, and *Ranger* in 1937.

In 1922, Burgess, A. Loring Swasey, and Frank C. Paine formed the design firm Burgess, Swasey, & Paine in Boston. Lewis Francis Herreshoff worked with them, too. They designed several yachts, including the *Advance* for John S. Lawrence, the *Gosson* for Charles Francis Adams III, and the *Ellen* for Charles Foster. In 1926, he dissolved Burgess, Swasey, & Paine and created the firm Burgess & Morgan, Ltd. in New York City. At that time he designed some very successful yachts, such as *Niña* and *Ninette* (which will be described with more detail below). In 1930, he was commuting to New York City and living in Darien, Connecticut, with his wife, Else, and their two children.

Burgess was also active internationally. In the mid-1920s, Henry Rasmussen met Starling Burgess, and by 1926 Rasmussen had completed two small motor boats for him. What followed was a close and successful business relationship. Burgess designed the yachts, which A&R built, for United States customers. This represents an example of successful international cooperation across a distance of more than 4,000 miles—in the twenties of the last century!

In 1930 Burgess designed the America's Cup winner *Enterprise*, once more introducing revolutionary innovations such as the duralumin mast. He followed this in 1934, with the design of the equally successful yacht, *Rainbow*. In 1937, together with Olin Stephens, he designed his last America's Cup challenger, *Ranger*.

After designing a streamlined shaped skyscraper in 1927, he joined forces again with R. Buckminster Fuller in 1933 to design the revolutionary aerodynamic three-wheel vehicle, Dymaxion. For this, he carried out extensive wind channel tests.

From 1935 to 1942, Burgess worked as a freelance yacht designer for the Aluminium Company of America, where he applied aluminum as a building material. He designed the *Alumette*, a ship built entirely out of aluminum (including the propeller).

In 1937, he developed a fast destroyer made from aluminum for the U.S. Navy. In 1942, Burgess began working as a civil designer in the aviation department of the Navy, where he focused on submarine defense. In 1946, Burgess came to the Steven's Institute of Technology, where he researched in the area of damage limitation.

In addition to his engineering interest, Starling Burgess also had poetic talent. At least in the early years of his career, he found enough time to write poetry. He published his work in 1903 under the title *The Eternal Laughter and Other Poems*, a 76-page collection of his most notable poems.

Burgess' private life was complicated. Numerous affairs, five marriages, five children, high-profile divorces, and endless scandals, the accidental death of one of his sons and other private details were often connected to his business life, led to numerous problems, many of which were financial in nature. At one time he even had to declare bankruptcy due to his lack of business knowledge.

His daughter, Natascha, wrote this about his death in 1947:

> *Papa had a recurring dream all his life of a beautiful, walled medieval city. He would approach it in his dream but he could never enter. The doors and gates were always locked. He would look at all the towers and balustrades and know that it was beautiful within. He longed to enter but never could.*
>
> *One morning as he was reading the newspaper, he looked up and said to Majorie, his last wife, "Majorie, I had my dream again last night and I finally found the key to the city." With that, he fell over dead. He must have entered that city at that exact moment. What a wonderful way to step forth into something new!*

NIÑA

Type: two-mast staysail schooner
Designer: Wm. Starling Burgess
Year of Construction: 1928
Shipyard: Ruben Bigelow, Monument Beach, Cape Cod, Massachusetts
Length (sparred): 70'
Length on Deck: 59'
Length on Waterline: 50'
Beam: 14'10"
Draft: 9'7"
Displacement: 44 tons
Height of Mainmast: 85'
Height of Foremast: 65'
Sail Area: 2,500 sq. ft.
Construction: mahogany over white oak, bronze fastened
Owner: David A. Dyche, III
Home Port: Wilmington, Delaware

***Niña*: The First "Small" Transatlantic Racing Yacht**

In the first ocean races at the end of the nineteenth century, only very few yachtsmen could afford to participate. To illustrate, the fourth transatlantic race, held in 1905, was won by the 171' three-mast schooner *Atlantic*, driven by a cloud of 1,720 square meters of sail. Legendary skipper Charlie Barr skippered the vessel together with a large professional crew, needing 12 days, 4 hours, 1 minute and 19 seconds to navigate the distance of 3,014 miles between Sandy Hook and Cape Lizard, setting a record that stayed unbeaten for many decades. The *Atlantic's* best daily log was 341 miles. No small yacht could ever compete with this massiveness.

It took many years to organize the first transatlantic race intended for small sailboats. Their time came in 1928, when the yachts starting at the transatlantic race were divided into two classes, one for yachts over 52' and another one for

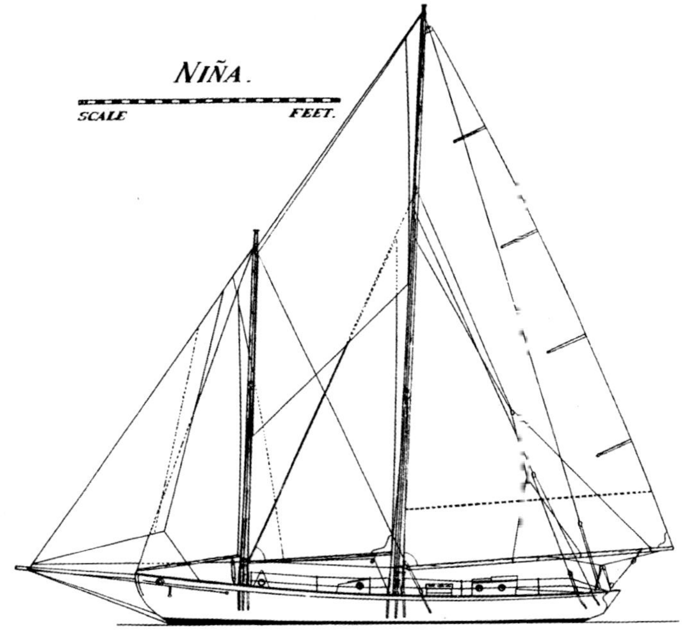

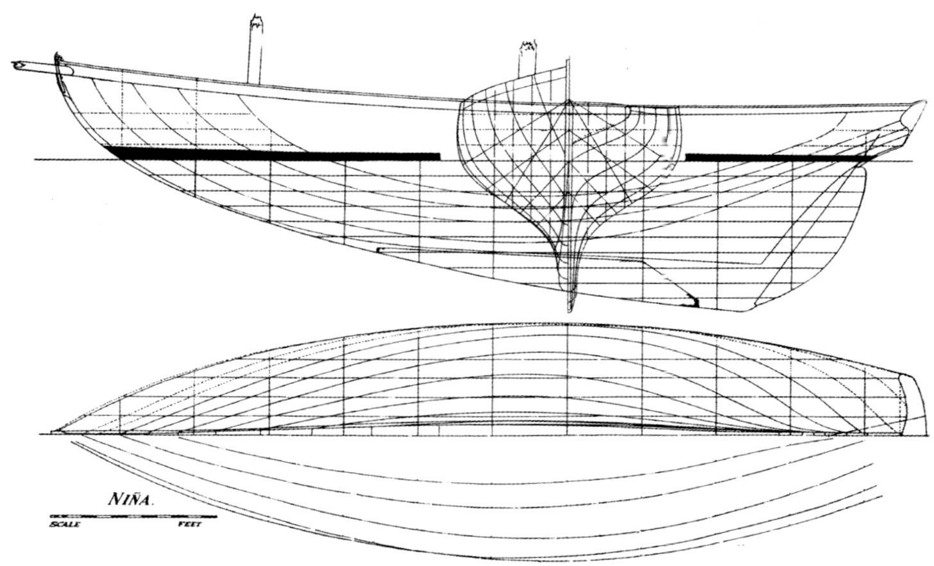

smaller yachts, between 33' and 52' in waterline length. The apparent small size of this last division provoked criticism for the unprecedented risk going out into the ocean with these small boats. Another innovation in this race was the adoption of a compensation system for the elapsed times between the different boat lengths, a system that led to the handicap system denominated "American Ocean Racing Rule," which was then used for the first time on small boats, and which has been very successful ever since. These rules led to the design and construction of yachts especially for the ocean race. The first regatta of 1928 was sponsored by the Spanish King Alfonso XIII, himself an avid sailor, and went from New York to Santander.

The winner of this first race was the schooner *Niña*, which had been specifically designed by Starling Burgess for the race. *Niña* won the 3,900-mile race in 24 days and was greeted by King Alfonso from his launch. As he came alongside *Niña*, he waved his cap and shouted, "Well sailed, *Niña*, I congratulate you! I am the King of Spain."

In the next transatlantic race in 1931, between Newport and Plymouth, the 18 participating yachts had been designed specifically for racing. The smaller yawl *Dorade* won by surprise over the *Niña*. *Dorade* had taken the perilous route over the Northern part of the Atlantic, racing at an amazing speed. This yawl was an Olin Stephens design; Stephens was only 23 years old at that time, and had barely started his great design career.

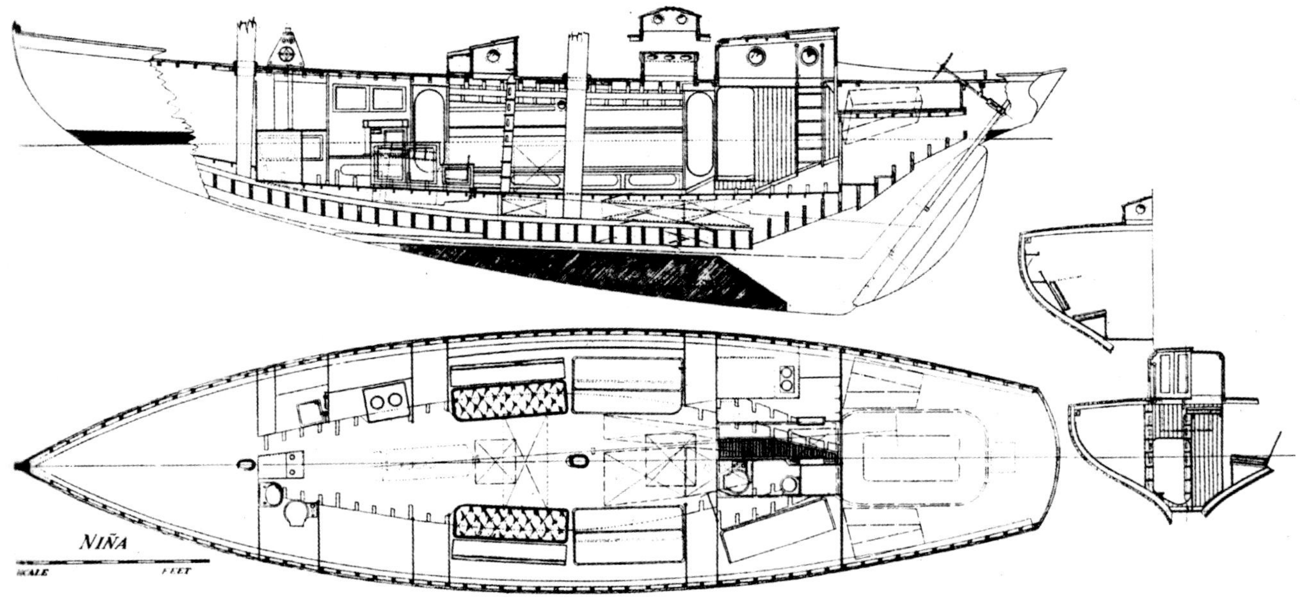

Niña's Design

Starling Burgess opted for the schooner rig because it was easier to handle than a ketch or sloop. In Burgess' design, the mainsail was the main element of propulsion. The mast is positioned at the place of most beam, at 55% of deck length measured from the bow. It was also the first yacht to use the triatic stay, which is rigged from mainmast head to foremast head above the place where in a gaff schooner would be the fore-gaff. Both masts are stayed independently of each other, which allows for the foretopsail to remain set when tacking. Her short ends are the result of the American Ocean Racing Rule; otherwise, *Niña* would have had longer overhangs for and aft. With her small amount of wetted surface, she is easily driven, while the outside lead ballast enables her to stand up to hard weather.

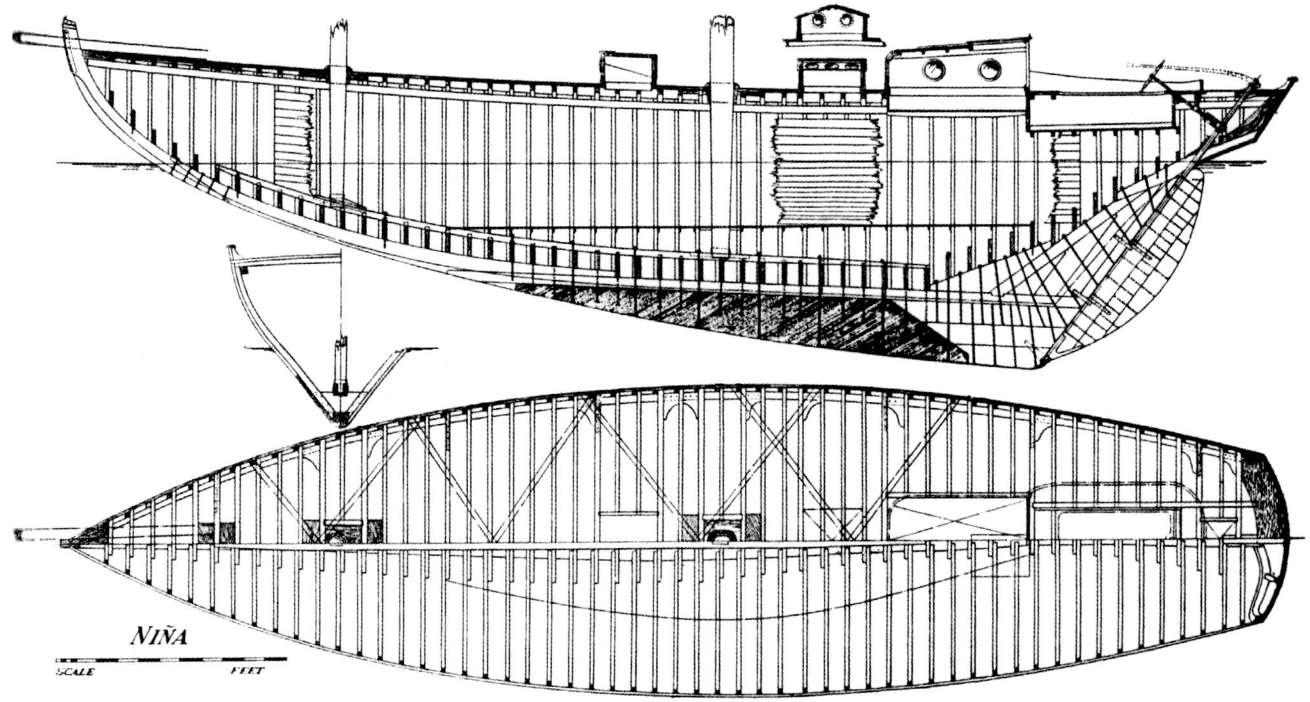

The sails before the mainmast helped to balance the boat in the different wind speeds. The disadvantage was that the mainmast had to be stayed by running backstays, instead of the more popular fixed backstay. On the forefront of the foremast a staysail and a jib are set. The use of booms at all masts and the foresail made the control of the three respective sails (main, main-staysail, fore-staysail) easier with strong winds.

The staysail rig was innovative in 1928. It had been introduced in America in 1922 on the schooner, *Advance*. When sailing windward it is unquestionably faster than the ordinary schooner rig with gaffs. In addition, the staysail schooner rig is easier to handle than a gaff rig, or even a conventional cutter rig, because of the split-up sail area in so many pieces, which all run on stays instead of on gaffs. Some even describe the staysail schooner rig like the ones used by Burgess on *Niña* and her little sister, *Ninette* (see the section on *Rose of Sharon*), as "a cutter with a small mainsail and a large fore triangle."

The greatest advantage of the staysail schooner rig is its diversity of use. It can be used either for hard racing or an easy cruise. On the one hand, when racing the staysail schooner-rig, it allows one to set a wonderful assortment of sails forward of the mainmast, from the three small lowers to the great spinnaker, set on the bowsprit and running past the foremast head to the main topmast head, thus filling the whole space forward of the mainmast. On the other hand, the jib, fore, and main staysails, with a three-quarter-sized mainsail, make a very easy and simple cruising rig.

For her first ocean races, *Niña* had no bulkheads at all, but only one large cabin, in which her crew lived all together. After the first racing season and the transatlantic trip, the owner, Paul Hammond, altered her accommodation to that generally found in a cruiser of her size, with three cabins for owner and guests.

After the Transatlantic Race, More Racing

Still in 1928, when *Niña* headed out of Santander, she was bound for England to sail the 600-mile Fastnet Race, which takes place in the stormy waters of the English Channel and the Irish Sea. In fact, she became the first American yacht to win that race. Her overall time was 4 days, 12 hours, 48 minutes, 13 seconds. *Niña* had one more major win in that season, the 1929 race from London back to the United States, to Gibson Island in the Chesapeake Bay. When Paul Hammond became involved in the 1930 America's Cup race, *Niña* was temporarily laid up.

In 1934, a New York banker, DeCoursey Fales, bought *Niña*, and each year of his life he became more and more devoted to her. He would talk for hours about the "old girl." The rest of *Niña's* career was probably foreordained as she won the New York Yacht Club Astor Cup in 1939 and 1940. Just before World War II, she won, for the first time, an event that was to become her specialty, the 233-mile Stanford-Vineyard Race in the Long Island Sound.

After this 1940 race, she was laid up for the duration of the war. *Niña* was not allowed to rot, however, and after the war she came out in better shape than ever for a three-year stint as flagship for the New York Yacht Club. Fales became the Club's commodore in 1949, and *Niña* earned her honors by taking first place in three out of four of the yacht club's squadron races, as well as winning the Cygnet Cup in 1949. She made such a habit of winning races that Commodore Fales put the trophies back in competition. It became almost a stock joke that *Niña* would proceed to win back her own trophies. In 1960, to thunderous cheers, the then 34-year-old *Niña* became the oldest yacht to win the Newport to Bermuda Race, under the command of 72-year-old Commodore Fales. In 1966, the then 78-year-old Commodore Fales passed away while his crew was attempting to repeat the Bermuda win.

The schooner became so famous that the *New Yorker* published an article about the *Niña* in the 1980s, saying that when she appeared under full sail it was "like seeing Garbo on the street."

From Ocean Racer to Hippie Community Home

After Fales, ownership passed to the King's Point Academy, where she was used as a training ship for young cadets. After that, for a brief time, from approximately 1972 to 1974, Gilbert Seifer, a psychologist from Northport, New York, owned the yacht. Before buying her, he started a spiritual commune in his house. The commune decided to sell the house and purchase the *Niña* from the Kings Point Merchant Marine Academy to move onto the boat and further develop their communal lifestyle.

The commune, which consisted of one other couple, and assorted children, called themselves the "Motley Crew," and they had decided to leave Northport forever, sailing off to spread a vague message of peace and love to the savages along the intercoastal waterway. Gilbert Seifer told a newspaper reporter it was a "spiritual adventure." And for him, that's exactly what it turned out to be. Roseanne Scamardello (the inspiration for Gilda Radner's Roseanne Roseannadanna) came out in *Niña's* dinghy with her camera crew. She instructed the Seifer's two children, Sandi and Jon, to dive into the jellyfish-infested waters of Northport harbor. The two children did as they were told, coming up with welts and translucent blobs all over them. They all seemed to like extreme situations where a strong dose of psychological strength was needed.

The boat had been immaculately maintained by the Academy before ending up in the hands of the commune, who outfitted her sleek but hollow hull with makeshift bulkheads to create rooms and bunks. The walls did not go all the way up, so unless one was sleeping in the captain's cabin, there was little privacy. But the schooner was still a sight to behold under full sail.

However, what was supposed to be an around-the-world voyage turned into a trip to North Carolina. After weathering a nighttime storm in the Atlantic on the way down, and later running aground, the commune decided to go their separate ways in Southport. Gilbert Seifer flew off to England, moved into another commune, met his third wife there, and continued his spiritual journey.

Niña, on the other hand, ended up being owned by Morehead City Boatyard, North Carolina, in exchange for some cash and repair work, before being bought by the Chalet Club in Manhattan, New York, where she was used for charters. From there she came into the hands of Hans Van Ness, who sailed her as a private yacht for some years.

Under the Dedicated Ownership of Captain David A. Dyche, III

In 1988, Captain David A. Dyche, III bought *Niña*. At that time he did not know *Niña's* extensive history, but he soon found out her exciting history and her enormous sailing potential. The vessel was brokered by Alan Viase, a well-known specialist in fiberglassing bottoms of wooden boats. Although David Dyche had heard much criticism about this method, he knew that it would be a very effective way to prevent *Niña's* hull from further deteriorating, make it stiffer and have less water in the bilge, which ultimately would help keep her in better shape. *Niña* had a history of leaking and pumping, as she was very often going in rough weather conditions. The fiberglassing was done very thick, so that it actually became the new hull, adding to her displacement in such a way that she sat about two inches deeper in the water. At present, *Niña* has had this second skin for over twenty years, and she has sailed almost 30,000 ocean going miles without the least trouble or need of pumping.

With these improvements, David Dyche was able to sail her hard again. He felt that everything was right some years after he had purchased her when he was one morning under the lee of Nantucket with 20 knots of wind, sitting on the low side. He could set his coffee cup down at the water's edge as the rail was under water, the water's edge running beside him, while the boat was powering ahead at 10 knots with all sail set. At that moment he realized that he was sailing one of the finest yachts that has ever existed.

Under Dyche's ownership, *Niña* won the New York Mayor's Cup in 1989 and the Schooner class at Antigua in 1994. David Dyche has expanded *Niña's* horizons by cruising her to the Mediterranean Sea as far as Istanbul, Turkey, and the Black Sea, and as far south as Grenada in the Caribbean Sea.

After sailing her to the Mediterranean in 1992 and cruising through the Greek archipelago, it became evident that *Niña* needed more work. Her decks were loose, and carlins had lost their structural strength. He had to replace the deck, as well as the deck carlins and beams. This took place in Miami over a period of three years, finishing in 1997. The end result was startling. Not only did he rebuild the deck, but he also replaced interior faults within bulkheads. All new deck hardware was installed, including new Lewmar winches and custom-made ventilators and hatches. Also, the doghouse was rebuilt and revarnished.

Essentially, with a new hull—if we count the new fiberglassed exterior hull and the new deck—*Niña* sailed the Gulf of Mexico and the Bahamas, with home port Wilmington, Delaware. She was regularly berthed in Panama City, Florida.

In 2000, David Dyche's father suggested sailing her around the world. In preparation for that endeavor, he decided to address the original wooden hull by rebuilding her from the inside out. Most all of the interior was removed all the way to the interior ceiling. Fourteen feet of the keelson was replaced, a new stainless steel mast step and cabin sole beams were installed. Every item that was removed was brought to the shop, such as fuel and water tanks, doors, paneling, etc., anything that could be removed was rebuilt or newly made, all with the emphasis of applying the finish coating of sprayed Awlgrip®. Also, the fasteners and bolts of the keel were replaced with mainly stainless steel.

After David Dyche's restoration, *Niña* sailed again as proudly as in 1928 (*David Dyche*).

At that time new plumbing and electric wiring was installed throughout the entire vessel to the highest standards. The masts were removed and painted. The spreaders and rigging were replaced as needed.

On September 1, 2008, David Dyche, his wife, Rosemary, and son, David, set off on their dream to circumnavigate the globe, meet diverse people, learn about different cultures and see the beauty of the world.

The trip started in Panama City, Florida, and from there they headed through the Caribbean to Cartagena in Colombia, and then to Panama. Once they arrived in Panama, they decided to take the opportunity to sail through the famous San Blas Islands. After sailing for five weeks in the San Blas Islands, they finally reached Cayos Limon, and from there they headed for the Panama Canal. Their trip brings them to Tahiti, Australia, South Africa, and Europe.

This photo shows the current sail plan on *Niña*, after she had received a new aluminum rig. Note the taller foremast, although it is still stayed independently from the mainmast, as it was with the original wooden rig. On top of the main-staysail she can carry different types of fishermen, depending on the wind (*David Dyche*).

Niña sporting her nicely shaped stern. William S. Burgess designed several yachts with this cut-away stern, which still was elegant due to her fine ends (*David Dyche*).

Captain David Dyche, III, owner and current caretaker of *Niña* (*David Dyche*).

Niña in port with her covers set. David Dyche replaced the entire teak deck between 1994 and 1997 (*David Dyche*).

Niña's uncluttered and wide decks show her racing potential (*David Dyche*).

Niña's brass and bronze is always polished. Together with her teak cabin houses and hatches, the boat has a very fine classic feel (*David Dyche*).

Another detail of *Niña* shows the main sheet traveler. Everything is kept as original as possible in layout and rigging (*David Dyche*).

The compass was embedded into the deck to free space in the cockpit and allow easy reading while steering (*David Dyche*).

Sailing in the Gulf of Mexico, off Panama, Florida (*David Dyche*).

In 2008, David Dyche and his family decided to sail around the world. They took the schooner through the Panama Canal into the Pacific Ocean, where they are continuing a long voyage through yet undiscovered seas for this yacht (*David Dyche*).

ROSE OF SHARON

(Ex- *San Cristobal II*; Ex- *Rose of Sharon*)

Type: two-mast gaff-marconi schooner
Designer: Starling Burgess
Year of Construction: 1930
Shipyard: Eastern Shipbuilding, Shelburne, Nova Scotia
Length on Deck: 51'2"
Length on Waterline: 42'
Beam: 13'3"
Draft: 8'4"
Displacement: 25 tons
Construction: fir planked on oak frames
Engine: Perkins Model 4-236, built 1994
Owner: Byron Chamberlain
Home Port: Newport Beach, California

Rose of Sharon: The Little Sister to *Niña*

Rose of Sharon was designed by Starling Burgess and built by Eastern Shipbuilding in Shelburne, Nova Scotia, in 1930. She was launched just in time for the 1930 Bermuda Race, where she would make a remarkable fourth place. One of the other schooners in the race was *Dauntless*, a 61'10" John Alden schooner. It is noteworthy to say that 82 years later, the two boats are still racing each other, but now on the West Coast of the United States.

Since Burgess' schooner *Niña* had been so successful a few years earlier, he thought that if he could design a smaller *Niña*, there might be a better market of buyers, so he designed *Ninette*. Three boats were built to this design: *Ninette*, *Cayuse,* and *Rose of Sharon*. Of these three, only *Rose of Sharon* remains today.

In the February 13, 1930, edition of the magazine *Fore and Aft*, Burgess wrote these words about *Ninette*, which are directly applicable to her sister, *Rose of Sharon*:

> When a design appears that seems to carry out all of our hopes, it becomes an event. Such a boat is the *Ninette*, tinged with the romance of the sea, smacking of the speed and sport of racing, a worthy daughter of a famous dame. For the *Ninette* is in reality but a miniature, as the diminutive of the name implies, of a boat known wherever sails are hoisted or starting guns fired, the *Niña*.

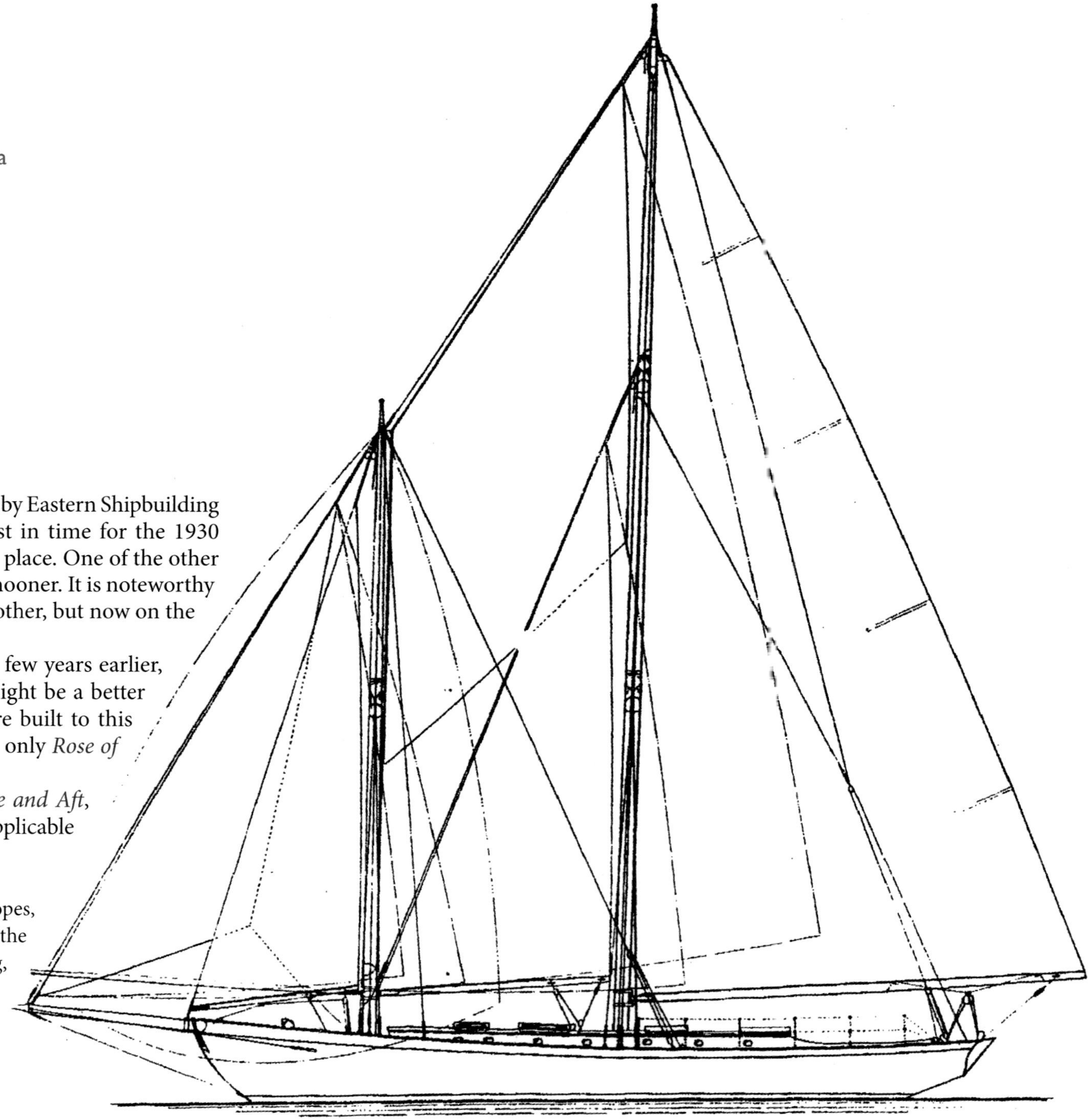

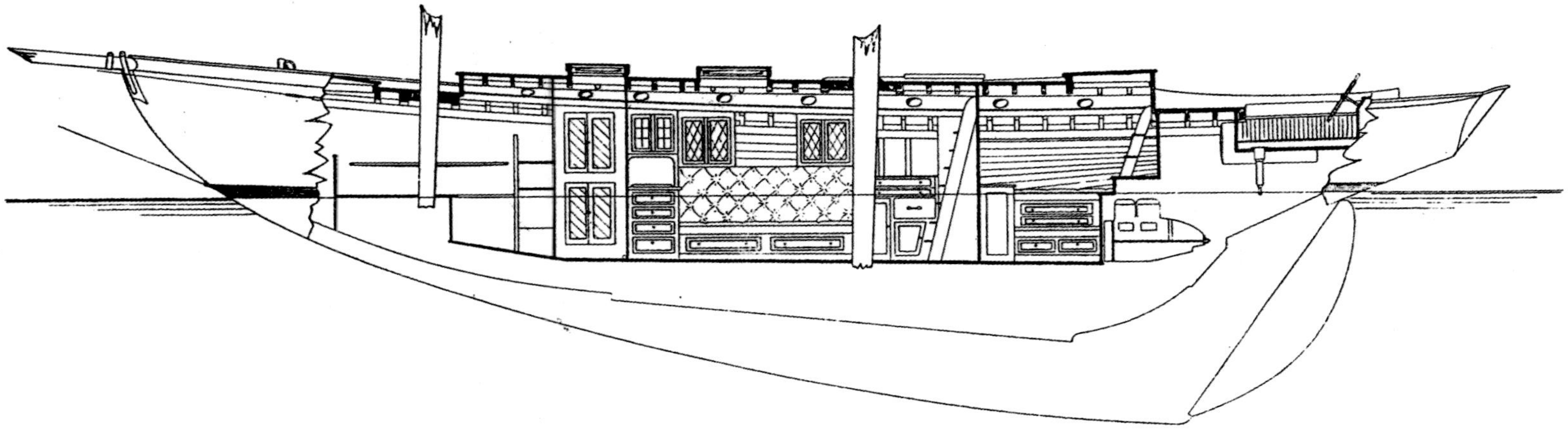

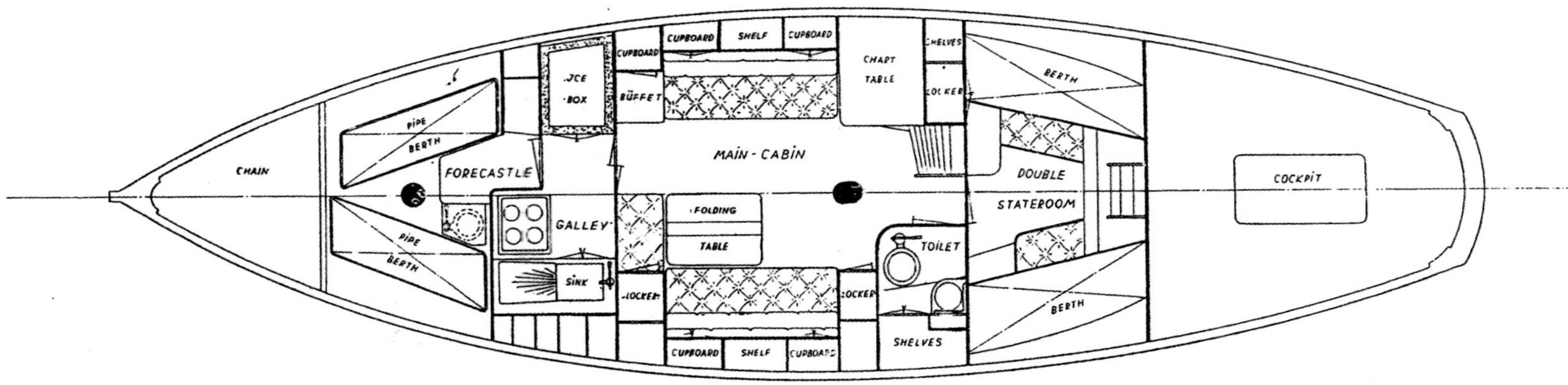

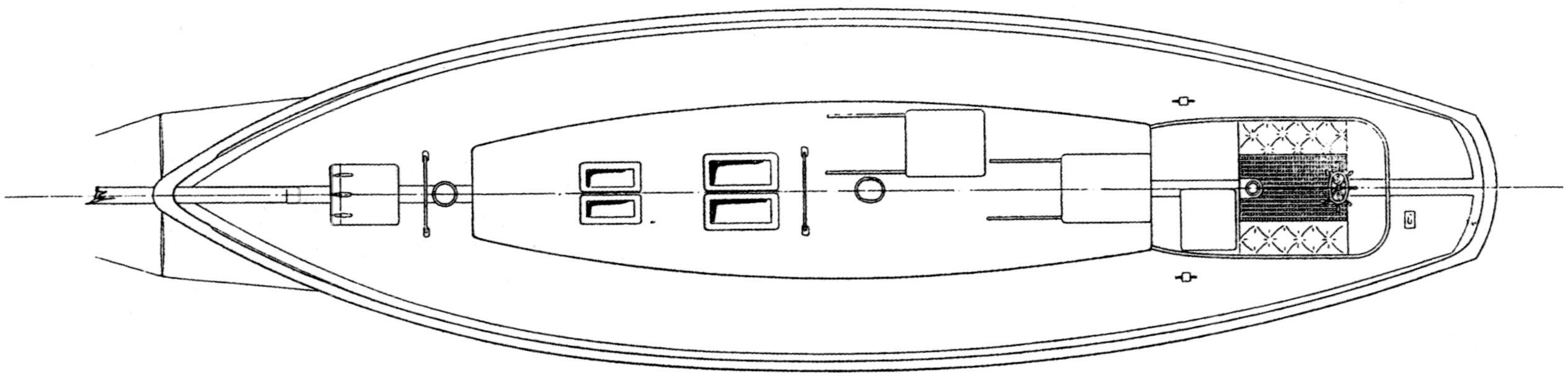

Niña won the Queen of Spain Cup in the 1928 Ocean Race from New York to Santander skippered by owner Paul Hammond with a Corinthian crew. Burgess and Morgan Ltd. of New York designed the *Niña*, and reasoned that if a miniature *Niña* could be produced at a lower cost, it would "meet with a hearty response from American yachtsmen."

Starling Burgess began the task. Racing performance influenced her design. The mainmast position, at 55% of the waterline length measured from the bow, ensured that there was no possibility of even a technical argument over whether or not the *Ninette* was a true schooner. They figured that she would top Class B under the 52' overall rule (Universal Class). Further, her designer favored the gaff over the staysail rig for this boat, because the staysail rig is heavily penalized in racing, as happened with *Niña*.

The designers went looking for a yard that could build the boat ruggedly but economically, and found it in Canada. Eastern Shipbuilding Corporation's shipwrights were unique—almost all were young, enthusiastic yachtsmen for whom shipbuilding was an avocation. Burgess' account continued: "It would be difficult to get together a more ardent group of racing and sailing enthusiasts than these young men, two of whom were with the *Niña* on her famous Santander race, and one of whom was on the *Mohawk* as a Corinthian

This was *Rose of Sharon* when Byron Chamberlain found her half-way through the restoration in 1976. He continued the work and finished the restoration (*Byron Chamberlain*).

Here, *Rose of Sharon* is completely replanked over the course of the 1976 restoration (*Byron Chamberlain*).

In 1996, another major refit was due. She received a completely new caulking and new garboards (*Byron Chamberlain*).

During the 1996 refit, some planks were also replaced (*Byron Chamberlain*).

This photo shows the rebuild of the cockpit. Note that Chamberlain had "parked" the schooner in such a way that her stern was at the height of one of the shipyard's windows. This allowed him to comfortably step on and off the boat and into the house without the need of a ladder (*Byron Chamberlain*).

In this photo her lovely stern becomes apparent (*Byron Chamberlain*).

In 2006 a new refit was due. The schooner, still in excellent condition, was hauled out for six months to have a long list of minor work done on her. In this occasion the varnish was updated. She looks newly built in these photos (*Byron Chamberlain*).

crew member." All loved a fast sailboat and considered the new *Ninette* a pride and joy that transcended commercial enterprise.

Early Racing on the East Coast and Lake Michigan

The first owner of *Rose of Sharon* was Thomas Lamont, president of the J. P. Morgan company. Lamont owned the boat from 1930 to 1935, but had little time to sail and sold it to Fred Pape. Pape was a very active yachtsman and sailor, who renamed the boat *San Cristobal II* and campaigned the boat on the East Coast of the United States. With World War II on the horizon, Pape sold the boat to Charles Stoll from Escanaba, Michigan, in 1940. Stoll changed the name back to *Rose of Sharon*.

Until Stoll's death in 1970, *Rose of Sharon* raced and cruised all over the Great Lakes. Helen and Roy Wildman bought *Rose of Sharon* from Stoll's estate. Fully loaded, they brought the boat down the Erie Canal to New York, and entered the first race of their lives, the New York Yacht Club Mayor's Trophy Race. They won first place. The Wildmans spent two and a half years cruising the boat down the East Coast, around the Caribbean and through the Panama Canal to Newport Beach, California. The boat was hauled out of the water and stored in a boatyard where Wildman, a boat builder, began the restoration. Part way through the rebuilding, Byron Chamberlain purchased the boat and completed the restoration, winning the 1982 VREB Best Restored Sail Award.

A West Coast Racing Career

Since December 7, 1976, Byron Chamberlain has been the owner and meticulous caretaker of *Rose of Sharon*. He worked in Newport Beach and calls Poulsbo, Washington, home. Chamberlain has had a life-long relationship with classic wooden schooners. His first two were Alden designs: the 46' *Golden Hind* and the 43' *Revenge*. On this last schooner he won the 1973 San Francisco Bay Master Mariner Regatta.

After acquiring *Rose of Sharon*, he continued the restoration and has maintained her in perfect condition ever since. Overall, during the time he has had the boat, he either added or replaced the stern, floors, frames, keel bolts, planks, mast steps, deck beams, carlins, deck, covering boards, bulwarks, caprails, bowsprit, transom, engine, generator, water maker, refrigeration, diesel furnace, water and fuel tanks, and wiring and plumbing. The rig and keel are original and the boat has been renovated with little change to the design in the interior and exterior.

Racing in the 1980 Newport Beach, California, to Ensenada, Mexico, race, *Rose of Sharon* was first overall, competing against 580 boats, and using PHRF handicapping. There could not have been a better tribute to her 50th birthday than this race. In 1981, she raced from San Diego, California, to Lahaina, Maui, in the Ancient Mariner Race, finishing first and establishing a new elapsed time record which remains today. Over the years she has raced and cruised from Acapulco, Mexico, to Sitka, Alaska, and Hawaii, and participated in many races along the way.

In 1996, *Rose of Sharon* was due for the second large refit of Chamberlain's ownership. By this time, Chamberlain had brought her up from California to Poulsbo, to entrust the local shipyard at Boat Harbor to do most of the work. Her restoration entailed replacement of her entire deck. She received new deck beams, new carlins, a new plywood sub-deck and a new teak deck with a total thickness of 1 1/4". They also rebuilt the 12' spruce bowsprit and the teak cabin house. Because the old deck had caved in, the interior had to be taken apart, reassembled, and refastened.

They removed all rig hardware, stripped the masts down to bare wood, made repairs and revarnished. It was a big job that had been in the planning stages for a long time. Byron Chamberlain had bought teak five to ten years before this restoration, and waited for the right moment to perform this work. This is only one example of his dedicated love to this exceptional schooner yacht. The boat has become a part of the identity of Newport Beach, California, where everybody knows and admires this masterpiece of American yachting history.

Though *Rose of Sharon* is now 82 years old, she still actively campaigns in various classic yacht races and cruises along the west coast.

After relaunching in 2006, the rig had to be put on her again. This photo shows her narrow cabin trunk. The wide side-decks are ideal for working on deck. She is truly a racing machine with the elegance and outfit of a proper classic cruising yacht (*Byron Chamberlain*).

Rose of Sharon sails again. She can have a good turn of speed even in light winds, thanks to her gennaker and gollywobbler. These two sails are essential on a staysail schooner when there is not much wind (*Byron Chamberlain*).

The schooner *Rose of Sharon* sailing in spring 2011 out of Newport Beach, California, under genoa, fisherman, main staysail, and main. She honors Burgess' heritage very well (*Byron Chamberlain*).

Rose of Sharon's original wooden wheel (*Byron Chamberlain*).

Albert S. Chesebrough: The Larger the Better

BIOGRAPHY OF ALBERT S. CHESEBROUGH

The late Albert Stanton Cheseborough was one of the foremost figures in the field of naval and marine architecture on the East Coast of the United States until his death. He descended maternally from a family that for generations had been famous for its interest and skill in naval architecture. He was born in Bristol, Rhode Island, in 1868, as the son of Lieutenant E. Stanton and Caroline Louisa (Herreshoff) Chesebrough. Lieutenant E. Stanton Chesebrough was a member of a family long prominent in New York; his wife was the daughter of Charles Frederick and Julia Ann (Lewis) Herreshoff, of Bristol.

Their son, Albert S. Chesebrough, went to school in Bristol, and was prepared for college at Mowrey & Goff's English and Classical School in Providence. Then he studied for three years at Brown University. Following that, he learned naval architecture with his uncles, the Herreshoffs in Bristol, Rhode Island. Under the mentorship of such men as Nathanael G. Herreshoff and John B. Herreshoff, Chesebrough received training in every stage of the design and construction of vessels for pleasure and warfare. He finally adopted designing as his profession, and in 1892 he established himself in Boston as a designer of steam and sailing yachts. Later he moved to Wilmington, Delaware, where he became connected with the firm of Harlan & Hollingsworth, designing and building the steel-hulled schooner yachts *Hildegarde* (146') and *Invader* (136'). *Invader* is still sailing today and is featured in this chapter. Chesebrough also designed many great steam yachts, such as the *Alcedo* for George W. Dhilds Drexel in 1897, and the *Alvine*, a 177' yacht for Charles E. Fletcher, of Providence. In 1898, he moved to Baltimore as designer for the Maryland Steel Company, where he was engaged mainly in the design and construction of torpedo boats. In 1900, Chesebrough returned to Bristol, where he established an independent design office. He became widely known in architectural circles as a designer of large pleasure and racing yachts. Among these was the *Cassandra*, one of the largest seagoing steam yachts of his time. He supervised *Cassandra's* building in Scotland at the celebrated yards of the Scotts Shipbuilding Company at Greenock in 1907 to 1908. The *Cassandra* was built for Roy A. Rainey, of New York, as one of his last vessels. He then built the high-speed gasoline yacht *Conejo* in Bristol in 1915, with a length of 93'. This craft attained the unusual speed of 33 knots. He also built a number of destroyers for the United States government, particularly towards the end of his career.

Chesebrough was an ardent sportsman. He was a member of the Bristol Yacht Club and took part in all its activities. He was well known in Philadelphia, New York, and Boston. He was prominent in club and social circles in the United States and abroad, and was considered an authority on all subjects pertaining to the design and construction of ships.

On May 6, 1897, Chesebrough married Emma Russel Bullock, who was born September 25, 1869, and died December 8, 1908. Bullock was the daughter of the late Hon. Jonathan Russell Bullock and Emma (Westcott) Bullock. Albert Chesebrough was sincerely beloved by his many friends for his personal virtues and genial qualities in both social and public life. He was instantly killed in an automobile accident on May 18, 1916.

INVADER
(Ex- *Empress*; Ex- *Invader)*

Type: centerboard (now fixed keel) two-mast gaff schooner
Designer: Albert Stanton Chesebrough
Year of Construction: 1905
Shipyard: George Lawley & Sons, Neponset, Massachusetts
Length (sparred): 154'4"
Length on Deck: 130'4"
Beam: 24'3"
Draft: 13'/23'5" (centerboard up/down)
Displacement: 184.32 tons
Sail Area: 13,455 sq. ft.
Construction: nickel steel, teak deck
Engine: 700-hp

In 2003, after almost 100 years of racing, cruising and chartering, *Invader* turned up for the public in a corner of the Portosole Marina in San Remo, right after the previous year's Classic Week races in Monaco. With her two towering wooden masts on a narrow hull, she didn't go unnoticed. This chapter will recount *Invader's* history, her racing career (such as at the Transpac), her moments of glory, her adventures, and also her decline, which began with the Second World War. Now, at more than 100 years of age, *Invader* is again sporting in as-new condition, set to tell everyone about her past.

Invader's Design and Construction

Invader was designed by Albert Stanton Chesebrough, a disciple of Nathanael Herreshoff and Edward Burgess, who were considered to be the most brilliant designers of their time. The schooner was built by the famous George Lawely & Son shipyards in South Boston and registered in New York. They launched the vessel on July 11, 1905.

Lawely & Son in Boston, and Herreshoff Manufacturing in Bristol, Rhode Island, were the most famous American shipyards for yacht construction at the time. They were known for their construction techniques and for

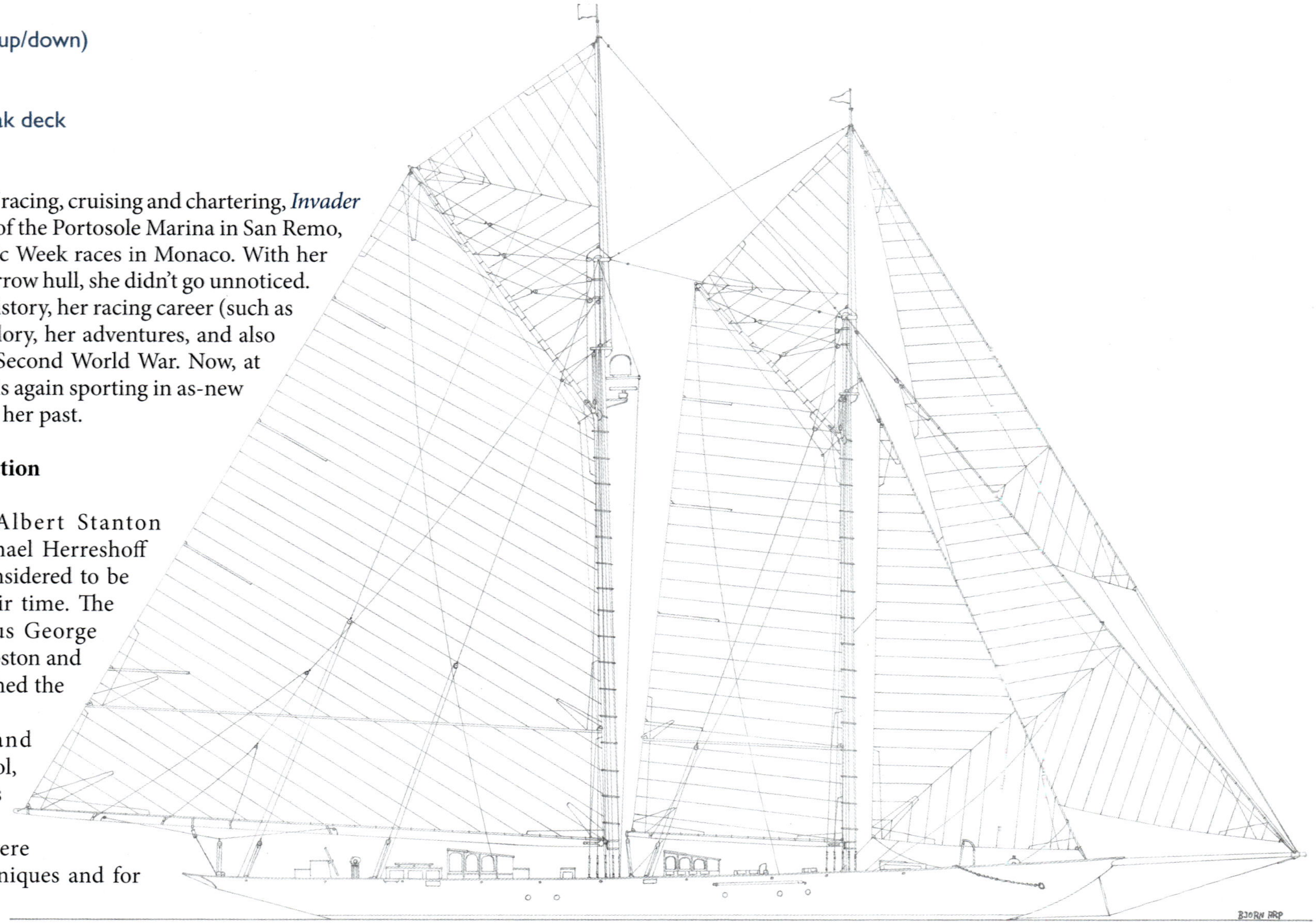

Invader at anchor in the Long Island Sound. She originally had a black hull, which underlined her elegant lines and low profile (*Mariner's Museum, Virginia*).

Invader is shown here sporting a cloud of sails in a race in the Long Island sound, c. 1920s (*Mariner's Museum, Virginia*).

using high-quality materials, which made their boats better than the British-made in many aspects. Just to mention a few examples, Lawley produced two yachts designed by Edward Burgess, the *Puritan* in 1895 and the *Mayflower* in 1896, both of which challenged and won the America's Cup. More than 200 yachts and tenders have survived from those built by Lawley between 1866 and 1945, when the shipyard closed down. Some of them are lovingly restored today. *Invader* is the largest of the Lawley fleet.

Invader's structure and planking were in nickel steel, the ballast was made of lead, and the deck was teak. The ship had a centerboard that brought her draft to 23'5", enhancing the sailing capabilities while allowing the yacht to access shallow waters. Very few designers dared to use a centerboard in ships that size. The harmony of the yacht's lines, which ran from bow to stern uninterrupted by shafts or propellers, must have been a wonderful sight to see on the day of her launch. The ship's hull had been designed and built to move through the water without impediments of any type, powered by more than 13,455 sq. ft. of sail.

Invader's first owner was Rainer A. Roy of Cleveland, a coal magnate. While the ship was under construction, Rainer Roy sent coal to the shipyard to be scaled with concrete under the keel. The coal was only discovered many years later, during her complete refit in Italy in 2003. In addition, Roy did not forget, as the tradition commands, to put a gold coin onto the mast step where the mast sits on. Only four months after the keel was laid, *Invader* was ready for delivery to her owner, with all her masts and rigging, as well as her internal furnishing.

The launch took place at high tide on July 11, 1905, at 6.25 P.M. The owner was not present at the ceremony. In his place, Albert Chesebrough and his wife launched the ship and broke the traditional champagne bottle, adorned with red and white ribbons, against the bow. As soon as the hull started to slide down towards the water, Chesebrough's wife pronounced the usual words: "I christen thee *Invader.*" The yacht was the largest and the most magnificent to join the fleet of the Larchmont Yacht Club, where Rainer Roy was vice-commodore.

Once launched, *Invader* was fitted out until she was able to sail. Her first departure from harbor was a widely celebrated spectacle. She was towed out of Boston Harbor with Rainer Roy on board, his wife, and Albert Chesebrough. There was still much disorder on board. The sails were only partially attached, and others were still packed, with all the adjustments to be made for the imminent racing season. The main mast was 123' high above deck. After the first trials at sea, it was decided to cut the main mast by as much as 7'6" and the foremast by 6'6".

Rainer Roy was, indeed, an impatient character. He was determined to have *Invader* racing at the coming regattas from New York to Halifax, and then to Shelburne, Nova Scotia. It would be no surprise, if we consider his penchant for gambling, that his urge was due to some kind of bet with a member of the New York Yacht Club.

The last shipyard worker went off the yacht just seconds before the tug rope was cast off. The schooner had no auxiliary engine, so she immediately set sails and further trimmed them while heading towards Cape Cod on her way to Newport at the Narragansett Bay.

Roy was keen for *Invader* to take part in the 1906 Spring Cup regattas, but the boat needed more preparation and the crew of 28 to 35 men needed more training. Without more preparation, there would be no hope for competing against the large America's Cup yachts that were already sailing the waters of New York and Newport. The adversaries were the Vanderbilts, Morgans, Astors, and Goulds, not to mention the ones from the Old Continent like Kaiser Wilhelm II or Sir Thomas Lipton, the richest men in the world who also owned the fastest yachts built at the time.

Participating in the First Large Yacht Races of the Early Twentieth Century

Invader finally managed to take part in the 1906 Spring Cup regattas and, most likely, in the following years as well. There is no evidence, though, of any victory. While Roy owned *Invader*, the boat never left the New York and Newport waters, and there is no news of summer cruises taking her anywhere north or south.

Chesebrough definitely showed that his uncle, Nat, could be proud of him. The profile of *Invader's* hull was perfect and sleek, although Chesebrough's special merit was in her structure, where he demonstrated a particular genius. The mere 184.32 tons' displacement made the yacht easily maneuverable. It enabled quick accelerations, and at the same time it was still possible to handle her well with the wheel. Especially in broad reach, with the centerboard up, which gave the schooner a moderate draft of only 13', it is very likely that she could almost surf the seas.

After some years' sailing in the Long Island Sound, *Invader* went into an unstable situation with many owners. It seemed that she was too large for any owner to handle on the Long Island Sound. So she was sold, first to John Bordon, then to Henri D. Whiton, who subsequently sold the vessel to John Barneson a little after Christmas Day in 1919. He in turn sold her on August 31, 1921, to J. Percival Jefferson. At the beginning of 1924, Don Lee became *Invader's* new owner. Just like J. Barneson, he was well known in California. He created a fortune out of his business managing exclusive rights to sell cars such as Cadillac, La Salle, and Woods Electric. He was also a supporter of new communication technologies. He founded and bought some radio stations so as to achieve a complete coverage of the coast of California. He owned the Don Lee Mutual Network and San Diego's Station KGB as well as stations in Los Angeles, Santa Barbara, and San Francisco.

Don Lee was surely aware of *Invader's* sailing potential. It is rumored that he paid a high price for the purchase. Many more dollars were invested to bring the boat back to perfect condition, including new sails and equipment. The initial work focused on a complete servicing of the rig, on 7,535 square feet of canvas for the main and schooner sails, and the light jibs.

He also changed the name of the vessel to *Nancy Lee*, like his daughter. Nevertheless, *Invader* came back to her original name on February 9, 1925, when the ownership was transferred from Don Lee to Don Lee Incorporated. The reasons for this decision, which occurred a few months after the new name was chosen, are not known.

Invader's Golden Age

Invader came into the hands of Joseph M. Schenk, in charge of the United Artists Studio, an independent company created in 1919 by Charlie Chaplin, Mary Pickford, William S. Hart, and Douglas Fairbanks. Mr. Schenk worked out a pragmatic way to combine business with pleasure by shooting a film with his schooner in the fascinating South Seas, along with a series of travel documentaries. The *Los Angeles Times* of February 10, 1932, reported the yacht's departure from San Pedro, with Fairbanks and his wife, Mary Pickford, waving goodbye on the pier. John Haga was in command of the yacht; he had been *Invader's* captain before, during some races, and he brought along much racing experience from other great schooners, such as *Windward* and *Cutty Sark*. First mate was Patrick Ryan, a Pacific war veteran. The engineer was O. Schonsted, and for boat handling there were 14 paid hands. Since the 3,400-mile trip to Papetee would take at least 20 days at sea, the film crew (among them the director E. Sutherland, Douglas Fairbanks, and the leading character, played by Spanish actress Maria Alba) left some weeks later on the passenger ship, *Makura*. *Invader's* schedule included a stop at Tahiti and Moorea for another film, then she continued the voyage heading for Tuamotu, Fiji, Tonga, New Hebrides, Solomon Islands, Java, Bali, and Hawaii, before returning to California after 12,000 miles of sailing.

On one occasion, they avoided the shipwrecking of *Invader* during a storm that pushed them onto an unmarked coral reef between Tahiti and Moorea. The schooner was refloated with a clever handling by Captain Haga, who succeeded in keeping the damage down to a torn sail, a damaged launch, and a torn-off control pillar. The film crew on board *Invader* took the shots for the film *Mr. Robinson Crusoe*, a personal interpretation of De Foe's novel written by Fairbanks himself. The film, still available on video and DVD, has high artistic quality and represents an important document of *Invader*; the schooner appears in it while under full sail.

Once back on the West Coast, *Invader* sailed frequently to Catalina Island off Los Angeles with United Artists actors and other VIPs of the show business. The schooner had a private mooring buoy in Avalon Bay, near the new casino. On board were gamblers who went on the boat out of the territorial waters to gamble. This activity was alternated with social events for people who made cinema history, like Charlie Chaplin, Clark Gable, Mary Pickford, Douglas Fairbanks, Buster Keaton, Gloria Swanson, and many others. Stars of another planet, certainly, but still with earthly needs: Just to mention one example, Robert Decker, a former crew member, remembers that he had to rub sun lotion on Clark Gable's back, despite the respectful distance that had to be held with such guests. It was also aboard *Invader* where Greta Garbo, the great cinema diva of the time, discussed for a whole weekend her imminent film *Queen Christina* with her producer.

In his autobiography, Charlie Chaplin—frequently invited on board by Joseph Schenk—describes with poetical lightness the first encounter with one of the most important women in his professional and private lives: "...his guests were rarely exciting, usually poker players...but he usually also embarked a collection of beautiful girls and, being desperately lonely, I just hoped to find a tiny, pretty, sun ray." This is precisely how he met Paulette Goddart, his future wife and favorite actress. Chaplin remembers the *Invader* as "...a beautiful sailing boat, 138' long, that can comfortably welcome fourteen people."

Difficult Years and Return to San Francisco

Harry H. Hunnewell of Boston bought the schooner from Joseph Schenck. Hunnewell fitted her out in San Pedro, California, for a six-month cruise through the South Seas. *Invader's* departure was scheduled for March 1, 1936. But unlike a simple tourist cruise, Hunnewell undertook a real expedition to the little explored Tuamotu Archipelago. Scientists and researchers from the University of Southern California, the Museum of Los Angeles, the Smithsonian Institution, and Scripps College of Oceanography took part in this expedition. A designer, Nicholas S. Potter, was in charge of modifying *Invader's* rig to be easily sailed by a small crew on this long offshore cruise.

After the trip, in October 1941, the vessel was sold to Paul Noyes, who sailed her to San Francisco and converted her into a floating hotel for sailors. It is probably about this time that the SUP, Sailors' Union of the Pacific, founded in 1885, thought of taking over the management or buying the boat to use her as a school ship. Previous attempts at buying a school ship for merchant seamen had failed due to lack of funds. The promoter of this SUP initiative was Harry Lunenberg, who wanted to safeguard the SUP from the Maritime Committee's repeated attempts to fill merchant vessels with reserve trainees from the Navy. To this end, Lunenberg moved to obtain political support and founded a trust for buying *Invader*, the Andrew Furuseth School of Seamanship, which still functions today. Some sources say that the actor John Barrymore was behind this trust and that it had been he who, knowing *Invader*

After the extensive restoration at the Italian port of Viareggio, *Invader* sailed again with her original gaff-rig in the Mediterranean (*Rudolph Arp Archive*).

The deck houses on *Invader* are not as originally designed, because when she was first built she had an entirely flush deck that did not offer shelter for the crew or guests. She was laid out exclusively as a large racing day-sailor. Today, the interior and deck, while preserving the classic appearance, are suited to comfortably accommodate passengers for long trips (*Rudolph Arp Archive*).

The main boom on *Invader* extends more than 12' abaft the stern. This can be a challenge when maneuvering in the narrow modern ports (*Rudolph Arp Archive*).

well, had given the ship to the SUP in 1942. The SUP managed to cover the high maintenance costs by using the insurance fund contributions to the "Union" made by its members at war.

The necessary changes were made to *Invader* to make her a school ship. A large deckhouse was added, the interior compartments were adapted to suit a much larger crew, and the necessary work of substituting the lead ballast with concrete was carried out. The lead could be used for making bullets, as the United States had just entered World War II and it was for this reason that the SUP, in true practical American style, made the painful decision to sell the lead to contribute to *Invader's* running costs.

Invader, camouflaged as a coaster according to Navy records, was used until the end of the war for patrolling the stretch of coast between San Francisco and San Diego with orders to signal foreign presence to the land through light signals.

On January 8, 1943, only a few months after Paul P. Noyes had acquired *Invader* and started her transformation into a school or training ship, he retained only two shares of ownership from a total of 300, having sold 98 shares to United Textiles and 200 to Paul J. Steffen. Steffen sold his 200 shares to William A. Ducharme on August 31, 1943, and on September 23, 1943, United Textiles sold their 98 shares to Joseph Rosenberg. Once the war was over, Steffen bought back his 200 from William Ducharme.

Although it is not known what happened to *Invader* during the war, it is clear that the war coincided with the yacht's decline, which was marked by the fact that just a few months before the end of the war, a fire in the sail locker burnt the last remaining original sails from before the war. As we shall see, this was just the start of a series of accidents to befall *Invader* over the following 30 years.

Gambling and Flowerpower

At the end of World War II, *Invader* was moored at the Ferryboat Station and had three owners, Joseph Rosenberg, Paul Steffen, and Paul Noyes. These three tried to create a floating club without the permission of the local authorities. It proved impossible to legitimize their business which, it is thought, focused on gambling. The main obstacle was the state of California, which before the war had succeeded in cleaning up a whole fleet of floating casinos run along the coast by Benjamin "Bugsy" Siegel. The state of California did not want to create a precedent by helping organized crime start up business again even though, at that time, Tony Cornero, a.k.a "Captain of the fleet of casinos," was trying to relaunch his business in great style. The owners of *Invader* decided to move the ship to the shipyard of George W. Kneass, a less frequented place in Redwood in the south of San Francisco Bay.

On New Year's Eve of 1946, a fire, which turned out to be caused by arson, spread from the cabins to the kitchen and then through the ceiling to the teak deck. The fire did not deter the owner's plans, despite the newspaper attacks on their "Club" project, and the project continued secretly. Ben Black, the fourth owner, tried without success to put an end to the journalists' rumors, which persisted until 1948 and which had been further fuelled because Tanya Barber, a.k.a. "Belle Silver," had appeared on the San Francisco scene declaring her wish to buy several yachts like *Invader* on which to organize long cruises for fishing and gambling.

Towards the end of 1947, news appeared about Tanya Barber in connection with the purchase of *Invader* for $35,000, and gossip abounded about her wish to install a sumptuous circular bar at a cost of $6,000 or to transform *Invader* into a yacht with no privacy, i.e. into a large open-plan area for guests and crew to live promiscuously "like one big happy family."

At the end, it all vanished. While *Invader* continued to languish in the Kneass dockyard, Warren C. Holst, who lived not far away, decided, with renewed enthusiasm, to buy the schooner to restore and cruise around the world. The change of ownership, according to the official documents, took place on January 15, 1948.

But Holst never sailed around the world; instead, he had to offer her again for sale because he had overestimated his capacity to restore this large schooner yacht. George Koykendahl bought her, transferred her to Redwood and started work on fitting her as a coaster in order to sail along the Peruvian Coast. The agreement with the workers was such that they would not be paid for the refitting work, but would be embarked as crew to Peru. Koykendahl discovered that two of the hands were alcoholics and refused to take them. On the eve of departure, the two came on board and cut the copper fuel tube and set fire. The damage was serious; the interior and the deck were completely destroyed and the foremast was badly damaged but not totally destroyed. After this disaster Koykendahl sold *Invader* to a gentleman from Berkley, who used her as a houseboat on the San Francisco Bay.

In 1958, Roger J. Henderson, a San Francisco businessman, purchased the schooner with the aim of restoring her and again racing the Transpac. He changed *Invader's* name to *Empress*, but he did not manage to do any meaningful work on her. One year later *Empress* had not been touched, and somebody suggested towing her up the Sacramento River and turning her into a floating restaurant. But nothing became of these plans either. In 1960, having borrowed sails and masts, *Invader* took part in a regatta for classic yachts in the bay of San Francisco. The only work carried out by R. J. Henderson was the substitution of the Hall-Scott engines with two Superior diesels, each of 150 horsepower and which powered *Invader* for many years to come.

The "Wood Era"

Just after having replaced the engines in December 1961, R. J. Henderson sold *Invader* to R. L. Wood, owner of the Wood Brothers, a salvage business based in Sacramento. He bought her for $10,000 in Oakland and moved her to a dock in Alameda, California. Wood drove every weekend the hundred miles to Alameda to work on *Invader* and returned home late Sunday night. It took him four years to complete the work. Among many other things, there was a large hole in her bottom, which needed repair, and entire trees were towed from Coos Bay, Oregon, to Alameda to be used for new masts. When she was restored, she was like a wonder: five state rooms, three bathrooms, galley, dining room, and a saloon. *Invader* was moved to

Jack London Square in Oakland, where she served as breakwater for the marina. She may have been inactive but was never abandoned in that period. She took two cruises to Mexico, the first around 1965, and then in 1970. On both trips she stopped in San Diego. Thanks to R. L. Wood, *Invader* survived for these 10 years.

The to-ing and fro-ing of the ownership of *Invader* between Warren C. Holst and R. J. Henderson in the 1950s continued throughout the 1960s between Robert L. Wood and Richard Waters. This then became a foursome from 1972 to 1976 among Richard Waters, the Brotherhood of the Sun, Erick N. Paulsen, and Robert J. Halcro, who, as owner of Windjammer Cruises, used *Invader* to set up a charter business out of Honolulu.

In April 1974, her registry was officially transferred to Long Beach, Los Angeles. It symbolized a transfer of ownership, which took place between the Coast Guard of San Francisco and the Coast Guard of Los Angeles–Long Beach. No value was assigned to this transfer of *Invader*. However, the Central Bank sold or rendered the boat on the same day for $31,875, the same amount as the previous two transactions, to Richard Waters.

Invader came to be berthed in Los Angeles. Rumors running in the area say that *Invader* either sank suddenly one day or fell prey to a ship breaker. Given that the Brotherhood of the Sun were always concentrating upwards to the sky, they would have been unaware of what was going on under their bare feet!

In 1975, Robert J. Halcro from Montreal bought *Invader* for the first time and registered her in Honolulu. After two years of alternate ownership (August 1974–September 1976) among Erick N. Paulsen, the Brotherhood of the Sun, and Robert J. Halcro, as well as that of the Crocker National Bank, on October 10, 1977, *Invader* became the stable property of Robert J. Halcro, who had apparently already sailed her to Hawaii in 1975 to fit her out for passenger tours and island cruising under the banner of Windjammer Cruises.

Dillingham's Shipyard carried out the first work on *Invader* in Honolulu; all the double plates of the plating were taken away and an eight foot high upper deck was built for the length of the whole yacht and covered in wood to give the passengers shade.

In order to conform to the safety regulations imposed by the Coast Guard, the partners of Windjammer Cruises sent *Invader* to the Honolulu shipyard of Armstrong Builders Ltd., who had to raise the bulwarks by 36" with a suitable structure. The majority of the riveting of the plating was replaced with soldered curbing, the teak deck was removed and replaced by 6-mm steel plating, the masts were reduced, and the gaffs and topmasts were removed. Even the main masts were shortened and tapered and the main boom was mutilated in such a way that the yardarm was 9' inside the taffrail.

Small, flat Marconi sails were hoisted from her shortened masts, useful only for reducing roll and completely overwhelmed by the propellers of two powerful GM 6-71 220-horsepower engines and a bow thruster for ease of docking. These radical changes also had the effect of reducing the vessel's gross and net tonnage to 95.4 tons and 72.0 tons, respectively. This tonnage reduction made it possible for *Invader* to be classified as a motor vessel with "oil screw propulsion," and she lost her classification as a sailing yacht. But the most visible change was the addition of a long ferryboat deckhouse with orange lifeboats on top. It gave the yacht a crossbred and unfinished appearance.

This was one of the saddest moments in *Invader's* history. She had lost not only what little remained of her as a great sailing ship, but also her role as a treasured reminder of a great past.

Invader as a Booth Cruiser and the Subsequent Decline

It is not clear when exactly the work on *Invader* in the Honolulu shipyard was completed and when the Windjammer Cruises tours started. However, J. Halcro took on William J. Lambie from Chicago in 1975 as operational assistant, and the following year he signed the Coast Guard declaration that the name of the ship and port of registration had been duly marked on the ship "in characters (Roman) of the correct size, 4 inches, and in the correct place on the bow and the stern."

In February 1983, *Invader* changed her port of registry from Honolulu to Miami. Larry Briggs of Fort Lauderdale had purchased her. In April 1983 he sailed *Invader* to San Diego because there were better opportunities for chartering the vessel. Among other things, Larry Briggs chartered the yacht as a spectator boat during the 1988 America's Cup races. After a few years chartering out of San Diego, he transferred the boat to the Caribbean, where he continued living on board while chartering the yacht out to tourists. During the hurricane seasons he kept the boat in the relatively safe harbor of Chaguaramas in Trinidad and Tobago, in order to have the boat ready for a new charter season when the hurricane season was over.

The Rebirth

In October 2000, the Italian captain Guiliano Mussone was engaged by the Blue Sea, Inc., which is a marine business affairs company based in Anguilla, to find a prestigious sailing ship for promotional purposes. He set out on his search to discover the whereabouts of what he remembered as being the most beautiful ship he had ever seen. After months of research, he found the *Invader* in Germany, at the Lürssen shipyards in Bremen. There was only a bare hull with no masts, but he recognized her great potential.

The company's idea had been to purchase a hull as a base for a sailing vessel with modern rigging. However, as he gathered more information about *Invader's* history, he realized that it was a truly classic sailing yacht that deserved to be restored to her original splendor. Luckily, he arranged for the *Invader* to undergo an accurate and precise restoration. The hull was brought to Viareggio in Italy, where it was completely gutted, sandblasted, and restored where needed. All the interior and deck equipment was new. Once the hull was launched again, between 2001 and 2003, the finest Italian craftsmen in La Spezia fitted the yacht out. The restoration was officially finished on

November 23, 2003, when the *Invader*, under full sail for the first time in many years, left La Spezia for Nice in the Côte d'Azur, where a place of honor had been reserved for her in the Bassin Olympia, located in the heart of the old city.

On December 13, 2003, the shipping company Blue Sea, Inc. and the city arranged a rechristening ceremony for *Invader*. The event was organized with no cost spared, a sumptuous banquet, music, and a master of ceremonies in charge of the protocol: the speeches, the blessing, the naming of the boat with a bottle of champagne hurled against her bow.

Invader Today: A Challenging Combination of Modernity and Classicism

Invader is in many aspects a very special classic schooner yacht. The total restoration undertaken by Italian shipyards between 2001 and 2003 has lead to a distinctive combination of a classic exterior with a neo-classic, sometimes even modern, interior.

The saloon is situated amidships and hosts a dining area to starboard with a settee in leather and an extendable table, plus a cozy bar with antique brass stools. The oak floor with marqueterie and the cherry wood wall paneling evokes a long bygone era of elegance.

The passageway leading aft to the guest cabins splits to pass either side of the main mast. A beautiful circular lobby leads towards the curved double doors of the twin-bed main cabin, which is spacious and very traditional, with curved deck-beams, double skylights overhead and an adjacent double bathroom.

On both sides the lobby opens to two twin-bed guest cabins, each en suite. Forward to the saloon are a fully equipped modern galley, dinette, and two twin crew cabins, while the captain has a double cabin. The engine room is immaculate, with tanks for 1,000 gallons of water and 4,330 gallons of fuel. Except for the original compass binnacle, everything else on the yacht has been replaced. The schooner stands out for an easily driven hull with a classic wineglass underwater body, deep draught, long overhangs and a large sail area.

An exceptional event was the presence of the direct descendants of the owner who had commissioned the *Invader*, Rainer Roy. Emotions ran high in seeing the *Invader* restored to her original splendor and the presentation of a piece of coal, which had been found in the keel during the restoration, and which most likely had been put there by their ancestors "par bonheur."

During the following months after the rechristening ceremony, *Invader* made sailing trials, offering an evocative sight in the waters off the Côte d'Azur and navigating in the Mediterranean until she was ready for her official presentation in the world of classic sail during the 2005 Monaco Classic Week. In 2006 and 2007, *Invader* spent her time in Valencia on the regatta fields as guest boat of the America's Cup. The America's Cup organizing committee used her as a VIP boat. From her wide classic deck, the spectators could view the race of the 24-meter (79 feet) high-tech sailing yachts. *Invader* was also protagonist for a fashion shoot with a top Australian model.

During the intense season of the America's Cup, unfortunately, began a sad period in *Invader's* new life: Captain Giuliano Mussone's cancer, which had already been diagnosed some months before, worsened. He stood ahead of the fight against the inevitable with great force but ultimately died on February 12, 2008, leaving behind this magnificent vessel and his spirit of integral seamanship.

After a short period in Barcelona, *Invader* moved to Puerto Tarraco in the port of Tarragona. From there the large schooner moved back to Barcelona, where she was moored at the Marina Barcelona 92. Since then, she has been sailing in the Western Mediterranean.

Cox & Stevens: Designing Large Steel-Hulled Cruising Yachts

HISTORY OF COX & STEVENS

The firm Cox & Stevens began in yacht design and commercial brokerage in New York City in 1905. The firm's original principal partners were Daniel H. Cox, Irving Cox, and marine engineer Colonel Edwin Augustus Stevens. Daniel was concurrently in partnership with William Francis Gibbs, and after a company-reorganization in 1932, the firm of Gibbs & Cox, Inc., took on all the commercial work, while Cox & Stevens retained the yacht design work. The firm specialized in large motor and sailing yachts, producing the design for the largest yachts built at the time. The most salient example was the four-mast barque *Hussar II*, today known as *Sea Cloud*. This and many other yachts designed by Cox & Stevens were built in Germany at the Friedrich Krupp-Germaniawerft in Kiel, which was famous for the high-quality craftsmanship in steel construction.

Philip L. Rhodes became associated with the firm by 1934, and after the death of head designer, marine engineer, and vice president Bruno Tornroth in 1935, Rhodes became head naval architect for the firm. In 1946 the firm of Philip L. Rhodes succeeded Cox & Stevens Inc., and the business ceased altogether with Philip L. Rhodes' death in 1974.

DEVA

(Ex- Te Vega; Ex- *Vega;* Ex- *Juniata (IX-77);* Ex- *Etak)*

Rig: two-mast gaff schooner
Designer: Cox & Stevens, Design No. 354
Year of Construction: 1930
Shipyard: Friedrich Krupp-Germaniawerft, Kiel, Germany
Length Overall: 156'
Length on Deck: 137'
Beam: 28'2"
Draft: 17'5"
Displacement: 242 tons
Sail Area: 10,500 sq. ft.
Engine: Built with a 200-hp Winton marine diesel engine; replaced by a 400-hp English Mirrlees in the 1950s; from the mid-1990s a 700-hp German MTU
Speed Under Engine: 11 kn
Homeport: Le Grazie, Italy

The American Schooner Yacht *Etak*

Etak was a two-mast, gaff-rigged schooner designed by New York naval architects Cox & Stevens in 1929 for American businessman and sailor Walter Graeme Ladd and his wife, Catherine ("Kate") Everit Macy Ladd. *Etak* ("Kate" spelled backwards) was built at the Friedrich Krupp Germaniawerft shipyard in Kiel, Germany, and launched in 1930.

This schooner was a fine addition to the New York Yacht Club fleet. She was intended to be very comfortable to her owners, guests, and crew, and at the same time have a good turn of speed under sail and under power. These multiple requirements were only possible to fulfill with an overall length of 134'2", a waterline length of 100', a beam of 28' and a draft of 16'. The construction at Krupp was conformed to Lloyd's highest standards for steel-hulled yachts. The schooner was equipped with a Winton Diesel engine of 200 hp, with which she could go under motor at 9 knots. In addition, two Hill diesel auxiliary engines were installed, that were connected to a battery. With this electric power, the boat could run electric lighting, electric sail and boat hoists, capstans, etc.

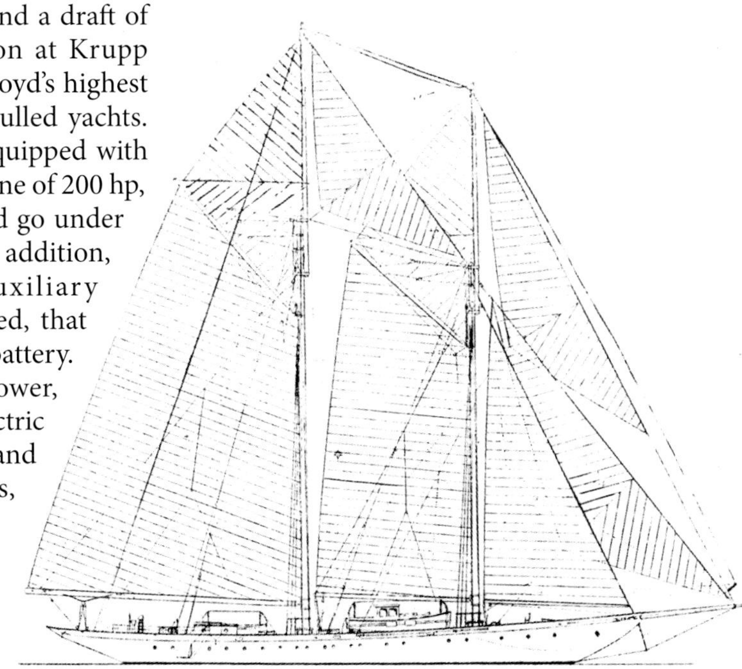

(Schiffbau, Schiffahrt und Hafenbau, January 1931)

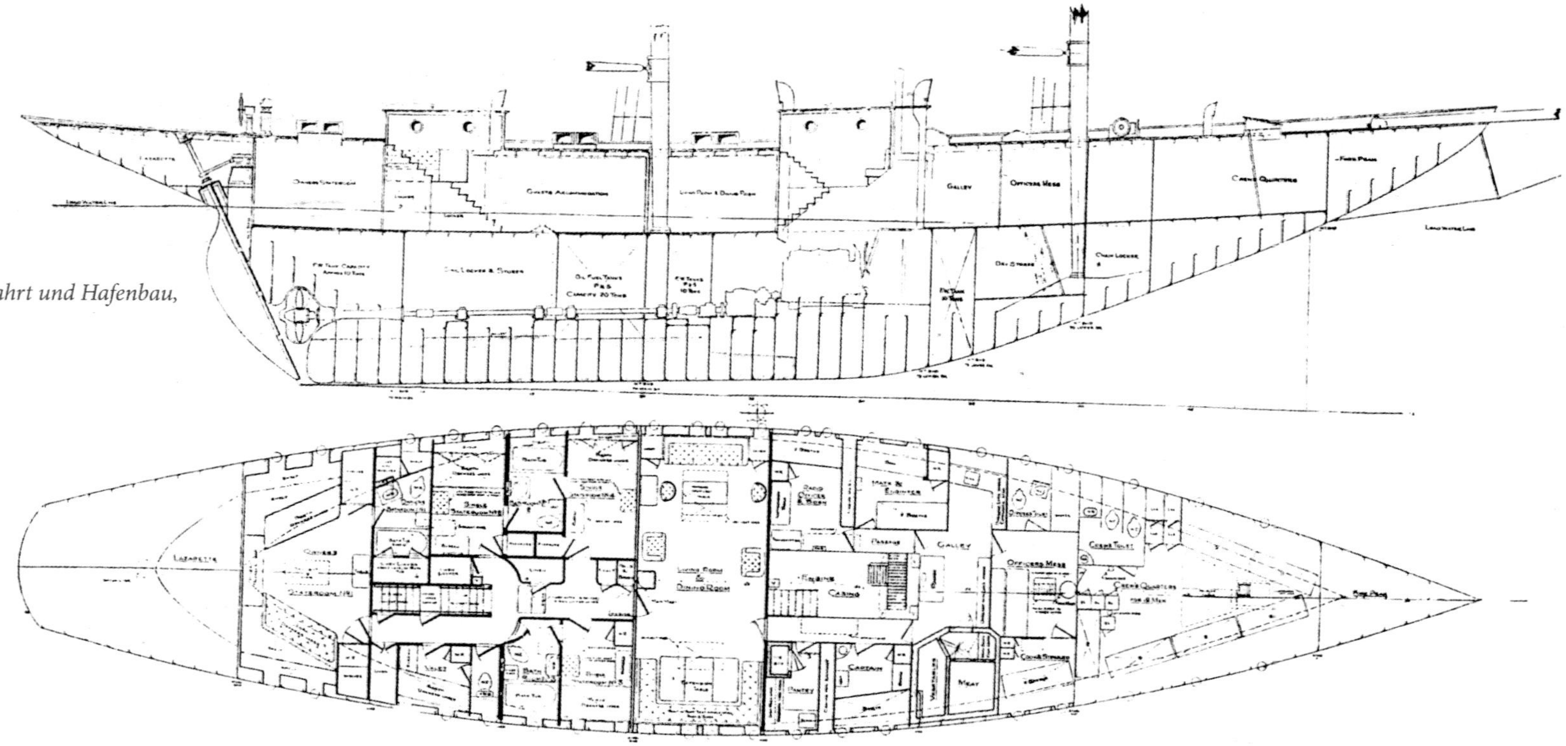

(Schiffbau, Schiffahrt und Hafenbau, January 1931)

This painting of *Etak* represents her shortly after launching in 1930. She had a black hull and a long deckhouse between the two masts (Yachting, *1930*).

These two early photographs of *Etak* show her deck layout and sailing performance in the Atlantic, during her crossing from Germany to New York (*Schiffbau, Schiffahrt und Hafenbau, January 1931*).

The accommodations below decks included a large double stateroom for the owner, three bathrooms, a combination living and dining room the full width of the ship, deck salon, and unusually fine quarters for the crew.

Walter Graeme Ladd died in 1933, and the schooner was bought by Adolph Dick of the Dick sugar and banking family of New York. He was of German ancestry and well-known, among many other things, because of his board membership of the National Sugar Refining Co. Then the yacht came into the hands of another German, Hans-Wilhelm Röhl, who co-owned the Rohl-Connolly Co., which specialized in building ports. Among others, the Rohl-Connolly Co. built the Port of Los Angeles breakwaters. Röhl himself was later, in 1942, investigated for pro-Nazi sympathies.

World War II Service

In 1942, the United States Navy purchased the schooner from H. W. Röhl, and renamed her *Juniata* (IX-77), and placed her into service on August 11.

Juniata was assigned to the Western Sea Frontier and was based at San Francisco, California. She alternated with other ships on patrol for the great circle route to Hawaii, steaming to and from her station some 500 miles west of Eureka, California. *Juniata* was placed out of service at Treasure Island, San Francisco, on January 1, 1945, returned to the Maritime Commission, and was sold to Thomas Hamilton in June 1945.

Vega with Thomas Hamilton in the Pacific

When *Juniata* became property of aviation pioneer Thomas F. Hamilton, he named her *Vega*. Thomas Hamilton was a serious yachtsman, who also owned the Herreshoff-designed schooner *Vagrant*. The name *Vega* comes from the evening star, and an apocryphal legend perpetuated on board contends that Pacific islanders, impressed by her handsome lines added the adjectival prefix Te, meaning beautiful, before her name. This is how the name *Te Vega* evolved, and ultimately ended up in the registry books.

Hamilton sold the vessel in 1951 to Cornelius Crane. As conditions of the sale, the hull color was changed from black to white and deck houses were added. The actual transfer took place in Hawaii, and Thomas Hamilton personally, together with some friends and his professional crew, delivered her there.

Chartering in the Pacific

Cornelius Crane was the heir to the plumbing fortune of the Crane Co. He put the famous Honolulu-based Capt. Omar Darr in charge of the vessel, who sailed her from Hawaii to Los Angeles and then to Tahiti and Bora Bora to do charter work.

The captain sailed the schooner with a crew of 18 and embarked 12 passengers. In Tahiti, the schooner was transferred to French registry to work as a passenger ship between Hawaii and Tahiti; since air service, mostly chartered air service, was only to Bora Bora. When on her shakedown cruise from Long Beach, California, to Hawaii with some paid and some Corinthian crew, they sailed the schooner hard, so that they popped a main topmast backstay and, at a different time, the bobstay. The schooner reached 15–17 knots at one point but the lee rail was well under water at the time and the main engine and one of the generators were flooded. So the captain did not indulge again in such a hard sailing.

The transfer of registry to French flag took months. When *Te Vega* left Tahiti in December, 1951, she had a sad catastrophe at sea when the main mast broke off at the deck, killing two and injuring many others. At that time, none of the big schooners doing charter in the Pacific, such as *Invader*, carried topmasts anymore.

Chartering in the Atlantic

At the end of the 1950s, *Te Vega* was bought by Stimson Lumber Co. scion Harold Miller, who was originally from the Northeast of the United States. Miller put the schooner into the charter trade under the command of Capt. Willoby and the Swedish Capt. Boisen. The vessel was based at English Harbor, Antigua, and carried charter passengers on one-week cruises in the Windward and Leeward Islands. The schooner was represented by R.E.B. Nicholson charter agents, of English Harbor. At that time *Te Vega* sailed with a white hull, and it still carried the gaff rig. However, the main had been blown out in a storm and was replaced by a triangular sail. Even that smaller sail was enormous. It was raised by a halyard wrapped around an electric winch.

Te Vega had a crew of seven sailors, plus captain, first mate, second mate, engineer, pursar, two cooks, chief steward, assistant steward, and mess boy. There were usually 10 or 12 passengers. The officers and sailors were all from Sweden. The sailors were teenage boys who attended a maritime academy in Sweden and at certain intervals left school to work on ships. Among the many famous guests on board at that time were such stars as Anita Edberg. While chartering, the crew was encouraged to enjoy themselves with the guests and sometimes they invited steel bands to play on deck as the crew barbecued foods for their guests.

At the end of the summer of 1961, *Te Vega* sailed to Oyster Bay, New York, where she was to be converted from a gaff rig on both masts to a staysail rig. Although she arrived in New York, the conversion of the rig never happened. Instead, the vessel was abandoned and lingered at some port for many years. The ship ultimately was taken over by Stanford University, which invested some money into her restoration and fitting out, keeping her gaff rig.

The schooner's name plate in 1972, when she sailed as *Te Vega* for the Flint School out of Florida (*Palmer Stevens*).

Te Vega sailing in the North Sea under Dutch flag in 1990. She was used as a private yacht at the time (*Palmer Stevens*).

Currently, *Deva* is located in Italy and restored to the highest standards. The charthouse features all imaginable navigational instruments (*Palmer Stevens*).

Researching for Stanford

Once the schooner was ready to set sail again, she was used by Stanford University as a research vessel off the California coast. But there were also some longer trips. In the summer of 1964, *Te Vega* sailed from Mombasa, Kenya, to Singapore. The University had set up a scientific expedition studying the Deep Scattering Layer, i.e. the D.S.L., of the ocean, a sonar layer deep in the sea, which moves up and down with the daylight and nighttime hours. They dragged a fine net many thousands of feet down, catching organisms thought to be the cause of the D.S.L. The research found out that the organism responsible for this phenomenon was a siphonophore, which is a light-sensitive organism.

The boat traveled across the Indian Ocean stopping at the Seychelles, Maldives, and Sri Lanka. At each stopping point, the researchers aboard also collected reef fish to identify and catalog. The trip took about eight weeks, and was done by five faculty members, twelve marine biology students, and a crew of fifteen.

In 1965–66 the schooner was managed by the Johns Hopkins Marine Laboratory in Monterey, California, an offshoot of Stanford University. The captain was again Omar Darr, who previously had sailed her during her Honolulu-Tahiti days. The vessel did some research in Monterey Bay in a large volume of water near the Monterey Marine Canyon, which was strangely deficient in oxygen. During that time *Te Vega* also underwent extensive refitting at Bethlehem Shipyard in San Francisco.

Under the Flag of the Flint School

In the fall of 1970, *Te Vega* was leased by the Flint School, with owner George Stoll and his son Capt. Jim Stoll on board. The Flint School was a private land-based school from Sarasota, Florida, that moved aboard *Te Vega* in the fall of 1970. Shortly after her acquisition, the first students embarked in the Bahamas. *Te Vega* sailed in company with *Te Quest*, which is now the *El Boughaz*, also featured in this book.

In Dutch Hands

At the end of the 1980s the schooner belonged to the Dutch financier Pieter Schoonheim Samara. Samara was, in addition to his financial talent, a talented kundalini yoga teacher. He allowed the ship to be used by the Watermark Program at the Landmark School in Beverly Farms, Massachusetts, which specializes in working with dyslexic students. The crew consisted of 17, and there were 32 students. Captains Steve Wedlock, and later Niels Lindiger were in command of the schooner. *Te Vega* sailed from Amsterdam to St. Malo, France and Vigo, Spain, to the Mediterranean, where they cruised around Ibiza, Menorca, Almeria, and some other ports. From there they headed towards Tenerife in the Canary Islands. Then, it took them 17 days to sail to the Caribbean, stopping at Antigua, St. Baths, Isle de Saint, St. Kitts, and a few more islands. From there, they continued to Bermuda and New York.

In July of 1987 the *Te Vega* was delivered to the Netherlands from Lunenburg, Nova Scotia.

Restoring *Te Vega*

In 1995, Te Vega changed hands and the new owner realized that the old schooner needed a large restoration. The work started at the Bilbao shipyards in Spain and continued at the Beconcini shipyards in La Spezia, Italy. The goal of the meticulous restoration was to produce a comfortable and functional yacht, suitable for long cruises, while maintaining the style and appearance of the 1930s. The schooner was repowered with a 700-hp MTU diesel engine and classified under the Maltese Cross Class 100 A 1.1 Y, conferred by RINA to large yachts.

Te Vega was then owned by Calisto Tanzi of Parma (Italy) a tycoon involved in the food and travel businesses. He registered the schooner under Italian flag.

Deva: The Second Large Classic Yacht of an Enthusiastic Italian Sailing Family

In 2005, *Te Vega* was sequestered as a consequence of the Parmalat scandal. In December 2005, the schooner was auctioned off to the fashion magnates of the Diego and Andrea Della Valle family, who also own the 23-meter Class, J-Class rated, *Candida* and two classic motor yachts. The new owners christened her *Deva*.

Claudio Mottola was the skipper of *Candida*, and he was put in charge of a quick refit of the schooner. He had to bring her back to her original beauty for the upcoming summer of 2006, while *Candida* was laid up in the harbor. After the complete sanding down of the hull and repainting in Genoa's Amico Shipyard, Mottola sailed her to the Beconcini yard in La Spezia for a complete overhaul of the rigging, sails, deck, and machinery equipment. Her masts, booms and gaffs were removed, carefully checked and varnished. Her spreaders were rebuilt with Douglas fir and the main boom was lengthened. The diameter of higher and intermediate shrouds were reduced on both masts to reduce weight in the rigging. The four heavy davits and the two large tenders on deck were removed. Instead, a small service tender was put in place. A low, removable sundeck was added in the central area of the deck between the foremast and the entrance to the forward deckhouse. This was achieved without altering the lateral profile of the schooner but it had the advantage of making the deck very clean and functional. A new sail plan was designed and realized by Halsey, which is now "one" sail-maker in La Spezia. The new sails have a total area of 12,378 sq. ft., compared to the previous 9,041 sq. ft. The cream-colored sails are cross-cut and sawn to the highest standards in Dacron dimension Polyant. The engine room and machinery was carefully serviced and updated to modern safety standards to match all requested Class Register regulations and rules.

Deva's winter base is now the small and beautiful bay of Le Grazie, near Portovenere (La Spezia). She is based there along with *Lulworth*, *Astra*, *Candida* and other famous big classic yachts. When underway she usually cruises the Mediterranean. The boat can embark twelve guests, with a crew of eleven, which includes a chef and a waiter, who are both good sailors when needed. *Deva* can once again easily reach 11–12 knots under sail, with 18–25 knots of true wind. On October 12, 2009, *Deva* even reached an exceptional 16.1 knots in more than 60 knots of wind, with just the four lower sails, i.e. mainsail, foresail, staysail and working jib. The speed lasted for less than ten minutes before the main gaff broke and the boomed staysail was reduced to shreds!

Deva is currently among the largest and probably most impressive steel-hulled schooners afloat.

Deva's low profile bow, with her varnish always well kept up (*Palmer Stevens*).

Deva at her current slip in Italy. She sports a bright white hull to cope with the Mediterranean sun (*Palmer Stevens*).

Samuel S. Crocker: Innovation and Tradition

BIOGRAPHY OF SAMUEL S. CROCKER

Samuel Sturgis Crocker was born in Newton, Massachusetts, on March 29, 1890. He studied naval architecture at the Massachusetts Institute of Technology before he started working as a draftsman with George Owen, a famous naval architect of Newton, for the following four years. In 1916, Sam Crocker opened his own business in a small rented yard in Marion, Massachusetts, where he mostly repaired boats. However, occasionally he received orders to design and build new yachts. During World War I, he worked at George Lawley & Son in Neponset, Massachusetts. There he was in charge of a construction crew responsible for completing the planking of nine, 110' submarine chasers on a United States' government contract. In 1919, he was associated with Murray & Tregurtha, Quincy, in the building of F-5-L flying boats. Between 1919 and 1924, Sam Crocker worked as designer and draftsman with John G. Alden in Boston. This was probably the most influential experience in his career, because there he learned the detailed drafting of yachts which was so characteristic of Alden, and which he followed from then throughout the rest of his career.

With this huge experience accumulated at Alden's, Crocker established his own office as S. S. Crocker, Naval Architect, in Boston in 1924, and ran it successfully for 32 years. In 1956, he moved the enterprise to the yard of his son, S. Sturgis Crocker, in Manchester, Massachusetts. He continued his activities in designing and building at that location until he passed away in 1964.

Sam Crocker designed and supervised the construction of more than 300 vessels, including commercial craft for fishermen, yachts, and racing boats, each individually designed to the special requirements of the prospective owners. Many of his yachts were utilized for pleasure cruises in the waters around Florida and the Caribbean, as well as the New England coast. Fast cruising craft designed by him were frequent winners in races on the Great Lakes. Among these were the *Barbette*, winner of the Detroit-Mackinac Races in 1927 and 1929; the *Jacinta*, winner of the Wind Point Race in 1931; the *Nawanna*, winner in class B in the Detroit-Mackinac Races in 1933 and 1934; and the *Valkyrie*, winner of the Chicago-Mackinac Race in 1934. Among the salt water racing winners designed by Sam Crocker were the *Chantey*, winner of the New Bedford Race Week in 1930, 1931, and 1932, and of the Whalers Race in 1933; the *Retriever*, winner in Class B in the Jeffrey's Ledge Race in 1932; *Grey Gull II*, winner of the Huntington-Cornfield Race in 1932 and the Bayside Block Island Races in 1933 and 1934; and the *Pole Star*, winner in Class B in the Jeffrey's Ledge Race in 1933 and the Whaler's Race in 1934.

Sam Crocker also designed many remarkable schooners. His small schooners, with deck lengths ranging between 30' and 40', were very popular in the 1930s, as they were very much inspired in the Alden designs, with swept shear lines and handsome interiors. He usually used very good building materials, preferring bronze fasteners over galvanized steel, which led to his boats being preferred in southern latitudes. His yachts also had it easier to stand up against aging, which is shown by the fact that many of his boats are still sailing today.

This chapter will present two of his largest designs that are still actively sailing. One, the 54' *Mahdee*, was about to be broken up in 2006, and was only saved because of the strong effort of her current owners; and the other, the 60' *Tyrone*, has had a relatively stable record of caring ownerships, and she is currently as beautiful as she was at her launch in 1936. What both boats have in common is that they are different from the classic outfit of schooner yachts of their time, being laid out more as sturdy cruising yachts rather than racing machines.

MAHDEE

(Ex- *Privateer;* Ex- *Pandora;* Ex- *Mahdee)*

Type: two-mast gaff-Marconi schooner
Designer: Samuel Sturgis Crocker
Year of Construction: 1930–1931
Shipyard: G. F. Lawson, Dorchester, Massachusetts
Length (sparred): 68'
Length on Deck: 54'
Length on Waterline: 46'
Beam: 14'11"
Draft: 6'4"
Displacement: 28 tons (gross), 19 tons (net)
Sail Area: 1,500 sq. ft.
Construction: original fir on steam-bent oak; rebuilt mahogany on laminated mahogany
Engine: gasoline-electric-drive auxiliary, replaced with Cummins 6B5.9-M diesel
Owner: David & Brenda Hattery
Home Port: Washington, District of Columbia

Mahdee: A Revolutionary Yacht in Her Time

Alexander W. Moffat, known to family as "Skipper" and broadly among East Coast boaters as "Sandy," was a prominent member of the Cruising Club of America, and when he had *Mahdee* commissioned in 1931, he was commodore of the club. During his long life, Sandy owned at least 26 boats—each planned for the use to which he intended to put it. Sandy Moffat's desire, for his 7th boat, in 1930, was a new schooner to serve as a summer houseboat, a weekend cruiser, and it had to comfortably sail coastwise during his two-week summer vacation. For these purposes, the boat had to be roomy and seaworthy, and the intended auxiliary powerplant had to be a pleasure to operate, rather than the opposite. Essentially, Moffat sought safety, comfort, and silence. The result was an interesting schooner, the *Mahdee*, believed to be the first hybrid electric-drive sailing yacht built. The name *Mahdee* means "pretty woman" in eastern India, according to Mr. Moffats' writings; however, in the Moffat family, this word was known to refer to Moffat's mother-in-law, "Mother DeCamp."

For the design of the boat, Moffat turned to Sam Crocker. The vessel was built at Dorchester, Massachusetts, by G. F. Lawson and Son. She was launched in April, 1931.

The boat's length was determined by the fact that Moffat wanted 6'4" headroom, because of his own corporal characteristics. In addition, he wanted a shallow draft boat with a pleasing profile and sheer line. Given the requirements, the length on deck worked out to be 53'4". The draft was to be limited to 6'. Her waterline length was 45'11" and her beam, 14'11". She displaced 29 tons, with 10 tons of lead ballast, eight outside and two inside. Since the Cruising Club of America sometimes went out sailing to little-explored waters with limited opportunity for provisioning, it is understandable that Moffat had *Mahdee's* designer provide for 800 lbs of ice in the icebox, 500 lbs of coal in the hopper, and two large propane cylinders for her duel-fuel galley stove.

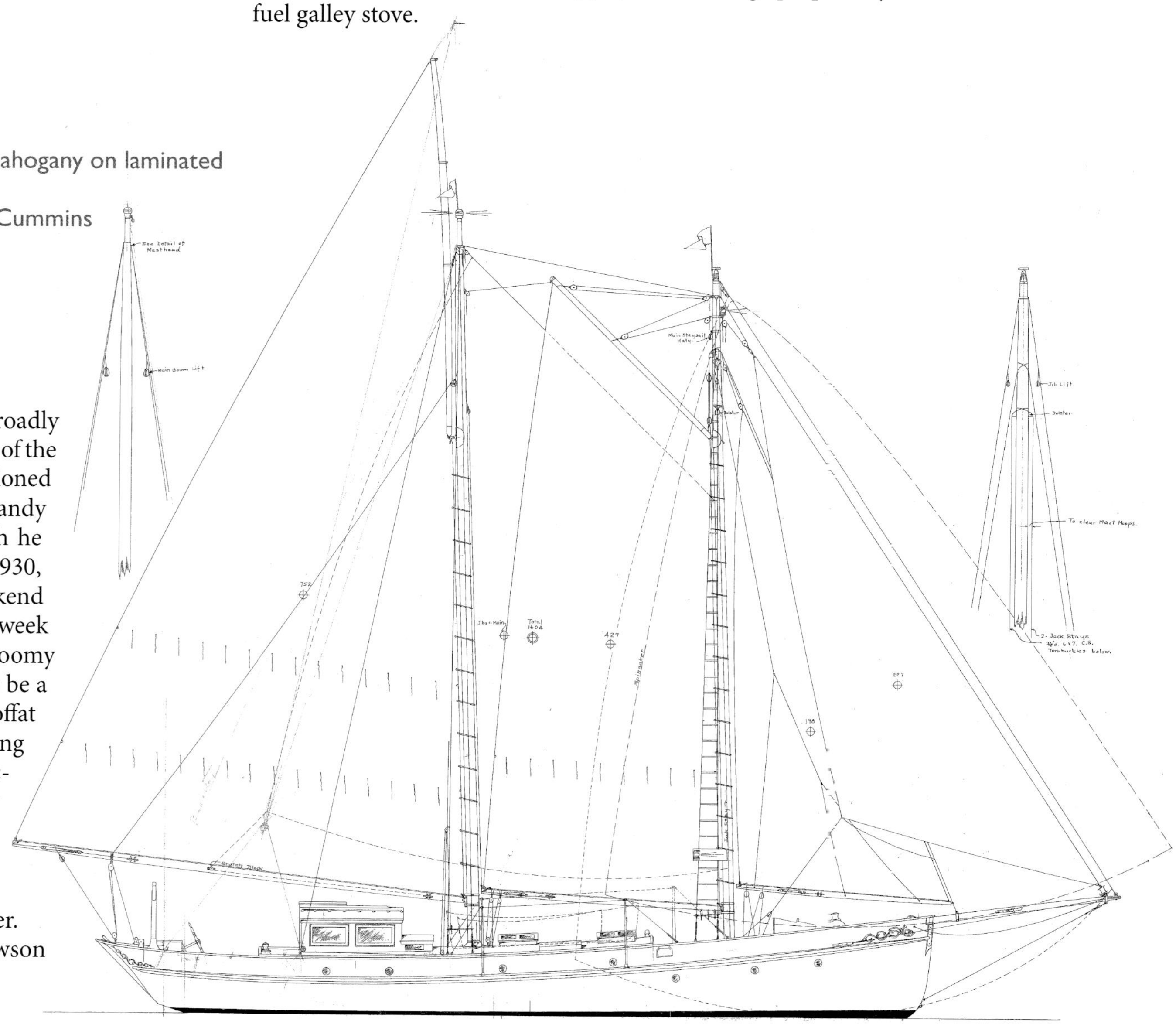

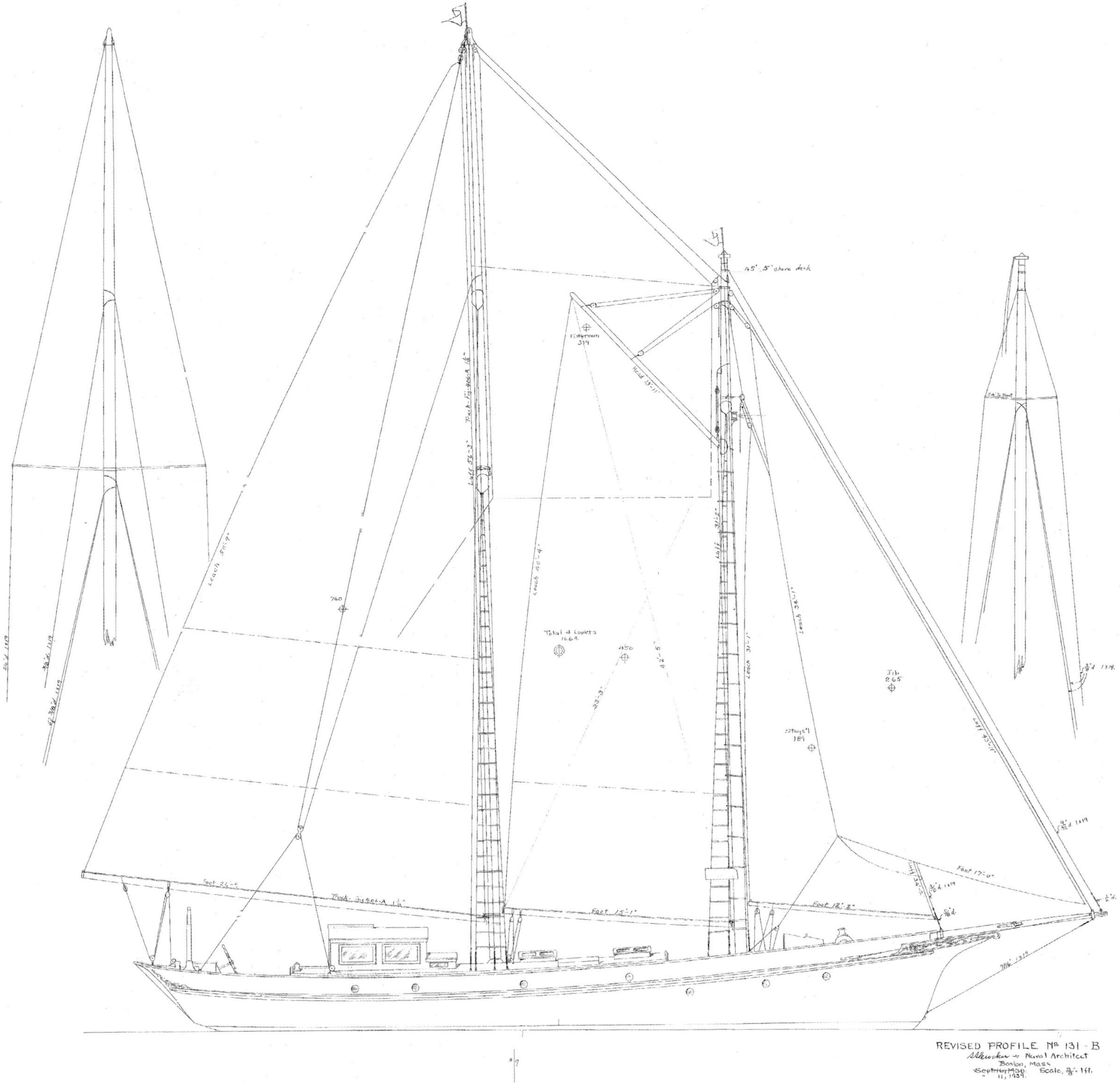

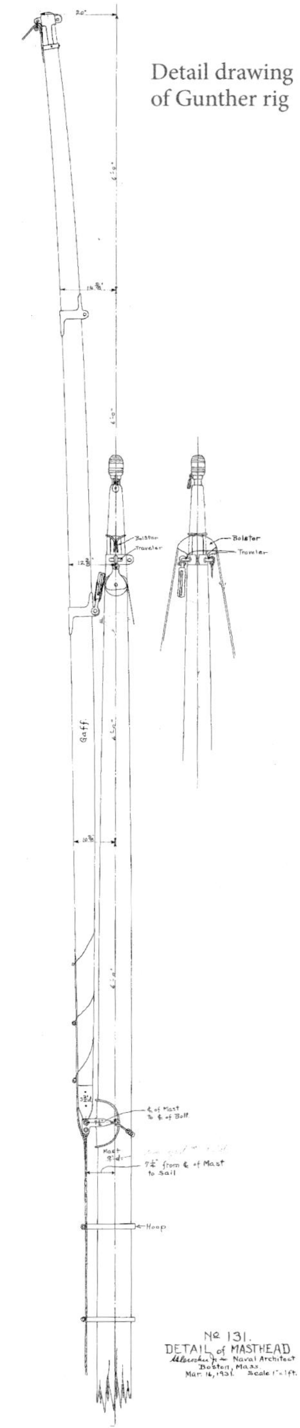

Detail drawing of Gunther rig

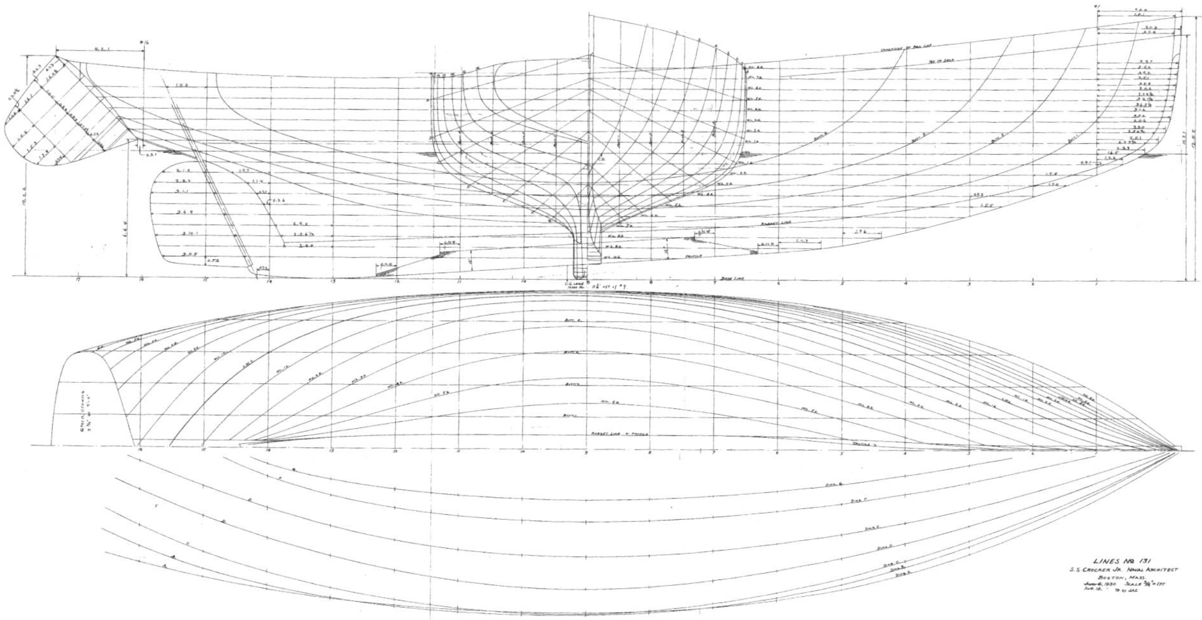

Moffat describes *Mahdee's* hull as that of a shoal-draft Brixham trawler. Although it can be largely discussed whether she has any real similarity to a Brixham trawler, she certainly has a powerful hull of the type that stands up to her sail. She has hollow waterlines forward and a nice run. Her limited draft would keep her from performing particularly well to windward, but that was not one of Sandy Moffat's objectives. In any case, with a good breeze this schooner can certainly sail given her conditions; she has been logged reaching 10 knots. *Mahdee* can steer easily with her long, straight keel and her big rudder set well aft. Yet her forefoot is cut away enough so that she can turn easily.

With a working sail area of 1,500 sq. ft., she has a moderate rig. Indeed, Moffat's intention was to start with a rig that already had the equivalent of a single reef tied in so as to avoid reefing the boat except in a real breeze. This impedes speed in light weather, but Moffat planned to use auxiliary power as necessary. And she has a huge, deep-footed balloon jib that overlaps half of the foresail.

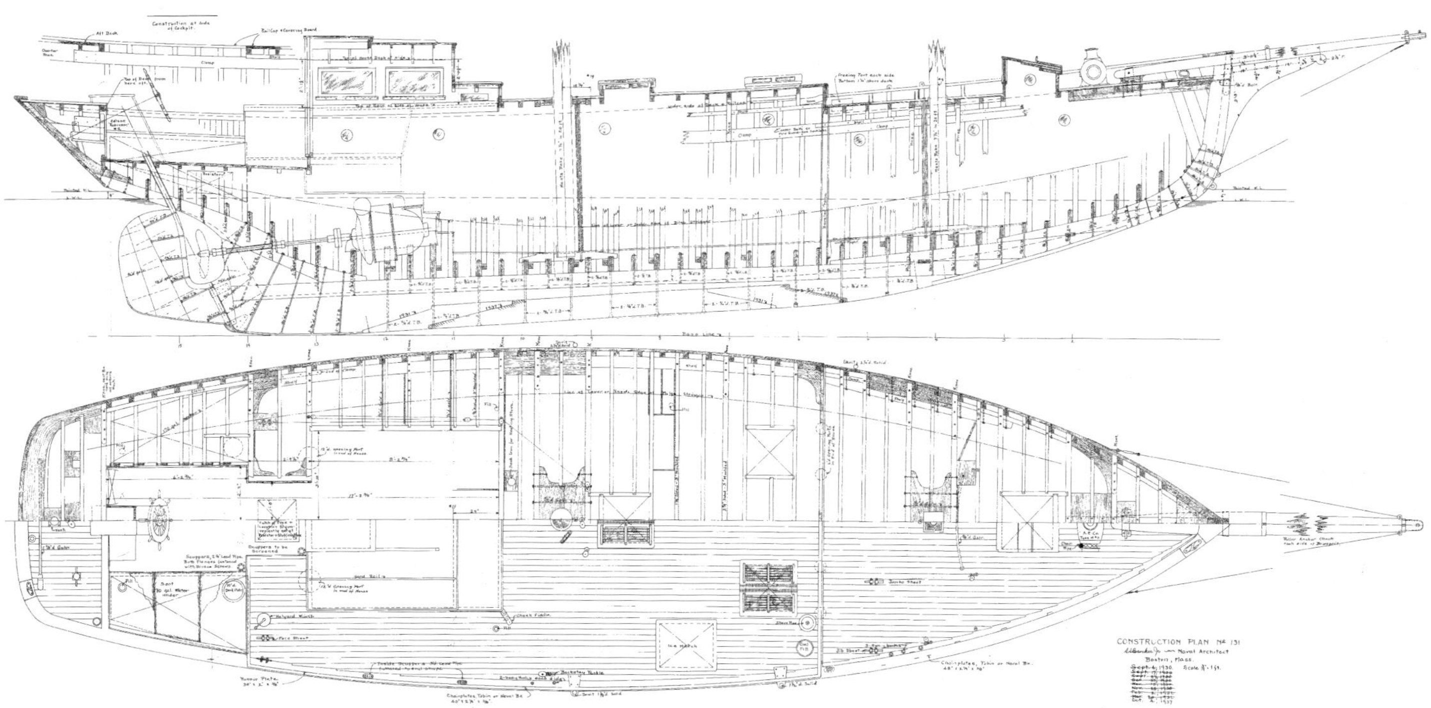

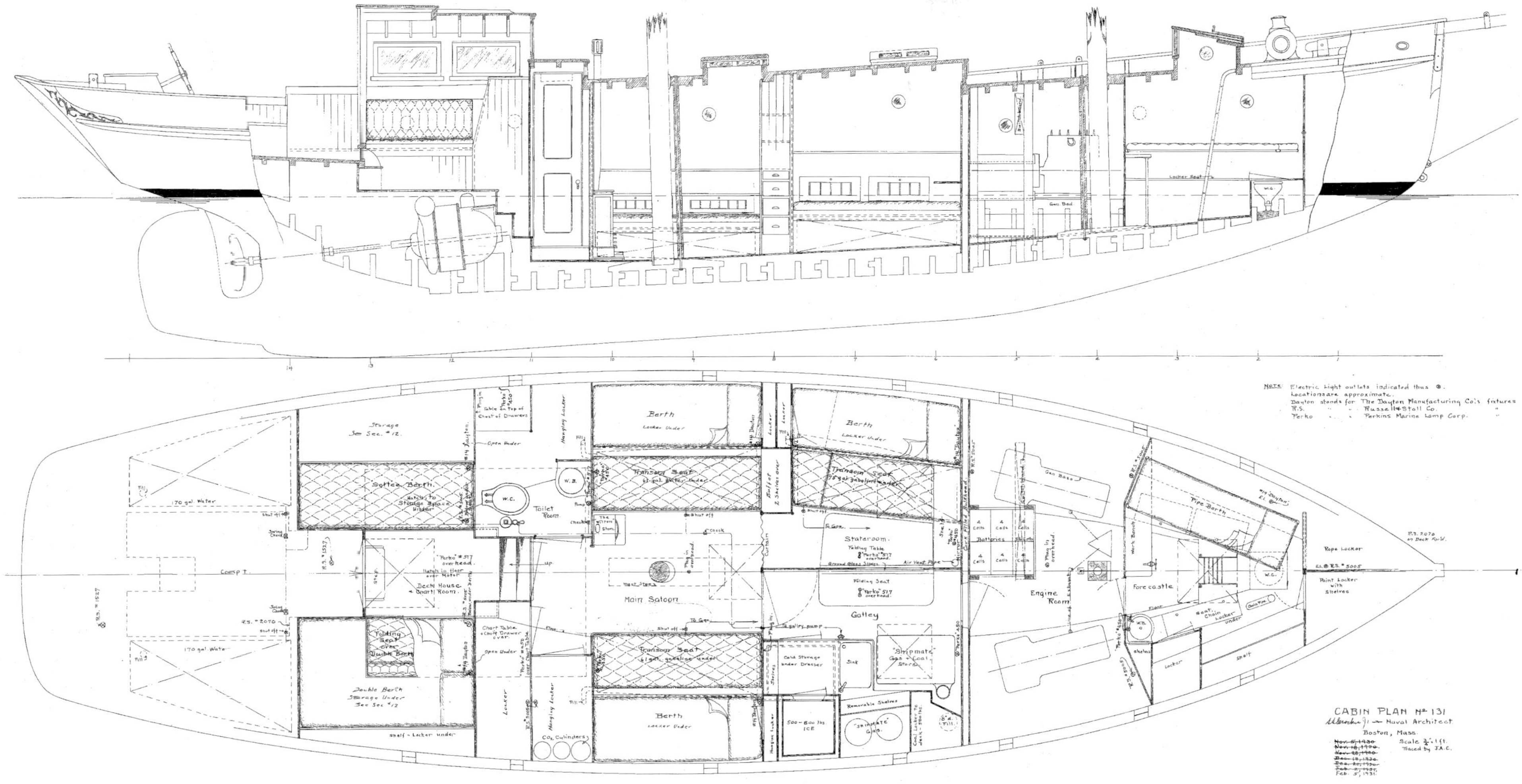
NOTE: Electric Light outlets indicated thus ⊗.
Locations are approximate.
Dayton stands for The Dayton Manufacturing Co.'s fixtures
R.S. " " Russell & Stoll Co. "
Perko " " Perkins Marine Lamp Corp. "
CABIN PLAN No. 131
Naval Architect
Boston, Mass.
Scale 3/4" = 1 ft.
Traced by J.A.C.
Feb. 5, 1931.
Main Saloon
Galley
Stateroom
Engine Room
Fore castle
Deck House & Chart Room
Toilet Room
Berth
Transom Seat
Settee Berth
Double Berth
Pipe Berth
Rope Locker
Hanging Locker
Batteries
Shipmate

The "Gunter Rig"

Her tall, narrow gaff-foresail has a vang to take the twist out of the sail. But it is the gunter mainsail that is the most interesting feature of *Mahdee's* 1931 rig. Gunters are usually relegated to small boats such as sailing dinghies. Moffat thought that if a gaff rig makes sense in a large sail, surely the gunter does also, for it is merely a high-peaked gaff. The gunter rig combines the advantage of the shape of a Bermudian sail together with the advantage of the gaff rig, namely, that the mast height can be kept moderate. In the late 1920s, Moffat had sailed several times on George Doane's sliding gunter-rigged yacht *Sea Lure*, including a trip to Bermuda, and wanted the same successful rig.

The gunter rig on *Mahdee* has raised some discussion among sailors in more recent years. In the book *The Sailmaker's Apprentice*, Emiliano Marino considers the advantages and disadvantages of the gunter rig for large boats, saying that:

> *[T]he gunter is a small-boat rig. It was attempted on a large scale by Sam Crocker on the schooner* Mahdee*, which originally carried a big jib-headed gunter-rigged mainsail. The havoc wreaked by a yard of those dimensions swinging widely about when making sail was more than Sandy Moffat could endure, and a conventional Bermudan main was rigged as a substitute.*

However, there is no evidence that Moffat himself did not like the gunter rig. Indeed, the contrary appears in an article written by Moffat and published in the magazine *Yachting*, where he states that:

Mahdee with her original gunter rig. This photo shows clearly how the gunter gaff is tightly hauled to the top of the main mast (*W. B. Jackson*).

> *[T]he advantages of the sliding gunter mainsail are in having the shape and size of a Marconi sail with a short mast which needs no spreaders. There is, therefore, a minimum of chafe to the sail. Mast hoops are used so there are no slides to jam if the sail has to be lowered while running off the wind; furthermore, there is the weight of the gaff to bring the sail down on the run. The short mast reduces windage considerably when going to windward under power alone, and saves top weight as well. In fact, I have found no disadvantages. The sail seems to set as well as the best of the true jib-headed sails. (*Yachting*, 2/1932, p. 100).*

A Revolutionary Concept in Her Time: The Hybrid Gasoline-Electric-Drive Auxiliary

Sandy Moffat wanted a quiet powerplant, so quiet that it would not have to be shut down to listen for fog signals. He achieved this objective with a hybrid system of an electric drive, a battery bank, and (gasoline) generators. He placed two gensets and batteries in a forward engine room and used a quiet exhaust-gas-water-separator system to both achieve quiet and ample accommodations. *Mahdee's* powerplant cost $9,200 in 1931 Depression-era dollars, fully installed; though Moffat wrote that one could be fully installed for perhaps half the price. His hybrid electric drive propulsion system was expensive due largely to the cost of systems integration and the choice of a large battery bank.

Set forward in the schooner, Moffat considered the engine room to be "well back from the bow." The 3,800 lbs equipment was centered abaft the foremast, 14 ft aft of the stem. The 25 kW electric drive propulsion motor, located beneath the deckhouse, was made by General Electric. It was directly connected to two, 6-cylinder Winton gasoline generators of 3" bore, 4" stroke governed to 1,300 rpm. These generators furnished current for a 220 volt General Electric motor, which is directly connected to the propeller shaft and which developed 25 brake horse power at 550 rpm turning a 28" by 18" propeller. Two propellers had been tried, one a two-bladed Thompson

Mahdee was launched in April 1931. She can be seen here sliding off the railways at Crocker Boatyard (*Crocker Boatyard*).

In this other photograph of *Mahdee's* launch, the scrollwork on her bow is clearly visible. This nice scrollwork has since been removed, probably when the clipper-bow was added (*Crocker Boatyard*).

feathering, which drove *Mahdee* at 7.6 knots, and a three-bladed Hyde of the same diameter and pitch, which drove her a strong 8 knots. The gasoline consumption has proved to be the same with either propeller, so that the three-bladed propeller was kept installed.

When only one generator was in operation, delivering 10 kW power to the 25kW motor, the latter turned 300 rpm and drove the boat at a speed of 5.5 knots. Normal operation took power directly from the running generators, carrying the batteries at zero float. With both generators running at 1,350 rpm, the schooner reached 7.6 knots and burned 4 1/2 gallons of gasoline per hour. On one generator, and with half the fuel consumption, she made 5.7 knots. She could also be run, of course, on the battery alone. Moffat noted that starting with a full charge, she could make 5.7 knots on the battery for a few minutes, or three knots for an hour.

An ampere-hour meter indicated battery levels at all times. When both generators were running simultaneously, the batteries were still charged by only one generator line or the other, depending on which side the battery switch was thrown. The switchboard was so arranged that it was impossible to accidentally apply excessive voltage to the 110-volt battery bank or lighting lines.

In starting the engines the battery current was thrown into the generators, making starting motors of them, and the switchers were then thrown to running position, when they took up their functions as generators. This switchboard is a masterpiece of simplicity. Moffat said that anyone who could read the plates on the switchboard had only himself to blame if he went wrong.

Much attention was paid to achieving a silent exhaust. The *Mahdee* had a water-cooled exhaust with an exhaust gas-water-separator in the engine room similar to those employed for gensets on large power yachts today. The hollow foremast, with a 2 1/2" copper pipe built into it, took the exhaust gas from both engines whilst a pipe carried the cooling water to exit at the waterline. The exhaust gas exited high above the sails and just below the truck of the foremast.

Moffat later wrote that if he were working out *Mahdee's* propulsion again, his only change would be to make her entire electrical system 110 volts, thus eliminating the 12-volt lighting system for the sake of simplicity. All the other details of the system worked out fine, he said.

Other Little Innovations in *Mahdee's* Design

The *Mahdee* has a flush deck with a break abaft the foremast. This arrangement gives her plenty of headroom below and a large, clear, working space on deck.

Ventilation was planned carefully. For example, her skylights are square so they can be turned to funnel air in from any of four directions and her opening portlights used a single-lever, watertight cam mechanism similar to that used in the breech of a gun.

The schooner design had permanent bunks for six but no fewer than ten berths, if we include seating converted to berths. In the daytime, the deckhouse is a charthouse and lounging place, at night, an upholstered seat folds back to reveal a full size double berth.

In commenting on the design and building of *Mahdee*, Sandy Moffat wrote: "We adhered to the three mottos that anyone building a boat should swear faithfully to follow: The best is none too good; the most expensive is generally the cheapest in the end; if you are going to sea and going in safety, you've got to be particular." Today these words are just as true as they were in 1931!

Changing Ownerships

Sandy Moffat owned at least 26 boats during his lifetime. Before *Mahdee*, he owned at least six other boats. However much Sandy Moffat liked all the innovations and engineering on *Mahdee*, he loved new boats and only owned *Mahdee* for five years before selling her in 1936 to Robert L. Ireland, Jr. This new owner most likely enjoyed the schooner, but he did not seem enchanted by the sliding gunter rig nor her plumb bow. In 1939 he changed the mainsail to a conventional Bermuda sail. Ireland also removed the innovative hybrid electric drive system from *Mahdee* in 1937. It can only be guessed that the gas-electric hybrid drive system was replaced because of the high cost of batteries and perhaps it was time to replace batteries in 1937. Ireland replaced the forward engine room with a stateroom and this required substantial rebalancing of the boat. It may have been that he just wanted another stateroom in his vessel as well. He added a billet to *Mahdee's* stem in 1939, giving her a clipper bow in profile. Almost 50 years later, another owner, Tom McHugh, removed the billet to reveal the original plumb bow.

After Ireland's ownership, she was sold a few times and was even owned by the War Department and served during World War II. The owner who sold her to the government served on a destroyer during the war and once saw *Mahdee* being sailed by a Navy man in uniform whilst the former owner sat miserably seasick on the destroyer as it motored along the United States coastline of Maine, probably remembering with romance his happy days on the schooner. After the war, *Mahdee's* name was changed to *Pandora* and then to *Privateer* in 1953, when Peter Paul Luce bought her. He sailed her for several years until 1960, when he sold the boat to a young couple, Charles "Mac" and Roswita McIntosh. They intended to use the boat in charter service on the United States' West Coast, for which they delivered *Privateer* from New York to Los Angeles through the Panama Canal in Spring 1961. The crew roster included one experienced sailor (Mac), as well as Roswita, their 16-month old baby girl, and four additional crew: Men interested in adventure but with no prior sailing experiences. They left Long Island Sound on December 23rd during an ice and snow storm. They safely weathered a horrible Nor'easter off Cape Hatteras that, at the time, was responsible for the sinking and grounding of a number of yachts and ships. They dropped off two of the crew members midway through the trip and transited the Panama Canal on their way to Los Angeles. Roswita McIntosh wrote her memories about this trip in her book entitled *Live, Laugh, & Learn*.

***Privateer* on the United States' West Coast**

The McIntosh couple was unfortunate in that their charter plans were dashed by new Coast Guard requirements for charter boats that were enacted during their trip. It is ironic that the requirements were largely due to the loss of a charter boat during the same storm off Cape Hatteras that they had made it through safely. They decided to offer the boat for sale in California. They subsequently sold her to a doctor and his wife, Richard and Mary Cavendish-Bentinck, of Belvedere, California, who continued sailing the schooner as a private yacht, doing some trips to the South Pacific.

Mahdee sailing in 1966, when she was named *Privateer*. This photograph was probably taken in the San Francisco Bay, where she was sailed by her owner at the time (*Brenda Hattery Archive*).

The Cavendish-Bentincks sold her to the David Allen family of Belvedere in 1965. In the 1970s, Allen became very interested in the new materials and designs of racing boats and in the late 1970s he was a well-known ocean racing sailor because of his innovations with the ocean racer *Imp*. With *Privateer* (*Mahdee*) Allen ran the 1967 Transpac Race. His crew was the large Allen family, many of whom were children at the time of the race. She finished second from last in Class B. Each class was set up according to the dimensions of the boat rather than their sailing qualities. Different handicaps allowed for comparing the yachts entered in each class. There were light winds in that year's race and this, along with a boat full of children, might explain the poor performance of the heavy, under-canvassed *Privateer*.

The Allen family recalls that the 38-year-old hull leaked very little during the Transpac race. The bilge was hand pumped for only an hour at most each day; however, during the homeward sail, they encountered a sizable Pacific blow during which the hull weeped alarmingly throughout; the family recalls that for a few days the bilge was pumped constantly. In 1968, the prudent David Allen had the Spaulding Yard of Sausalito, California, refasten all the planking as well as provide new standing rigging, main boom, and boom gallows. At the same time, Allen had new Dacron sails made to replace the boat's numerous cotton sails. The main boom's 1950s-era rolling reefing system was no longer desired by Allen. Not a wasteful man, the original boom went into service as the Belvedere U.S. Post Office flagpole. It is still in use there as of this writing.

The trail of *Privateer's* ownership around 1970 became a little muddy. The Allens were in real estate and David Allen almost lost *Privateer* to dishonest land schemers. He signed over the boat in exchange for land. When he went to confirm the surveyed land information, he realized that he had been cheated. He immediately called the Coast Guard to put a lien on the boat. *Privateer* was fast making her way for the

Privateer sailing in the San Francisco Bay in the 1970s. Note the stiffness of her sails, a sign that they are new and well trimmed (*Diane Beeston*).

This impressive photo was taken of *Privateer* reaching with her gennaker and gollywobbler. She appears to make good speed (*Diane Beeston*).

Beating to windward. Note her attached clipper-bow with figurehead. This addition was removed by a later owner (*Diane Beeston*).

Mexican border and the Coast Guard could board the vessel just a few miles away from the limits of the United States' territorial sea. They impounded her in San Diego while awaiting the federal court judgment. All ended well, with the Allens getting the boat back. However, she was in Los Angeles and the Allens, in San Francisco, sold her there to Robert and Harriet Goss in 1970. The new owners enjoyed the boat in the early 1970s and spent much time aboard in Port Townsend, Washington. The couple split in the mid-1970s and in 1976 the boat was signed over to Robert whilst Harriet kept their Port Townsend house. After the breakup of the marriage, Robert, alone or with one other crew, sailed *Privateer* up and down the Pacific Coast from as far north as British Columbia and as far south as Costa Rica and enjoyed much time in Mexico's Sea of Cortez. He also entered the boat into the Ancient Mariners of San Diego Transpac to Hawaii in 1980. There are many stories involving *Privateer* and that Transpac race. During the 14-day passage Robert became so frustrated with his crew that once in Hawaii he dropped them off at the dock and without reprovisioning, he set sail for Port Townsend. Solo, the trip exceeded one month and without a working radio he could not have called for assistance had he needed it.

Robert Goss sold *Privateer* to Tom and Denise McHugh in 1981 in San Diego, California. Tom was a former U.S. Navy frogman (now called a Seal) and Denise a schoolteacher. Patriotic, they did not like the idea of piracy or privateers and immediately rechristened the boat *Mahdee*. They raised Denise's three children from an earlier marriage, one adopted son, and two children of their marriage aboard *Mahdee*. Tom McHugh still smiles today when he explains that the boat fell into disrepair as the college savings for the six children "ate the hull." Despite financial challenges, the couple saved money to purchase parts for *Mahdee* over the years—they invested in everything from new engine, genset, breakers, to sail reconditioning as they prepared for their planned cruising retirement.

When, around 2003, the boat partially sank in her slip, Tom realized that the hull itself needed major work that he could not do alone in San Diego. Tom did not want to "part the boat out" but instead wanted someone to rebuild it and use it as he and Denise had planned.

When David and Brenda Hattery found *Mahdee* in 2006, she was sitting at a dock near San Diego. She seemed waiting there for her great comeback, not willing to give up her life. Indeed, she still sported her elegant lines from the 1930s (*David Hattery*).

Although her hull looked fair externally, because her owners had regularly kept up with paint as they used her as a houseboat, on the stern the rot was obvious. What David and Brenda Hattery did not know at that time was that these few spots of rot were an indication of the general degradation of the hull. Note that she was still substantially original, with many original fittings (*David Hattery*).

Mahdee's interior at the time when David and Brenda Hattery purchased the boat. Much of the interior was gone, and so the frames were easily accessible for inspection. However, it was necessary to get deeper into the structure of the boat, especially in the keel area, to ascertain the real condition of the hull (*David Hattery*).

The Big Restoration

David and Brenda Hattery of Washington, D.C., found *Mahdee* in 2006 in a sad state of disrepair. They wanted a cruising boat and they had determined that their ideal vessel would be a pre-World War II yacht designed by a well-known and respected naval architect and built, from the start, as a capable cruising boat rather than a work boat or racing yacht. Important attributes were the vessel be easily sailed short-handed, a capable blue water vessel but shallow drafted for gunkholing, small enough to be owner maintainable, but large enough for living and working aboard while extended cruising. It would have ample deck space for working on projects outdoors as well as a deckhouse or other reasonable inside steering station to be used in the high latitude sailing they intended. It would not have features nor scantlings inspired by or designed around a racing rule. They did not limit their search to the United States nor to schooners; they seriously considered pre-1950 yachts by German Frers Sr., John Alden, William Hand, and Frank Paine, among others. The findings were often either too large to sail short-handed, too small to realistically live and work aboard, deep drafted, or had undergone a poor rebuild/refit with many historic elements lost.

Before they flew across the United States from Washington, D.C., to San Diego to view *Mahdee*, they obtained copies of her drawings through the Crocker Yard and hired a surveyor to evaluate the boat. When they saw *Mahdee's* fast underwater lines, charthouse, and cruising layout on the Crocker drawings, they realized that the vessel had enormous potential as a cruising schooner and her restoration would be meaningful. Her shallow draft, cutaway fore keel, fine entry, open deck space, accommodations, and capacity seemed ideal.

After an inspection *in situ* at her San Diego dock, a meeting with Tom McHugh, and interviews with shipwrights and boatyards about the scope of work required to fully restore and bring *Mahdee* back to a seaworthy cruising yacht, they came to an agreement with Tom in February 2006 with arrangements to close on the deal and take delivery by August 1, 2006. In the spring, they came to terms with a shipwright and boatyard on the scope of work and a plan to properly restore and rebuild *Mahdee*.

Preparing for the Work to Be Done

The first month, August 2006, flew by with cleaning and inventorying *Mahdee* as well as assessing the project and capabilities of the boatyard. The spars were removed and the hull was shoe-horned into a covered shed at a small boatyard. If all went well in the first month, their plan was to keep *Mahdee* in the small yard where employees of that yard could work on the project; otherwise, *Mahdee* would be trucked elsewhere for the restoration or the project might even be scuttled. Due to unforeseen events with the restoration in that first month, the Hatterys radically revised their plans. They had not originally planned to be heavily involved in the rebuild but could see no way around it if the project were to succeed. They relocated from Washington,

For the restoration, David and Brenda Hattery had to remove the entire interior and deck, and start replacing all the rotten woods of the keel, frames, and planking. *Mahdee* can be seen here as an empty hull, exposing all her frames. This allowed them to carefully check all of them for rot (*Brenda Hattery*).

She received a new stem, which can be seen here with the new planking already installed (*Brenda Hattery*).

The form of the rudder was specially designed by Crocker at the time of *Mahdee's* building. The Hattery's kept the original form of the rudder, although they refurbished the old wood entirely (*Brenda Hattery*).

D.C. to San Diego to provide oversight, perform logistics, and physically work on the project; *Mahdee* spent the first ten months of her restoration in the small shed before she was moved and the remaining work completed in a more spacious location.

In the spring, they had hired a reputable shipwright with excellent references to provide an outline of the effort expected to bring *Mahdee* back to the seaworthy cruising vessel she once was and to either perform the work or to oversee structural aspects of it as they performed the work. The shipwright outlined a plan, which became the starting point of the restoration.

What the Hatterys did not know was that many owners undertaking classic boat restorations focus on having a pretty boat that will look great at the boat shows and will be capable of fair weather sailing, and that such owners often are unwilling to spend money on unseen structural elements. Retaining historic materials is not a

Brenda Hattery caulking *Mahdee* (*David Hattery*).

priority for these owners as historic materials are often not as easy, nor cheap to work with, to get to the ultimate "pretty" as new materials are. Finally, blue water sailing is not a typical goal for these owners.

What the shipwright did not realize when making his projections for a cost-effective scope of work was that the Hatterys weren't those sorts of owners but instead the opposite: They were exceedingly performance and safety-oriented; they really wanted a blue water-capable schooner and keeping original and historic materials was a priority for *Mahdee's* restoration. Many of the cost-saving methods and shortcuts that can be taken in wooden boat rebuilds which result in a pretty "harbor only" boat would not be appropriate for *Mahdee's* restoration nor acceptable to the Hatterys.

Two months into the project, looking at a significantly expanded scope of work to achieve a blue water-capable vessel and concerned about the capabilities of the small yard, the Hatterys hired Canadian furniture maker, John Fruehwirth, initially for a few weeks to assist Hattery in replacing keelbolts. The Hatterys were impressed with his work ethic and learned about his past work as a planker in a Canadian shipyard. He ended up working on *Mahdee* side-by-side with David Hattery for almost two years on all parts of the hull rebuild.

The Hatterys wrote Sandy Moffat's mottos for successful boatbuilding in the front of their restoration notebook and adhered to them. All materials used in the rebuild were of the highest quality and suited to the applications of their use. Many of *Mahdee's* galvanized fasteners had rusted away or were in bad shape and the ferrous metal had taken a toll on the white oak used in the boat. With the shipwright's advice, the Hatterys decided that silicon bronze fasteners were to be used 100% throughout the rebuild and refastening. If there was a question, for any reason—from rot to corrosion or fatigue—about the ability of an existing rigging or structural member to do its job—from foundation and planking to glazing and fasteners—it was replaced during the restoration.

Edensaw Lumber of Port Townsend, Washington, had sourced high quality planking materials for the restoration of the schooner *Martha* during two winters in 2006 and 2007 and *Mahdee* benefited by purchasing the extra planking wood that *Martha* could not use each winter. The *minutiae* of project logistics included things like establishing wholesale accounts for bronze fasteners; finding bronze clench rings for the large deadwood drifts; large dimensions of appropriate hardwoods; and researching use of esoteric materials like period-appropriate beeswax, Irish felt, and a shipwright-recommended "boat soup" of linseed oil, Stockholm tar, and turpentine to prevent overly fast drying out of the keel. With experience in the field of historic restoration and large-scale construction management, Brenda Hattery focused on obtaining the right quality at a good price, managing the historically appropriate use of a variety of materials on the project, and keeping the project moving at a good pace. Paper patterns were sent to a logger in Nova Scotia for the Tamarack (Eastern Larch) natural knees needed to replace 14 of the 24 hanging knees and two of the six lodging knees. Wooden patterns were made as needed and sent to foundries for bronze castings ranging from rudder gudgeon, mast rings, and boom bails.

The Restoration Step By Step

The important structural rebuild of stem, stem knee, floors, frames, new keel bolts, and counter timber was completed by the early spring of 2007 and enough planking performed by Fruehwirth and Hattery by June 2007 so that it would be safe to truck the boat to a more spacious boatyard where they would have more room to complete the planking, a new deck, new rudder, new cockpit combing, refinish the deck fixtures, and work on the spars. For the ten months *Mahdee* was in the small yard, a wooden-boat shipwright with 20 years of experience, though busy at another yard with a large project, joined *Mahdee* to work on major structural elements as needed; the Hatterys welcomed the shipwright's knowledge of the wooden boat world, materials, and traditional methods of construction using hand tools. The yard also provided a carpenter full time for the project.

There were many surprises during the restoration. In the first two weeks of the project, the garboard plank was removed to inspect frame ends and to have the boat steam-cleaned. Forward of the break deck, with no ceiling in place, several frames unexpectedly crumbled with the steam cleaning as it was just paint holding them in place. The planking, seemingly with no help from the frames, was holding the boat's forward shape.

Each project in the hull restoration had its own challenges, which often impacted other projects or even drove the path of the restoration entirely. In particular, seemingly small actions by boatyard employees drove the course of several larger projects. For example, the bobstay iron through the stem knee had been used by a previous owner as part of a grounding plate and the wood was degraded due to that use around the thru-bolts; further there was an old stem rot repair that had not been done to the highest standards—it was expected that the stem and knee would require replacement. Knowing the stem was suspect and needed inspection but without stopping to consider the impact to the project planning or the structural integrity of the hull, while Hattery and the shipwright were at lunch, a boatyard worker with a reciprocating saw cut straight away the planking forward of the first frame and removed the stem and knee for the shipwright's evaluation.

Upon return to the yard, with the old stem out of the boat, the shipwright could add "new stem and knee" to the growing list of projects. Hattery felt the gaping hole like a cut to his own body. Importantly, a pattern had not been taken before this drastic measure and all the planking, good and bad—without regard for condition—had been cut 1' away from the stem and knee. The decision to replace all the planking had not yet been made but now every plank would have to be replaced or scarfed some distance back from the stem. Worried about the tight space in the small boatyard and seeing different boat projects interfering with each other, the Hatterys had been mulling about the decision to go ahead and move *Mahdee* to a more roomy boatyard where work could progress more efficiently as soon as practicable.

But now, the boat could not be trucked from this boatyard without unreasonable risk until the stem was replaced; there was also an obvious need to install framing to support the forward hull which had held its shape amazingly well but now with both the stem cut away and the crumbled frames the forward section was at risk of losing shape even sitting in the yard. Station molds were quickly built and installed but shipwrights advised that the boat still shouldn't be moved. As such, work on the floors and frames started straight away and the Hatterys worked on *Mahdee* themselves, pushing the idea of moving the boat to a different yard to a few months out—when it would be safe to do so.

Many times, a worker would approach with a reciprocating saw to remove an original part of the boat and the Hatterys would stop them and force the item to be carefully removed, cataloged, and saved for reinstallation. Both Fruehwirth and the shipwright advised that it would be better to replicate things like the wood decklights, scuttle, teak grates, companionway ladder, and steering housing; this was true especially when the old materials were worn or damaged and would require repairs. While the Hatterys were willing to do what was needed to improve the structural integrity of the boat to being as seaworthy as new, they were also committed to saving as much of the original *Mahdee* as possible and focused on keeping as many of her original non-structural elements intact as possible. Through the years, *Mahdee* retained many of her unique original design features like the telescoping slide of the forehatch. The Hatterys had no intention of replacing these things with replicas or a different design.

With the removal of the stem and knee, there was need for new wood to replace the old. Originally, both were white oak, but no seasoned white oak of the needed scantlings could be found for this and other projects. Instead, in most cases, purpleheart was chosen due to its strength and rot resistance. It was ordered and upon its arrival, the shipwright ripped the purpleheart into strips for laminating the stem knee. The laminating was performed in three "lifts" with plenty of clamps. The old knee was laid on top of the new laminations to gauge how much more might be needed to complete the knee. Finally, the stem knee was ready to be planed and shaped. It took more than one person to run the heavy laminated knee through the planer. After planing, it was trimmed and cut to fit the forekeel.

The shipwright lofted the new stem from the drawings since he did not make a pattern of it on the boat before the stem and the knee were removed from the boat. After lofting the lines and beginning on lofting the important rabbet line from the 3/4":1' scaled drawings, the shipwright thought something was not quite right. So, he "recreated the as-built-stem" by putting it all back together and clamping it to the boat. Going back and forth between measurements pulled off the drawings and the "as-built-stem," a pattern was made for the new stem and later for the rabbet line. After creating the patterns, a 6 x 12" purpleheart timber was rough cut by a carpenter and literally "carved" to shape.

After the stem had been recreated, work could continue on the restoration of the bow. Hollow at the waterlines and with a plumb bow, *Mahdee* should cut through the waves rather than riding up over them. This bow profile with basically no rake was in keeping with the original owner's desire to own a "shoal-draft Brixham trawler." The Brixham trawler is a mid-nineteenth century fishing vessel from Devon, typically about 65 feet long. *Mahdee's* hull form was inspired by this design because of its outstanding seaworthiness and handling characteristics.

Mahdee's bow was reframed with a combination of angelique sawn frames in the forecastle and alternating mahogany (sapele) laminated frames and sawn frames where the forward engine room had been. Then, her mid-section was reframed with laminated frames. And finally, her stern was reframed. All her old oak floors were replaced with purpleheart floors. The original frames were steam-bent white oak 2 3/4 x 2 3/4" finished size.

Although steam bending new frames would have been the quickest way to reframe the boat and get her ready to move, the yard did not have a steambox nor crew to steam-bend frames and did not want to bring in an experienced contract crew and materials from Port Townsend to do the work. Instead, knowing that outstanding results could be achieved with laminated frames, Hattery, Fruehwirth, and a boatyard carpenter spent several months working through the boat, floor by floor and frame by frame to perform the work.

Along her 54' length, she has 49 floors spaced 12 inches apart. In addition to her 49 frame stations, she also has eleven intermediate frames, called "auxiliary frames" in the specification. The intermediate frames run from stringer to stringer and bolt into the aft side of the floors while the main frames bolt along the forward side of the floors.

The structural integrity of *Mahdee's* stern counter timber, what Crocker called the "tailfeather," had been in question but a need for replacement was not certain. Even so, at the very beginning of the entire restoration, a young and new yard employee, fresh out of wooden boat school and assuming the old timber would be replaced, used a reciprocating saw to cut away a large section in the middle of the long curving timber, weakening it, to investigate a spot of suspected rot. The Crocker Yard in Massachusetts was sent photographs of the counter timber including a weep area around the rudder post and softness around the stuffing box. Advice on replacement was requested. The Crocker Yard advised that the timber would be highly unlikely to ever fail due to the rudder post or stuffing box problems, though leaks there would be "irritating," and in that light, the big chunk of wood removed by the young employee, even when repaired, might be considered the "straw that will break the camel's back" and that perhaps replacement was in order.

Even so, the Hatterys wavered for three months on the decision. The supplies were dwindling as work progressed on floors and frames. Soon they were out of purpleheart for any more floors. They had enough mahogany laminates for about ten long frames and another ten short ones. They were out of silicon-bronze bolts for installing the last four intermediate frames they had just laminated. Furthermore, they had run out of bronze rod for attaching floors, mast steps, and keel fairings. The supplies the Hatterys had ordered were just about enough to complete the floors and frames back to the cockpit. That was how far their plan was. Once all the other work on the hull foundation was done, they decided to bite the bullet and also replace the entire tailfeather. That young employee had only worked in the boatyard a few short weeks before leaving, but his actions not only netted *Mahdee* a lovely new counter timber that might not have been installed otherwise, but also he helped push the Hatterys to become very active and protective of *Mahdee* in the restoration.

The tailfeather project included several dreaded tasks for Hattery and Fruehwirth to do. The first was removing the propeller housing that passes through both the rudder-post timber and the tailfeather. Lots of "two person pounding" with a 16-pound sledge hammer got the housing to move about 1/2' forward out of frame 41. The second dreaded task was dealing with the rudder shaft and stock. Once it was decided to replace the entire tailfeather, it was clear that they could just cut the side out of the tailfeather and slide the assembly down. Lifting and carrying the massive, solid bronze rudder stock, however, was a three-person job.

The third dreaded task was removing the bolts that fasten the tailfeather to the keel. Two of the bolts were especially worrisome. They pass around the propeller housing and come out in the propeller aperture. The wood is very sculpted and drilling new holes would take much alignment jigs and a minor miracle. Six more bolts go through more than 4 feet of the entire keel and deadwood. Again, drilling new holes would be very difficult so as not to punch out the side of the keel. Sam at Crocker's Yard told the Hatterys that these bolts would probably be impossible to remove and that they had to plan on installing the new tailfeather with spiral-cut drifts.

However, with these negative admonishments, Hattery and Fruehwirth managed to remove four of the six long bolts, and one of the two bolts around the propeller shaft—those bolts go through curved holes. Yes, curved! They could at least move the other propeller shaft bolt, generating confidence that they would get it out after the tailfeather had been removed, which would reduce the curvature in the hole. The process involved lots of pounding and periodic cutting of the bolts as they hit the ground. The aft one had to be cut every 4 inches of movement due to external constraints.

The fourth dreaded task was cutting the remaining bolts and drifts holding the tailfeather. A floor jack opened the joint enough for a 12" Sawzall® blade. Clean cuts were made to all the remaining fasteners. The tailfeather was then ready to be lifted out.

With their great and unexpected success in removing the six 3' to 4' long, 3/4" bronze bolts that hold on the tailfeather and pull together the deadwood and keel, they now needed all their stock of 3/4" bronze rod to make the new replacement tailfeather bolts. Meanwhile, they finished up the last floors and frames in the main cabin and forward. Floor 24 was made and ready to install. It originally had 3/4" bronze bolts holding it to the keel. The keel bolts were generally 3/4" diameter, but there were some 7/8" and 1" bolts. Frame 24 is a very wide "fat" floor near the middle of the keel. It seemed the ideal candidate for an upgrade to 1" bolts.

The two keel bolts for floor 24 were each 34" long. The holes for bolting on the tailfeather were a special challenge. Not only were they big (3/4" diameter and 3' to 4' long), but they also had fairly tight tolerances for their exits (center of keel at the bottom and between floors on top). For this reason, they pounded out the old bolts, leaving the holes in the keel. All they had to do was position the tailfeather and drill up through the existing holes into and through the new tailfeather. This was easier said than done.

Due to the positioning of the yacht in the shed, the keel had very little room between it and the asphalt floor of the shed. There was some talk with the boatyard owner about being able to dig down into the asphalt to increase clearance, but only after *Mahdee* was in the shed, did the yard owner state that there was a big sewer main just below the keel. This certainly discouraged them from digging into the asphalt. Under these circumstances, they had about 13" of room for the drill bit and drill. Then, they had to drill up about 4' (most of that through an existing hole); using a series of very short drill extensions it was possible. Once they had the tailfeather in place, they did not want to move it because not only was the 800-lb tailfeather heavy, but getting it realigned would be very difficult. Only long and tedious work from under *Mahdee's* keel made it possible to draw the necessary bolts into the stern deadwood to hold the new tailfeather.

Mahdee's scantlings were preserved, though it was a constant struggle because Fruehwirth had roots in the large scantling world of wooden fishing boats and the shipwright working on the foundation had roots in the racing world and preferred to reduce weight when possible. The final decision was usually made with an answer to Brenda Hattery's question, "What did Crocker specify for this boat?" Only regarding issues of safety was she willing to deviate from the original plans. For example, the shipwright advised that the intermediate frames were extreme "overkill" and might be omitted from the rebuild to save weight and construction cost. However, one of *Mahdee's* unique traits, as designed by Sam Crocker, were these intermediate frames designed to carry rig loading and protect the garboard plank, so they were included in the restored boat. Another example: The Hatterys, to meet the current standards for offshore yachts, had the deep cockpit sole raised 6" higher above the waterline than the original drawings show. Similarly, the companionway door modification needed for the Allen family to meet the requirements of the 1967 Transpac was kept.

Mahdee spent 31 months on the hard, 27 months with rebuild activities underway. Then, once *Mahdee* was relaunched in April 2009, the Hatterys prepared the masts and spars, the mast stepping and rerigging was completed later in 2009. The Hatterys and Fruehwirth performed the bulk of the work.

Like the accounts above of replacing the stem, tailfeather, and frames, each project during the restoration had its own challenges and most could be characterized by difficulty in obtaining appropriate materials and a tightrope of careful decisions to use the original parts or not, to preserve scantlings or not, to use traditional work methods or not, and so on. What cannot be understated is the dedication to authenticity as well as the skill, and finesse it often took to properly restore, conserve, repair or replicate all the parts and pieces needed for *Mahdee* to return to her original sailing ability.

The Final Balance of the Restoration: A Structurally New Boat with Original Fixtures

The results were as follows: *Mahdee* retained her original wood keel and fore keel of white oak mortised to receive heels of every other frame. The large, oak after counter timber "tailfeather" and stern timber were replaced with purpleheart. The stem was new of solid purpleheart and the stem knee of laminated purpleheart.

The white oak deadwood was kept but all old bolts and drifts were replaced with new silicon bronze of the original scantling. The inside and outside softwood stopwaters were used in place as appropriate on the entire foundation. All old stopwaters were replaced in kind. The white oak stern/transom framing was replaced with purpleheart ring timber and mahogany quarter logs; angelique stern knees were installed to replace those of white oak.

Original floor timbers were white oak and replaced with purpleheart. All drifts and keelbolts were replaced. Per the original construction, the new ones were installed with spacing 12" on center; 2" up to 4" alternating thickness every other floor. Over the lead keel, the 2" floors are drifted into the keelson whereas the thicker floors have two bolts fully through the lead keel. Forward of the lead keel, alternating floors are single fastened through the keelson with drifts and floors over the narrow forekeel are single fastened. Aft of the lead keel, back to the start of the tailfeather, the floors are fastened through the keelson and deadwood. Aft, the floors are fastened to the tailfeather with drifts and clench rings. All bolts, clench rings, and drifts are silicon bronze.

Main frames are spaced 12" on center. The first seven frames and frames 9, 11, 13, 15, 17 are constructed of double-sawn angelique with finished dimension of 3 1/2" x 3 1/2". All other main and auxiliary frames are constructed of laminated (West System®) sapele (African mahogany) with finished dimension of 2 3/4" x 2 3/4". Eleven auxiliary frames span bilge stringer to bilge stinger midships. Main frame heels are fastened to floor timbers with silicon bronze bolts and frames not in mortises were screwed into wood keel. Ample limbers are provided at every frame; the bottom of the boat is run with wax to the height of all limbers. All frames were replaced.

Original clamps and shelf were kept. They are long leaf yellow pine (LLYP) 2" x 6". The clamp which carries the forward deck frame runs through to the stern and is end-tapered. The lower edge is bolted through the outside guard rail at every frame. The clamp and shelf which carry the raised deck frame are 2" x 6" LLYP. Repairs were made during the restoration to the forward deck clamps in the area of frame 6 and forward. With old growth LLYP unavailable, new wood was clear angelique and scarfs per the Crocker specification for *Mahdee* of at least 3'6" long; scarfs are glued with West System epoxy and bronze bolts. Where there is both a clamp and shelf adjacent to each other they are bolted every 24".

The boat uses her original bilge stringers of LLYP 1 1/2" x 6", tapered at ends to 4 1/2". The mid-ships forward stringer and mid-to-aft section stringers overlap for 7' starboard side and 12' port side.

New mast steps were fabricated of purpleheart shaped per the Crocker plans. Because *Mahdee's* original main mast step had broken in half with the floor beneath the break crushed, both the fore- and main-mast steps were increased in length to have more bearing surface over two additional frames. The step was also made 1" thicker to increase load capacity. The original planking was 1 3/8" clear Douglas fir. It was replaced with clear sapele (African Mahogany) of 1 3/8" finish thickness. The planking schedule was with butts distribution such that no two butts come on the same frame or in the same frame space except where there are three clear planks between, and in no adjacent plank be nearer than three frame spaces. The average plank length was 22'; range of lengths from 8' to 37'. The sheer plank was scarfed (12:1) with no butts. Planking was lined out following the lines of the old planking. Planks were fastened with silicon bronze screws; hood ends and butts were fastened by silicon bronze screws into clear white oak butt blocks cut with 1/2" gap between the block and frame for drainage and 1/2" overlap onto adjacent plank strakes. The number of fasteners per plank follows Lloyd's Rules and Regulations for the Classification of Yachts and Small Craft. Planks show a tight seam inside and caulking seam of not more than 3/32" outside. Planking was cotton-caulked and paved with Interlux Seam Compound® (white above and brown below the waterline). All planking is new with this restoration.

Deck beams are of Douglas fir, with the exception of beams under the bridge deck and alongside the cockpit which are sawn white oak of the original design scantlings. The vertical scantling of deck beams replaced with Douglas fir was increased by 10% to compensate for material property differences between Douglas fir and white oak. New carlines for the cockpit and deckhouse are sapele and for the hatches are Douglas fir. All carlines and deck beams were replaced during this rebuild.

Originally specified by Crocker to be 1" straight laid teak over 3/8" plywood for torsional loading, the original deck had rotted and was leaking. From discussions with various prior owners, the Hatterys learned that at some point before the Allen's 1960s ownership, the plywood was removed. The new deck structure is laid double, of 3/4" thick clear Alaskan yellow cedar (AYC) overhead plus two 9 mm thickness British Standard 1088 Meranti Marine Plywood® (total 18 mm—approximately 3/4" thickness). The 3/4" cedar overhead is laid fore and aft, in strips 2 3/4" wide (grooved and splined) and fastened to the deck beams with both PL Premium waterproof adhesive and with silicon bronze screws. The two sheets of 1088 plywood are glued together with PL Premium® as well as to the AYC overhead. Raptor plastic nails were used to fasten the plywood to the AYC overhead while the glue set. The seams of the top layer of plywood are sealed with West System Epoxy. The deck is waterproofed with Metacrylic Roofing Membrane®. Canvas is laid over the cured Metacrylic and painted for a traditional looking deck surface. The plywood deck is laid to cover the top edge of the sheer plank and waterproofing covering exposed plywood edge. The new sapele 7" wide by 1 1/2" thick covering board is fastened over the deck with silicon bronze screws.

All major structural bulkheads are 3/4" thick (18 mm) British Standard 1088 Meranti Marine Plywood and are new this rebuild. Other bulkheads are Douglas fir (groove and splined) if original construction or 3/4" thick 1088 Meranti Marine Plywood if new this construction. The tamarack (eastern larch) hanging knees (24" all) are thru-bolted to frames and deck beams with silicon bronze bolts. Fourteen are new this rebuild, and the remaining 10 were refastened this rebuild. There are six lodging knees, two tamarack at the start of the break deck and four oak under the bridge deck; all lodging knees were refastened.

The breast hook, all deck blocking and mast partners were replaced this rebuild. Breast hook is purpleheart. All other blocking is Douglas fir. Steel tie rods and compression posts were replaced with silicon bronze.

The sole in the deck house and main cabin, consists of panels of 3/4" or 1" marine plywood with 3/8" teak laid fore and aft, in strips 4 1/2" wide. It was most likely installed by the Allens in the 1960s. In the head, 3/4" BS1088 marine plywood with

Amtico 12 x 12 tiles, new this rebuild. In the forecastle, a wet-room with shower floor with drain system was installed this rebuild.

The exterior hull and deck fittings include a new foredeck sapele bulwark. Foredeck bulwark includes 6" x 1 1/2" structural cap and 7" x 1 1/2" sapele rail that is a continuation of the raised deck covering board. A sapele 3" toerail tops the inboard edge of the covering board along the entire length of the raised deck from the break deck aft to the aft end of the cockpit. The combined covering board height of 1 1/2" and 3" toerail nets a 4 1/2" toe rail. The toe rail design is taller than the old and was added to enhance safety.

Originally of steam-bent white oak, the cracked and rotted wood guardrail was replaced with laminated (3 layers) sapele wood and is approximately 6" x 5" cross section midships tapering fore and aft to 2" x 1 1/2" section at stem and transom. The guardrail is thru-bolted to the clamp.

The original teak and bronze telescoping forehatch was refinished and reinstalled on the foredeck. During the restoration, its oak corner posts were refastened with silicon bronze screws and the forehatch refastened with silicon bronze screws to the deck beams and carlines; the glass in the two fixed portlights in the hatch were replaced with safety glass.

The three original teak skylights were refinished and reinstalled on the main deck with silicon bronze screws to the deck beams and carlines and the glass in the skylights was replaced with safety glass. *Mahdee* retains her 21 original Gustofson® opening bronze portlights—fourteen, 6" ports in the hull; four, 6" ports on the break deck; and three, 5" ports on the forward side of the deck house. In all *Mahdee* has thirteen fixed ports—the two bronze framed on the fore hatch and eleven wood framed on the deck house.

The original cast bronze hawse pipes were reinstalled in new blocking adjacent to the stem. New bronze deck drains were installed to replace the original lead ones. Two large 12" x 5" freeing ports clear the foredeck of water.

A new cast bronze 7" (Lunenburg Foundry) moat-style stove deck iron installed on sapele block adjacent the skylight over the galley accommodates a 6" or smaller stovepipe.

Mahdee's original fir and teak deck house was repaired and reinstalled on main deck. The deck house structure is of Douglas fir, solid wood siding on oak corner posts; 1 3/4" x 2" laminated fir coach roof beams with fir planked overhead (2 1/2" groove and splined). The deck house fixed windows were reframed in new teak by an earlier owner prior to this restoration. The companionway door framing and teak companionway hatch is original; the sliding companionway stainless steel rails and stainless steel and teak turtle for the companionway hatch was installed by a prior owner. The original deckhouse was fastened to new carlines and deck beams with 6" #24 silicon bronze screws driven vertically and 9 mm BS1088 marine plywood was fastened and glued to the inside of the deck house sides and thru-bolted to the carlines to act as a filch plate, further stiffening the deck house behind the built-in seating and chart table. A new port side aft oak deck house corner post was fabricated this restoration. The original fir companionway door was replaced with an identical sapele one. The deck house's original Douglas fir (groove and splined) coach top was roofed with Metacrylic and painted canvas stretched atop it for a traditional roof surface.

The cockpit was rebuilt with a reduced size, for safety reasons, by providing narrow sidedecks and a combing as well as raising the sole height. All Crocker's cockpit designs were reviewed by the Hatterys to establish a new combing in keeping with Crocker's designs. Original lazarette doors were groove and splined teak and not watertight by design so new groove and splined AYC doors were constructed and installed with a watertight latch and seal system.

The original teak steering gear housing had been enlarged over the years to accommodate the autopilot. The housing was rebuilt with oak and sapele framing and was modified, bedded and sealed to provide a more watertight enclosure than previously existed. The steering gear cover is hinged to provide access to inspect the steering gear. At the aft end of the steering gear box there is a new Dorade-type baffled ventilation box with a new 4" bronze ABI cowl vent with deck plate to aid in ventilation of the hull area under the aft deck and cockpit.

Mahdee's caprails, covering boards, cockpit combing and waterways, steering housing, compaionway hatch, front of break deck, break deck trim, and bridge deck trim, as well as forward scuttle and skylights, are bright-finished with varnish. Deck house, hull, cockpit seating, and spars are painted.

Mahdee retains the rig design implemented by the Allens and the Spaulding Yard in 1968, which is largely as-depicted on the 1939 rig plan. A bi-pod boomkin for a fixed backstay installed in the 1950s was replaced with a single boomkin. The currently used single spreaders on both masts are depicted in the 1939 rigging plan as well. Her mainmast is the original 1931 clear Douglas fir mast lengthened in 1939 during the gunter-to-Bermuda rig conversion. The bronze main masthead fitting from the 1939 conversion is in use. The foremast is clear spruce; other spars are clear Douglas fir. The masts and spars were stripped and prior repairs evaluated. Two small scarfed repairs to the mainmast were redone to ensure no rot in the old repair. A prior birds mouth repair to the mainmast top was reglued as well during this restoration. The spars are varnished, masts are painted.

Master rigger Jamie White, while at the San Francisco Maritime Museum, acted as a key advisor to the rerigging project. Because *Mahdee's* 1939 rig, which was being restored, included 1 x 19 wire which is difficult to splice properly, rigger David Burgess from the San Diego Maritime Museum spliced some of the shrouds and taught Brenda Hattery how to perform the required splices in 1 x 19 wire. All standing rigging wire and mechanical terminals and running rigging lines were replaced during the restoration with their scantlings verified against the 1939 rigging plan. The standing rigging is 5/16" 1 x 19 stainless steel on the forestay, running and fixed backstay; 3/8" 1 x 19 stainless steel on the shrouds; 3/8" 7 x 19 stainless steel on jibstay; and 5/8" rigging screws with 5/8" jaws and clevis pins were used throughout. Bronze and teak boom gallows and push pit from the 1968 refit were reused. The original fir bowsprit was modified to enable shipping and stayed with a new running bobstay of 1/2" dia.,

7 x 19 stainless steel for a fixed length and a 4-to-1 purchase of 3/8" Amsteel for the running length. The main halyard and jib sheets are 5/8" Samson VLS® 3-strand polyester w/Olefin® core, other running rigging is 1/2", 3/8", or 1/4" New England Rope polyester 3-strand line.

Sixteen of *Mahdee's* 18 bronze chainplates are new this restoration; they are 3/8" thick by 36" to 48"in length, of Tobin bronze, and all 18 have new 2 3/4" x 2 3/4" laminated sapele backing frames thru-bolted to the hull with 3/8" silicon bronze bolts. The two chain plates which were reused are cast bronze running backstay chainplates supporting the 1939 rig plan. New forestay-to-stem gammon chainplates and a gobstay (boomkin) chainplate of 1/2" silicon bronze were installed with the restoration.

Mahdee's sail-handling hardware is primarily traditional with approximately 50 wood-cheeked and bronze-sheaved blocks. The majority of the blocks are Merriman of the era of the Allen's ownership and were rebuilt by adding new axles, pins, or cheeks as needed; since the mast hoops were missing, new HDPE (high density polyethylene) mast hoops like those made by Pat Vineyard for the schooner *Alycone* were made by Pat for the gaff foresail and Brenda Hattery covered them with traditional latigo leather. Elsewhere, the 1 1/4" bronze sailtracks, including that installed during the 1968 refit, were retained. New angelique and sapele pinracks were made while the original turned oak belaying pins revarnished. The original teak fife rails at the base of the masts were reused with new 3/4" bronze rods bolted through the mast partners. Nine of *Mahdee's* 14 manual winches were reinstalled; they are of the era of the Allen's ownership and built by Barient/Barlow with bronze drums. The gaff foresail trims to a bronze horse traveler. To improve short-handed sailing, all sheets as well as the foresail halyards, run back to the cockpit with close proximity to the original 1931 rigging plan and winches in close proximity to those used in the original plan as well.

The sail inventory includes the Bermuda main (plus spare), gaff foresail, staysail, jib, *Yankee* cut jib, balloon footed jib, spinnaker, fisherman, and gollywobbler. All sails are old and of Dacron cloth and most are suspected to have been built when the Allens owned the boat. They were repaired, releathered, and bolt ropes resewn professionally in 2003 and by Brenda Hattery in 2010.

The Hatterys installed many new equipment items that had been purchased but never installed by McHugh, as well as reinstalled numerous equipment that McHugh had removed and stored. The first week of ownership of *Mahdee* in 2006, Tom took David Hattery into McHugh's large storage unit and explained the equipment therein and how to reinstall much of *Mahdee's* hardware. Two years later, the new Cummins engine and Onan genset as well as numerous electrical and plumbing components were pulled out of storage and installed in the boat. Entering the storage unit was like Christmas for the Hatterys and they developed a fondness for McHugh based upon the thoughtful selection that he had made in the purchase of so many things.

When evaluating *Mahdee's* systems during the restoration, the Hatterys were careful to keep intact and restore as needed the original elements in the boat. For example, in the cockpit, original to the boat, a beautiful Kelvin & White bronze and glass skylight compass binnacle and inclinometer sit on the original 37" tall teak pedestal inside of which reside a number of compensating magnets mounted in racks in both fore-and-aft and athwartships directions. The original double-arm worm gear in the steering system was retained as was the teak wheel. The Tobin bronze rudder stock was replaced in kind and a new oak rudder built to the 1931 plans. *Mahdee's* original Shipmate galley stove had been removed by an unknown previous owner and her soapstone saloon heating stove removed by McHugh while *Mahdee* was in San Diego. The Hatterys located a similarly sized multifuel Shipmate 134 coal, wood, and diesel stove which had been removed from an old tug boat in New Jersey and installed it in the galley. A suitable main saloon stove has not been located as of this writing.

Even when the systems were not original from the 1931 build, vintage hardware and systems on the boat have been maintained or upgraded. In addition to much rigging hardware, this includes an Ideal Windlass with bronze bollard, bronze wildcat, and bronze rope gypsy. The Cavendish-Bentincks installed a Wood Freeman Autopilot® in 1962 which, according to records on file with Wood Freeman, was maintained by the Allen and Goss families with replacement parts occasionally sent to tropical ports. Very few autopilots work reliably with the size of heavy worm steering gear *Mahdee* has. As such, the Hatterys contacted the manufacturer and upgraded the sturdy Wood Freeman with a later model control unit and remote.

Much of *Mahdee's* beautiful original interior remained intact until the mid-1980s. Though most of the remaining interior was removed during McHugh's work in 2003, numerous original pieces including doors, drawers, and hardware were kept by McHugh in storage and given to Hattery. Along with Crocker's very detailed interior drawings, those parts allowed Hattery to measure scantlings and finishing details so the interior may be rebuilt and restored as much as possible to its original interior plan.

In 2009, Hattery installed the basic electronics needed for safe cruising, roughed in the galley and head, installed a washer/dryer in what was formerly a closet for a 1931 CO_2 engine fire suppression system, built a double berth in the stateroom (as added by Ireland and shown on the 1937 drawings) as well as built the Crocker-designed charthouse furniture to replace that which was missing. At the same time he reinstalled parts of McHugh's storage lockers and a series of cargo netting walls and hammocks. This basic interior allowed the Hatterys to live aboard

Before relaunching the vessel, *Mahdee's* name was carefully written in gold-leaf letters onto her stern (*Brenda Hattery*).

and cruise *Mahdee* during 2009 and 2010. In 2011, Hattery spent several months rebuilding more of *Mahdee's* interior to the original Crocker plans and he plans to alternate between sailing and building out the interior for several more years.

Mahdee and the "Privateer Knot"

On their blog Brenda Hattery wrote an account of how she found out about the origins of the Privateer Knot:

> *I spent last evening, sitting in the charthouse with 4 candles lit (great heat and light) and re-installing the bronze sail slides to the mainsail. The slides/cars were knotted onto a rope in a bucket by* Mahdee's *previous owner. As I evaluated the nifty knotting of the strips of heavy latigo leather, I pulled out Marino's 2001* Sailmakers Apprentice *to see what the proper way of dealing with these sailslides might be. There, I found a full page with a lovely series of drawings of how to tie exactly the leather lashing that I was studying on my rope of sail slides. It is called the Privateer Knot and Mr. Marino states it's especially appropriate to large boat bronze slides. Within the flickering candlelight my thoughts turned to days of old and I quickly imagined big "privateer" type boats of long ago—something one might read about in O'Brian's books. Then I turned the page and was amazed, and pleased, to read: "I first encountered this aboard Bob Goss's schooner Privateer (formerly* Mahdee*) where it had been in use for several years. He'd devised and adapted the method, thus the name." Well, now I felt really that* Mahdee *was even more "special" knowing that I was looking at the "original" Privateer Knots. We keep finding little references to her and it's really fun to learn more about her past.*

Merging the Past and the Present

During the restoration and now sailing *Mahdee*, the Hatterys have enjoyed meeting and corresponding with former owners as well as relatives and friends of former owners, and have received special "re-launch" gifts that are reminders of *Mahdee's* varied history. In 2009, a San Diego sailor gave the Hatterys a bronze sink pump that had been removed some years ago from *Mahdee*. In 2010, Alexander White Moffat III, a.k.a. "Banner" Moffat, the grandson of *Mahdee's* original owner, brought two gifts from the Moffat family. First, a gift from Banner: He returned to *Mahdee* an original etching by Gardiner entitled *Out of the Fog* and signed "to *Mahdee*, a taut sheet and flowing seas." The gift was originally presented to *Mahdee* upon her launch in April 1931. The second gift was a small, porcelain figurine of a happy little Asian man with a fishing pole slung over his shoulder, a fish resting on his back. Banner said this little mascot had belonged to *Mahdee's* original owner and had served as a mascot on each and every of the 26 or more boats that Skipper Moffat owned throughout his long life. The mascot was affectionately called "musk ox" because Banner's father, as a small child, could not pronounce the word "mascot" properly.

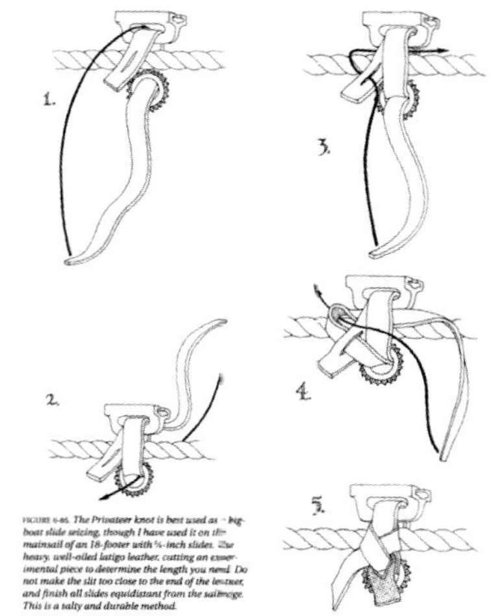

This drawing of the "Privateer Knot" was what Brenda Hattery found in the 2001 book *Sailmakers Apprentice* by Marino. The knot apparently was named after the schooner *Privateer*, formerly named *Mahdee*.

The Hatterys wrote:

> *We were touched by the generosity of the Moffats to share this wonderful family treasure with us and noted that little Musk Ox has been through a lot in his long life and it shows. With a little chip here and there; several parts of the hat glued back on and his fishing pole mostly missing. He's had quite a life on those varied boats, we're certain! Ah, but little Musk Ox also has a twinkle in his eye that says "lets go!"*
>
> *And, go we have! We're thrilled that Musk Ox was able to make the trip up the California Coast with us. His place, for now, is in a wood bin kept high on a shelf in the galley. He resides adjacent the olive and sesame oils, in front of the whiskey and just where he can usually see all that is happening below decks. I say usually because, well, when we're actually underway Musk Ox is shrouded in a bit of bubble wrap inside a tall Crystal Light Lemonade tube that protects him from coming to harm. He gets to look out and about once we've anchored.*

Since the relaunch, the Hatterys have cruised with *Mahdee* along the Pacific Coast. They first started out doing sea trials in San Diego, and from there they sailed the Channel Islands and up the coast north to San Francisco and took part in the 2010 Great San Francisco Schooner Race.

The excitement of slicing through the waves while beating to windward through a late season gale and the exhilaration of downwind sailing unexpectedly barreling down the wave faces at hull speed while offshore on a moonlit night reveal that *Mahdee* today performs brilliantly, and, much as Sandy Moffat knew, she's in her element in big winds and large seas. With countless days at anchor— whether lazy days eating blackberries in the Sacramento Delta or keeping the boat warm with the coal-fired Shipmate® while standing a late night anchor watch in the comfort of the charthouse during a winter blow—the Hatterys have found, in *Mahdee*, their perfect cruising schooner.

After the restoration, the first long cruise brought the boat to San Francisco to take part in the 2008 Mariner's Regatta. She is docked here in front of the San Francis Yacht Harbor early in the morning, waiting for the action to begin (*David Hattery*).

Mahdee motoring past Point Conception in a calm. Note the lowered foredeck, which offers some shelter when working with the foresails or the anchor (*Chris Kennedy*).

Mahdee under full lower in 2008, sailing in the Raccoon Strait, San Francisco Bay (*John Swain*).

Today, *Mahdee's* sails are as stiff and well trimmed as in the 1930s and 1960s. This is just another sign that she is in good hands (*John Swain*).

TYRONE
(Ex- *William H. Thorndyke*; Ex- *Tyrone*)

Type: two-mast gaff schooner
Designer: Samuel Sturgis Crocker, Design No. 202
Shipyard: Simms Brothers, Dorchester, Massachusetts
Year of Construction: 1939
Length (sparred): 75'
Length on Deck: 60'
Length on Waterline: 50'
Beam: 15'
Draft: 8'6"
Displacement: 29 tons (gross)/ 25 tons (net)
Sail Area: 2,200 sq. ft.
Construction: Honduras mahogany on oak, bronze fastened
Engine: Cummins, model 6B5.9, 120 hp
Owner: Matt Sutphin
Home Port: Harwich, Massachusetts

Tyrone: An Able Cruising Schooner

The schooner *Tyrone* was built in 1939 by the prestigious yard of Simms Brothers in Dorchester, Massachusetts, for Alexander C. Tener of Pittsburgh, Pennsylvania. He was a member of the Eastern Point Yacht Club of Gloucester, and later of the Boothbay Harbor Yacht Club and the Corinthians, headquartered in New York.

Tyrone was heavily built with attractive and traditional lines by Sam Crocker to be good for both long offshore passages and shoal-water weekend cruises. Her design was the subject of a lot of correspondence between Tener and Crocker until the plans were finished. Several different combinations of beam, draft, displacement, and freeboard were considered. The possibility of building her in steel was explored but found impractical and expensive. Tener wanted a rugged, able boat capable of weathering any kind of weather if given half a chance, and yet one that he and his captain could handle with some help from the cook. When in commission, she always carried a captain and a cook.

Being heavily built, she originally carried a Lathrop Mystic 125 gas engine, and she had a 3-kilowatt, 32-volt, two-cylinder generator to run her refrigerator and other electric powered gear.

She wintered in the water in Boothbay Harbor, Maine, and went into commission around April 1 each year. In 1959, she was brought to Manchester, where the Crocker yard replaced some soft wood around the corners of her stern. She was too big to be hauled out at the yard, so they did the job while at the dock. The yard workers used all sorts of barrels full with chain, moorings and other heavy materials to put on the foredeck to lift up the stern to work on it. While the boat was at the yard, the cook stayed on board, cooking for them. He made pies, cakes, or doughnuts every day, and on Fridays he made a fish chowder that put lobster stew to shame. He did it all on a coal-fired Shipmate that was kindled in April and never went out until the boat was laid up in the fall. During that refit, the schooner also received a new engine and new sails.

Tener owned the vessel until about 1968, when his son George took over ownership. He sold *Tyrone* in 1970 to Norman Matson of Boston, and he owned her until 1977. When he sold the boat to a new owner, she was renamed *William H. Thorndike*.

She has proved her capabilities and practicality as a liveaboard cruiser by her several transatlantic crossings and cruises in southern waters. She is also a veteran of New England waters and has cruised on the West Coast and in Hawaii.

In addition to her cruising capabilities, *William H. Thorndike* won the Billican Cup in San Francisco. Furthermore, she won the "most photogenic" prize at the Antigua Classic Yacht Regatta out of a field of exceptionally lovely classic yachts, including *Ticonderoga*. At the Antigua Classic Yacht Regatta, *William H. Thorndike* was beaten by only five minutes on a three-hour racecourse by the Burgess-designed schooner *Niña* and was reported to be faster than *Niña* on the reaches.

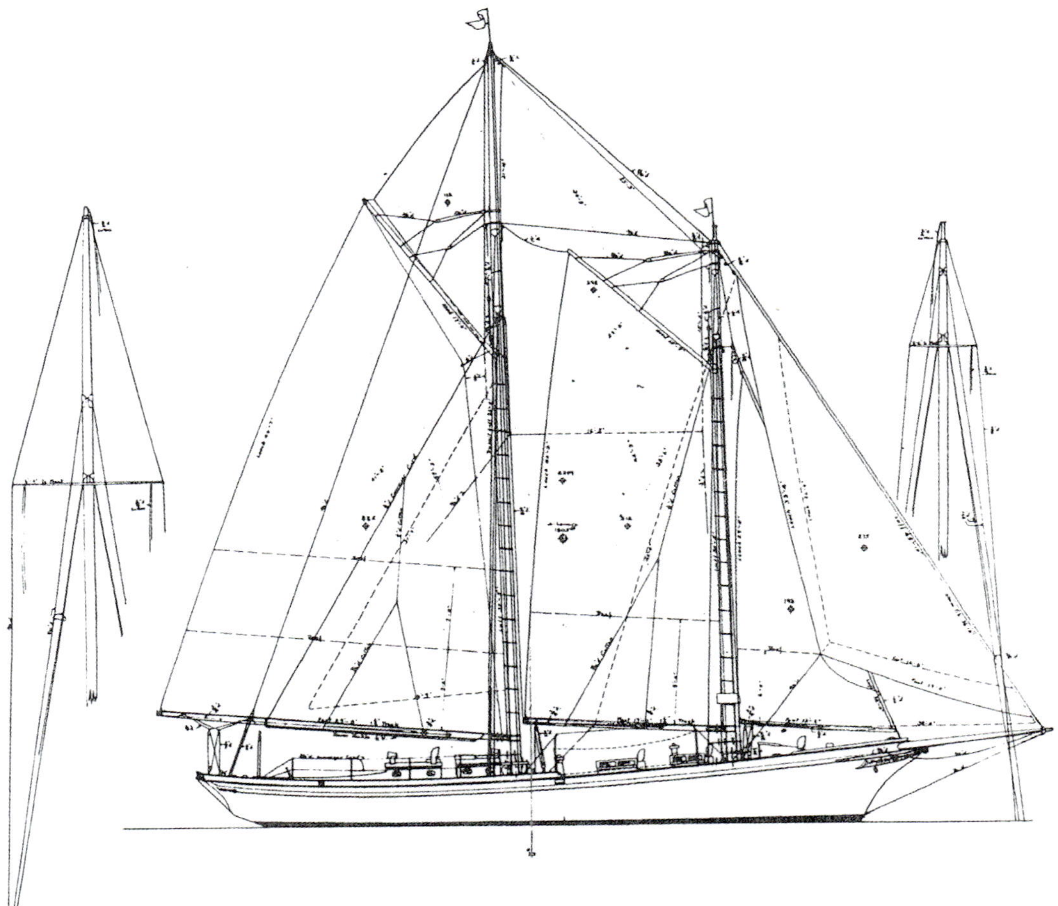

William H. Thorndike underwent a refit in 2001, and when she came into the hands of her current owner, Matt Sutphin, he again accomplished a mayor restoration aimed primarily to improve the structural strength of the boat. He changed the name of the boat back to her original name *Tyrone*.

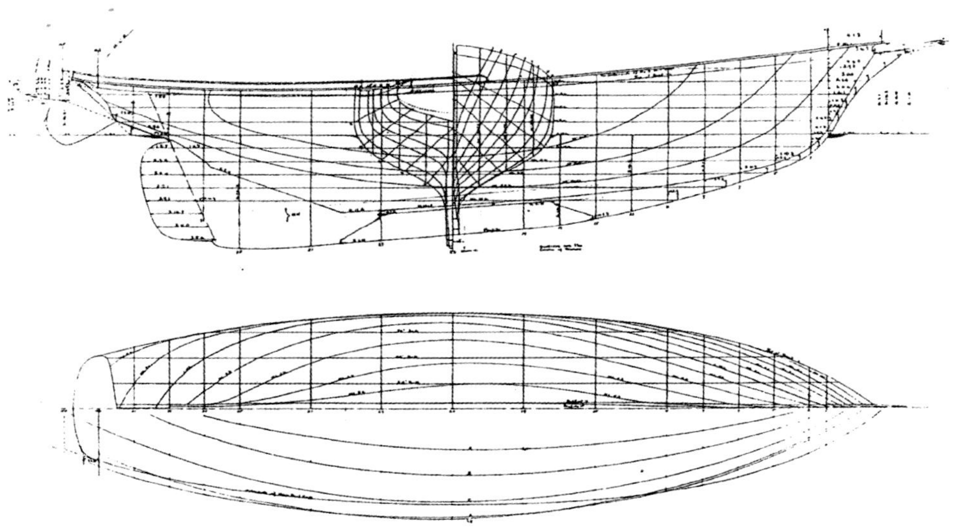

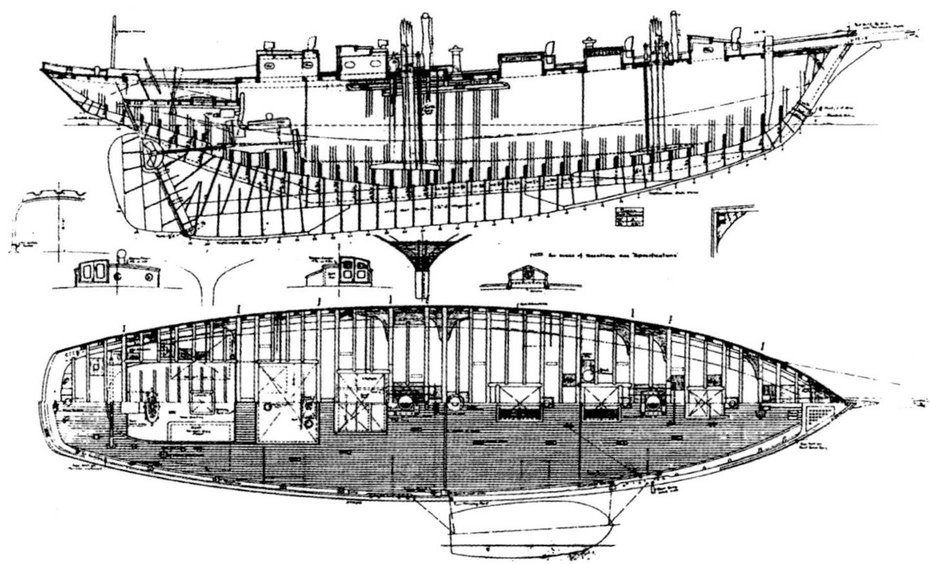

Tyrone gets ready to be launched in 1939. The man with the pipe and the blazer around his arm on the foredeck of *Tyrone* is probably Alexander C. Tener, who came out from Pittsburgh, Pennsylvania, to witness the launching (*Crocker Boatyard*).

The workers from the Crocker Boatyard stand for a last photo before the finished schooner glides into the water (*Crocker Boatyard*).

This stern-view of *Tyrone* shows her powerful lines. She truly was a masterpiece at the time (*Crocker Boatyard*).

Once she was launched, the work was not over. The riggers had to install all the standing and running rigging (*Crocker Boatyard*).

The schooner *William H. Thorndyke*, ex- *Tyrone*, taking part in a yacht race off Newport, Rhode Island (*Matt Sutphin Archive*).

Tyrone Today

Today *Tyrone* is a private sailing yacht out of Harwich, where she is kept in Bristol condition by her very enthusiastic owner. She is distinctive with her clipper bow, round bilge, full keel and transom stern. Her hull is constructed of 1 1/2" Honduras mahogany carvel planking, which is bronze-screw fastened to 2 1/2" double-sawn oak frames on 16" centers. Backbone, floor timbers, and deadwood are also oak. The schooner has a full keel with 7/8" bronze keel bolts and the rudder is GRP-sheathed mahogany. The ballast is external 10 tons of lead. In addition, there is some 1–2 tons internal lead ballast. The decks are caulked and consist of laid teak over oak deck beams. The superstructure is limited to a small mahogany deckhouse that stands above the engine and the galley.

Tyrone carries gaff sails on both masts. The chain plates pass through the deck and are bolted through the hull.

Tyrone has a very clean and uncluttered deck that offers ample working space for the crew. Here she is seen sailing wing and wing (*Matt Sutphin*).

Another view of *Tyrone* sailing wing and wing (*Matt Sutphin*).

The cockpit offers plenty of space for helmsman, or helmswoman, and guests…(*Matt Sutphin*).

Tyrone currently has a figurehead that seems to depict William H. Thorndyke, the person for whom she was named in 1970. Originally, her bow was decorated with golden scrollwork (*Matt Sutphin*).

The interior layout of the vessel has a chain locker forward followed by the forecastle. This cabin has an upper and lower berth to port and a head followed by a vanity to starboard. Next aft are port and starboard upper and lower berths. The main cabin is next aft. Forward to port and starboard are lockers and drawers. To port is an L-shaped settee and to starboard are berths with drawers below. Next aft is the navigation station to starboard and a full enclosed head to port. Steps up lead to the galley area. The galley is to port and to starboard is a U-shaped dinette. The companionway is aft to starboard with a door to the engine space behind. The engine room is behind the galley area, separated by a partition.

The high bow keeps *Tyrone's* decks dry and allow for her to smoothly take the waves. Note that her anchor gear is stored on deck, in the "old fashioned" way (*Matt Sutphin*).

A winter scene at her owner's dock in Harwich, Massachusetts. She is a great addition to the romantic landscape of that traditional seamen's village (*Matt Sutphin*).

Tyrone sails smoothly into the day. Her wide decks again become apparent. They invite one to go along the sails, check everything, and make sure the trim is right. On such a schooner this exercise could go on an on forever. *Tyrone* has done so for only seventy years, and she is ready for many more years of fighting the eternal contest between man and the sea (*Matt Sutphin*).

A detail of *Tyrone's* bowsprit shows the immaculate shape of her rigging. All fittings in the rig are the original bronze fittings produced by Crocker Boatyard in 1939 (*Matt Sutphin*).

Tyrone's stern is simple and elegant (*Matt Sutphin*).

The rigging work aboard *Tyrone* is still done the same way it was in 1939 (*Matt Sutphin*).

Waiting for many more years of sailing (*Matt Sutphin*).

Bowdoin B. Crowninshield: Elegance as Trademark

BIOGRAPHY OF BOWDOIN B. CROWNINSHIELD

Bowdoin Bradlee Crowninshield was born in 1867 in New York, and he grew up in Marblehead, Massachusetts, into the wealthy Crowninshield family with longstanding ties to the sea. His family was one of the most influential maritime families of the early United States. His father was Benjamin Williams Crowninshield (1837–1892) and his mother was Katherine May Bradlee (1844–1902). His great-grandfather Benjamin Williams Crowninshield (1772–1851) served as Secretary of the Navy, and his great-granduncle George Crowninshield Jr. (1766–1817) built the first luxury yacht in the United States, *Cleopatra's Barge*, in 1816. Because of his many relations, he was generally known as "B.B." Crowninshield.

After graduating from Harvard in 1890, he speculated in real estate before signing on as a draftsman with John R. Purdon, a respected yacht designer in Boston. Crowninshield struck out on his own eighteen months later, starting a yacht design and brokerage firm, which quickly prospered. He would rise to become one of America's most respected yacht designers during a period, which is now regarded as the golden age of American wooden yacht design.

In 1898, Crowninshield opened his office in Boston, originally in partnership with Frank Tandy. Crowninshield was involved in practically all marine-related activities during his career, including design, construction, brokerage, insurance, and personnel management. He designed the America's Cup contender *Independence* in 1902 and also the seven-mast steel schooner *Thomas W. Lawson*. Crowninshield served with the American Volunteer Motor Ambulance Corps in northwestern France in 1916, and was present at the battle of Verdun. From 1917–26 he was the president and general manager of the Crowninshield Shipbuilding Company of Fall River, Massachusetts. He was appointed Inspector of Hulls Building for the Navy in 1943. He died three years later, on August 12, 1948.

Crowninshield is now best remembered for his working schooners and his America's Cup contender *Independence*, built by George Lawley & Son in 1901 for Thomas W. Lawson. He was also responsible for designing the *Dark Harbor* sloop. He designed the unique seven-mast schooner *Thomas W. Lawson*, named for his patron. Crowninshield's work also contributed to the development of the Gloucester fishing schooner, well known for their sweeping and seaworthy lines. His synthesis of racing yacht and fishing schooner design led to many design evolutions that produced the American schooner yacht we know today. He designed the schooner *Adventuress*, which was launched in 1913 and has been named a National Historic Landmark. Also, the schooner *Martha* is a remarkable example of his craftsmanship. Both schooners are further described in this chapter.

In addition to his spectacular yacht designs, he was also widely known for his strong character. He married Priscilla Janet Macphail on May 12, 1900, and two years later, in August 1902, Crowninshield was fined $20 for using his fists on Adolphus G. McVey, the yachting editor of *The Boston Herald*. Aparently, McVey made some disparaging remarks about Crowninshield's designs for *Independence*, so there was bad blood between them. McVey happened to be on a boat dock as Crowninshield's motor launch approached. Crowninshield's wife said something along the lines of: "There's that wretch now; why don't you go up and throw him overboard?" To this, McVey replied: "You ought to have thrown her overboard when you met her first." This did obviously not set well with Crowninshield, and he proceeded to climb up and soundly trounce McVey. While the aforementioned trouncing was occurring, Mrs. Crowninshield was heard to loudly proclaim, "Kill the wretch." The other folks on the dock came to McVey's defense, and Crowninshield was forced to withdraw to his launch and leave. After Crowninshield was fined the twenty dollars, McVey sued him for $10,000, a princely sum in those days. *The New York Times* then gave this report of Crowninshield's reply to the problems with McVey:

> *I wish to state I had no argument whatsoever with A. G. McVey, as I consider my time too valuable to argue with a man of his caliber. He showed a desire to throw me overboard, which I cordially invited him to do, but instead of accepting my invitation he grossly insulted my wife, which I resented. But I didn't take him unawares, as I had to climb a ladder and walk ten feet before getting to him. Furthermore, he saw me coming and picked up a heavy stick with which he struck me before I reached him. He richly deserved all he got at my hands, and I hope he has learned a lesson.*

The suit was settled in 1911 in McVey's favor for $448. This was not the end of Crowninshield's troubles however. It seems that his wife decided to go shopping in Boston in 1915 without telling her husband and took a room under an assumed name. She was found in the Parker House Hotel dead in a tub of hot water. *The New York Times* reported that the medical examiner, George B. McGrath (a Harvard class mate of Crowninshield's) stated "that apparently Mrs. Crowninshield fainted as she stepped into the bathtub, the water of which was very hot." The death, he was certain, from his investigation, was neither suicidal nor homicidal. Interestingly, he did not make his report until conferring with Crowninshield.

Crowninshield later remarried Laura A. Wildar in 1916. He died August 12, 1948, in Marblehead.

ADVENTURESS

Type: two-mast gaff schooner
Designer: Bowdoin Bradlee Crowninshield
Year Built: 1913
Shipyard: Rice Brothers, East Boothbay, Maine
Length (Sparred): 135'
Length on Deck: 101'
Length on Waterline: 71'
Beam: 21'
Draft: 12'
Mast Height: 110'
Sail Area: 5,478 sq. ft.
Displacement: 82 tons
Construction: wood
Engine: 250-hp diesel
Owner: Sound Experience
Home Port: Port Townsend, Washington

Adventuress: A Schooner for Arctic Adventures

Commissioned originally as a private yacht to gather Arctic specimens, *Adventuress* was built in 1913 at the Rice Brothers shipyard in East Boothbay, Maine. Her first owner was John Borden, of Chicago. He had her built for a trip to Alaska by way of the Magellan Straits and Seattle. Once she had arrived in Seattle, her owner planned to sail into the Arctic Ocean, specifically to Wrangel Island in search of big game.

Adventuress was designed and built as an impressively elegant schooner. Very much in line with the usual racing yachts of her time, she had long overhangs, a large main sail and a long bowsprit. At 101' on deck and 21' beam she seems narrow for a cruising boat. However, taking into account the purpose for which she was built, her construction was very heavy.

To be able to fish in northern waters, the schooner was equipped with a 21' Atlantic Company dory launch; a regulation New Bedford 28' Arctic whale-boat by C. D. Beetle, of New Bedford, with full equipment including guns, lances, etc.; a Hiram Lowell & Son (Boston) haddock dory; and a 10' dinghy.

She carried an 80-hp three-cylinder Standard engine, for which her fuel tank had a capacity of 1,400 gallons of gas. The electric system was supplied by an Edison storage battery, charged by a 5-hp engine and an Eck generator. The generator also ran the refrigerator machine and an engine bolted under deck forward to operate the windlass.

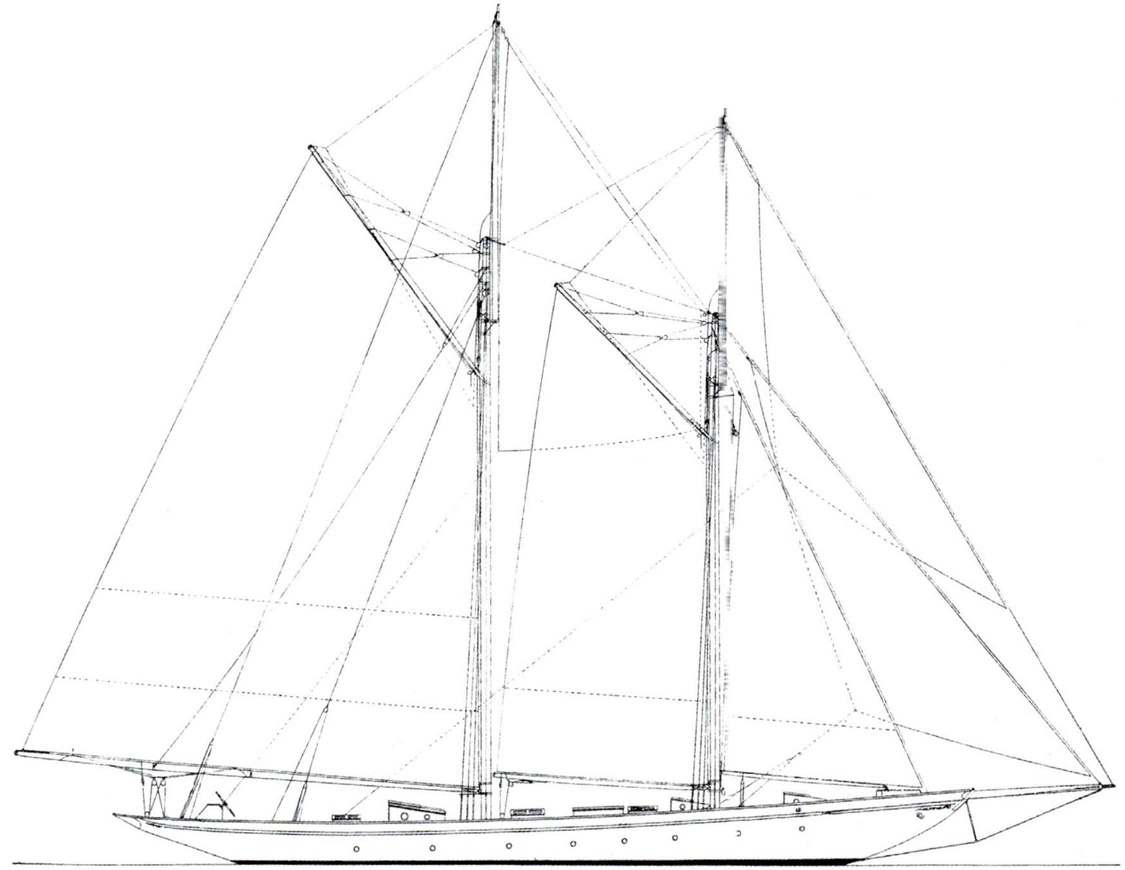

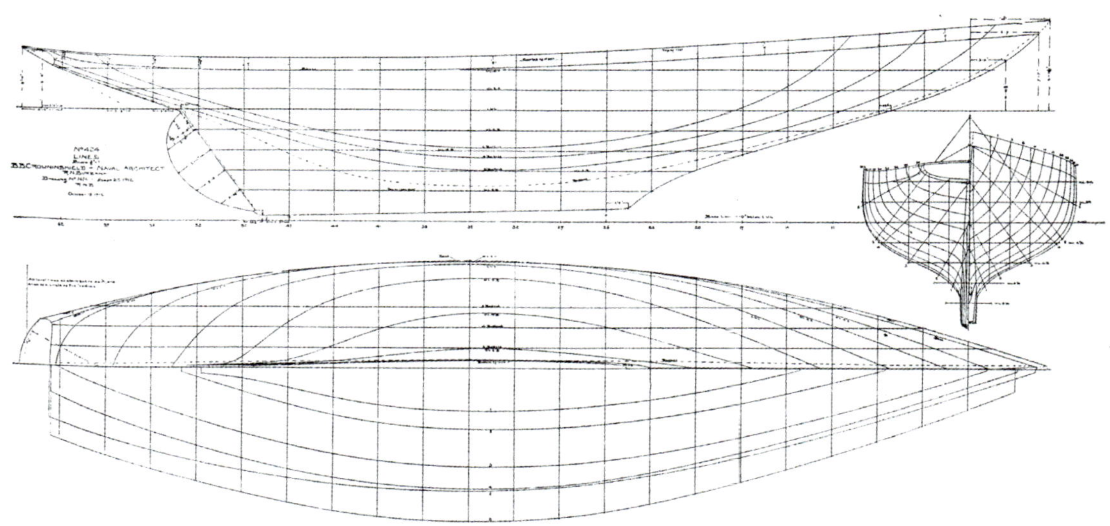

(The Rudder, *March 1913*)

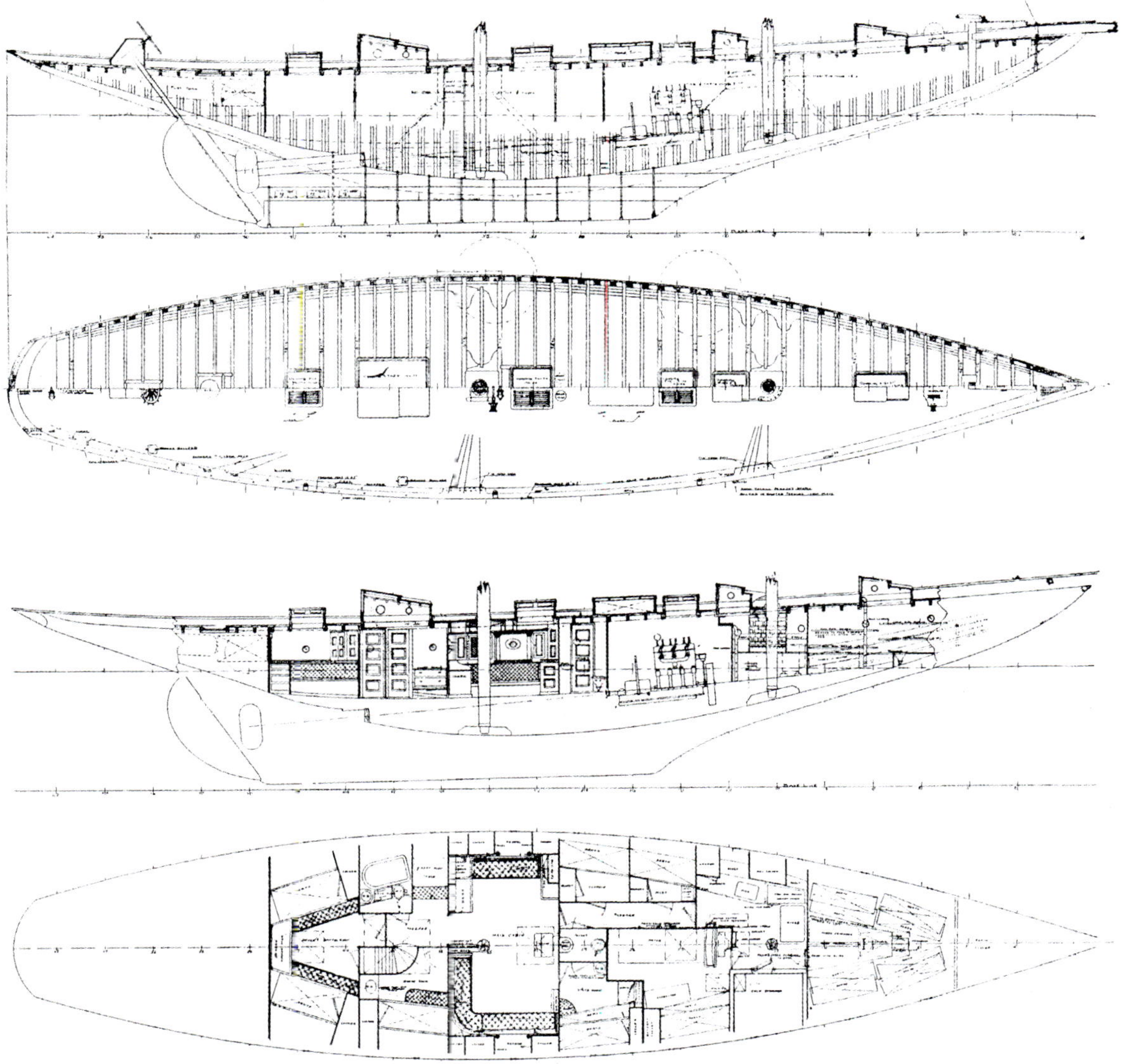

From Schooner Yacht to Harbor Pilot

However, already after her maiden voyage to the Bering Sea, John Borden sold *Adventuress* to the Bar Pilots of San Francisco Bay, where she served in commercial piloting until 1952.

In 1960, "Doc" Freeman of the Lake Union Chandlery in Seattle brought her to Washington's Puget Sound. Two years later Ernestine Bennett and a group of Girl Scouts seeking a challenge discovered *Adventuress*. Bennett became the helmswoman for a number of programs and ownership changes that led to the floating classroom program now known as Sound Experience.

At present, the schooner *Adventuress* sails to increase awareness of the majesty and vulnerability of Puget Sound. Since 1989, the non-profit environmental education organization, Sound Experience, has provided hands-on education aboard *Adventuress* in response to the area's urgent environmental issues. Volunteer and paid crew receive environmental and sail training. The ship's apprentice program for youth 14–18, and month-long internships for adult sailor/educators also feature extensive sail training. The non-competitive environment fosters cooperation, teamwork, and leadership skills. A National Historic Landmark and a Puget Sound treasure, the *Adventuress* is truly a boat for the people, providing empowering, life-changing experiences to more than 3,500 youth and adults each year.

The schooner *Adventuress* under all lowers. She sails the waters of the Puget Sound, where she is a very familiar sight (*Michael Berman*).

Adventuress waiting for wind. The crew must be expecting some strong gusts from the surrounding mountains. Being built for Arctic explorations, she is relatively heavy, although her lines promise some good speed in moderate breeze (*Michael Berman*).

MARTHA

Type: centerboard two-mast gaff schooner, rerigged as staysail schooner
Designer: Bowdoin Bradlee Crowninshield, Design No. 351
Year Built: 1907
Shipyard: William F. Stone, San Francisco, California
Length (Sparred): 84'
Length on Deck: 68'
Beam: 16'
Draft: 8'
Displacement: 84,000 lbs.
Construction: wood
Engine: diesel
Owner: The Schooner Martha Foundation
Home Port: Port Townsend, Washington

Martha's Origins

John Ryder Hanify, a West Coast lumber baron and an avid sailor and racing enthusiast, did not think long before choosing the famous yacht designer B. B. Crowninshield to draw the lines for his new schooner *Martha* in 1906. Design No. 351 was launched shortly after that by the William F. Stone Boatyard at San Francisco in May 1907. She had extremely sleek lines with low freeboard. A long bowsprit extended the foresails far ahead, and the large sail plan carried two gaff sails. With this configuration, she measured 84' sparred length, while she was only 68' on deck. As a centerborder, she was very beamy with 16'. Her centerboard reduced the draft to only a few feet while entering a harbor. She displaced 84,000 lbs. Early racing accounts about *Martha* in 1907 report, "She is a magnificent cruising boat besides being above average in speed" (*Yachting*, December 1907).

The Schooner Martha Foundation

When Robert d'Arcy and JoAnn O'Connor found the schooner *Martha* almost abandoned in a harbor in the Northeast of the United States in 1997, they created The Schooner Martha Foundation with the mission to restore and

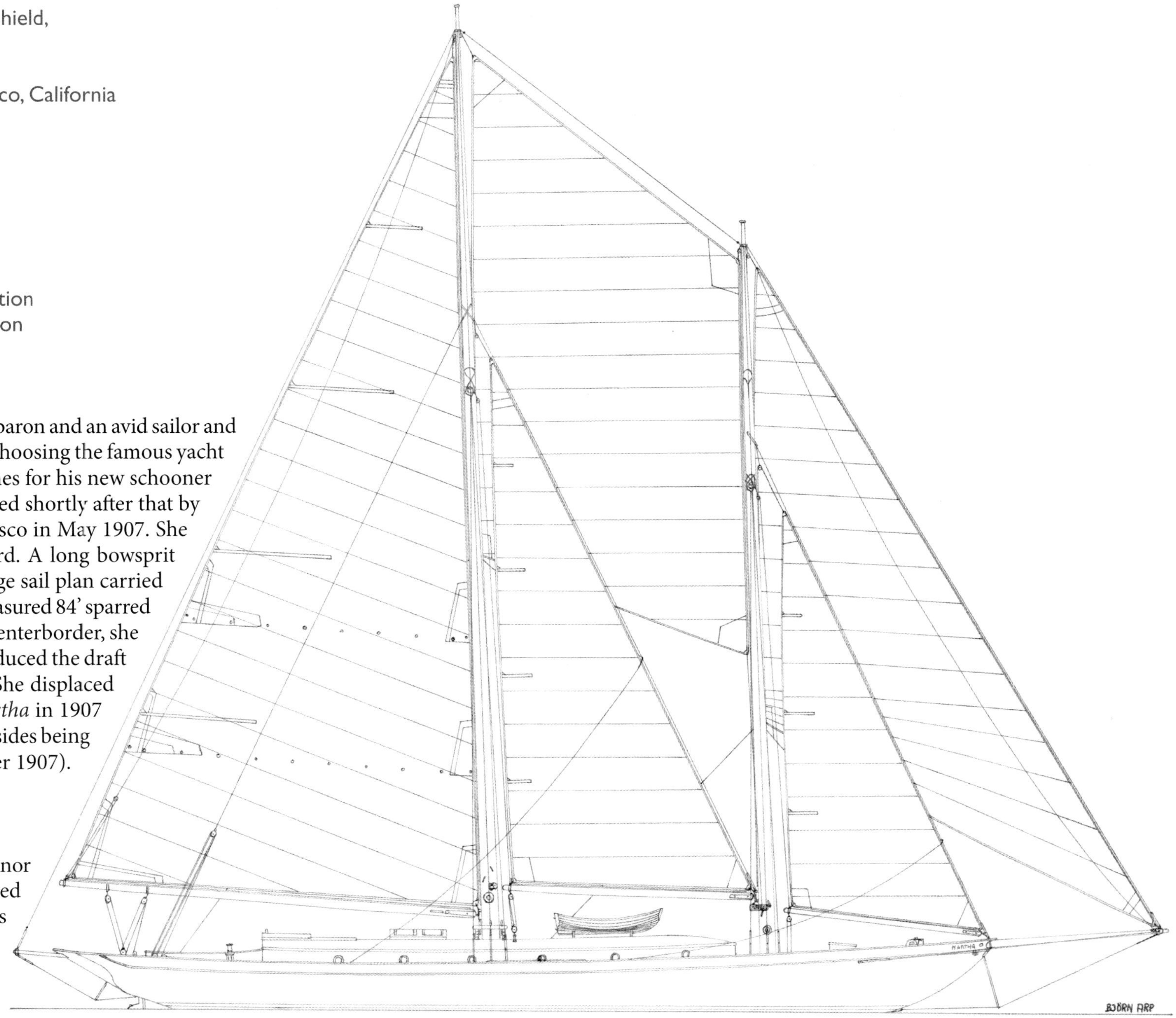

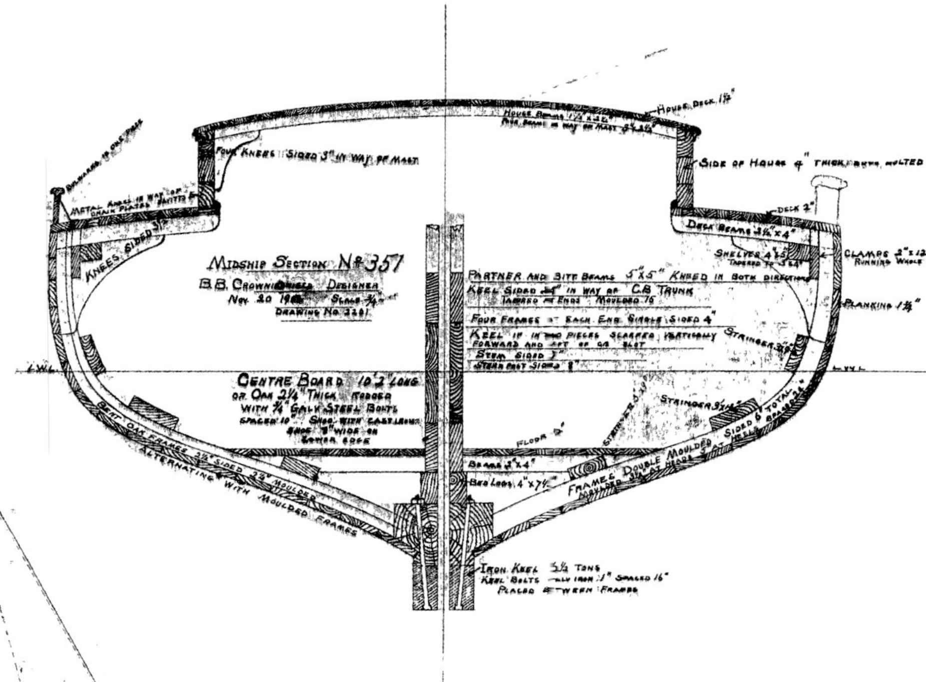

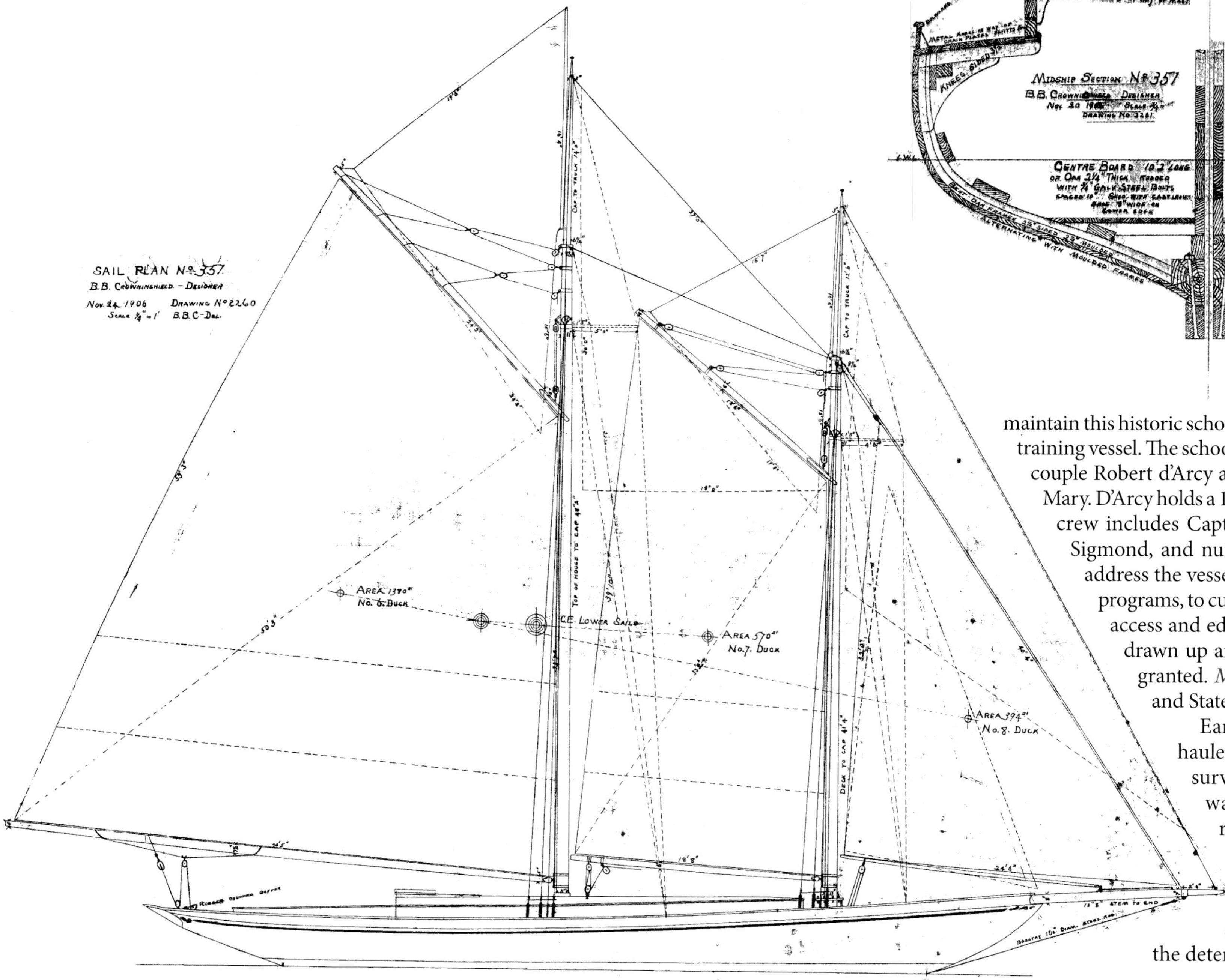

maintain this historic schooner and operate her as a youth sail-training vessel. The schooner is now operated by the married couple Robert d'Arcy and Holly Kays, and their daughter Mary. D'Arcy holds a 100-ton Master's License. Additional crew includes Captain Mary Beth Armstrong, Peter Sigmond, and numerous volunteers. Primary goals address the vessel's stewardship, youth sail-training programs, to curate the vessel's history, allow public access and education. A Board of Directors was drawn up and 501(c)(3) non-profit status was granted. *Martha* was placed on the National and State Historic Register in 2001.

Early in the year 1997, *Martha* was hauled out for a comprehensive marine survey from which a restoration plan was established. Analysis of old records, photographic evidence, and the survey, identified significant deficiencies which would need repair to keep the vessel seaworthy and to stop and reverse the deteriorating effects of hard use.

Martha's Long Restoration

A ten-phase restoration program was established. This way *Martha* could continue her summer sailing season work and allow the foundation time to gather resources for each year's work project. The Foundation had a staff of only volunteers, and it had minimal resources. Funding for restoration has been provided by a combination of income generated by the foundation's sail training programs, private donations, and in kind donations of materials and labor from local business and industry. The importance of donation of time, energy, and money by a handful of local (Seattle) volunteers cannot be emphasized enough, especially in the early months and years of the foundation. This kind of dedication and volunteer effort has followed *Martha* to her new home port of Port Townsend. People see the beauty and importance of *Martha* and give of themselves repeatedly to see that the necessary work is able to happen.

Martha's New Lease on Life as a Sail-Training Vessel

Since 1997, *Martha* has engaged in programs designed primarily for youth 12–18 years old and families of all ages. The trips range from 1–3 weeks with a capacity for six students at a time. The programs consist of an interdisciplinary education experience combining piloting, navigation, sail theory, history, teamwork development, and leadership skills. Students are engaged in just about every aspect of the use of the ship. Students on *Martha's* sail training program are immersed in the life of a crew on board a working sailing vessel. This is not a summer camp but rather an opportunity to learn, practice, and test skills. Robert d'Arcy and his crew believes strongly in the benefits of sail training; the lessons learned by participating in a sailing adventure permeate into a person's daily life and can give them a new perspective towards their future.

The schooner *Martha* is currently in superb condition sailing out of Port Townsend, Washington. Port Townsend is the same place where another iconic Crowninshield schooner is berthed, the *Adventuress*. Both schooners take part in such yacht races as the Classic Mariners Regatta, held yearly out of Port Townsend.

The schooner is not only beautiful on deck, but also below decks. Her interior is largely original, finished in varnished wood. The fact that she has a cabin trunk slightly reduces the space below decks. However, since she was designed as a racing yacht, this reduced space is an acceptable compromise (*Robert d'Arcy*).

Martha's saloon looking forward (*Robert d'Arcy*).

Martha sailing in a smooth breeze in the Puget Sound (*Michael Berman*).

The schooner *Martha* sailing out of Port Townsend under full sail and gollywobbler. She has very graceful lines, which are characteristic of B. B. Crowninshield (*Michael Berman*).

Theodore E. Ferris: A Naval Architect for Large Steel Ships

BIOGRAPHY OF THEODORE E. FERRIS

Theodore E. Ferris was born in Stamford, Connecticut, on August 17, 1872. He was the son of Nathaniel Betts and Louise (Keeler) Ferris. Theodore Ferris started his education in the public schools of Stamford and continued at Greenwich (Connecticut) Academy, from which he was graduated after a course of technical training. Once graduated, he was hired by a shipyard on Long Island, where he had his first exposure to the construction of wooden ships. After this first work experience, he moved on to work at John Roche's shipyard at Chester, Pennsylvania, where he learned about the construction of steel ships. He was also employed in the drafting office. He continued doing this same type of work in other shipyards in Baltimore, Philadelphia, Chicago, and Detroit. In about 1890, he became associated with A. Cary Smith, a distinguished marine painter and naval architect, and in cooperation with him he designed a number of sound and river steamships, yachts, and other vessels.

Theodore Ferris worked for the Townsend and Downey Company, which now is the Standard Shipbuilding Company, at Shooters Island, New York, from 1898 until 1903. There he was involved in the design of many large yachts, among them the three-mast schooner *Shenandoah*, which is still sailing today and featured in this chapter. After 1903, he left Townsend and Downey and again became associated with A. Cary Smith, with whom he established the firm of Cary Smith & Ferris. The firm continued until 1910, when Ferris created his independent practice as a naval architect and marine engineer. He specialized in merchant vessels, becoming a recognized leader in this field. Occasionally, he also designed passenger ships.

In April 1917, he was asked to become naval architect and consulting engineer for the Emergency Fleet Corporation, but he initially declined the offer. At the time of the offer he had 35 ships under construction, which represented an aggregate cost of about $17 million at the time. Nevertheless, he was persuaded to enter the new engagement and renounce his privileges as private naval architect.

He designed and built many well-adapted merchant vessels that served safely during World War I. The authorities have highly commended the Ferris type vessels for their special adaptability to the emergency needs of the government in the field of marine activities connected with the war, and whatever advantage may be gained through the process of standardized shipbuilding must be chiefly credited to the high abilities, marked originality, and tireless industry of Theodore Ferris. He became especially famous for the idea, and the first practical application, of the "fabricated ship." This meant standardization, as well as simplification of design and coordination of different industries in order to make it possible to give out the manufacture of various sections and parts of ships to different workshops and factories, leaving to the shipyard the assembling and launching of the assembled ship. This way, in a short period of time about 1,000 vessels were built to plans of merchant vessels designed by Ferris.

After resigning from the position of naval architect of the Emergency Fleet Corporation, Theodore Ferris resumed his practice in designing and supervising the construction of steamers and ships of all types.

Ferris married Lois Davis, daughter of James Blake, of New Bedford, Massachusetts, on August 25, 1912. They had two children, Nathaniel James and Theodore Louis Ferris.

SHENANDOAH
(Ex- *Shenandoah of Sark;* Ex- *Atlantis;* Ex- *Shenandoah;* Ex- *Lasca II;* Ex- *Shenandoah)*

Type: three-mast gaff schooner
Designer: Theodore E. Ferris
Year of Construction: 1902
Shipyard: Townsend & Downey Shipbuilding Co., Shooters Island, New York
Length (sparred): 180'7"
Length on Deck: 145'
Length on Waterline: 100'
Beam: 28'2"
Draft: 15'5"
Gross Tonnage: 280 tons
Net Tonnage: 225 tons
Displacement: 300 tons
Construction: Iron, 8 mm plates, riveted, now largely replaced by welded steel
Sail Area: 8,589 sq. ft.
Engine: 2x 470 horsepower, Lugger diesel engine, Model L6140A
Cruise Speed Under Engine: 10 knots
Top Speed Under Engine: 12 knots
Home Port: Antibes, France

Built in 1902 for the New York banker Gibson Fahnestock, *Shenandoah* is one of the few big three-mast schooner yachts that still exist from the early twentieth century, and which is still in perfect condition. This little wonder is due to two recent owners. The first was the great French sailing enthusiast (and co-founder of the company that makes Bic brand pens) Baron Marcel Bich, famous for his repeated participation in the America's Cup, who rescued her from demolition in the 1970s. And another private owner rescued her again from demolition in 1993, when he brought *Shenandoah* to McMullen & Wind in New Zealand for a total restoration.

The Launch of a Great Yacht

If Baron Marcel Bich, while in search for a large yacht as mother ship for his America's Cup challenge, had not fallen in love with the wreck named *Atlantis* in 1970, the yacht would most likely gone aground at Cannes or fallen into the hands of a ship scrapper. But let us start the story at the beginning...

Shenandoah was built in 1902 for the New York banker Gibson Fahnestock at Townsend & Downey Shipbuilding Co. on Shooters Island, New York, arguably the most prestigious shipyard of that time for luxury yachts. This might be demonstrated by the fact that even the German Emperor Wilhelm II had his famous *Meteor III* built there. Although drawn by different designers (*Meteor* by A. Cary Smith, *Shenandoah* by Theodore E. Ferris), the yachts had significant similarities: The yachts' keels had the same shape.

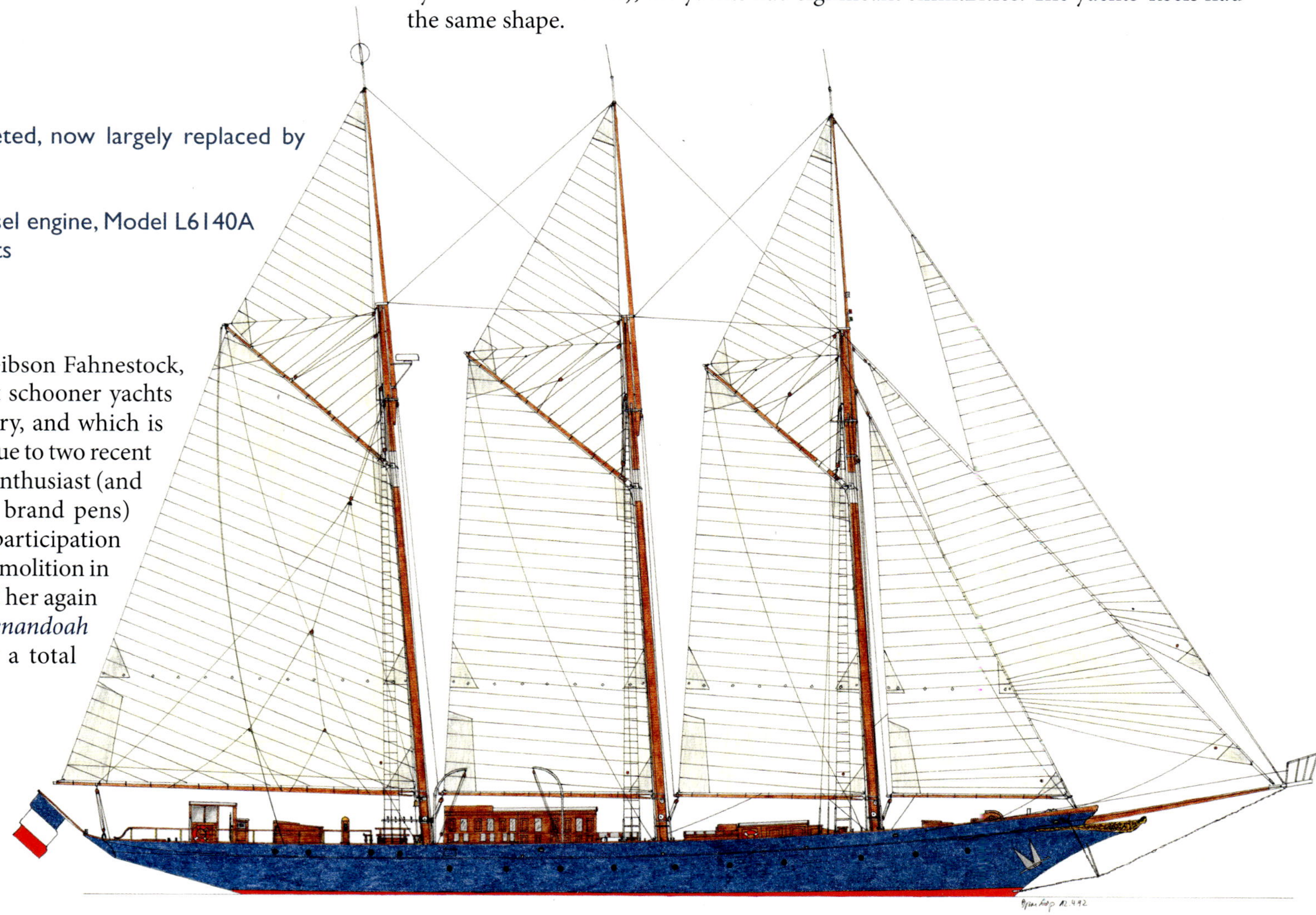

Gibson spent the first summer aboard *Shenandoah* in Newport, where he possessed a summer home, as any honorable member of the New York Yacht Club did. Then he sailed to Europe. The schooner then cruised for the next ten years in Italian waters, welcoming many well-known personalities of the time, from politics, arts, and business, on board.

Noble History

In 1912, the yacht was sold to the German Count Walther von Brüning. Renamed *Lasca II*, the schooner was based out of Kiel. On a trip to England, she was surprised by World War I, and subsequently seized.

In 1919, Sir John Esplen bought the yacht, and renamed her again *Shenandoah*. However, two years later he passed her over to Godfrey H. Williams. At that time the schooner was equipped with two engines. In 1925, the schooner was again for sale. The new owner was the Italian Prince Ludovico Potenziani. As *Atlantis*, the three-mast schooner cruised in the western Mediterranean off the coasts of France and Italy. A new sale took place in 1930, when she was bought by Count Viggo of Copenhagen. He renovated her extensively and equipped the yacht with the latest technical achievements, such as electric power and a diesel engine. It seemed that in 1952, the end of her career as a luxury yacht had arrived because Viggo bought a more contemporary, much smaller yacht...

Like almost all the big boats, *Shenandoah* went through a dark time. She had come along as many aristocrats did themselves over the years: The "old lady" had to work for a living for the first time. Gone was the era of pompous receptions in Cannes or Monaco, of uniformed crew and loving care from professional hands. Meanwhile, the ownership went to the mysterious Compañía de Navegación San Agustín of Honduras, where she traveled for some years as a cargo ship in Central America to return in the early sixties to the Mediterranean and Côte d'Azur. Behind the name of the company was a hidden gentleman who generated a great deal of polemics. It was the banker Travers, who later got into severe difficulties with the judiciary. For these reasons, the three-mast schooner was seized in 1962 by the French authorities. Since then, *Shenandoah* spent nine long years in the port of Cannes, slowly rotting and fading. She seemed only to wait for the day when she would go on her last journey.

Baron Marcel Bich and *Shenandoah*

When Baron Bich first saw her, he was immediately caught by the smoldering beauty of the yacht and her exquisite lines. He managed to free the *Shenandoah* from the French administration. The pen king had been involved in the America's Cup and was looking for a great, truly exceptional yacht. Captain Joe, a sailor from Cannes, had been trying to locate such a ship for him, and it was "love at first sight." *Shenandoah* was in a deplorable state, almost a wreck, but what did it matter—the Baron had fallen in love! This was the beginning of a wonderful story. Thanks to his good relations with the New York Yacht Club, Marcel Bich traced down the original plans and old photographs, as well as other useful documents for a faithful restoration. The first step, however, was the baptism of

The schooner *Shenandoah* is among the few large three-mast schooners that still exist. She carries the traditional configuration with three gaff lowers and three topsails. Her rig is well balanced with the many different small sails (*Copyright © Benjamin Mendlowitz*).

Her deck has plenty of brass and teakwood. Her steering wheel, which is positioned inclined backwards, reveals that she most likely is an American design. In Europe the wheels on yachts are usually mounted in a straight position (*Copyright © Benjamin Mendlowitz*).

Atlantis back to her original name, *Shenandoah*. After a year, the mahogany interior was again perfectly varnished, the cabins and passageways were finely paneled and the teak deck was newly laid. A few electric winches, new rigging, and Dacron sails were the only, almost imperceptible, concessions to modern times. Polished brass, selected hardware and loving woodwork dominated the appearance of this fine yacht, and even the line around the dark-blue hull was decorated with gold leaf.

After her launch in 1974, *Shenandoah* made a come-back in Newport, Rhode Island, for her first return to United States' waters in 69 years! The guests on board were taken back some 60 years, to the great time of Sir Thomas Lipton or T.O.M. Sopwith.

The schooner followed the preparations for the America's Cup, with more than seventy people on deck to watch the sailing spectacle. For the formal dinners in the evening there were less people invited. Until 1980, the yacht accompanied all preparatory races, until Bich dedicated his time only to his two, 12-meter yachts, *France II* and *France III*. He put *Shenandoah* up for sale in 1982, but one of the sons, François Bich, bought the yacht back for his father to let them continue sailing under French flag. As Bich lacked the means to keep *Shenandoah* up as a private yacht, he had to do as many boat owners had done, i.e. he had to charter her out to paying guests. It was no longer necessary to linger for an invitation from the Baron or try to smuggle into his group of followers to come on board, because "anybody" could charter the yacht. That seemed to come close to destruction, but it is quite understandable if we consider how much the maintenance of such a yacht costs.

In 1986, Philip Bommer, a Swiss businessman, fulfilled a lifelong ambition by buying *Shenandoah*. Bommer had a great deal of respect for the heritage of this yacht. A major refit was immediately undertaken and he continued sailing a few years in the South Pacific and Thailand. He renamed her *Shenandoah of Sark*, in order to have her registered in the British Channel Islands.

Shenandoah's Second Renaissance

But Bommer's plans failed to keep her up through charter, and he was forced to sell her. A Japanese owner came into command of the ship, but he apparently did not keep up the boat, because in 1993 *Shenandoah of Sark* arrived in New Zealand in an advanced state of decay, just a short step away from no repair. It appeared as if her fate, experienced in France twenty years earlier, was going to be repeated. It seemed that now she would definitively be scrapped. Nevertheless, a group of investors took on again the challenge of restoring her. Arriving at McMullen & Wing as a bare shell, *Shenandoah* filled the new slipway shed, remaining there until her launch in July 1997. The restoration required around 80% of the original steel plate-work to be replaced, and involved staff from all trades to face the rebuilding and restoration of the many details that are found on a three-mast yacht of the early twentieth century. The aim was to get *Shenandoah* back into shape so that she would continue to be considered by most who know her as one of the world's most beautiful classic yachts.

This restoration produced a strong link between the yacht and the sailing community in New Zealand, where many people are enthusiastic about classic yachts. Once McMullen

Shenandoah's deck after her restoration in New Zealand in the early 2000s. Her deck gleams again in the sunlight, reflecting the light in the bright varnish (*Rudolph Arp Archive*).

The central area for social life aboard *Shenandoah* is the seating area between the fore- and mainmast. It has an elegant awning to protect from sunlight (*Rudolph Arp Archive*).

had finished the restoration, *Shenandoah* participated in the superyacht events taking place during the 2000 America's Cup, especially the New Zealand Marine Cup (Kiwi Kawau Challenge). During that race, *Shenandoah* joined *Celandine* and *Drumbeat* in the one-day race from Auckland to Kawau.

Since then, *Shenandoah* has sailed again as a private superyacht, with an intensive schedule, which regularly brings her around the world. The owners tend to come back to New Zealand every three to four years as part of their world cruising plans, scheduling regular and major maintenance work to be done while in Auckland. *Shenandoah* can also be seen racing at some classic yacht races. Her participation in the Millennium Cup in Auckland in 2000 became widely advertised at the time.

The yacht is now flagged in the United Kingdom, the official registry port is Southampton and her home port is Antibes, France. *Shenandoah* is classified under the Maritime & Coastguard Agency (MCA) Large Yacht Code and has a maximum capacity of 10 charter guests. The yacht carries a crew of 14 people to manage the huge sails on the three masts.

The yacht has a range of 2,000 miles under engine, if driven under a speed of 10 knots. This range is made possible thanks to a fuel capacity of 5,019 gallons of diesel. The fresh-water tank capacity is 1,585 gallons.

Leslie E. "Ted" Geary: A Real West Coaster

BIOGRAPHY OF LESLIE E. "TED" GEARY

Leslie Edward "Ted" Geary was born in Kansas in 1885 and grew up in Seattle, Washington. He is considered by many to be the most prominent naval architect who designed vessels in the Puget Sound region. Geary is best known for designing a series of elegant fantail yachts in the late 1920s, but he got his start in Seattle designing, building, and racing sailboats. Geary moved to Seattle with his family in 1892, and much of his youth was devoted to boating. He designed his first sailboat in 1899 at age 14, a 24' centerboard racing sloop, and he continued to design, build, and race boats through his high school years. During a brief stint at the University of Washington's School of Engineering, he designed the *Spirit*, a 42' sloop, which he skippered in a 1907 race between the Seattle Yacht Club and its rival in Vancouver, British Columbia. Geary won this race, and this victory helped to establish his reputation in the Pacific Northwest as an outstanding designer and sailor.

A group of prominent Seattle businessmen and Seattle Yacht Club members, many of whom were leaders in the local lumber and fishing industries, admired both Geary's design skills and his sailing skills. They paid his tuition to attend the Massachusetts Institute of Technology, where he graduated with a degree in naval architecture in 1910. Returning to Seattle, Geary established a professional design practice and many of his patrons became clients, commissioning him to design a variety of commercial boats such as logging tugs, cannery tenders, fishing vessels, and power boats.

Three of Geary's early boat designs reflect his wide range of interests and expertise. In 1911, Geary designed the *Helori*, an elegant motor vessel for Seattle pioneer and developer O. O. Denny. In 1913, he designed the *Sir Tom*, an R-class racing sailboat named in honor of Sir Thomas Lipton, who had donated a trophy to be awarded annually in a contest between racing sloops in Washington and British Columbia. In 1915, Geary designed the *Chickamauga*, the first diesel-powered tugboat in the United States.

During World War I, Geary designed cargo vessels and other workboats for military use, and retained his connections to commercial clients through the Seattle Yacht Club's social network. After the war, Geary expanded his design portfolio with his first major yacht commissions. These included the schooner *Katedna* (now *Red Jacket*, described in more detail in this chapter), completed in 1920; the motor yacht *Wanda*, built for Seattle lumber baron C. D. Stimson in 1922; and the motor yacht *Samona*, completed in 1923 for California businessman Willits J. Hole. While Geary worked with several Puget Sound area shipbuilders, two of his frequent collaborators were the Blanchard Boat Company on Lake Union and Lake Union Dry Dock, both in Seattle.

In 1923, Geary started to design the *Westward*, an upscale cruising vessel based on a traditional cannery tender design, combining the sturdy lines of a work boat with the elegant profile and luxurious cabin spaces of a yacht. Geary and Campbell Church Sr. selected the John A. Martinolich Shipbuilding Company of Dockton to build his innovative design, which represents a stylistic evolution and shift in emphasis from work boats to pleasure boats in Geary's career. The *Westward's* abstract of title identifies Geary as the Master Carpenter.

During this period, Geary frequently returned to his original inspiration, sailboats, and in 1926 he designed the *Pirate*, a very successful R-class racing sloop listed in the National Register of Historic Places. In 1928, he also created the famous 18' Flattie class (later renamed the Geary 18) as an inexpensive and unsinkable sail-training boat for junior members of the Seattle Yacht Club.

Following the 1924 delivery of the *Westward* to the Alaska Coast Hunting & Cruising Company, Geary received several commissions from Seattle Yacht Club members to design elegant motor yachts, lighter and finer than work boats, and all with the graceful fantail sterns which became Geary's signature feature. The first of these were the *Malibu* and the *Mariner III* in 1926. Geary was at the height of his career when he designed a series of four distinctive fantail yachts between 1928 and 1930: the *Principia*, built for San Francisco yachtsman L. A. Macomber; the *Blue Peter*, built for Seattle architect John Graham; the *Electra*, built for A. W. Leonard, President of Puget Sound Power and Light; and the *Canim*, built for *Seattle Times* publisher Col. C. B. Blethen. Each boat was 96' LOA, and characterized by a plumb bow, elegant cabins, and the gracious curved lines of the "fantail," the overhanging portion of the vessel's stern, which extended the deck and provided extra space for dancing and other entertainment during the Roaring Twenties.

As the economic climate worsened following the Stock Market Crash in October 1929, Geary looked south for more commissions, because he realized that the market for luxury yachts was more likely to survive in Southern California than in Seattle. He received significant commissions from well-known figures such as millionaire J. Paul Getty and actor John Barrymore. For Barrymore, for instance, Geary designed the *Infanta* (now the *Thea Foss*). Geary served as the commodore of the Seattle Yacht Club in 1930, and shortly afterward he relocated to Los Angeles to be closer to his client base.

As the Great Depression wore on, Geary had few new design projects and his work shifted to redesigns and repairs. He worked through World War II and then for several years at Craig Shipyard in Long Beach, California, on restoration projects and some new designs. Ted Geary died on May 19, 1960 at the age of 75.

RED JACKET
(Ex- Katedna)

Type: two-mast gaff schooner, later changed to staysail schooner
Designer: Ted Geary
Year of Construction: 1920
Shipyard: N. J. Blanchard Boat Co., Seattle
Length Sparred: 72'
Length on Deck: 62'
Beam: 14'
Draft: 8'
Height of Main Mast: 70'
Gross Tonnage: 36 tons
Sail Area: 2,050 sq. ft.
Home Port: Tacoma, Washington

Katedna's Design and Construction

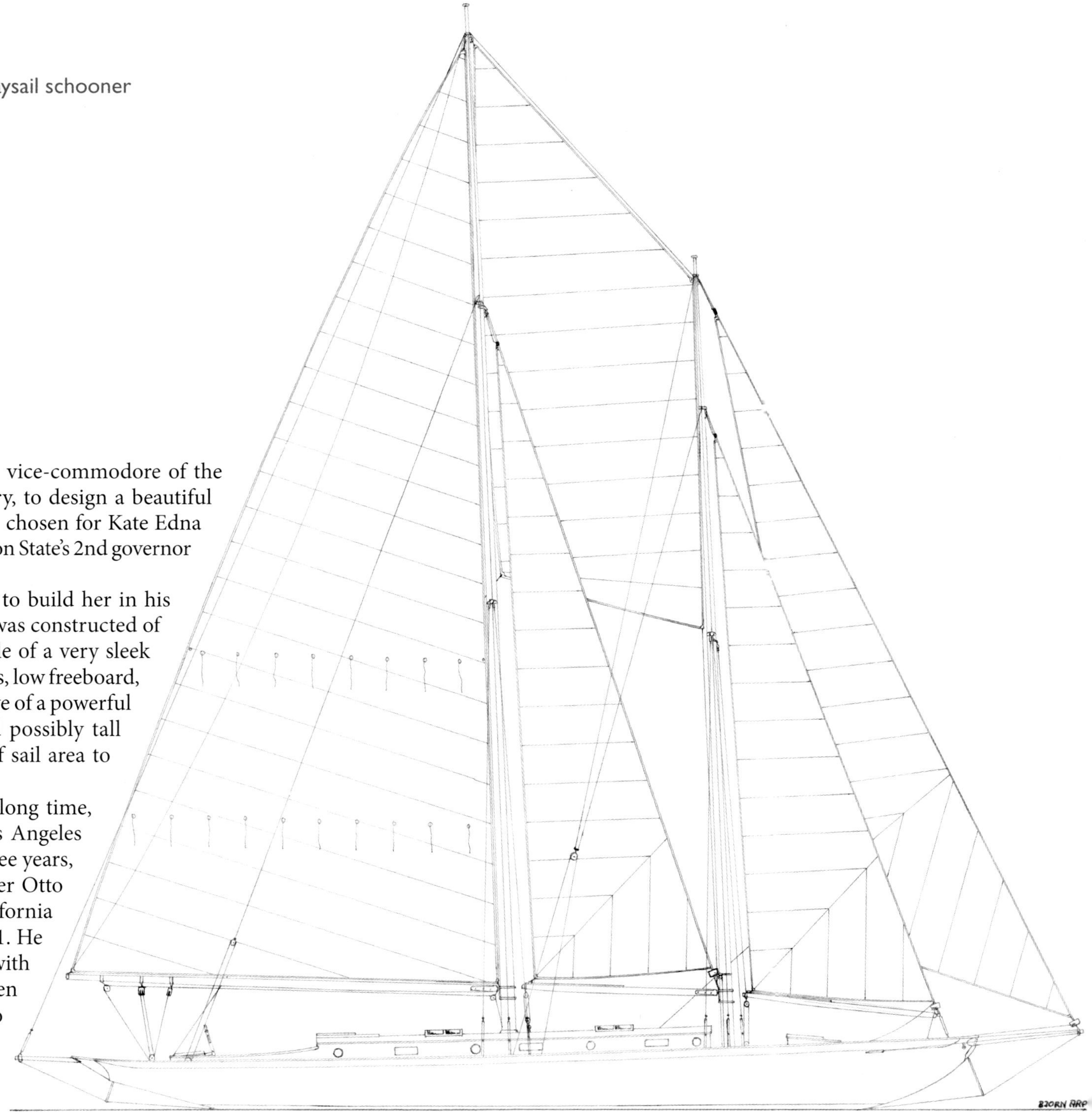

In 1919, Fred Baxter, the prominent Seattleite and vice-commodore of the Seattle Yacht Club, commissioned his friend, Ted Geary, to design a beautiful and fast schooner, the *Katedna*. The name *Katedna* was chosen for Kate Edna McGraw, Fred Baxter's wife and the daughter of Washington State's 2nd governor between 1893–1894.

Baxter hired another friend, Norm Blanchard, Sr., to build her in his famous Seattle boatyard on Lake Union. The schooner was constructed of cedar, oak, teak, and spruce. *Katedna* is a good example of a very sleek racing-schooner design by Ted Geary. The long overhangs, low freeboard, and reduced beam of only 14' and draft of 8' are indicative of a powerful racing machine. The schooner rig, with gaff sails and possibly tall topmasts with topsails on both masts, offered plenty of sail area to push the hull hard.

However, Baxter did not enjoy his schooner for a long time, because he sold her two years later in 1921 to the Los Angeles banker, E. N. van Bergen. He sailed the schooner for three years, when he sold her to Southern California land developer Otto G. Wildey. Wildey was the first commodore of the California Yacht Club in Wilmington, California, between 1920–21. He changed her rig from gaff to Marconi, and in 1925 he left with the schooner for a five-year South Seas cruise. They even sailed to Australia in this occasion. On her trip back to the United States in 1930, she was dismasted in a storm in the Pacific Ocean between Hawaii and Los Angeles.

Difficult Times

Back in the United States, *Katedna* witnessed the neglect of which the California Yacht Club had fallen victim, until it burned entirely down. The boat then did not even have an appropriate moorage, so that she was put up for sale. Geary informed friends in Seattle that *Katedna* was available, and in 1933 she was purchased by Seattle businessman George Webb and brought home to the Northwest on a freighter.

Webb made a total restoration of this schooner and renamed her *Red Jacket*. Chief *Red Jacket* was a prominent Seneca orator who wore a uniform coat given to him by a British soldier. Three months after her refit, *Red Jacket* caught fire while moored in front of Webb's Medina home on Lake Washington. The burning schooner was shot from the shore with large-bore elephant hunting rifles to sink and save her.

Frank Prothero bought the soggy, burnt out hull for $1,000 and rebuilt her at his own yard, the Prothero Boatyard on Lake Union. Prothero gave her a leg of mutton rig, a spartan interior and the cabin configuration with square and round portholes still in place today. Prothero's skill with wood may be seen today in the wheel and dove-tailed gear box below it. Once the schooner was operational again, he used her until 1935 for day sailing at Four Winds Camp on Orcas Island in the San Juans. While at the camp, she was called *Sea Gypsy* because of the Gypsy theme the camp used, although she always kept her name of *Red Jacket* on the registry papers.

In 1935, Paul Henry acquired the boat. He was the incoming commodore of the Seattle Yacht Club for the 1936–38 term. Ted Geary designed a new Marconi sail rig with hollow spruce spars and booms for her. Both Blanchard Boat Co. and Jensen Boat Works labored on *Red Jacket* simultaneously for three months to transform her into the most elegant sailing yacht on Lake Washington.

The Schooner *Red Jacket* Under George Parsons' Ownership

Sadly, Paul Henry died of a heart attack in late 1938, so *Red Jacket* was again up for sale. The next year, George Parsons acquired her from Henry's widow. *Red Jacket* remained in the Parsons family and in the Seattle Yacht Club for the next twenty years. She raced all the Swiftsures with Parsons and a crew of his Seattle Yacht Club friends and University of Washington students.

During World War II she was stationed in Friday Harbor with the Coast Guard to snoop for enemy submarines. She was painted entirely gray with a doghouse built over her cockpit. Her skipper was a friend of Parsons, Dan Trefethlen. Anchor Jensen removed the Coast Guard gray in 1944.

Red Jacket: From Boy Scout Boat to Wreck

When the happy Parsons years were over, Rex Kelley acquired the schooner. That was in 1959, and he sailed her to Tacoma. Terry Paine, a 17-year-old Sea Scout at the time, crewed on her that summer. Kelley used Sea Scouts to help maintain and sail his big schooner. However, the boy scouts could not do all the necessary work on such a schooner. The crisis came nearer and nearer, and manifested through signs such as the fire *Red Jacket's* gasoline engine caught in 1974 while sailing near Salmon Beach. She ran aground on the narrows that extend in this area, and one woman fell overboard but was rescued by the Coast Guard under the Tacoma Narrows Bridge. Probably as a consequence of the grounding, a few years later, in 1979, her 15,000 lb lead keel dropped off her bottom while she was at her moorage in the Tacoma Yacht Club basin.

Finally, in 1983, a 20-year lack of proper maintenance and continual jury-rigging had taken a heavy toll. *Red Jacket* left Tacoma Yacht Club under a 5-year lease to a Port Townsend shipwright. He was to rebuild the rotten interior in exchange for using her in chartering. The brown paint was removed from her teak, the rusted bathtub was tossed out, and the orange-like color of her hull was painted black.

After the restoration, many tourists enjoyed the charter cruises the shipwright organized out of Port Townsend.

Back in Tacoma

Finally, in 1987, *Red Jacket* returned to Tacoma and began her years as a Northwest Maritime Treasure in the Kelley Maritime Museum with Terry and Renée Paine. Both have 100-ton Coast Guard Masters Licenses. But even under their very dedicated ownership the schooner was not safe from misfortune. In 1990, the winterized schooner went on a ghost cruise in a December ice storm and did $50,000 damage to herself while bashing the Murray Morgan Bridge. She broke her bowsprit, destroyed her cap rail and crushed planks.

After the rebuild, in 1993, *Sail Magazine* elected her as among the "One Hundred Greatest Sailing Yachts in North America." She currently maintains a busy schedule of wooden boat festivals and tall ship rendezvous.

The Ted Geary-designed racing schooner *Red Jacket* under full sail. She sails out of Tacoma, Washington, and she is a common participant in classic yacht races in the Puget Sound (*Copyright © Benjamin Mendlowitz*).

Henry J. Gielow: Yacht Designer and Inventor

BIOGRAPHY OF HENRY J. GIELOW

Henry J. Gielow was a young designer who fast came to the front of yachting and design. He built several yachts that have done remarkably well. Among his schooner yachts, the *Black Douglas* stands out as a particularly impressive yacht. She is still sailing today as state yacht of the Moroccan Royal Family, with the name of *El Boughaz*. This chapter will discuss more in detail this large schooner.

Gielow was a native of Wisconsin and received a thorough classical education. When young he always did well in mathematical and scientific studies, and when he started out in life for himself he entered the United States' Engineer Corps. This was in 1874, and he remained in this service for thirteen years, when he started yacht designing in New York. In the first few years of his time in that city, he designed fifty-two craft, of which nineteen or twenty were yachts. One of his first yachts was the *Nydia* for Dr. Pierre of Brooklyn. She gained worldwide reputation as being a safe, comfortable, and speedy yacht. He then designed and built the *Theresa* for G. Seidenberg, the *Vesta* for H. Laughlin, and the *Marietta* for Harrison B. Moore. This last yacht could go up to 18 miles on the Long Island Sound. His most famous sailing yacht in his first years as designer was the *Loyal.*

Henry Gielow was a thoroughly practical and inventive man. He became famous for inventing a chiseling machine to be used to remove rocks and other obstructions from under the water. In 1883, Gielow became a member of the American Society of Civil Engineers.

Henry J. Gielow's successor was Joseph A. MacDonald. MacDonald joined Henry J. Gielow, Inc. shortly after World War I and became his top salesman and eventually president of the company after Gielow's resignation. The years between 1923–1929 were one of the wealthiest periods of American history and Gielow, Inc. took the opportunity to sell large private yachts to wealthy clients.

MacDonald succumbed to a fatal heart attack, passing away on January 11, 1935. Henry J. Gielow also succumbed to a heart attack shortly afterwards. The next president of Gielow Inc. was W. M. Rice, who turned the company over to a new prospect—floating power plants—as America's wealthy were no longer interested or capable of purchasing the ornate vessels of the past.

EL BOUGHAZ
(Ex- *Aquarius;* Ex- *Te Quest;* Ex- *PY-45;* Ex- *Black Douglas)*

Type: three-mast staysail schooner
Designer: Henry J. Gielow, design No. 131
Year of Construction: 1930
Shipyard: Bath Iron Works, Bath, Maine
Length (sparred): 175'
Length on Deck: 156'
Beam: 32'
Draft: 12'5"
Internal Room Height: 17'7 1/2"
Displacement: 331 tons light ship, 416 tons fully loaded
Internal Ballast: 60 tons
Sail Area of Original Sail Plan (1930): 9,111 sq.ft.
Sail Area of redesigned sail plan (1982): 11,400 sq. ft.
Construction: steel
Engine: 2 auxiliary diesel engines, 325 hp (in 1930, later updated; now 2 Volvo Penta TAMD, 120B/360 hp at 1,800 rpm)
Owner: King Mohammed VI of Morocco
Home Port: Casablanca, Morocco

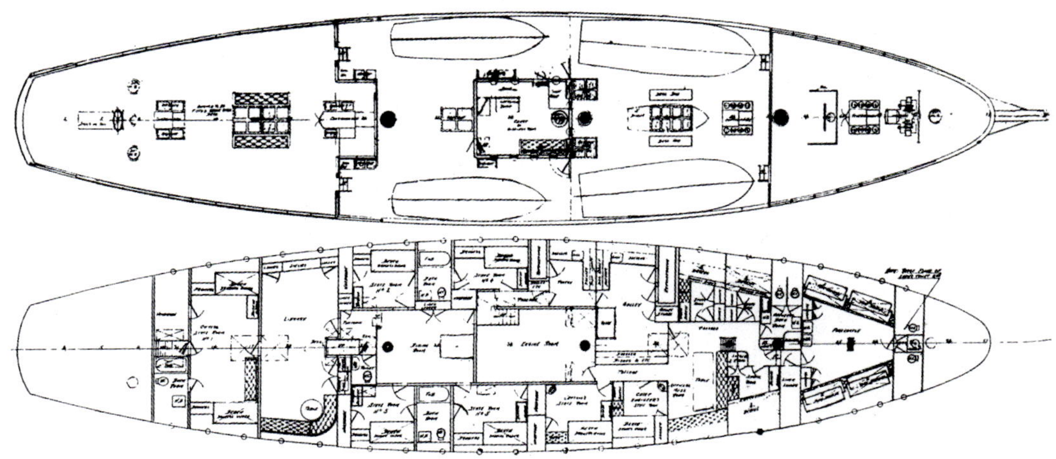

(Yachting, *August 1930*)

The American Schooner Yacht *Black Douglas*

The *Black Douglas* was built as a three-mast staysail schooner for Robert C. Roebling, who was the great-grandson of John A. Roebling and grand-nephew of Washington Roebling. This large yacht was built at the Bath Iron Works of Bath, Maine. The keel was laid on November 22, 1929, and the finished yacht was launched on June 9, 1930. The schooner was delivered to its owners on July 29, 1930. Designed by renowned New York naval architect Henry J. Gielow, she was one of the largest steel-hulled schooners ever built. The *Yachting* magazine described the *Black Douglas* in 1930 as "probably the largest and roomiest of craft of her type yet to be built." The schooner was 175' long, 32' wide, and had a draft of 12'5". The hull, interior, and rig had been designed as a floating home for her owner. Her auxiliary power was a 300-hp Cooper-Bessemer diesel engine, with which she could cruise for 10,000 miles on her fuel tankage of 16,000 gallons. She carried 14,000 gallons of fresh water.

The rig was designed for easy handling, with electric sail hoists and rugged spars and adequate shrouds to take care of any weather that may be met with in her intended voyages through the Atlantic, Mediterranean, Red Sea, Southern Atlantic, and Pacific.

The accommodations were very spacious thanks to the huge beam of 32'. The owner's suite was 28' long by 14' wide. The yacht had a library forward of similar dimensions as the owner's suite. There were four big guest staterooms, and a dining wardroom abaft the engine room casing.

Both the forecastle and poop deck were raised. Amidships was a sunken charthouse, which hosted the gyroscopic compass, instrument panels, etc. Duplicate steering wheels were placed fore and aft. The awning abaft the mizzenmast could be left standing at all times, affording complete shelter in tropical regions. The entire interior was ventilated with slanting skylights from the deck, in addition to a forced air system.

Originally, Robert Roebling wanted the schooner to be named *Grenadier*. He aimed at a name that was associated with strength and adventure. But, the yard foreman at Bath, who was closely involved with her construction, suggested the name *Black Douglas*. This man, called Mr. Main, was born and raised in Scotland. As a boy, he was fascinated with the stories of the Black Douglas and felt that it was a fitting name for this new and impressive yacht. Roebling loved it and immediately named her *Black Douglas*. A helmeted wooden figurehead of the famous Scottish knight was carved and set in place on her bow.

After she was launched, Roebling and his wife, with a couple of friends and a crew of 14, took the *Black Douglas* on her maiden voyage down the west coast of South America, through the Straits of Magellan, and back up the east coast.

After purchasing Modena Island near Savannah, Georgia, the Roeblings used the *Black Douglas* to shuttle supplies from the mainland to build their home while living aboard. All the plantation animals and the beginning of the black angus cattle herd that Robert Roebling developed and built were brought to the island aboard the schooner.

World War II Service

In 1941, she was sold to the United States Government's Fish and Wildlife Service by a special Congressional appropriation to do seal research in the Aleutian Islands off Alaska. The vessel was repaired and altered in Savannah, Georgia. When she was on her way to Seattle, stopping by at San Pedro, California, the Japanese bombed Pearl Harbor. After the bombing, and since all available public ships were immediately drawn for military service, the *Black Douglas* was incorporated into the Navy as a patrol craft. On her way to Seattle, a Japanese submarine lobbed a couple of shells across her bow off the Oregon coast, but she escaped. She even had a torpedo fired at her but came out unscathed.

She was stripped of her sails, sailing tackle, masts, spar, and the *Black Douglas* figurehead. Guns and sonar were mounted on her. She was painted haze gray and renamed *PY-45*. From 1942 through part of 1944, she patrolled the waters of Neah Bay, Washington.

After World War II: Back as a Survey Vessel And Treasure Hunter

After the war, the *Black Douglas* was again refitted for service as a research vessel, this time in Seattle. In April 1947, she made her shakedown cruise off the Olympic Peninsula in Washington State.

The schooner *Black Douglas* in her original configuration. Note the flush deck and the various tenders. She has since been largely modified, although her rig has stayed the same (*Steven Palmer*).

Black Douglas on a research mission, without rig, and a large deckhouse and bridge added. Only her clipper-bow still indicated that she was a former sailing ship (*Steven Palmer*).

Equipped as a floating laboratory, the *Black Douglas* left Seattle on May 28, 1947, for an eleven-month study in North Pacific waters tracking the migration routes and food habits of the Alaska fur-seal herd that breeds on the Pribilof Islands in the Bering Sea. The expedition was led by Dr. Victor B. Scheffer, a biologist, who wanted to seek new data on where the seals go when they leave the Pribilof Islands, what food they eat, and whether the young seals are preyed upon by other marine mammals.

After she had fulfilled her first mission in the Bering Sea, she spent 18 more years as the flagship of the Scripps-Southwest Fisheries ocean survey. From Seattle, and later from Treasure Island in San Francisco, the *Black Douglas* would follow the fur seal herds on the spring migration to their breeding grounds, conduct sealing and tagging operations on and around the islands, and later in the fall she would follow the herds south to continue the study of migration routes to winter waters. Extensive studies of the stomach contents of the seals were carried out to determine if they were feeding upon valuable commercial food fishes. The *Black Douglas* did also gather information on other marine life such as killer whales, hair seals, sea lions, and sea otters to ascertain if any of these mammals prey upon the young seals after they leave the islands on their winter migration. The vessel also served in the California Co-OP Sardine Research Program, later known as California Cooperative Oceanic Fisheries Investigations (CalCOFI).

On October 20, 1949, the *Black Douglas* was involved in the rescue of 17 sailors from the Panamanian vessel *Salina Cruz*, which burned the night before about 100 miles off Portland, Oregon. The crew of the *Black Douglas* picked up the Panamanian crew from lifeboats, after being directed to the spot by Coast Guard planes. The *Black Douglas* was then on her sixth cruise, which had begun on October 3, 1949. The cruise was to determine the amount and extent of sardine spawning, survival rates of sardine larvae, productivity of the area, the current patterns of the region, and other related characteristics of the marine climate off the West Coast.

In 1966, she was bought at auction by Louis Black of Santa Monica, California, to be used as a treasure hunter in the Caribbean. Black sailed the ship through the Panama Canal and then spent eight years treasure hunting in the Turks and Caicos. He was particularly interested in finding the famed Spanish galleon *Atocha*.

Training Ship for the Flint School

In 1972, the *Black Douglas* was sold to George Stoll of Sarasota, Florida. He probably saved her from becoming a rusting hulk for divers somewhere off the beaches. Apparently, the *Black Douglas* had been tethered to someone's private island and used for power generation for about 6 years. The previous owners went bankrupt after running aircraft parts around the Bahamas. During her time in the Turks, little maintenance, if any, was performed. When George Stoll bought her, he brought the ship to Fort Lauderdale to be reskinned because the hull was very thin in many places from rust. Since the old Enterprise engine had a clogged cooling system, she boiled water on her trip to Fort Lauderdale. Stoll had her masts replaced to be able

When she came to Florida in 1971, she was renamed *Te Quest* and largely restored to serve as a floating establishment for the Flint School. This photo shows her being sandblasted and primed in 1972 (*Steven Palmer*).

Te Quest made many trips around the Caribbean and the Mediterranean during her years with the Flint School. She usually sailed in company with the schooner *Te Vega*. The schooners were handled by young students, who learned seamanship and experienced the cross-cultural adventure of exploring far away places. They sailed as far as Saint Petersburg in the Soviet Union (*Steven Palmer*).

Between 1982 and 1983, *Te Quest* was transformed into the superyacht *Aquarius* at Abeking & Rasmussen in Lemwerder, Germany. The deckhouse that was added over the years was transformed into comfortable lounges and reception rooms. A bridge was added on top of the deckhouse between the main and the mizzen masts (*Steven Palmer*).

to sail her again. He renamed her *Te Quest* and turned her into a floating classroom for intellectually gifted children in his Flint School. *Te Quest* often sailed jointly with *Te Vega*, now *Deva*, another famous American schooner yacht. The two yachts voyaged throughout the Caribbean, Mediterranean, North and Baltic Seas, along the coast of Africa and far up the Amazon, all under the flag of the Flint School.

From Training Ship to Megayacht

The school closed in 1981 and the schooner was sold to be reconditioned in 1982–1983 at the prestigious Abeking & Rasmussen shipyard in Lemwerder, Germany. Behind the project was a group of investors who completely rebuilt and restored this schooner to her present majesty in Germany. She was completely gutted, her plating renewed, and totally rebuilt from the frames up. Once the hull was restored, the interior was redesigned by James M. Stoll, who conceived, organized, and supervised the construction of a unique multi-level interior comprising seven double guest cabins with baths, an owner's suite with six-person spa and sauna, an office, and living and bedroom with his and hers baths. There is also a library, enclosed sunken wheelhouse, two bars, two galleys, and six double crew cabins with baths. A bottle of water from the Kennebec River, where she was originally christened, was flown to the rechristening ceremony. Her new name was *Aquarius*. Then, the schooner was purchased by the King of Morocco, Mohammed VI, to serve as his state yacht. The vessel spends most of its time in Monaco and other ports of the South of France. Her name is now *El Boughaz*.

Her bare teak decks and internal woodwork are impeccable. Her new massive 120' tall masts are made of aluminum. At full sail, she can move the all-steel clipper-bowed hull through the water at a brisk 10.5 knots. She is also equipped with twin Volvo in-line engines that drive a single propeller. She grosses 480 tons and carries 11,400 sq. ft. of sail. She has a range of 7,500 miles at 10.5 knots under power, but under sail her range is indefinite! She carries 9,990 gallons of fuel and 8,800 gallons of fresh water.

She requires a crew of 12 to sail and care for her. She can be steered from an enclosed wheelhouse completely equipped with the latest electronic navigational gear or from a massive wooden wheel on the fantail equipped with only a magnetic compass, in the "old way."

Aquarius in Nice, France, in the early 2000s, right before she was purchased by King Mohammed VI of Morocco (*Steven Palmer*).

The yacht features a long clipper bow, although she does not have any decorative scrollwork or figurehead (*Steven Palmer*).

El Boughaz performs majestically as a state yacht for the Moroccan monarchy. However, most of the time the schooner is in the South of France (*Guilain Grenier*).

El Boughaz sailing in her current configuration in the Mediterranean. On the fantail is the wooden wheel, which is covered because the vessel is usually steered by autopilot from the main bridge deck between the main and the mizzen masts (*Guilain Grenier*).

Henry Gruber: Beauty in Simplicity

BIOGRAPHY OF HENRY GRUBER

Heinrich A. "Henry" Gruber was a very versatile yacht designer. He could design everything from a square-rigger to a 12-meter yacht, always beautiful and graceful, with harmonious lines and strong, thoroughly calculated construction. He had careers designing yachts in both the United States and Germany from the mid-1920s until 1956.

Henry Gruber was born in 1899 in the small village of Steinberghaff on the shores of the Baltic Sea in Germany. His father was a marine engineer whose skills served the family well during this time of rapid technical progress.

During his childhood, boats and ships captured Gruber's imagination, and he decided they should make up his professional career. He finished his secondary education in 1919 after spending two years in the coastal artillery of the navy at the end of World War I.

Gruber's first job was at a local shipyard in Flensburg, where he gained practical experience before attending Technical University in Berlin. He received his diploma in shipbuilding in 1924 and worked in Kiel building small boats and yachts. Renewed business relations between the United States and Germany made it possible for Gruber to consider designing yachts in the United States. He moved to New York City in 1925.

He spent the next ten years working for such well-known designers as Wm. Starling Burgess, where he assisted in the design of *Niña* in 1928, and the J-Class America's Cup defender *Enterprise* in 1930. Later, in 1933, he worked on the design of *Rainbow*, the 1934 America's Cup defender, again with Burgess. He also worked with New York designers Cox & Stevens. Then came a partnership with Megargel, soon followed by the merged firms of Burgess and Donaldson, Megargel and Gruber.

Two notable yachts Gruber designed in this period were the 65' schooner *Barlovento* and the 39'10" cutter *Binker*. *Barlovento* is described in more detail in this chapter.

While living in the United States, Gruber never gave up thought of returning to Germany, and in 1935 he and his family finally moved abroad. Hitler had been in power for two years, and economically Germany seemed to be recovering. Yachts were being built, and the 1936 Olympics were held in Berlin. Gruber became known as the "German genius from America." He first lived in Flensburg, the city where he had started his design career. He set up his own office, Gruber Yachts, and worked closely with the Burmester Shipyard in Bremen, which became a major competitor of Abeking & Rassmussen in yacht construction. His first big success there was his 1936 design of the composite-built, 59' yawl *Roland von Bremen*. She was shipped to Boston, fitted out at the Herreshoff Manufacturing Company in Bristol, Rhode Island, and with Gruber's friend, Sherman Hoyt, among the crew, finished eighth out of twenty-seven in her class in the 1936 Bermuda Race. He subsequently designed a second *Roland von Bremen*, which was cutter-rigged. Another famous design of the time was the 80' yawl *Nordwind*, which today sails primarily in the Mediterranean. Another schooner worth mentioning is Gruber's 24 KR staysail schooner yacht *Ashanti IV*, which is still sailing today as the *Ashanti of Vegesack*.

Gruber retired about 1956 and died three years later at age sixty.

BARLOVENTO

Type: two-mast gaff-Marconi schooner, later converted to staysail schooner
Designer: Henry Gruber, while at Cox & Stevens
Year of Construction: 1932
Shipyard: Pendlton Shipyard, Wiscasset, Maine
Length (sparred): 80'
Length on Deck: 64'5"
Length on Waterline: 50'
Beam: 15'6"
Draft: 9'6"
Displacement: 43 tons
Sail Area: 2,500 sq. ft.
Construction: long leaf yellow pine on oak
Engine: Perkins 6354-T, 165-hp Turbo
Owner: Craig Downey
Home Port: Paulsbo, Washington

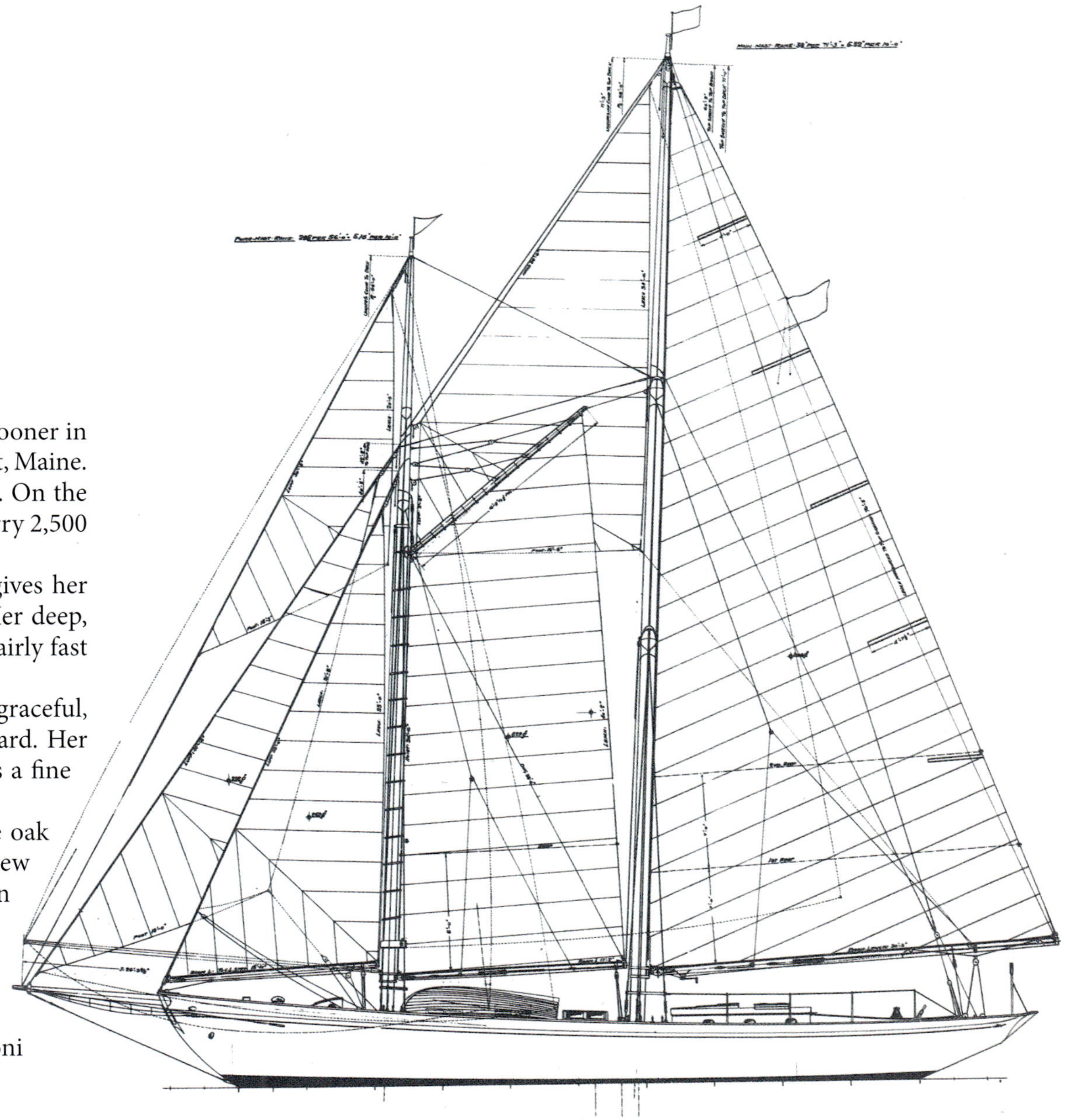

The Design of a Capable Racing Schooner: *Barlovento*

The schooner *Barlovento* was designed and built as a gaff-Marconi schooner in 1932 from the board of Henry Gruber at the Pendleton Shipyard in Wiscasset, Maine. She had external lead ballast, and measured 64'5" on deck and 80' overall. On the waterline, she was 50', with a beam of 15'6" and a draft of 9'6". She could carry 2,500 sq. ft. of sail.

With almost ten feet of draft, *Barlovento* had a very deep keel that gives her remarkable stability. At the same time, she has significant lateral plane. Her deep, heavy hull will bring her into her own in a big seaway, when she will sail fairly fast yet have a reasonably comfortable, easy motion.

She has a bit of curve and tumblehome in her topsides to give her a graceful, powerful look. Forward, at the bow, there is more than six feet of freeboard. Her overhangs are moderate. While she has these deep bow lines she also has a fine entry with a little hollow at the waterline.

The schooner was strongly built to a high standard. The frames were oak and the planking was done in yellow pine, held together with Everdur screw fastenings in bronze. The deck was teak, and she had diagonal strapping in hull and deck, and heavy bilge stringers running nearly her full length.

Gruber designed four different rigs for this schooner, in advance of the eventual changes required by the final settlement on the particulars for the ocean-racing rating rule. Henry Gruber drew her up gaff-rigged with three working topsails and then drew alternate sail plans with a taller Marconi

Henry Gruber drew three alternative rigs for *Barlovento* (Yachting, *May 1931*).

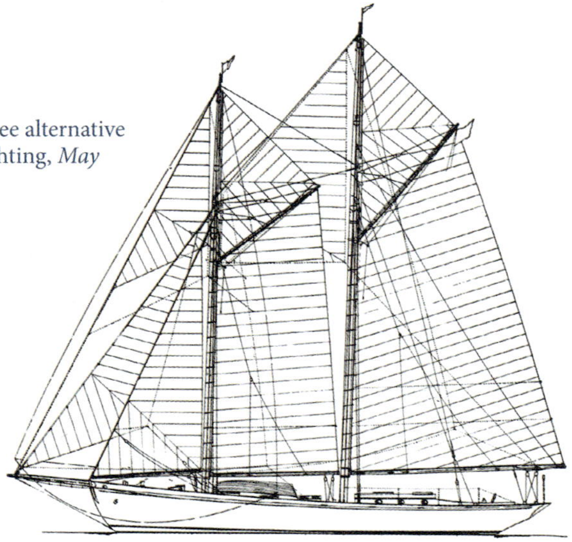

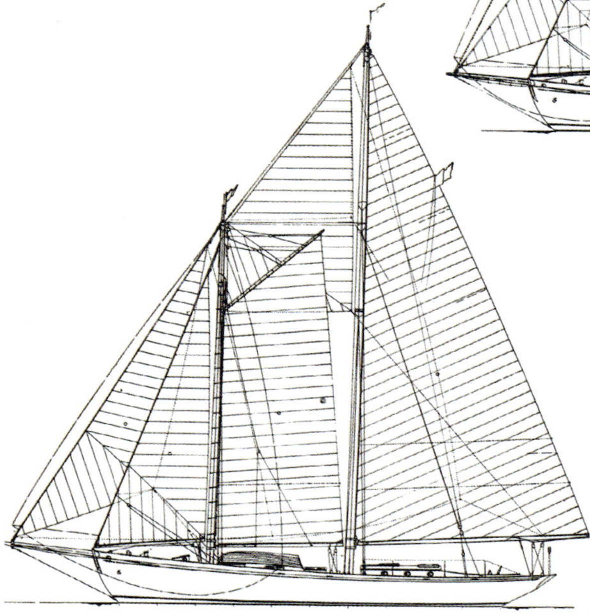

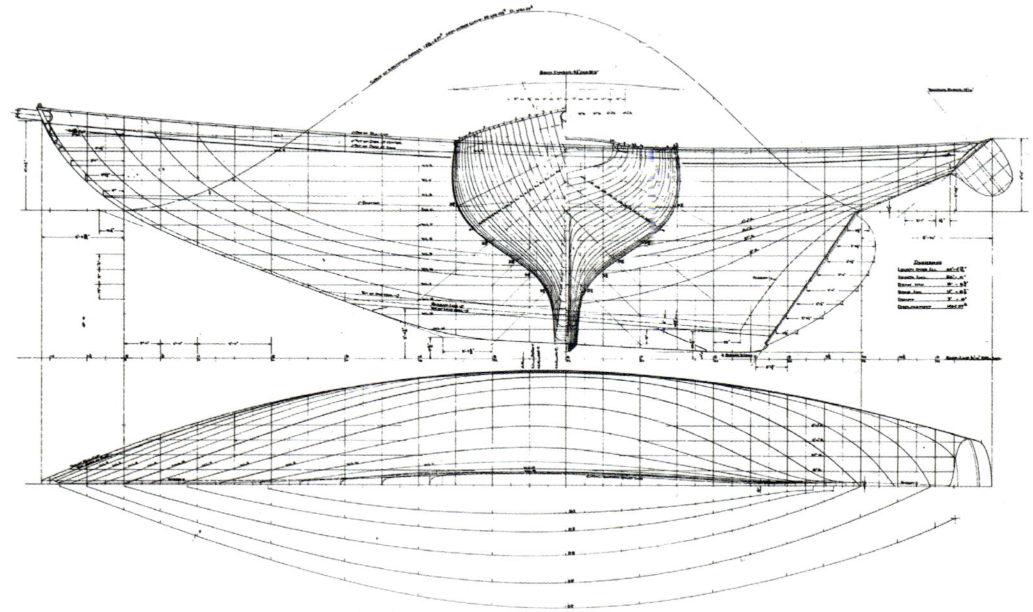

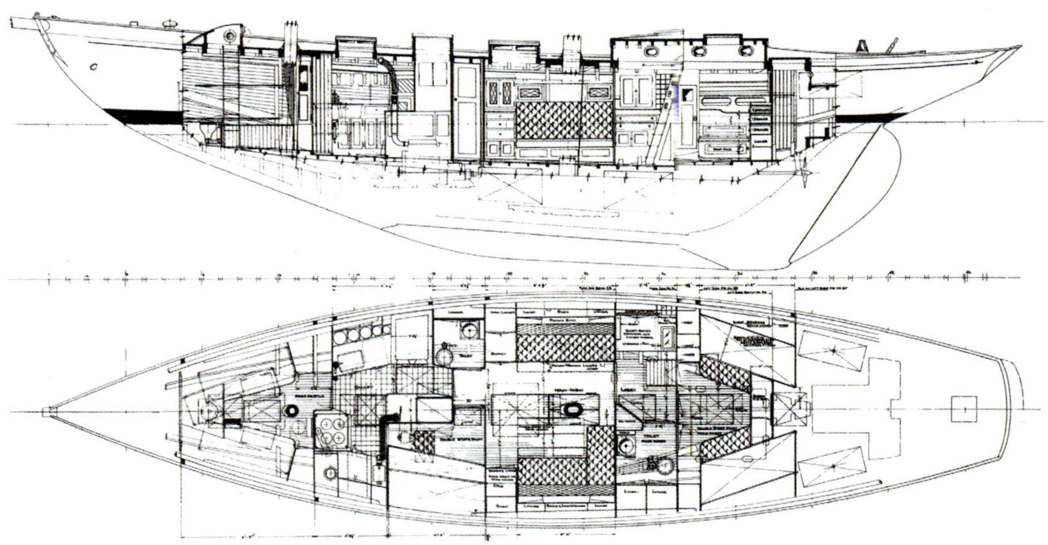

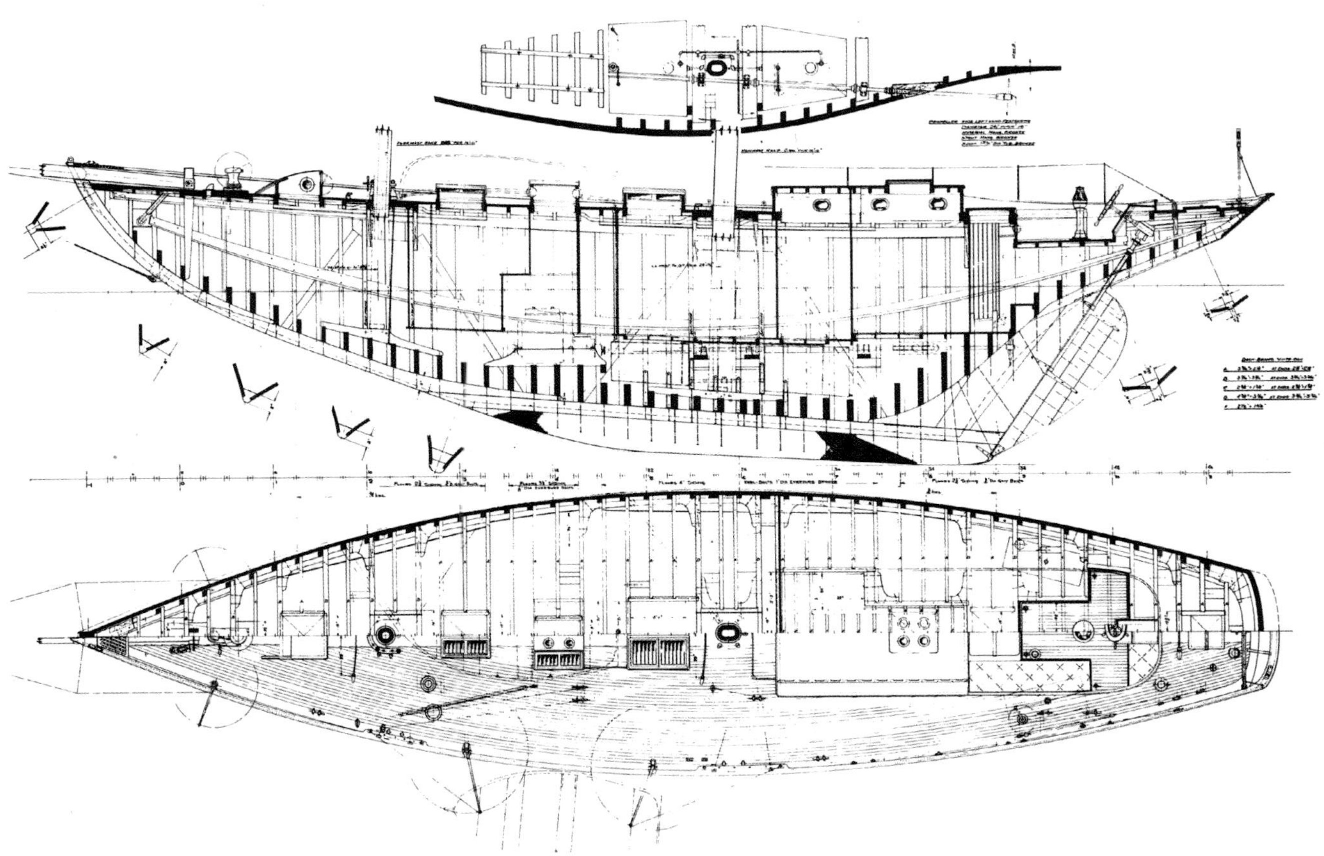

mainsail and shorter foremast, one with a gaff foresail and the other as a simple staysail schooner. The gaff rig had 2,315 sq. ft. of sail, while the Marconi and staysail rigs each had 2,250 sq. ft. Areas and rig allowances were cranked into the rule to see how she would rate with each rig.

The rig that finally was decided upon for the *Barlovento* was a fourth one, with a Marconi mainsail and a gaff foresail, but with a taller foremast, so that a jib topsail could be set, as well as a bigger balloon jib and spinnaker.

The Marconi mainsail is simpler than the gaff mainsail and topsail, but not less effective, if we keep in mind that the Marconi mainsail alone adds up to 1,000 sq. ft. of canvas to the rig. The mast was 72' above deck.

The fore-gaff was trimmed with a vang, as it became usual on many schooners in the 1930s. This was an easy and effective feature in such a rig, as it allowed close-hauling the gaff and improved the windward capabilities of the gaff sail.

An important advantage of the schooner rig is that it offers many light-wind sails and sail combinations. *Barlovento* could carry a big, high-cut *Yankee* jib topsail when beating to windward in light or moderate weather, and, on a reach, could break out her huge balloon main topmast staysail, or gollywobbler, lead its sheet through a block on the end of the main boom, and go running along even in light air.

On deck, *Barlovento* was flush-decked with just a small trunk cabin aft. She can stow a 12' tender on deck between the masts and she is big enough to carry it in davits on the port side most of the time. Her engine was placed well forward, up between the masts. The shaft was off-center to port. The engine compartment had a fidley to the deck for light and air, but considerable woodwork would have to be removed to get at the engine, which was a 4-cylinder Hill diesel with 40 hp and running a 1 kW generator as well as swinging its 24" diameter by 18" pitch feathering propeller. She carried 130 gallons of fuel in wing tanks in way of the cockpit, giving her a range under power of 500 miles. Beneath the cabin sole were tanks for 350 gallons of water.

There was a steerage under the bridge deck and cockpit for stowing sails and bosun's stores. The companionway was in the forward starboard corner of the house. Right at its foot was a chart table. The schooner's staterooms were tucked away where it was quiet. Her forecastle was all right for sleeping except when punching into a head sea. For larger crews, four could be accommodated in the main cabin, where upper bunks swung up over the transoms. There was a four-hole Shipmate stove forward in the galley.

Early History

Barlovento's first owner was Pierre S. DuPont III, of the famous Delaware industrialist family. In the same month she was launched, she entered the Bermuda Race, which ultimately was won by the Alden schooner *Malabar X* in her second attempt in Class A, and by the yawl *Dorade* in Class B. Nevertheless, *Barlovento* showed a promising performance, and she would win many races throughout her long life. Indeed, the DuPont family was so satisfied with the design that they kept her for racing and cruising for thirty years, until they sold her to a captain who enrolled her into the charter trade out of the Caribbean. Then, under the ownership of other yachtsmen, *Barlovento* completed two around the world cruises, in the wake of which she ended up on the United States' West Coast in the early 1970s. There, she raced and cruised, and made two trips to the South Pacific. In 1983, she moved to Washington State, were her state of maintenance substantially worsened over the years.

Barlovento's Second Life

It did not seem that *Barlovento* would ever make it into the high seas again; she was lying abandoned in wrecked shape at a dirty dock in the Puget Sound in 1991. But Craig Downey did not waste time lamenting her sad condition. Instead, he purchased her, knowing that she had no interior, no sails, and no working systems. It was essentially the bare hull with the two masts.

Between 1993–1994, the boat was hauled to Port Townsend, Washington, for a period of eight months. In this haul out, the entire topside planking was removed and replaced with new wood. During this operation many frames were found to be in need of total or partial replacement. Also, new chain plates were prepared out of bronze and newly installed. The cabin house, hatches, and comings, which were made of teak, were carefully restored, and a completely new interior was installed. This interior was made of Honduras mahogany. A new 24", 3-blade max-prop was connected to a 165-hp Perkins turbo diesel, which gives her a cruising speed under engine of eight knots. New Barient and Lewmar winches were installed to help with sail handling. Of course new sails also had to be purchased, new fuel tanks installed, etc. *Barlovento* came out of the shop for the 1994 sailing season almost as a new boat.

Although newly built, her accommodations below decks were classic and are a reminder of the original layout from 1932. From stern to bow, there is now a double-bunk stateroom aft, two single-bunk staterooms amidships, and one double-bunk stateroom forward, in addition to the saloon. There is also a wide chart table and a comfortable galley with double sink, a Force 10 propane stove, and a Narcold refrigeration system.

Her rig was also done new. She was laid out for cruising and racing alike, thus the decision to opt for a staysail schooner rig. This rig had the advantage of performing very well as a racing rig due to the considerable capability of carrying many large sails, as well as being manageable by a reduced crew when doing family sailing. So although a family boat, when she now sets her fisherman, her huge gollywobbler, or even the asymmetrical spinnaker, she needs a well-trained racing crew to handle the enormous amount of free-hanging canvas aloft. The Downey family always has many good friends available to lend a hand when racing in such a fashion.

Barlovento has been very active in both classic and PHRF racing where she has had great success. The Downey family has also enjoyed many seasons of sailing in the Pacific Northwest.

Barlovento sailing in 1932 in the Long Island Sound, preparing for that year's Bermuda Race. She still had a white hull then (*Mariner's Museum, Virginia*).

When Craig Downey purchased *Barlovento*, he changed her rig into a staysail schooner for easy handling. This rig also allowed him to use her as a well-performing racing yacht (*Craig Downey*).

Racing *Barlovento* has always been a great experience, now and then (*Craig Downey*).

Barlovento can carry a large spinnaker on her tall foremast, as well as an impressive gollywobbler. These sails make her 43 tons sail fast even in a light breeze (*Craig Downey*).

William H. Hand: A Traditional Schooner and Motorsailer Designer

BIOGRAPHY OF WILLIAM H. HAND

William H. Hand was born in Portland, Maine, in 1875 and lived in several different coastal communities on the United States' East Coast, owing to his father's assignments with the Navy and the Coast Guard. He briefly attended Brown University, but he was largely self-taught as a designer. For most of his career, his office was in Fairhaven, Massachusetts. He was also closely associated with the Hogdon Brothers yard in East Boothbay, Maine.

Hand began his career designing small racing sailboats around 1900. He also drew designs for cruising boats rigged as catboats, yawls, and ketches. The gasoline engine, however, lured Hand away from sail.

Prior to World War I, Hand was one of the first to work in high-speed, V-bottom powerboat-types, which were designs that he evolved from the dead-rise workboats of the Chesapeake. He held a patent for one such configuration, and his boats were well known for speed, looks, and good behavior. Many of them held speed records.

After the war, Hand did some of his best work on several excellent offshore Gloucester-style schooner yachts, including the famous Arctic voyager *Bowdoin*, built in 1921, which is still sailing actively in Maine today. Compared to other schooners of the 1920s, Hand's were more reminiscent of their commercial ancestors, with stronger sheers and a more rugged appearance. A total of twenty-three such schooners were built. Today, the schooners *Nathaniel Bowditch* and *Zodiac* are among the best examples of his talent.

In the resurrected Bermuda Race of 1923, five of the seventeen schooners entered were designed by Hand. There were four yawls and ketches, including the 32' Hand-designed ketch, *Sea Call*. Hand's schooners, such as *Black Hawk*, *Yankee Girl II*, and *Flying Cloud III*, continued to do well in subsequent races.

Despite the success of his schooners, by 1926 Hand started using more powerful engines, which had become increasingly reliable. He only used sails for auxiliary power and steadying. He also changed from schooner rig to ketch. This way the Hand motorsailer was born.

These motorsailers were clearly engine-driven vessels, designed to be fuel efficient, seaworthy, and comfortable. Good examples of the Hand motorsailers are the *Nor'easter*, built for the DuPont family in 1927, and the *Guildive*, built in 1934. Both are still lovingly maintained and preserved today.

William Hand died in 1946, shortly after World War II.

NATHANIEL BOWDITCH
(Ex- *Joseph Hawkins;* Ex- *Jane Dore;* Ex- *Ladonna)*

Rig: two-mast gaff schooner
Designer: William H. Hand
Shipyard: Hogdon Brothers, Boothbay, Maine
Built: 1922
Length Sparred: 107'
Length on Deck: 82'
Beam: 21'
Draft: 11'
Sail Area: 3,700 sq. ft.
Engine: 140-hp Detroit Diesel
Current Owner: Captain Owen and Cathie Dorr
Home Port: Rockland, Maine

***Ladonna*: Of a Large Racing Schooner**

The schooner-yacht *Ladonna* was built in 1922 by Hogdon Brothers in East Boothbay, Maine, from a William Hand design. The yacht was built in the heyday of Hand's schooner design career and represented, together with *Zodiac*, one of his greatest creations. The rig and hull were very much inspired by the fishing schooners, which made them also resemble the famous Alden schooners. Indeed, it was difficult to distinguish a typical Hand-designed schooner from an Alden-designed example. *Ladonna* had a flush deck on a hull with moderate sheer and relatively short ends. While the spoon-bow was very short, her stern was impressive with a very large and flat transom stern. Compared to a typical Alden design, she had a longer bowsprit. Originally, she carried a gaff-foresail and a main-Marconi on a tall mast. This rig was subsequently changed to a gaff fore and aft, as she was used as a "charter-windjammer" off the Maine coast. In her first racing season in 1923, *Ladonna* took part in the Bermuda Race.

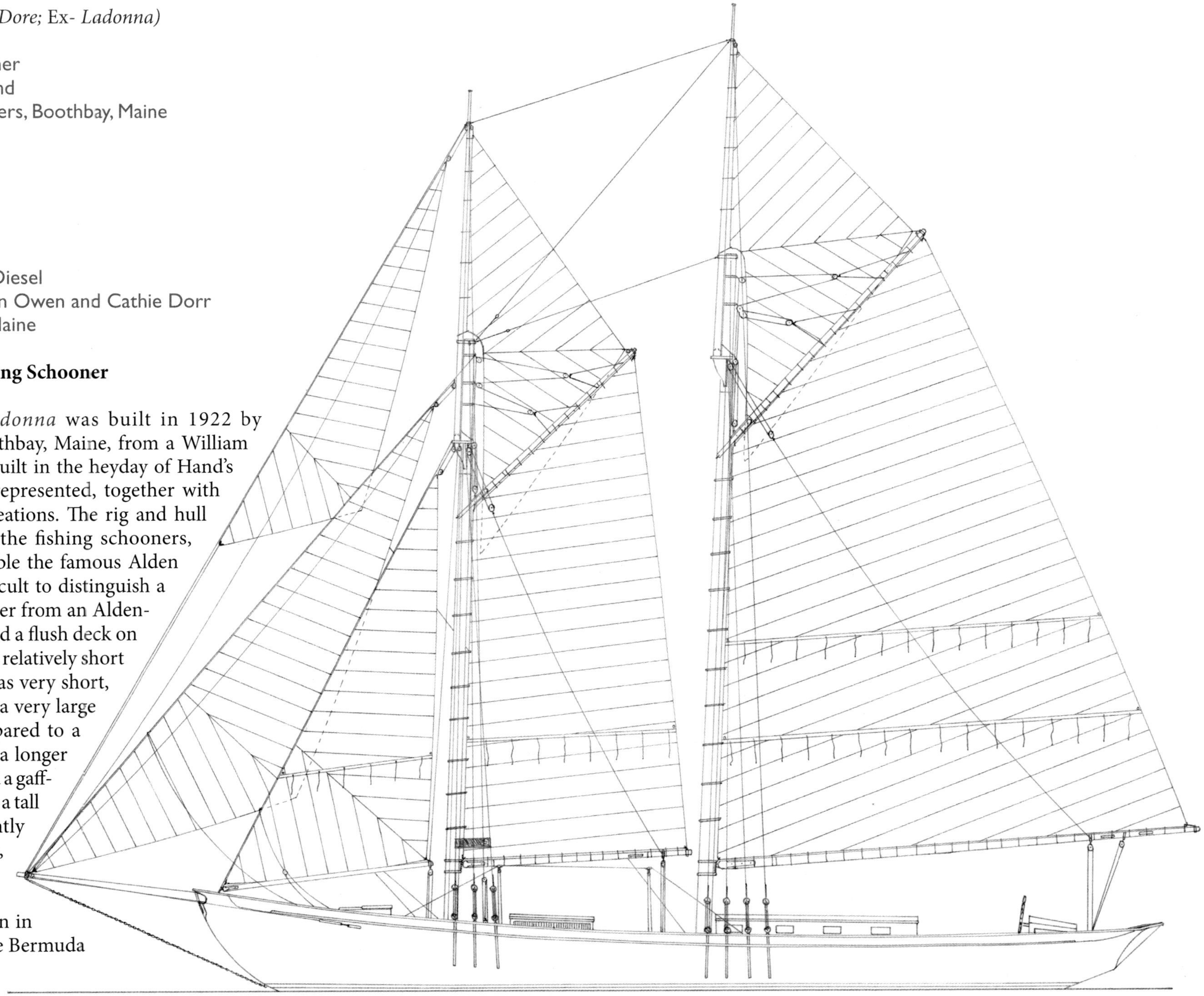

Her second owner renamed her *Jane Dore* after his daughter. As many large yachts of that time, in 1942, she was commissioned by the United States Coast Guard and assigned to offshore patrol to search for German submarines off New York Harbor. During this time she received two citations by the Commander of the Eastern Sea Frontier United States Coast Guard for seaworthiness in poor weather.

After the war, she got into the fishing industry as a commercial dragger out of Stonington, Connecticut. The beautiful classic interior was removed and the hull was accommodated for holding the captured fish.

In 1971, the *Jane Dore* was purchased by American Practical Navigators, Inc. This company completely rebuilt her for passenger trade and renamed her *Nathaniel Bowditch* after the brilliant mathematician and author of *The New American Practical Navigator*.

Nathaniel Bowditch Under the Caring Ownership of Captain Owen and Cathie Dorr

Captain Owen's love of sailing began at a very young age and runs deep in his family. He spent his summers on Vinalhaven, an island in Penobscot Bay, where he worked for the local fishermen. He later joined the Maine Windjammer fleet, working in a variety of positions on most of the boats in the fleet—including mate on the *Nathaniel Bowditch*. He earned his captain's license in 1989. Capt. Owen later went on to teach sailing and to command several vessels from Newfoundland to the West Indies, but has always come home to Maine.

Cathie Dorr grew up in upstate New York. She earned a degree in occupational therapy and later specialized in hand therapy. Her career led her to travel throughout the United States as a traveling therapist and later to own a private practice hand therapy clinic. In 1998, her parents organized a family trip on a Maine Windjammer. It was on that trip that Owen and Cathie met. They have been together ever since, working toward their goal to own and operate their own Windjammer. They realized their dream when they acquired the schooner *Nathaniel Bowditch*, and put her into the charter trade within the Maine Windjammer fleet.

Nathaniel Bowditch: A Yacht to Charter

Nathaniel Bowditch currently sails out of Rockland, Maine, offering day trips and overnight charters to passengers who wish to experience the natural beauty of the New England coast. The charter activity has granted this great schooner yacht a new lease on life, which allows her to remain actively sailing in very good shape. She sometimes takes part in the local traditional yacht races and windjammer contests, always sporting her distinctive and graceful lines, which honor her designer's ability to combine strength with elegance. Her traditional rig certainly adds to the fascination of this yacht. She carries her two large gaffs, which have to be hoisted in the traditional manner without winches, but only with block-and-tackle. Only the material of her sails has changed, which are now of Dacron, which is somewhat lighter than the old cotton sails, and less prone to degrading in the sunlight.

The schooner *Nathaniel Bowditch* has two large areas for passengers below deck, each with its own head. The forward compartment, or foc's'cle, has three double beds, one of which could be used as a triple, a traditional bunk style cabin, and a pullman berth. There is an open skylight in the companionway and louvered doors for good airflow. Following aft is the midship compartment with four large and comfortable cabins. These cabins have several graduated bunks along the side of the hull and which follow the hull's external shape. A large skylight allows for good ventilation and sunshine down below.

Captain Owen holds a 100-ton masters license through the United States Coast Guard. Boat, captain, and crew undergo a rigorous safety inspection annually, which includes emergency drills and a check of all emergency equipment. He and his wife are assisted by a crew of three to four, who also have ample experience in sailing and handling traditional wooden boats.

Nathaniel Bowditch was built as the yacht *Ladonna*. However, she does not preserve her original rig or interior, because at some point in her history she was transformed into a working boat. Her lines are reminiscent of her former glory as a private sailing and racing yacht (*Copyright © Benjamin Mendlowitz*).

Sailing hard in a breeze, guests can enjoy the power of this large schooner (*Copyright © Benjamin Mendlowitz*).

ZODIAC
(Ex- *California;* Ex- *Zodiac)*

Rig: two-mast gaff schooner
Designer: William H. Hand
Shipyard: Hogdon Brothers, Boothbay, Maine
Built: 1924
Length on Deck: 127'
Length sparred: 160'
Beam: 26'
Draft: 16'
Height of Main Mast: 127'
Sail Area: 7,000 + sq. ft.
Engine: 450-hp Caterpillar diesel
Hull Speed: 13 knots
Gross Tonnage: 147 tons
Owner: The Vessel Zodiac Corporation
Home Port: Bellingham, Washington

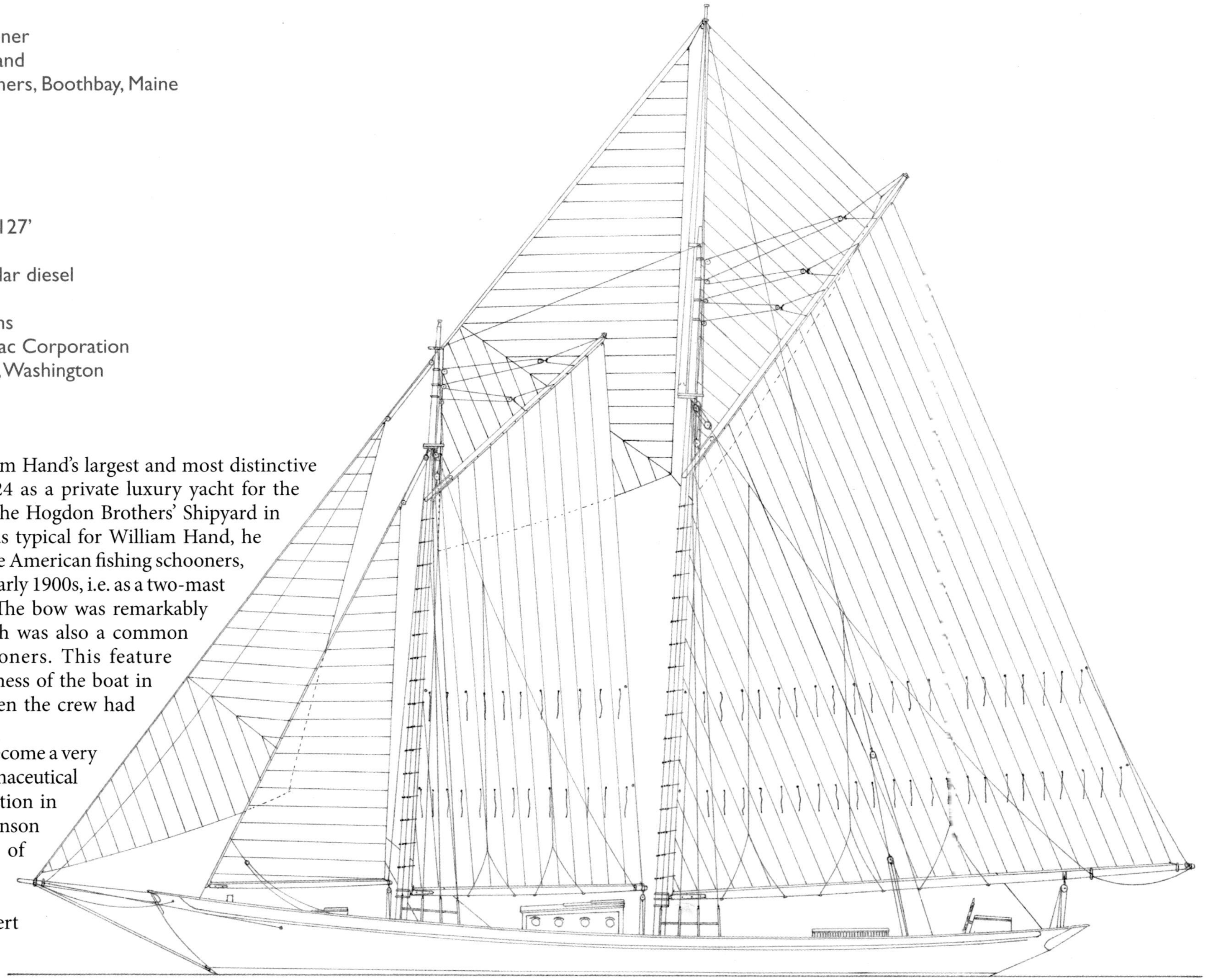

Zodiac's Early History

Zodiac was among William Hand's largest and most distinctive designs. She was built in 1924 as a private luxury yacht for the Johnson & Johnson heirs at the Hogdon Brothers' Shipyard in East Boothbay, Maine. As was typical for William Hand, he modeled the schooner after the American fishing schooners, popular in the late 1800s and early 1900s, i.e. as a two-mast gaff schooner with topsails. The bow was remarkably high-raked for a yacht, which was also a common feature of the fishing schooners. This feature contributed to the seaworthiness of the boat in heavy weather, especially when the crew had to furl the foresails.

Johnson & Johnson had become a very important sanitation and pharmaceutical enterprise since its incorporation in 1887. Based in New Jersey, Johnson & Johnson also became one of the largest pharmaceutical companies in the world. In the 1920s the chairman was Robert

Wood Johnson, who most likely was *Zodiac's* beneficial owner. Among many other races, in 1928, the Johnson's competed the schooner in the Transatlantic Race for the Kings' Cup where she finished only in fourth place, due to very light winds.

During the Great Depression, the *Zodiac* was sold to the San Francisco Bar Pilots, and renamed *California*. She worked the rugged waters outside the Golden Gate for forty years, retiring in 1972, as the last working pilot schooner in the United States. In the mid 1970s, the Vessel Zodiac Corporation was formed to operate and maintain the schooner, whose name was promptly restored to *Zodiac*. Drawing on an experienced crew of sailors and shipwrights, the ship was restored to her former beauty and sailing strength.

Zodiac Now: Chartering the Puget Sound

In 1982, *Zodiac* earned a spot on the National Register of Historic Places by the United States Department of the Interior. She continues to work the waters of Puget Sound, San Juan, and Gulf Islands to this day.

The Schooner *Zodiac* is a Coast Guard-certified charter vessel that can carry up to twenty-six passengers on overnight cruises and forty-nine passengers for day sails. She sails with a licensed captain, first mate, and experienced crew. The schooner *Zodiac* takes passengers on windjammer voyages throughout Puget Sound, the San Juan's, and Canadian Gulf Islands, as well as excursions into Desolation Sound. She is a proud member of the American Sail Training Association and of the Pacific Northwest Schooner Association.

The schooner *Zodiac*, sailing under the name of *California*, in 1940. She worked then for the San Francisco Bar Pilots. Note the large deckhouse on the aft deck. This deckhouse required the mainsail to be made smaller. It's very possible that she had to rely on her engines more often than if she had kept her original rig (*Zodiac Corporation*).

Another view of *Zodiac*, showing her from her stern sailing to windward (*Zodiac Corporation*).

Zodiac today sails the Puget Sound. Her rig is close to original, although in the 1920s she also carried a topmast on her foremast, with the corresponding sails. A distinctive sign of this vessel is her high bow, something William Hand took from the Newfoundland schooners (*The Schooner* Zodiac *Corporation*).

Nathanael G. Herreshoff: Unsurpassed Beauty

BIOGRAPHY OF NATHANAEL G. HERRESHOFF

By almost any reckoning, Nathanael Greene Herreshoff, the "Wizard of Bristol," was the greatest American yacht designer and builder of all times. Beginning just after the American Civil War, his career of more than seventy years spanned an era of exuberant industrialization. He was a natural offspring of this fast-paced industrialization. He dominated the America's Cup races from 1893 to 1920, designing and building all of that period's five successful defenders. He was responsible for a series of significant improvements in the design of steam engines, and invented numerous items of yacht hardware and rigging that are in common use today.

The seeming modernity of the surviving N. G. Herreshoff boats, their quantity, and the apparent youthfulness of adequately maintained examples make it somewhat startling to realize that the midpoint of his career was approximately a hundred years ago. Herreshoff has been the standard against which other designers and builders have been judged throughout the modern yachting era. A very important part of this standard is good, timeless design.

Herreshoff grew up on the harbor in Bristol, Rhode Island, in an intellectually stimulating family of avid sailors. His father was an active yachtsman who designed and built himself a series of yachts, and his brothers were also active in boatbuilding and racing. While a teenager, Herreshoff designed and built several family-owned yachts.

In 1869, after graduating from the Massachusetts Institute of Technology, Herreshoff started out as draftsman at the Corliss Steam Engine Company in Providence, Rhode Island. He remained there for nine years and gained valuable experience in the design and construction of steam boilers and power delivery systems. In 1874 he and his blind brother John built a 17' sloop named *Riviera* and another boat named *l'Onda* on the shores of the Mediterranean. They cruised *Riviera* on the inland waters and canals of France, Switzerland, Germany, and Holland, and crossed the Channel to England, where they went up the Thames. They brought her back to New York on a steamer and then sailed to their home in Bristol.

At age thirty-five, Herreshoff married Clara DeWolf, with whom he had six children. Two of them also became yacht designers: Lewis Francis Herreshoff and A. Sydney DeWolf Herreshoff.

In 1878, Nathanael and John Herreshoff founded the Herreshoff Manufacturing Company. John handled the financial side of the business, while Nathanael was in charge of the design and construction of the yachts. He became world famous for his successive America's Cup yacht designs, which all in a row steadily won the race and consolidated the United States as the leading sailing nation in the world. At the same time, Herreshoff produced hundreds of yachts for the American and international yachting scenes. High quality in construction, combined with light materials and good sailing performance, were his particular trademarks.

Most of his boats were rigged as sloops and cutters with some yawls and ketches. But Herreshoff also produced some remarkable schooner designs, albeit less in number. Over the years, Herreshoff built a total of nine large steel schooners, in addition to the composite schooner *Vagrant* (*I*). These schooners were the following:

Contract year	HM Co. Hull No.	Name	Length	Overall Length on Waterline	Beam
1903	590	*Ingomar*	127'	86'	24'3"
1906	657	*Queen*	126'	92'6"	24'
1909	692	*Westward**	135'4"	96'	26'8"
1910	698	*Vagrant (I)*	78'	56'7"	18'
1910	706	*Elena**	136'6"	96'	26'8"
1912	719	*Vagrant (II)*	109'	79'1"	23'8"
1913	722	*Katoura*	162'	115'	30'
1915	772	*Mariette*	109'	80'	23'8"
1919	827	*Ohonkara*	109'	80'	23'8"
1922	891	*Wildfire*	95'	68'	20'6"

Note: The yachts with grey background are those still afloat today, and the asterisk marks two yachts that have been built anew based on the original plans and specifications by Herreshoff.

To this list should be added a few smaller wooden schooner yachts, such as the *Mary Rose*, the only still sailing.

Despite the fact that today many hundreds of Herreshoff yachts remain actively sailing, it is surprising to observe that only very few of his great schooner yachts ever made it to the twenty-first century. The schooner *Mariette* certainly stands out as the best-preserved yacht of this type. Good fortune, generous and dedicated owners, and high-quality construction at the beginning, made it possible for her to sail through the years looking as new as she did when first launched. Another schooner that seemed to follow *Mariette's* fate is *Vagrant* (*I*), which received a massive restoration in the late 1980s and with it a new lease on life. Nevertheless, this lease is about to expire now, due to the total lack of attention her current owners devote to her. But she is still there, floating, and for this reason she will be featured in this chapter, jointly with her larger sister *Mariette*. In addition, the second *Vagrant* (*II*), sister to *Mariette*, is still afloat, in Trieste (Italy), where attempts at restoring her are made. She now carries a staysail-schooner rig. And there is yet another large Herreshoff schooner still sailing, albeit not restored to original specifications, under the name of *Atrevida* along the Brazilian coast.

Atrevida was designed in 1922 as a heavy-displacement schooner yacht aimed at cruising rather than racing. She was built the following year and launched as *Wildfire*. She had been commissioned by then New York Yacht Club Commodore Charles Harding, who won the 1924 Schooner Cup and several other important regattas with this yacht. She was sold in 1950 to Jorge Bhering de Matos who sailed the yacht to Brazil and renamed her *Atrevida*. The boat then passed to Dirceu Fortouta, who used her for four and a half decades for entertaining influential guests out of Rio de Janeiro, such as Elvis Presley, Rita Hayworth, Henry Kissinger, and many Brazilian presidents. After neglect over the years, the yacht was deemed scrap by 2002. However, Gilberto Miranda purchased her and completely restored her over a period of more than a year at the shipyard of MCP Yachts, located in Santos. While originally built as a main-Marconi and fore-gaff schooner, *Atrevida* now carries a modern staysail schooner rig with furling sails.

MARIETTE

(Ex- Janeen; Ex- Le Voyageur; Ex- Guinevere; Ex- Evening Star; Ex- Gee-Gee III; Ex- Cleopatra's Barge II; Ex- Mariette)

Type: two-mast gaff schooner
Designer: Nathanael Greene Herreshoff
Year of Construction: 1915
Shipyard: Herreshoff Manufacturing, Bristol, Rhode Island
Length (sparred): 138'
Length on Deck: 109'
Length on Waterline: 80'
Beam: 23'7"
Draft: 14'6"
Working Sail Area: 7,839 sq. ft.
Max Sail Area: 11,114 sq. ft.
Construction: Steel
Engine: 2x Caterpillar

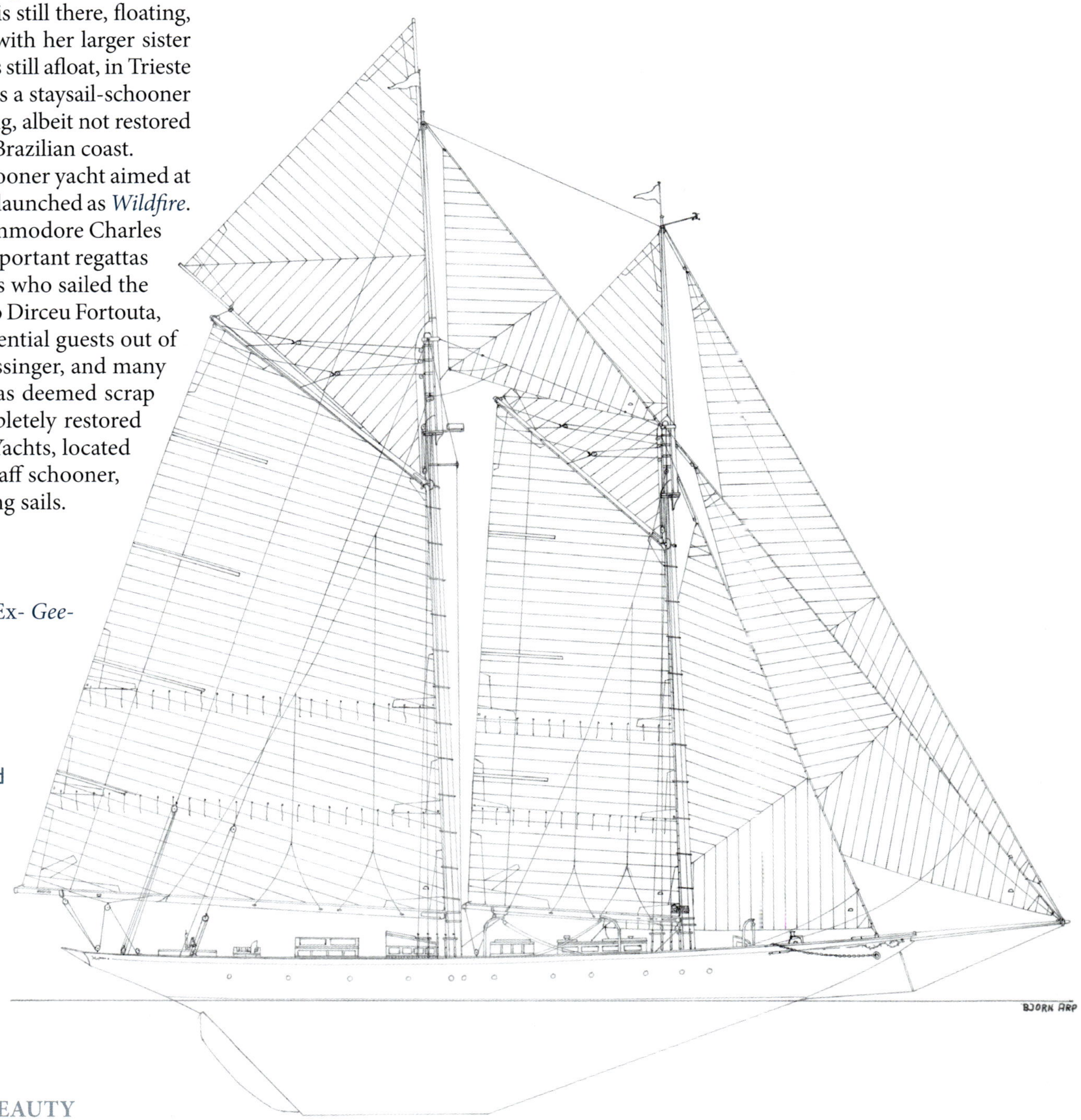

Mariette is arguably the finest surviving example of Nat Herreshoff's large luxury schooners. She is the larger sister to *Vagrant* (*I*), and signaled a development of large racing/cruising schooners that has not been able to trump her until today. Launched in 1915, she is still the epitome of a classic American schooner yacht.

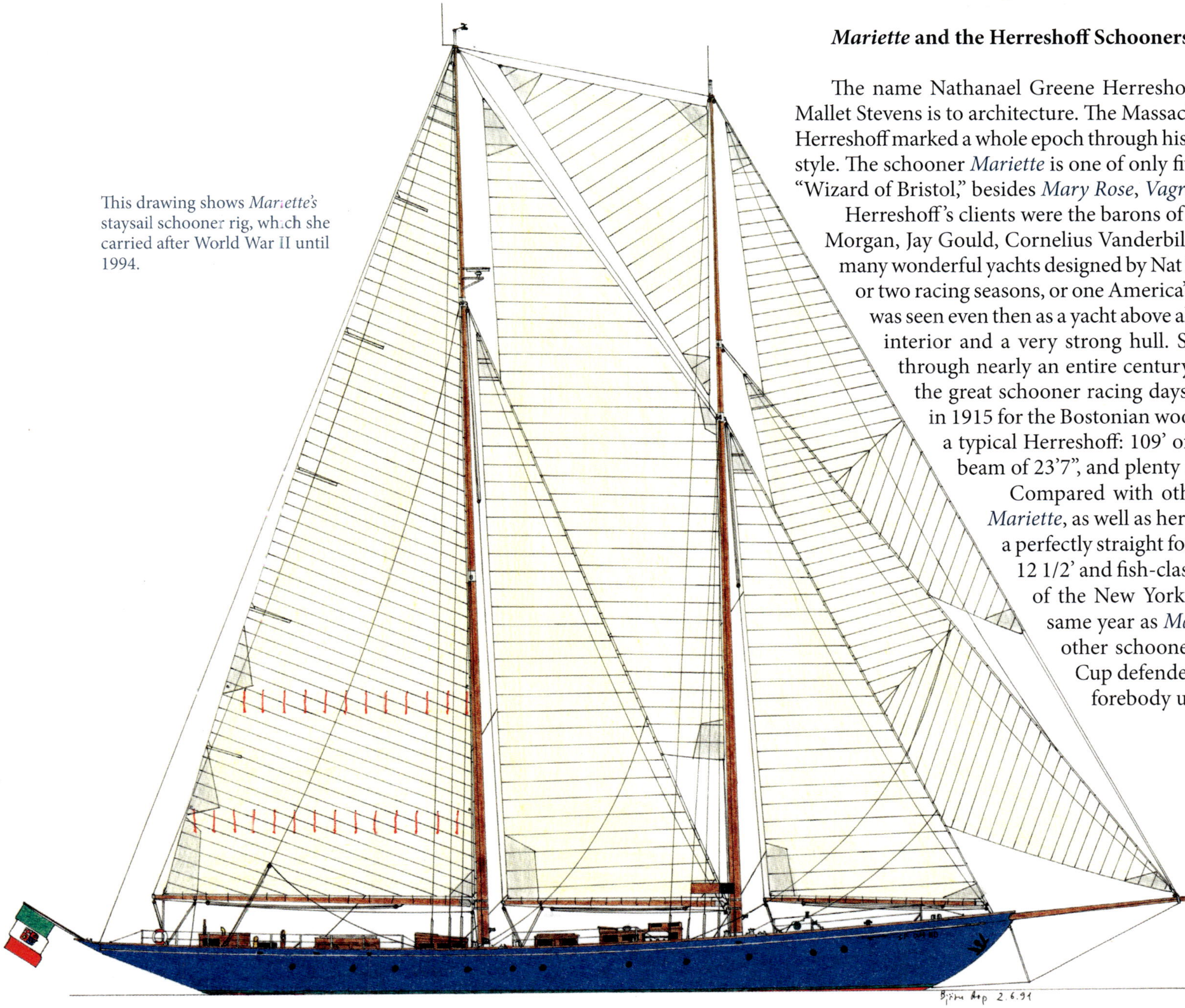

This drawing shows *Mariette's* staysail schooner rig, which she carried after World War II until 1994.

Mariette and the Herreshoff Schooners

The name Nathanael Greene Herreshoff is to the field of yacht design what Mallet Stevens is to architecture. The Massachusetts Institute of Technology-trained Herreshoff marked a whole epoch through his technical innovations and his particular style. The schooner *Mariette* is one of only five remaining schooner yachts from the "Wizard of Bristol," besides *Mary Rose*, *Vagrant* (*I*), *Vagrant* (*II*), and *Atrevida*.

Herreshoff's clients were the barons of his day: William Randolph Hearst, J. P. Morgan, Jay Gould, Cornelius Vanderbilt III, and Harry Payne Whitney. While many wonderful yachts designed by Nat Herreshoff were built only to last for one or two racing seasons, or one America's Cup edition, the white-hulled *Mariette* was seen even then as a yacht above all others, boasting a stunning Edwardian interior and a very strong hull. She indeed had the chance to struggle through nearly an entire century, so that we have here a testimonial of the great schooner racing days of the early twentieth century. Drawn in 1915 for the Bostonian wool merchant Frederick J. Brown, she was a typical Herreshoff: 109' of almost uncluttered deck space, with a beam of 23'7", and plenty of space on and below decks.

Compared with other large sailing yachts by Herreshoff, *Mariette*, as well as her predecessors *Vagrant* (*I*) and (*II*), show a perfectly straight fore keel, reminiscent of the much smaller 12 1/2' and fish-class sloops, and not too far from the shape of the New York 40s, a dozen of which were built the same year as *Mariette*. This contrasts with Herreshoff's other schooners, sloops, cutters, and even America's Cup defenders, that have noticeable hollows in their forebody underwater profile.

In 1927 Brown sold the schooner to Francis Boardman Crowninshield, descendant of the first great American yacht enthusiast, who in the eighteenth century built the amazing *Cleopatra's Barge*, and brother of Bradlee B. Crowninshield, the famous yacht designer.

With the name of *Cleopatra's Barge II*, she sailed until World War II, when she was seized by the Navy and then served as a patrol vessel for the United States Coast Guard. In 1946, Crowninshield got his yacht back in a lamentable state of disrepair, so that the captain recommended selling her.

After World War II the schooner sailed under the names of *Gee-Gee III*, *Evening Star*, and, when Edgar Palmer bought her in 1953, *Guinevere*. Her home port at that time was Oyster Bay, New York. Later on, she served as the Caribbean charter yacht *Le Voyageur* for the Canadian Walter Boudreau. He sold the schooner to one of his guests, but then Boudreau repurchased her and renamed her *Janeen*, after his daughter. In 1979, *Mariette* was acquired by the Italian publisher and yacht-lover Alberto Rizzoli, who restored her in La Spezia under the knowledgeable direction of skipper Erik Pascoli. At first glance, *Mariette* impresses with her extreme lines and low profile. The deck plan is very clear and demonstrates the ability of the designer to combine complex rigging with the appearance of ease. Despite the predominant materials of teak, bronze and brass, on board the schooner there is a feeling of being on a "racing machine."

While the deck is for the sportsman, the interior is for the gentleman. The interior of the yacht consists of a large full-width saloon, an owner's cabin with adjacent office, two guest cabins, and a separate crew's quarter for six persons. The mahogany staircase has a hand-carved handrail, the chairs in the saloon are covered with red leather, the saloon itself paneled in walnut; the fireplace, light wood and white lacquered furniture of the cabins extend a pleasant and warm atmosphere. But most of all, *Mariette* offers some masterpieces from her owner's art collection: a nude by Picasso, a still life by Sutherland, a Russian icon...that transform the old boat into a floating museum.

Mariette in 1916. She had a white hull at that time, and she always carried with her the tender hanging in the davits. This photo shows her towing a dinghy, and the awning set. She was probably relocating from one anchorage to another in the Long Island Sound (*The Mariner's Museum, Virginia*).

In 1994, the Silicon Valley venture capitalist Tom Perkins bought the schooner. He started another total and massive restoration, including the replication of *Mariette's* original gaff rig with fidded topmasts, two gaff topsails, one fisherman staysail, three headsails, and inherent complexity of standing and running rigging. It took one year to restore *Mariette* to her original beauty. While the work took place in Italy, Perkins himself spent hours carefully stripping and refinishing her walnut-pannelled main saloon. In that time he also came to know his new yacht intimately as she fulfilled his quest for an all-consuming project.

Although Perkins personally took part in *Mariette's* restoration, he could not be on site all the time, so he hired Tom Eaton, who had formerly worked on *Puritan*, to oversee the work and, later, to be her professional captain. Under Eaton's supervision the yacht's rig was pulled out and her original gaff rig was authentically recreated and installed. This included new varnished wooden spars by Spencer Rigging; new replica Herreshoff polished cast-bronze fittings; 180 new, wood-shelled blocks; new beautiful hand-sewn, cream-colored, narrow-panel sails by Ratsey and Lapthorn; downwind and fisherman sails by Doyle France; and some of the best examples of marlinspike seamanship that one could imagine.

While the new rig was the most visible aspect of the restoration, entirely transforming the appearance of the yacht, *Mariette* was also provided with a new pair of Caterpillar diesels that drove Luke feathering propellers, a sunken cockpit for steering (originally the wheel stood directly on the flush deck), and a new on-deck lounging and dining area designed to not disturb the classic deck layout of the schooner. Carefully designed and outfitted accommodations were installed below deck. The topsides were painted deep-blue with a mirror-like Awlgrip finish. The result was another extraordinary classic yacht restoration, in line with the previous stunning projects done on *Altair* and *Vagrant*. With *Mariette* back on the water in her original fashion, the big schooner started the timid revival of the big schooner class, which only years later was fully accomplished with the building of such replicas as the Herreshoff schooners *Westward* (*Eleonora*), *Elena,* and the mythic *Atlantic.*

Racing in the Mediterranean

The first debut after the restoration was at La Nioularge in Saint-Tropez in 1995. La Nioularge was the name of the classic yacht regatta before it was changed into Les Voiles de Saint-Tropez, precisely after what happened to *Mariette.*

The start of a sailboat race can influence who turns out to be the overall victor, and jockeying for the best position makes it the hairiest time of any race. La Nioularge was no exception. The yachts were moving at ten to fifteen knots, under the fresh breeze for which the Golf de Saint-Tropez is so famous. With many boats at the start, the scene was orderly chaos, putting *Mariette* into a particularly precarious position. She was sailing on port tack, approaching the start line of her division's race. Another boat on port tack was the 36' sloop *Taos Brett IV*, approaching from a sharp angle. Tom Perkins assumed she was part of the spectator fleet and did not notice that she was the lead vessel from the first division that had started more than an hour earlier. He also assumed the smaller boat would get out of the way and, being a hyperaggressive helmsman, he was not about to give in. But *Taos Brett IV* was not altering course and instead was plowing her way by all the big yachts crowding the starting line for their own race. Her skipper wanted to win no less than Perkins did.

With both boats on the same tack, the rules dictated that the leeward boat—the one furthest from the wind, which was *Taos Brett IV*—prevailed, unless the windward boat, here *Mariette*, was obstructed by some other boat or even land. In that event, the leeward boat had to give way. In this close situation between the two boats, *Taos Britt IV* was the leeward

Mariette was a typical Herreshoff schooner. This could be seen by her moderate, sheer, wide beam and open, uncluttered deck. The sails stand very stiff (*The Mariner's Museum, Virginia*).

boat, and her helmsman believed he had right-of-way. But *Mariette* had two huge yachts bearing down on her from both sides—coming from the opposite direction, on starboard tack. Perkins could not turn in either direction without ramming into one of them. With *Taos Brett IV* nearly upon him, Perkins' only hope was for her to realize that *Mariette* was obstructed.

Not only did *Taos Brett IV* arguably lack right-of-way, she was about to violate the universal rule that it is better to veer off than to risk a collision. Perkins' panicked crew, as well as the crews on the other boats nearby, began bellowing at the French skipper, Claude Graff, to get out of the way. Standing on the high side of the heeled-over *Taos Brett IV*, Graff saw exactly what was happening. But according to Perkins, Graff gave him the finger and continued to hold his ground, trying to slip by *Mariette's* bow with just enough room to spare.

Perkins kicked his two diesel engines into reverse to reduce *Mariette's* speed to a few knots. At first, it seemed that *Taos Brett IV* almost cleared *Mariette's* bow, avoiding a direct hit. But the schooner's long bowsprit clipped the rigging on the port side of *Taos Brett IV*, and began carrying the smaller boat along, and then under *Mariette's* bow. The rigging was one of the wire stays that supported *Taos Brett IV's* mast and the wire failed to snap. Within seconds, *Taos Brett IV* capsized, filled with water and sank.

The doomed sailboat had five sailors aboard, three in the cockpit and two in the cabin who were packing a spinnaker for use in the race. The pair inside had no idea what was happening in the duel between *Taos Brett IV* and *Mariette*. One of those people, a fifty-year-old physician from Nice named Jacques Bourry, did not make it out alive. Horrified at the collision and Bourry's downing, Perkins immediately dropped out of the race, which was soon canceled anyway, as was the regatta itself, for several years, because of the tragedy. Perkins was so shaken he gave the helm over to his captain, Tom Eaton.

Forty-five minutes later, after *Mariette's* sails had been furled and stowed, Perkins was arrested by armed French authorities and charged with manslaughter. He did not learn until midnight, ten hours after the collision, that *Taos Brett IV* was actually racing and in the lead in her division, and that the race committee had recklessly set up a course that brought the smaller boats directly into the starting line of the bigger ones. Eaton was arrested as well, even though he was not at the wheel. So, too, were the skipper of the other boat and the chairman of the race committee. Perkins was certain he had done nothing wrong, that the other boat had erred, and that it was all a terrible accident, but he was nonetheless not surprised by being taken into custody.

Evidently, Bourry's family agreed that it was an unfortunate accident. The next morning, his wife, as well as his mistress, came by *Mariette's* slip to see Perkins. They had just driven to Saint-Tropez from Nice. Perkins assumed they had come to berate him. Instead, over cappuccino and cookies, they hugged him and told him that he was not to blame for Bourry's death and, oh, one other thing—the widow wanted

Mariette's rig is impressive. The crewmember seems lost in the rig aloft in the fore-top. However, she is currently sailed by a highly professional crew who knows how to sail such a complex vessel (*Rudolph Arp Archive*).

to know if Perkins would take on her teenaged son as crew the following summer. Perkins felt he could not say no, though his lawyer subsequently told him that if he really hired the boy, Perkins would be looking for a new lawyer. Notwithstanding the widow's forgiveness, the local French prosecutor wanted Perkins' hide. Bourry was much loved in Nice. Egging on the prosecutor was the French press, which was having a field day with photos of the collision: "Monster American Yacht Kills French Doctor!" is how Perkins remembered the end-of-the-world front page headline in one of the Paris tabloids. Hyperbole aside, French law typically required a criminal inquiry in homicides, even if accidental. The sensationalist overlay of the regatta and its millionaires virtually ensured there would be a prosecution.

Perkins attended Bourry's funeral and, after he got his passport back from French police, he left the country. In theory, Perkins could have avoided prosecution by choosing not to come back. But he did return for the trial, exactly a year after the accident, timed to coincide with the anniversary, to be held in the old military village of Draguignan. While this was not the O. J. Simpson trial of France, the prosecutor was still scoring media points and kept saying he wanted Perkins to spend some time in the pokey. The American was big game and a risk-free target in the provincial countryside. Though friends gave him the names of top-flight criminal-defense counsel in France, Perkins underestimated the storm into which he was heading. So he hired a prominent Parisian lawyer who specialized only in such maritime accidents as major oil spills (including the *Amoco Cadiz* disaster off Brittany in 1978). It would prove to be a strategic miscalculation, because the lawyer was of little use in a court where the solution to the legal issues was negotiated between the defense and claimant counsel, and the judges, who had known each other since childhood.

After a three-day trial, the court convicted Perkins of involuntary manslaughter—excoriating the ruthlessness of sailing competitions—and found the other sailors guilty as well. But the judges did not heed the prosecutor's cry for prison time for any of them. Perkins received a sixty-day suspended sentence and a $10,000 fine, barely a rounding error in his bank accounts. Perkins paid his own captain's fine, too. Apart from having to notify the Securities and Exchange Commission of his conviction, which he was obligated to do in his capacity as board member of several publicly traded companies, the conviction had no consequence in the United States. In contrast to the French news media, which went nuts, the American press curiously missed the story altogether; these were the ancient days of the 1990s, before it became easy to use the Internet to keep tabs on a corporate official.

Perkins sold *Mariette* in 2008 in the wake of the construction of his latest sailing yacht, the *Maltese Falcon*. With a new owner, *Mariette* continues to compete in the major classic yachting events, such as the Veteran Boat Rally of Portocervo, Les Regattes Royales of Cannes, and Les Voiles de Saint-Tropez. The schooner is regularly inspected and refitted by Pendennis in Falmouth, United Kingdom, to make sure that she remains in perfect condition. Among the latest improvements of the schooner's performance was the installation of new folding propellers. Every possible improvement is done to enhance her competitiveness in races against other large classics.

Wherever *Mariette* appears, she is a sight not to be forgotten. In this occasion she shows off in 2007 in the bay of Palma de Mallorca in Spain. She took part in the classic yacht race of Palma that year (*Rudolph Arp Archive*).

Mariette trimming her fisherman staysail (*Rudolph Arp Archive*).

Mariette at anchor. The large deck invites relaxation in the sea breeze after a day of racing (*Copyright © Benjamin Mendlowitz*).

Although the schooner has a number of winches on board, most of the work is done by hand. For this reason, she requires a large crew to sail her efficiently. Between twenty and thirty strong crew members are needed on board for races (*Rudolph Arp Archive*).

This is another shot of *Mariette* sailing in a fleet of racing classics. She is truly the "queen of the fleet" (*Rudolph Arp Archive*).

VAGRANT
(Ex- *Queen Mab;* Ex- *Vagrant)*

Rig: two-mast gaff schooner
Designer: Nathanael Greene Herreshoff
Year of Construction: 1910
Shipyard: Herreshoff Manufacturing, Bristol, Rhode Island, hull number 698
Length (sparred): 109'
Length on Deck: 78'
Length on Waterline: 56' 7"
Beam: 18'
Draft: 11'4"
Displacement: 68 tons
Sail Area: 5,005 sq. ft.
Construction: Composite
Engine: Cummins 504-M diesel, recently replaced
Owner: Windward Ocean Sailing Club
Home Port: Nishinomiya, Japan

***Vagrant*: Herreshoff's First Schooner**

Nathanael G. Herreshoff signed the contract with Harold Vanderbilt to design and built *Vagrant* on March 23, 1910, with a cost for the completed schooner stipulated at $26,800. Very shortly afterwards Harold Vanderbilt took commission of the yacht and immediately won the Bermuda Race. *Vagrant* was among the smallest offshore racing schooners Herreshoff had designed. She was "only" 109' overall, with 78' on deck and a modest waterline length of 56'7". She displaced 68 tons, which were easily driven by her cloud of 5,005 sq. ft of sail area. Her construction was composite, with a steel structure and steel frames that were planked in pine. The main mast was made of two pieces of Douglas fir, which stirred up into the sky for a total of 92'. Harold Vanderbilt was so satisfied with this first schooner, that three years later, when he ordered a second *Vagrant*, he essentially only wanted the boat to be larger, but without any other relevant modifications

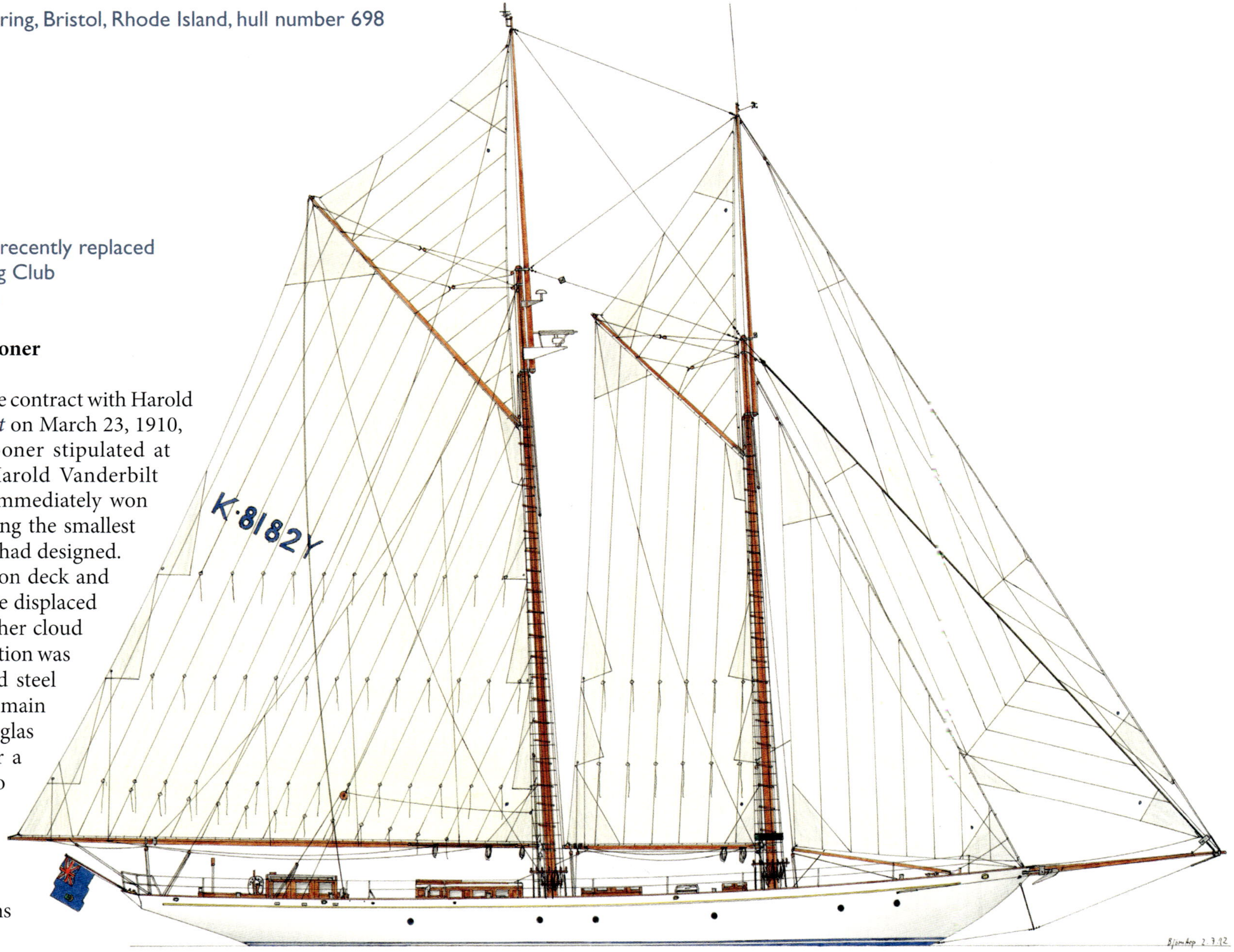

(except, of course, that Herreshoff built all other schooners entirely of steel). This way, *Vagrant* (*I*) served as a model for *Vagrant* (*II*), but also for *Mariette* and *Ohonkara*. The rescaling of *Vagrant* (*I*)'s plans resulted in a 43% increase in length and a 35% increase in beam, draft, and freeboard. The general hull form, with a straight fore-foot, long overhangs, and low freeboard, stayed the same for all three yachts.

Below deck, *Vagrant* (*I*) had room for four passengers and six crewmembers. *Vagrant's* owners usually occupied the two cabins in the aft part of the boat that had their own bathroom and toilet. There were separate cabins for the crew. The main saloon featured stained glass for the cabinets and mahogany trim on white bulkheads, all typical of Herreshoffs' style and highlighted by the emphasis on the smallest details.

But however beautiful this schooner was, for Harold Vanderbilt she was too small. While he ordered from Herreshoff a second and larger *Vagrant*, he put the first one up for sale. He sold the first *Vagrant* in 1913 to Hendon Chubb, who renamed the schooner *Queen Mab*, a name under which the boat became famous throughout the globe in the voyages that followed. He also changed her heavy gaff rig by substituting the main gaff for a main Marconi sail, with a tall main mast in one piece. While her windward capabilities were most likely improved and the boat could be sailed more easily by a reduced crew, the rig still proved to be impressive from an aesthetical point of view. After Chubb had sold the schooner *Queen Mab*, she was successively owned by several members of the United States' East Coast racing scene. Around 1954, Robert Pringle became *Queen Mab's* new owner. He was based out of Los Angeles, California. He sold her around 1968 to other people. At some point in time the rig was further simplified and definitively changed into a staysail schooner rig. The redesign of this rig was done by naval architect William "Bill" Lapworth.

After a few years' sailing with the name *Vagrant* for Harold Vanderbilt, she was renamed *Queen Mab* and her main gaff sail was converted into a Marconi. With this rig she still proved to be impressive, as this early photograph shows (*The Mariner's Museum, Virginia*).

Queen Mab in a powerful reach with all her sails up. Note the bent bowsprit, which makes her appear even more spectacular (*The Mariner's Museum, Virginia*).

From Glory to Near Destruction

Queen Mab had a bad time in the 1980s. In May 1983 she was in Antigua in a sorry state. There, she changed hands again. This time it was to those of Hans Lammers, a 53-year-old Dutch man with a penchant for classical beauty. Lammers had been doing charter work in the West Indies mainly on classic yachts since he was 21 years old. Lammers decided to change the name of *Queen Mab* back to *Vagrant*, as she had originally been called.

After doing some refitting, Lammers chartered the semi-restored *Vagrant* for about a year, until the end of 1984. He realized that the proceeds of his charter business could not generate the needed resources for the restoration she deserved and needed. He thus put her up for sale again.

Three years passed until the real estate developer and yacht owner Peter de Savary learned of the availability of the schooner and rescued her from her Caribbean mooring. He brought her to Britain for a total restoration.

After Peter de Savary's restoration, *Vagrant* again sported her original gaff rig and was stronger and faster than ever (*Rudolph Arp Archive*).

Precision Surgery

Until that moment, only very few large classics from the early twentieth century had received a total restoration such as *Vagrant's*. The only comparable work that had been done previously was the restoration of the Fife schooner *Altair*. In this sense, Peter de Savary was a pioneer, marking the way for many other restorations that followed during the 1990s. Under de Savary's personal direction, *Vagrant* was fully refurbished by a team of highly qualified craftsmen in a period of almost three years and a cost of several million dollars. The boat originally had no engine, but in the refit an engine was installed beneath the saloon floors. This engine was a Cummins diesel with 143 kW and 195 hp. She had a range of 1,000 nautical miles under this engine at a cruise speed of 8 knots. She received a single propeller on a center shaft. Tanks were installed to carry 840 gallons of diesel fuel, and about double that amount of fresh water.

The new rig was built by Spencer Rigging on the Isle of Wight. Spencer used the original Herreshoff plans for the gaff rig fore and aft, with an impressive main boom that seemed to glide endlessly over her flush teak decks. Regarding navigation equipment, it is understandable that she was equipped with the state of the art of her time.

Vagrant's nicely varnished skylight seen from the main saloon. It provides both ventilation and light to the saloon. Together with the white paneling of the saloon, this room becomes a bright and comfortable space to live (*Rudolph Arp Archive*).

Sailing Again!

Once restored, Peter de Savary crossed the Atlantic twice with *Vagrant* and sailed the Mediterranean, the Caribbean, and the Atlantic. The schooner reached speeds of up to 13 and a half knots. Yet in 1991 he decided to sell her to a Japanese owner, who subsequently sold her to the Windward Ocean Sailing Club in Japan. After sailing her from Southampton, United Kingdom, to Nishinomiya, their idea was to put *Vagrant* into service as a sail training and promotional yacht for the club. But the club lacked the needed human and financial resources to effectively sail and maintain the boat. For this reason, she has remained at her dock since her arrival in Japan, without any work being performed on her. Over the years, her exposed steel framing has corroded heavily, as have other important structural parts of the boat. The spars have severely suffered from the lack of varnish, causing the lamination of the Douglas fir to spring open, weakening the rig to a point that it is only a question of time before it all falls apart. The boat would need urgent attention if she were to be saved.

The electric panel was custom made in de Savary's restoration. It provided for state-of-the-art electric and electronic control of the vessel. However, besides this control panel, nothing else below decks are modern. Every detail has been lovingly restored to its original 1910 configuration (*Rudolph Arp Archive*).

After twenty years rotting in Japan, *Vagrant* was still a sight to be seen. However, a closer look reveals that she is literally falling apart. This photo shows her in February 2009 (*Rudolph Arp Archive*).

Hidden in a deckhouse close to the wheel is the nav station with a wide chartable and the necessary displays of the electronics needed to safely captain the vessel (*Rudolph Arp Archive*).

Due to lack of the most basic maintenance, the steel of the frames has rotten so thin that any stress on the hull would easily break it open (*Rudolph Arp Archive*).

Vagrant's deck looks like it is waiting for a new crew to arrive and set sails. However, the plywood deck below the teak is rotten and needs replacement (*Rudolph Arp Archive*).

The yacht still has the original home port of Southampton on her stern, from the time Peter de Savary owned her. The owners who purchased her in 1990 did not bother to update the port of registry (*Rudolph Arp Archive*).

Vagrant is one of the last relics of the great times of schooner racing in the United States. After rotting in Japan for more than twenty years, will she ever sail again? (*Rudolph Arp Archive*)

Lewis F. Herreshoff: A Proper Yacht Designer with a Traditional Twist

BIOGRAPHY OF LEWIS F. HERRESHOFF

Lewis Francis Herreshoff (1890–1972) was born in Bristol, Rhode Island, as Nathanael Greene Herreshoff's son. L. Francis Herreshoff started out working on the family shipyard and under the direct supervision of his knowledgeable father.

During World War I, L. Francis Herreshoff designed underwater shapes for the Navy, and later worked for Wm. Starling Burgess. In 1925, he started designing yachts on his own, and became a very successful small racing-yacht designer. In addition, L. Francis Herreshoff not only designed racing yachts, but also created cruising yachts, canoes, and small sailing craft. His interests and experience were as broad as the yachting industry. In the 1940s he began writing his famous articles for *The Rudder* magazine. These articles led to a number of books that now form part of any standard marine library.

Among his notable racing designs, there was the 1930 America's Cup J-boat, *Whirlwind*, the incredible *Istalena*, and the remarkable and innovative R-class sloops *Yankee* and *Live Yankee*. His graceful cruising boats such as the ketches *Bounty*, *Tioga*, and *Araminta*, and the schooners *Joann* and *Mistral* are still considered the pinnacle of perfection in form and proportion in boat design. These last two schooners are still sailing today and will be explained in more detail in this chapter. Some other famous designs were intended for home builders, and included the *Nereia*, *Marco Polo*, and the ultra-shoals *Meadow Lark* and *Golden Ball*. Also, the highly successful ocean-racing ketch *Ticonderoga*, built in 1936, maintains some features so typical of L. Francis Herreshoff that were already present in *Joann* and *Mistral*, such as the long cabin trunk, low freeboard, clipper bow, and traditional transom stern. Due to her good balance between seaworthiness for long passages and sailing performance, *Ticonderoga* was one of the most successful maxi ocean racers in yachting history, so successful that she was still winning races and setting records three decades after she was built. She still today continues to win classic yacht regattas.

L. Francis Herreshoff made his home "The Castle" in Marblehead, Massachusetts, where he was known locally by his nickname, "the Skipper," famous not only for his design work but for his strongly held and strongly expressed opinions. Herreshoff worked on design right up to his death in December 1972, at the age of 82.

L. Francis Herreshoff was quite a character and about as opinionated as one could be. He knew what he liked, and did not care about what anyone might think of him. In a *Boston Globe* interview published on June 11, 1967, he is quoted as saying, "Almost all the people today who have any money in this country have been here only a generation or two and have little education, little taste, little sense of beauty." And in regard to the plastic-hulled and aluminum-rigged sailboats, which dominated Marblehead Harbor (and still do), he comments, "The harbor looks to me just like floating swill." When asked about up and coming young boat designers, he abruptly responded, "At the present time there isn't one designer in the whole world that's any Goddamned good. No one knows how to draw. No one has any decency."

BRIGADOON
(Ex- *Joann)*

Type: two-mast gaff schooner
Designer: Lewis F. Herreshoff, Design No. 257
Year of Construction: 1924
Shipyard: Britt Brothers, West Lynn, Massachusetts
Length (sparred): 65'
Length on Deck: 49'11"
Length on Waterline: 43'
Beam: 13'2"
Draft: 4'8"
Sail Area: 1,620 sq. ft.
Construction: wood
Engine: Westerbeke diesel, 40 hp
Owner: Patti & Terry Klaus
Home Port: Alameda, California

Joann: A Small L. Francis Herreshoff Schooner

The 50' schooner *Brigadoon* was the first schooner in a long line of two-mast, clipper-bowed designs by L. Francis Herreshoff. She was commissioned in 1924 while Herreshoff was working for Burgess, Swasey, and Paine. She was built for Waldo H. Brown by the Britt Brothers' yard in West Lynn, Massachusetts, and named *Joann.*

She is a traditional schooner from the earlier part of L. Francis Herreshoff's career. She is heavy and full, though the draft has been kept moderate and she has a nice run. She is no great performer to windward, although she has a good potential for reaching. Her bow is as full as that of most Herreshoff's designs; there is only a slight hint of hollow at the forward end of the load waterline. Her hull has many of the essential characteristics of later, well-known Francis Herreshoff designs, such as the *Nereia* and the *Mobjack* ketches.

Joann's rig was designed relatively old-fashioned. The deadeyes and lanyards, elaborate lazyjacks, and lug foresail with its brails all seemed outdated already when

the boat was built, yet all of this is cruising gear that has proven its value in terms of making sail handling easier over a period of many years. Her mainsail had 614 sq. ft., the foresail 496, and the jib 312, for a total of 1,442 sq. ft. of working sails, plus fisherman. She had deep reefs to make it possible to snug her right down.

The schooner's arrangement was dominated by the two separate cabin houses that stand on the otherwise flush deck. In the after house, there is a chart table to port and the galley to starboard, with the saloon immediately forward of these. The forward house hosts the engine room with a work-bench to port. The head is to starboard, with a sleeping cabin forward. There is a heating stove at the forward end of this cabin.

Racing and Cruising in California

In 1948, *Joann* was purchased in New England by the sailor, film star, adventurer and author, Sterling Hayden. He renamed her *Brigadoon* and worked her hard for three years before selling her to a Californian yachtsman. He took her on the 1959 Transpac, and then to Tahiti for six months. *Brigadoon* came to the San Francisco Bay Area in 1960. She was owned by land developer Gary Reese for fifteen years, and he sold her to Dino Valenti of the Quicksilver Messenger Service.

Patti and Terry Klaus purchased the boat in 1976, rebuilt her over the years, and have been successfully racing and sailing her for the past 30 years. *Brigadoon* has been the flagship of the St. Francis Yacht Club, the Master Mariners, and has been a consistent winner in MMBA, Jessica Cup Races, and the MMBA/Corinthian Wooden Boat Show held each June in Tiburon, California. *Brigadoon* has been sailed by two generations of family and friends over the last thirty years, with the third generation starting to come aboard. She is berthed at the family home in Alameda. They have done much work on her to always keep her in very good condition. Along the way, they redesigned her rig to enable her to carry topsails and thus improve her sailing characteristics. In addition, they restored the deck, including entirely new deckhouses.

The schooner *Brigadoon* seen from the deck of the schooner *Yankee* in San Francisco Bay. Owner Terry Klaus had *Brigadoon's* rig altered to carry topmasts with gaff topsails and a fisherman. This considerably enhances her sailing performance (*Terry Klaus*).

In the purest Francis Herreshoff tradition, *Brigadoon's* stern is decorated with a golden eagle attached to the varnished counter stern. From this angle, she looks like a little *Ticonderoga* (*Copyright © Benjamin Mendlowitz*).

Brigadoon in a strong breeze. This type of weather is her favorite. The schooner can thus show her full potential (*Copyright © Benjamin Mendlowitz*).

MISTRAL

Type: two-mast gaff-Marconi schooner
Designer: L. Francis Herreshoff, Design No. 73
Shipyard: Britt Brothers, West Lynn, Massachusetts
Year of Construction: 1938
Length (sparred): 82'
Length on Deck: 64'
Length on Waterline: 54'9"
Beam: 15'1"
Draft: 6'3" (7'1" after the restoration)
Displacement: 43 tons
Sail Area: 2,099 sq. ft.
Construction: Pitch pine on oak frames sheathed with three layers of sipo mahogany
Engine: Nanni diesel, 114 kW (155 hp)
Owner: Dieter Krügel
Home Port: Flensburg, Germany

Mistral: A Shoal Draft Schooner for Coastal Cruising

The big schooner *Mistral* was designed by L. Francis Herreshoff as a refined and somewhat modernized version of the smaller *Joann*. The hull is finer and more shapely, and the rig was modernized in that *Mistral* carried a main Marconi sail instead of a gaff. Even with the Marconi sail, she still had a traditional air about her, with her handsome clipper bow, topgallant rail, and exposed, curved rudder head. *Mistral's* design has inspired many sailors and designers, creating a "Herreshoff"-saga for beautiful cruising boats with clipper bow. Many boats have been built to the Lewis F. Herreshoff's plans, including quite a few to *Mistral's* design. Some were built in ferrocement in the 1970s, when this material became popular in the United States. Others were built using the cold-molding method, and yet others in fiberglass. They all enjoy the highest respect from their owners and other sailors for their seaworthiness and wonderful lines.

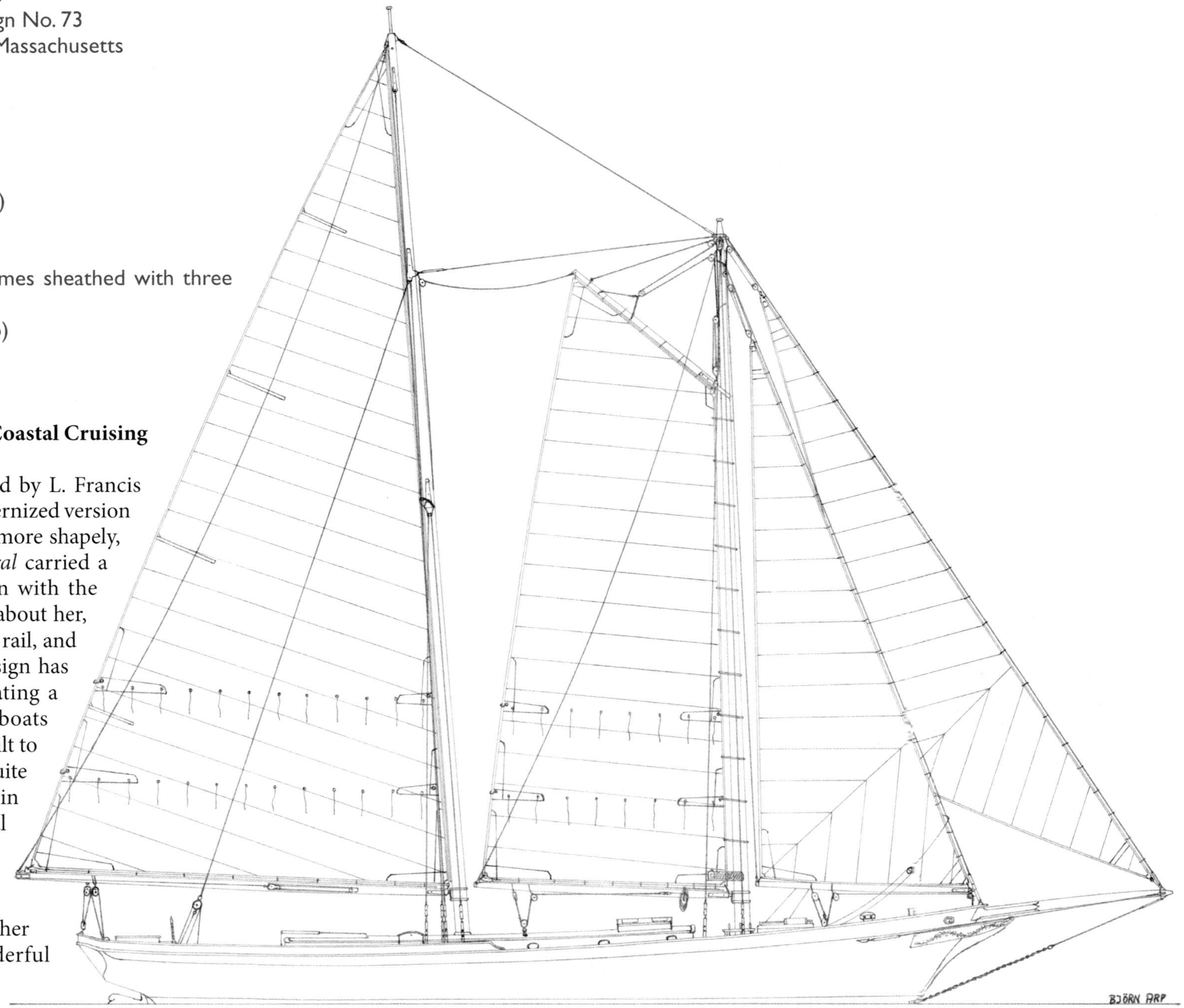

The schooner *Mistral* was built in 1938 at Britt Brothers in West Lynn, Massachusetts. The keel was cast of lead, and then the rest of the boat was built (*Dieter Krügel Archive*).

A close view of the inner side of her planking (*Dieter Krügel Archive*).

The frames are being put into place and the first planks are screwed and bolted to them (*Dieter Krügel Archive*).

The stern is planked. The yard worker continues with the starboard side planking (*Dieter Krügel Archive*).

Once the hull was finished, she was moved outside the boatshop to prepare for launching (*Dieter Krügel Archive*).

This view shows *Mistral* already in the water. There was still a lot of work to be done before she could start sailing. Note, for instance, that the mainmast spreaders still needed varnish (*Dieter Krügel Archive*).

Mistral stands ready to be launched, already with her spars laid on deck. The yard probably did not have the necessary crane to put the rig in, so she was going to be moved to another location for mast stepping (*Dieter Krügel Archive*).

The finished schooner at her mooring in West Lynn. She was ready for Theodore S. Little to take command of her (*Dieter Krügel Archive*).

Mistral's draft was kept moderate at 6'3" on a waterline length of 54' 9", with the result that the buttock lines are easy and sweeping throughout. In addition to the main Marconi sail, the foresail was designed to be self-tending, which all added maneuverability with a small crew, but it was also less efficient than the loose-footed, overlapping version that was common in other boats of the time.

Mistral's interior allowed for significant room due to a 15'1" beam. While there were many small compartments, her saloon was roomy and cheerful with its generous skylights. On the starboard side of the long cabin trunk was a companionway just abaft the mainmast. The accommodations were laid out to host eight persons, which seemed more than enough to handle her simple rig.

Her total sail area was 1,972 sq. ft. with 895 sq. ft. in the mainsail, 517 in the foresail, 260 in the forestaysail, and 300 in the jib. The shipyard entrusted with the construction of this schooner, under close scrutiny of her designer, was Britt Brothers, in West Lynn, on the Saugus River, Massachusetts, for Mr. Theodore S. Little. She was hull number 73.

Herreshoff personally machined much of her deck hardware, and it has remained intact over the years and has been scrupulously preserved. Her construction was of the best materials of the time, with bronze fasteners, teak, and mahogany.

Louise Burke: The First Woman to Captain a United States Government Vessel

Mistral has received the loving care of only five owners since her launching. One of these owners was the United States Naval Academy, where she was used as the flagship for carrying naval officers across the Atlantic for promotional campaigns. During her time as the flagship of the United States Naval Academy, she was the only American yacht that ever had communication with a German submarine, that was saluted by the Royal Navy, and that had the first woman, Louise Kevin Burke, in command of a United States Government ship.

Burke was the civilian captain of this schooner in the late seventies. Her actual job title was "operations and repair leader." A daughter of the New England coast, she had a nautical dream that had consumed her ever since her childhood. Born and brought up in Swampscott, Massachusetts, she vividly remembered *Mistral* riding at anchor in nearby Marblehead when the schooner was still privately owned. She told reporters that, "Every afternoon I'd grab some cookies and row out in my boat. It was a sure sign of autumn when *Mistral's* bowsprit hung out over the road behind Graves Yacht Yard."

A scuba diver and a pilot as well as a sailor, Louise Burke carried a restlessness wherever she went. After high school she got a job programming computers for General Electric, but the sea lured her away. Part of the lure included Les Burke, an aerospace researcher whom she married in 1962. The two together launched a seafaring career in the Caribbean as one of the first husband-and-wife crews in the charter trade.

But tragedy struck when Les died of a heart attack in 1972. As a reaction, Louise sailed about 15,000 miles the following winter. Anxious to keep busy, she moved from boat to boat, taking the jobs as they came: paid hand, race-crew member, bilge scrubber. Gradually the sea restored her, and in the process she became a superbly accomplished yachtswoman. In 1975, as navigator, she steered her first Atlantic crossing to deliver the 55' sloop *Dyna* from Marblehead to Sardinia.

It may have been coincidence, but on the day in November 1976 when Louise Burke reported for civilian duty at Annapolis, the battered *Mistral* first sailed into port. The schooner was desperately in need of attention. No one was more capable of giving it than Louise. Though the Navy reacted coolly to her application at first, she competed for the job and got it. Readying *Mistral* for an 8,000-mile round-trip voyage meant a thousand details were begging for her attention, and she only had a green crew of midshipmen to help her. Her mission on the month-long crossing was to train the nine middies (including Sandy Daniels, the only other woman on board) in all phases of seamanship, then join Queen Elizabeth's Silver Jubilee ship review on June 28, 1977. She fulfilled this task to the full satisfaction of the Naval Academy, and made history by being the first woman to command a United States Government ship. Only a very special person could dare to break the conventions and become an example for young women.

To Germany via San Francisco

After sailing for the Navy, *Mistral* was sold to private hands and she ended up in San Francisco. The German racing sailor, Dieter Krügel, discovered *Mistral* in

After many years of sailing, *Mistral* appears in San Francisco harbor in this seemingly beautiful fashion. However, she only looked so good thanks to a lot of paint, which held the aging planks together. Once her current owner, Dieter Krügel, took ownership of her, he realized that there was not much to save on her (*Dieter Krügel Archive*).

Dieter Krügel sailed her carefully from San Francisco to Newfoundland, where he planned to do a thorough restoration (*Dieter Krügel Archive*).

In Lunenburg, *Mistral* was put into a shed and completely dismantled to access all the rotten wood, which then was meticulously reconstructed and put back together (*Dieter Krügel Archive*).

After several years of continuous work, the restoration is complete and *Mistral* gets back into the water. She looked like she did when she was newly built in 1938 (*Dieter Krügel Archive*).

November 1995 through an advertisement for the Florida-based Ardell Yachtbrokers. He only had to see the elegant lines, low freeboard, and impressive sail area to make a decision about getting involved with this vessel. An entirely new chapter in his sailing life had begun.

Krügel's new-found love with *Mistral's* captivating lines was aglow. However, after the delivery from Newport Beach, California, to Fort Myers in Florida, the show was over: Frightful discoveries brought the happy owner plummeting back down to earth from his heavenly euphoria. After this relatively short trip through the Panama Canal, the schooner showed her true face: many rotten areas of the hull and superstructure had astutely been masked by a coat of white paint to spruce her up for sale. The situation became so extreme that in Cape Coral the bilge pumps failed and water filled the hull to the floorboards. It seemed that the surveyor Dieter Krügel had hired in California had been blind. Obviously, in this condition he could not undertake the Atlantic crossing to Europe, as he had planned. An alternative for going forward had to be found. The search for a suitable shipyard on the East Coast brought him up to Nova Scotia, where there were still some experienced woodworkers who could deal with the work *Mistral* needed so urgently. He very provisionally stuffed all the leaks on *Mistral* and brought her up to Lunenburg, leaving Florida in the middle of the hurricane season, in July 1996. The permanent wind warnings caused many stopovers during this trip, which otherwise proved to be without mayor incidents.

Once in Lunenburg, *Mistral* was brought ashore and Dennis Greenwood was named project manager on the spot, while owner Krügel commuted between Germany and Nova Scotia. They started by building a specific shed for housing *Mistral*—it was later to be called "the Cathedral," due to its church-like architecture.

At that point the extensive assessment of the work to be done was made. Everything indicated that the schooner would have a long stay in Canada. One surprise after another was found in a boat that was essentially a total restoration-project. Two keel bolts were heavily affected by electrolysis, and what initially were four rotten frames

Mistral has been sailing the Atlantic Ocean again since 1999. She has taken part in the Newfoundland schooner races as well as the Antigua Classic Yacht races (*Dieter Krügel Archive*).

Mistral holds pace with other classic schooners in a race off Antigua in 2002 (*Dieter Krügel Archive*).

gradually amounted to 26 broken ribs. It was a different story from the flashy color brochures Krügel had received from Newport Beach only one year earlier.

As work progressed, a new sternpost was installed, and the propeller shaft was installed amidships, instead of to one side of the centerline, which makes maneuvering the vessel a tough job. Frames had been replaced or older laminations renewed, deck beams had been fixed or reinforced, new planks installed, and the forward cabin house was completely rebuilt.

On the aft end of the boat, new cockpit lockers were installed, additional stowage space and four new cockpit drains were added. In addition, a new seat for the helmsman was built. Down below, the work on the keel timber was still in progress. By August 1998, the largely redone interior was installed. The original bronze fittings were reused, but many had to be newly made.

While putting the interior together, the builders observed that the original Herreshoff drawings did not provide for a load-bearing bulkhead located in the area of the main mast and cap shroud chain plates. For this reason, as a precautionary measure, the suspected structural weakness was counteracted by building beautiful bronze hanging knees into the cabin structure.

After a three-year restoration, it was time to launch her again. From 1999 onwards, *Mistral* has taken part successfully in the Nova Scotia Schooner races. However, despite this extensive restoration, under racing conditions, significant weaknesses of Herreshoff's light construction became apparent. On a windward course the cap shroud chain plates compressed the hull with such a force that it lifted the deck and superstructure. Below deck, cracks up to one inch wide appeared in the upper corners of the bulkhead. Attempts were made to remedy the hull weakness with bronze rod as bracing in the main mast area, and between the masts from the deck to the keel, additional deck beams and stringers around the superstructure and six more bronze knees.

Thus equipped and reinforced, *Mistral* set off from Newport, Rhode Island, in June 2003 on the Daimler-Chrysler North Atlantic Challenge, which unfortunately ended abruptly for the swift schooner, when in the middle of the Atlantic, 1,000 miles from Ireland, she broke her rudder. After a four-week stay in Kilrush, she finally set sail again for Flensburg, *Mistral's* home port in northern Germany.

The Second Restoration

Since the Baltic Spring Cup in 2004, when the old hull weaknesses became noticeable again, Krügel had to look again for a boatyard. He decided this time to work with one of Germany's foremost wooden boatyards, Yacht und Bootswerf Matthias Paulsen, located in the little village of Arnis on the river Schlei.

So, in November 2006, *Mistral* was standing stripped down to bare wood in a historic boatbuilding shed behind stacks of sawn sipo mahogany logs, from which later her new "corset" would be glued up, and from which new deck beams, covering board, and an additional exterior skin would take shape.

With her green hull, *Mistral* is not to be overlooked (*Dieter Krügel*).

In order to reconstruct the ailing deck, which had gained additional layers at almost every previous restoration, the shipyard machined away layer after layer and afterwards chiseled off the residue.

As there are no main bulkheads where the main-mast passes through the middle of the saloon, the only solution for absorbing the pressures of the rig were strong ring-frames, which naval architect Dieter Sharping calculated and constructed according to the classification societies' specifications. They were glued up in the form of a ring from 28 layers of 5-mm-thick sipo mahogany veneers. For installation, however, the frames must be scarfed and dismantled in order to be able to fit them below deck. The ring frames not only serve to strengthen the hull; each chainplate is bolted to these frames to take the strength of the rig. The new frames completely encircle the hull above the keel and under the engine bed. At the same time, a new Nanni engine was installed.

In addition, Sharping recommended reinforcing the hull with two diagonal layers of 6 mm and a longitudinal layer of 10-mm-thick sipo mahogany. This was later glued over *Mistral's* hull, which had previously been sanded and dried out; also, the caulked seams were replaced by wooden splines.

And again some "surprises" were found on the way through this second restoration. In order to remove the partially rotten covering board, it had to be sawn away. This subsequently revealed that some built-in frames underneath had delaminated at the top. Thus another repair was needed.

The boat also got a new teak deck, which was glued onto a new bed of thick plywood, which was meant to add strength to the deck.

Regarding the reinforcement of the planking, the seams of the planed and sanded long leaf yellow pine hull were first splined with similar resin-rich Siberian larch. Over this the first diagonal layer of 6-mm-thick sipo mahogany veneers were epoxied, which were stapled in place using hundreds of small pressure blocks. After the resin had cured, and before the hull was sanded in preparation for the next layer, all the blocks had to be knocked off again and the staples removed one by one—a Sisyphean task in which the owner himself, Dieter Krügel, actively assisted. With this procedure, layer after layer was applied, using literally thousands of small blocks and staples to hold the laminate in place for curing. An additional lead ballast keel was casted and bolted onto the already existent one, to lower the center of gravity and increase the surface area of the keel. In addition, the lead keel protects a mahogany "fender" keel. The entire keel area then was encapsulated into the mahogany laminate.

After a final sanding of the additional outer skin, the keel was reinforced by four layers of fiberglass before the entire hull got a two-layer fiberglass sheathing saturated with epoxy resin.

On May 22, 2008, the time had finally come for the new launch! *Mistral* left the boat shed where she had been undergoing the restoration for almost two years. On this fourth launching, on her 70th birthday, she was in far better condition than on her first in 1938 in West Lynn, Massachusetts. In *Mistral*, Herreshoff's ingenuity was now matched with German boatbuilding quality.

Mistral is the most famous schooner designed by Francis Herreshoff. A true sailing legend, which has profoundly marked the design and building of yachts in the twentieth century (*Katrin Storsberg*).

In June 2008, the final trim pieces for the interior were installed. The navigation station by the companionway was equipped with state-of-the-art yacht electronics. A NAV-net® electronic chart plotter with radar overlay was networked with a laptop over which, via satellite data, one can superimpose wind and weather information onto the electronic charts. In the saloon the new ring-frames create a sense of security. In the saloon there is also a Refleks oil stove to ensure comfort and warmth in northern latitudes. All the new interior was crafted in light cherry wood. Heads and cabins retain their simple traditional Herreshoff style. The light-colored furniture is accentuated by natural varnished trim.

Mistral now features nine berths in four cabins. There is a forepeak, next aft the very nice fore cabin with two berths up/down, writing desk, and companionway up on deck. Then there is a door to a passage cabin with two berths up/down. Another door leads to a passage with head/shower to port and an owners' double cabin with head/shower en-suite to starboard. The saloon has settees to port and kitchen to starboard. Aft is a quarter berth to starboard, nav-station amidships, an additional double cabin aft port and forward of that a head/shower as walkthrough to the engine compartment.

With this great cruising schooner, Dieter Krügel left Flensburg on June 20, 2008 on a several-year journey, which included regattas from Kiel to France and Monaco, up to Canada.

C. Sherman Hoyt: A Seaman and Yacht Designer

BIOGRAPHY OF C. SHERMAN HOYT

Charles Sherman Hoyt was born in Ohio as the son of a wealthy and established family. When the Hoyt family moved to the Hudson River Valley, they began summering at Oyster Bay, Long Island, where Hoyt learned to sail at an early age, achieving considerable proficiency as a helmsman and competitor during his youth and college days. He became a member of the Phi Beta Kappa association, and in 1901, he graduated from Brown University in Providence, Rhode Island, with the determination to become a naval architect.

After some early positions in shipbuilding and drafting, Hoyt enrolled and completed the naval architecture course at the University of Glasgow, Scotland, under Professor John Harvard Biles, the only available degree course in naval architecture in the world at the time. Here he began to make friendships and contacts that were to last throughout his entire life while working at the famed John Brown Shipyard at Clydebank and at Denny's in Dumbarton.

Hoyt returned to the United States at age twenty-six, and formed the company Hoyt and Clark with his longtime friend Montgomery Clark. After the split up of this company only a few years later, Hoyt obtained an engineering position with the Panama Canal Commission and then worked with Bethlehem Steel Company at their Wilmington, Delaware, factory. Following that, Hoyt became affiliated with the firm of Gielow and Orr, and when Alex Orr retired, he became a partner in the newly formed Henry J. Gielow, Inc. Besides his 6-meter designs—*Saleems*, *Lea*, *Pauponok*, and the Q-Class *Capsicum*—Hoyt's best-known design is the 60' schooner *Mistress* and the 45' schooner *Reveler*, both designed and built in 1930. Both schooners are further described in this chapter.

In addition to his career as designer, he was also a very able helmsman on racing yachts. He played an outstanding role in some America's Cup races. In the third race of the 1934 challenge, for example, *Rainbow* was down by two races and behind in the third when Hoyt took the helm. This was the closest that the New York Yacht Club had come to loosing its treasured cup until 1983. Hoyt was known for taking the helm in light weather because of his uncanny ability to note slight wind changes, and this time was no exception. He outfoxed T.O.M. Sopwith, pointing well above the course finish and forcing Sopwith to make a covering attempt. *Rainbow* sailed a straight course to the line while *Endeavour* fumbled. The Cup was safe as the tide of the challenge was turned by Hoyt's matchless genius at the helm and Harold Vanderbilt's ability to utilize the various talents of his crew to the best effect.

This was certainly not Hoyt's first experience with the America's Cup. A Cup enthusiast since childhood, he served as the New York Yacht Club representative aboard *Shamrock IV* in 1920. Of this experience, he later said that "conditioning an America's Cup yacht is no sinecure. It requires no end of hard work, but it is absorbingly interesting, frequently amusing, and never dull."

Hoyt served on the afterguard of *Enterprise* in 1930, and *Rainbow* in 1934, and would later broadcast the *Ranger–Endeavour II* series of 1937 for CBS. This he found trying, as there was sparse action except at starts and rounding marks. There was little question, however, of *Ranger's* superiority.

After an extraordinary life that took him around the world in adventures and voyages, Hoyt died in 1961.

MISTRESS

(Ex- Commodore; Ex- Mistress)

Type: two-mast gaff-Marconi schooner
Designer: Sherman C. Hoyt
Year of Construction: 1930
Shipyard: Eastern Shipbuilding, Shelburne, Nova Scotia
Length Over All: 74'6"
Length on Deck: 60'
Length on Waterline: 50'
Beam: 15'8"
Maximum Draft: 9'6"
Displacement: 41 tons
Height of Main Mast above Waterline: 75'
Sail Area: 2,000 sq. ft.
Engine: 90-hp Ford Lehman diese
Owner: Chris and Glenn McCormick
Home Port: Baltimore, Maryland

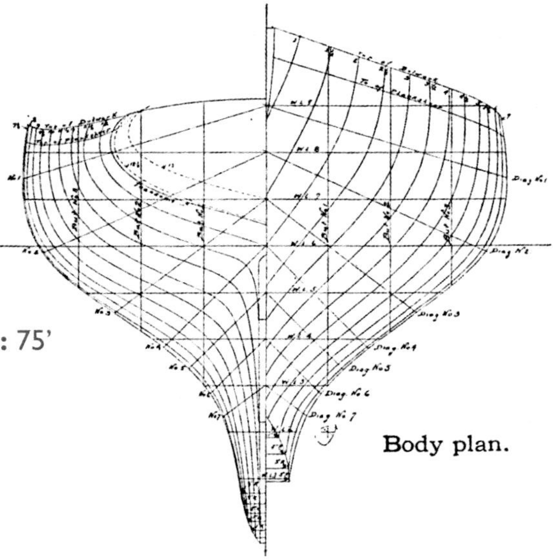

Body plan.

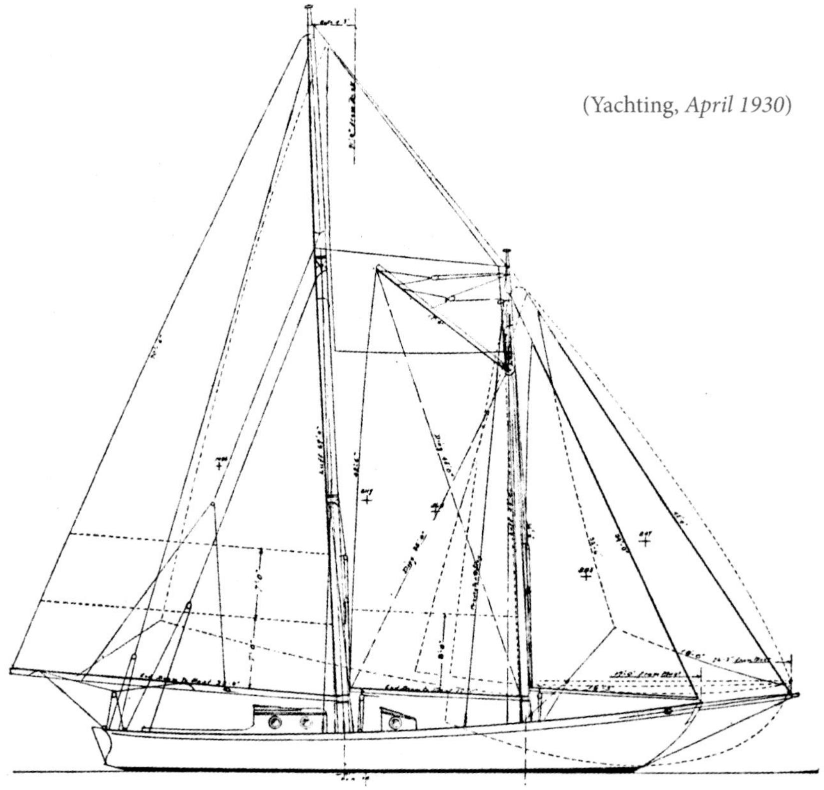

(Yachting, *April 1930*)

***Mistress*: An Unusual Schooner**

The schooner *Mistress* was built as a two-mast gaff-Marconi schooner in 1930 at Eastern Shipbuilding in Shelburne, Nova Scotia. The first owner was George Roosevelt of Oyster Bay, New York. He was the nephew of Theodore "Teddy" Roosevelt, President of the United States between 1901 and 1909.

She had a very different design than that of cruising schooners of her time, especially because of her "chopped-off" stern. This type of stern was undoubtedly due to the influence of the Bermuda Race Rule, under which Sherman Hoyt had designed her. She featured a flush deck with high freeboard, generous beam, moderate sheer, and very short ends. The sections were firm, yet easy, and the fore and aft lines were unusually sweet for a boat with the considerable beam she had.

Quickly, the spectator starts drawing comparisons with the design of Burgess' *Niña*, which had been built only two years before. *Mistress* had some differences to this design, in particular the fact that her lines seemed somewhat easier on the buttock lines. This was done to improve her in running and reaching, which were points where *Niña* was not so good.

The schooner rig featured a jib-headed mainsail and gaff foresail. The forestaysail and foresail are both relatively large, which gives a fine hard weather rig, and which would allow a cloud of light canvas to be set in the area forward of the mainmast.

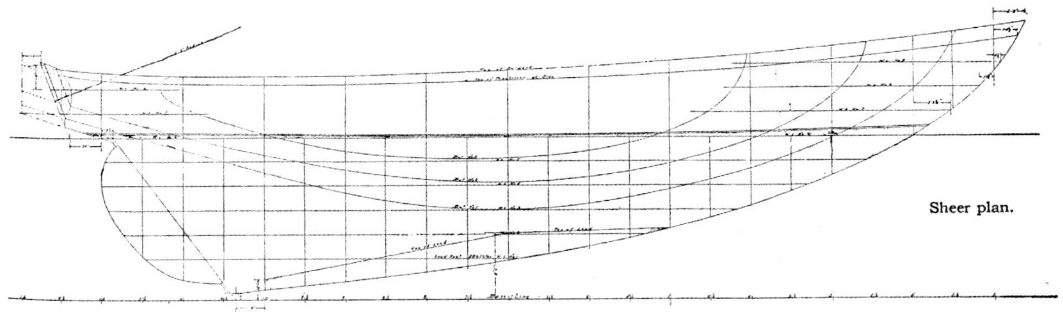

Sheer plan.

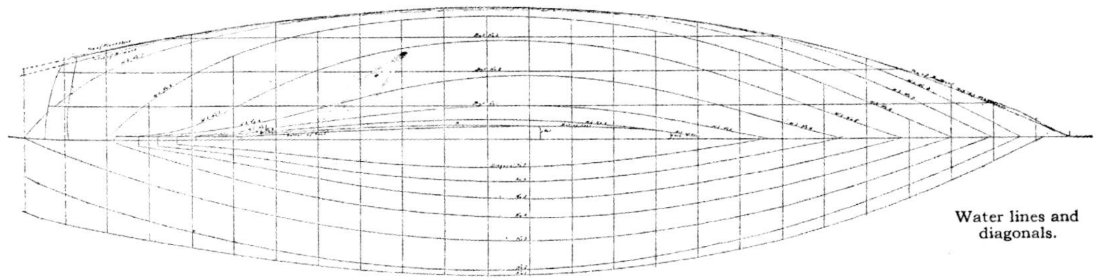

Water lines and diagonals.

Mistress' Early History

After her launch in Nova Scotia, she was immediately entered for the Sarah's Ledge race on June 22, 1930. Roosevelt competed her in many races after that. He sailed her in the 1932 Transatlantic Race to Plymouth and the Fastnet Race, the 1934 Transatlantic Race to Bergen, Norway, and numerous offshore races on the United States' East Coast. During one of the Bermuda Races, *Mistress* was the first private yacht to use a radar reflector to help prevent collision at sea.

Roosevelt loved his yacht and kept *Mistress* for more than thirty years. In the early sixties he sold or donated her to be used as a sail-training vessel at the New York Maritime Academy. The academy installed the first engine in *Mistress*. They also changed the name to *Commodore* (as George Roosevelt was known). In 1974, she was bought by four partners who used her as a charter vessel in St. Thomas, United States Virgin Islands. After a few seasons of chartering, she was again sold to someone who took her to the West Coast and Hawaii, apparently to take part in the TransPac Race. From there she came into the hands of a couple who sailed her around California and Mexico, returning her afterwards to the East Coast. That is where, in February 1987, her current owners bought her, the Brothers McCormick, Chris and Glenn. They were determined to rebuild her, as the frames were rotten and the fasteners nothing but needles.

Mistress' Restoration and Current Use

Once Chris and Glenn McCormick purchased *Mistress* in February 1987, the search for a suitable shipyard to do the restoration of the hull began. They finally decided to haul her out at the White Rocks boatyard in Annapolis, where she was totally gutted to gain access to the rotten frames. During the following nine months, most of the steam-bent frames were removed and new laminated frames constructed in place. In addition, new garboard planks, chainplates, and the planks around the chainplates were all replaced. Upon launching in August 1988, the brothers sailed her through the Chesapeake and then embarked on a passage to Key West. At that point she did not yet have any interior structure. Although it was not a wise decision to sail *Mistress* offshore without the proper

The schooner *Mistress* is still sailing as actively as when George Roosevelt owned her. She can be seen here sailing in the Caribbean, where she usually spends the winters (*Glen McCormick*).

The McCormick brothers lovingly care for her, and thus take her out of the water ever year to clean and repair the bottom. In this occasion, in 2009, they also had the mainmast out for major repairs (*Glen McCormick*).

The interior was redesigned anew in the late 1980s. Different woods have been used to create a welcoming atmosphere (*Glen McCormick*).

interior structure in place, which would reinforce the hull, they arrived safely in Key West in January 1989.

For the next 10 years, work slowly progressed on rebuilding the interior from paycheck to paycheck. Jimmy Wray, of Key West Woodworks, was the inspiration and artist for most of the design and construction effort below decks.

Even though they had repaired the hull to a great degree, she still wept uncomfortably when the seas were active. This led to the suggestion to cold-mold the hull, which was revisited several times and agreed upon. Such a decision would have far-reaching consequences for the boat, with negative and positive effects. The positive would be to make the hull tighter and more durable, while the downside would be that it would become almost impossible to replace rotten planks or even frames, not to mention the keel.

Once the decision for the cold-molding was taken, another 54 weeks were spent in the yard giving *Mistress* a new skin of two layers of 1/4" cedar laminate and many gallons of epoxy.

Since then, *Mistress* has sailed up and down the East Coast several times, from Key West to Maine. She participated in the Newport to Bermuda Race in 1998 (after a 40-year hiatus), the Tall Ship Operation Sail 2000, several Great Chesapeake Bay Schooner Races, and the Classic Yacht Regatta in Antigua (2003, 2004, and 2008).

During the summers she can be found in Baltimore, Maryland, where she is available for daysail charters or overnight excursions.

The berths in an artfully built cabin (*Glen McCormick*).

The schooner *Mistress* off Tide Point in Baltimore, Maryland, where she has her home port (*Glen McCormick*).

Mistress competing in the Antigua Classic Yacht Regatta. In the background, Dykstra schooner *Borkumriff IV* (*Glen McCormick*).

Mistress sailing in company with the traditional ketch *Iris* in a light breeze (*Glen McCormick*).

Another view of *Mistress* during the Antigua Classic Yacht Regatta (*Glen McCormick*).

Mistress on port tack sprinting through the Chesapeake Bay, her home waters (*Glen McCormick*).

When *Mistress* does not sail down to the Caribbean, she stays in the water in Baltimore harbor. There she rests, sometimes covered with snow, patiently waiting for the new season (*Glen McCormick*).

Mistress features the typical brass binnacle and teak wheel (*Glen McCormick*).

The schooner sails in the Caribbean in 1988. Note that at that time she did not have a gaff. Instead, the gaff sail was held to the mainmast with the vang (*Glen McCormick*).

Mistress' stern is cut away. It is still an impressive sight, and is reminiscent of the stern on *Niña*. *Mistress'* spreaders on the mainmast are extremely wide. They are indeed wider than the hull's beam. This was done to improve the stability of the rig (*Glen McCormick*).

REVELER

Rig: two-mast gaff-Marconi schooner
Designer: Sherman C. Hoyt & S&S
Year of Construction: 1930
Shipyard: Dauntless Shipyard, Essex, Connecticut
Length Over All: 45'
Beam: 11'6"
Maximum Draft: 7'8"
Displacement: 13 tons
Engine: Westerbeke 4-107, 40 hp
Cruising Speed: 6 mph
Owner: Karl Anderson
Home Port: Harwich, Massachusetts

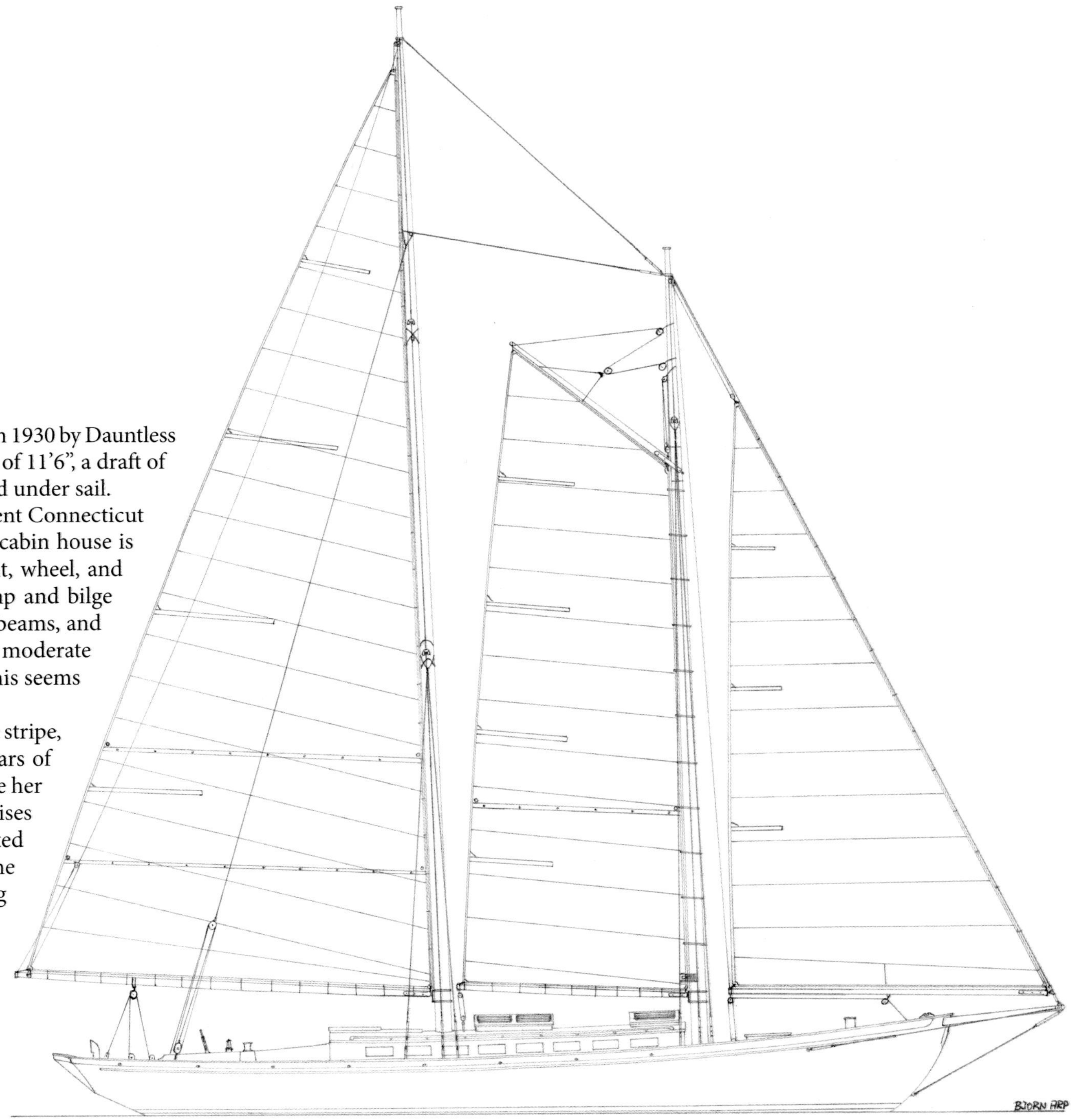

Reveler: A Fine Little Racing Schooner

Reveler was originally designed by Sherman Hoyt and built in 1930 by Dauntless shipyard in Essex, Connecticut. She is 45' on deck, has a beam of 11'6", a draft of 8'7", a displacement of 13 tons, and can reach 10 knots of speed under sail.

The vessel is Honduras mahogany planked on 84 steam-bent Connecticut white oak frames. She has a solid teak deck and toe rail. The cabin house is in Honduras mahogany, as are the hatches, coamings, cockpit, wheel, and compass pillar. She features long leaf yellow pine shelf, clamp and bilge stringers, white oak butt blocks, futtocks, floor timbers, deck beams, and ash interior cabin house beams. With 13 tons, she has only a moderate displacement for her length, with 4.53 tons external ballast. This seems to make for a fast hull.

Reveler's hull has always been colored black, with a gold cove stripe, a white boot stripe and green bottom. In 1990, after sixty years of hard sailing, Timothy Strange rebuilt the boat entirely, and gave her many years more to sail. Then, she took off for long-distance cruises from Newfoundland to Key West and the Islands. She participated in tall ship parades in Hyannis and was two-time winner of the Wickers race in Key West. The schooner was also used for filming a TV commercial on Little Palm Island in 1998. At one point in her history, she belonged to an owner who used her to bring oysters up north from the Chesapeake to Massachusetts.

Reveler splashing through the Caribbean in the 1990s. She belonged then to Timothy Strange, who used her for filming a TV commercial on Little Palm Island (*Karl Anderson*).

A Terrible Ferry Accident

Reveler has also suffered many accidents. She was sunk twice at her mooring when hurricanes hit her, and once she was dismasted at high sea. But fortunately she has always come back, in many ways better than before.

However, an almost definitive end for her was very close when she fell victim to a disastrous accident in 1997; she was sunk by a ferry at the entrance to the harbor of Hyannis, Massachusetts.

Reveler was sitting on a sandbar in front of the harbor, where she had been put inadvertently by her captain. They tried to set back under engine, but without avail. While from afar the ferryboat *Nantucket* approached, she suddenly wrenched in a strange arc off the bar. *Reveler's* propeller is offset to port, which makes her difficult to maneuver in reverse. So as she looped into the channel, the captain realized that nothing could prevent the collision any more, and thus told everyone to jump overboard.

As *Nantucket* closed in on *Reveler*, the captain ordered a crewmember forward to fend off. That crewmember managed to scamper up the foremast as *Reveler* was ground under and leapt from there onto the bow of the ferry, through the open car doors. Luckily, the captain and the two remaining crewmembers in the cockpit took to the water unhurt.

Reveler was refloated and the owner spent some years rebuilding her. After the rebuild, he took off to Florida with the schooner. Finally, the schooner came back to Massachusetts and is now in Cape Cod.

***Reveler* Today**

The schooner belongs now to Karl's Boat Shop in Cape Cod, where she has undergone a thorough maintenance schedule since 2004. New sails and diesel engine were installed in 2009. The schooner features all safety equipment required by the Coast Guard.

Despite being a racing schooner, the interior is relatively comfortable. There are two single berths and two double berths. The boat further features a complete bathroom with shower, a galley with sink, oven with two burners, and an icebox. Ventilation is provided through five hatches and slides with one opening port and three ventilators. Tank capacity is 60 gallons for fuel and another 60 gallons for fresh water.

The rig consists of a Marconi main sail and gaff foresail. The boat has approximately fifteen sails; in addition to the standard set of working sails, she carries a fisherman, a reacher and a spinnaker. The masts are Sitka spruce; the foremast is 45' above waterline and built of solid wood, while the main mast is 56' above the waterline and hollow round with the bottom 8' solid. The mainmast is stayed with running backstays.

When *Reveler* came out of restoration and rebuild as a consequence of a ferry accident, she was stronger and more impressive than ever (*Karl Anderson*).

Reveler under sail is a sight to be seen. Although she is a little schooner with only 45' on deck, she performs like a large yacht, and can carry a considerable crew on a sail. For racing, she needs such a crew to get the most out of her (*Karl Anderson*).

Walter J. McInnis: The Rugged Beauty of Traditional Crafts

BIOGRAPHY OF WALTER J. MCINNIS

Walter J. McInnis was born in 1893. Already at a young age he started his professional career as an apprentice with the famous commercial schooner designer and builder Thomas F. McManus. Spending only a short time there, he soon moved to the George Lawley & Son shipyard in Neponset, Massachusetts, where he worked as a draftsman in the design office for twelve years. After leaving in 1924 to manage the Frederick S. Nock yard in East Greenwich, Rhode Island, and to head the design office there, McInnis was offered to rejoin the Lawley yard as chief naval architect and assistant general manager in 1925. Only a year later, Albert E. Eldredge, vice president and general manager of Lawley's, and Walter J. McInnis formed their own firm of Eldredge-McInnis, Inc. in Boston, Massachusetts. While not a designer, Eldredge had worked at the Gas Engine & Power Co. and Charles L. Seabury & Co., Consolidated, managed the Milton Point Shipyard in Rye, New York, and worked with the United States Navy in World War I. He brought many years of experience in sales, promotion, marketing, and financial expertise to the partnership, leaving the design work to Walter J. McInnis. Some of the most influential contracts the new firm attracted were with American Car & Foundry Company and Richardson Boat Company, Inc., designing lines of stock cruisers. Hundreds of these cruisers were built for the newly affluent American market. Continuing in this line, the Eastward, Eastward Junior, Eastward Ho, and Eastward Ho Senior classes were popular for their ease of handling and maintenance and their ability to be easily driven under sail or power.

Eldredge-McInnis was also closely associated with the United States government, designing Coast Guard patrol vessels. During World War II, the firm had so much business that they joined forces with the John G. Alden Co. for five years and did $3 billion worth of work for the war effort, including tugs, salvage ships, minesweepers, and small transports. The company also built commercial fishing vessels, especially for Canadian owners. Although Albert E. Eldredge died in 1936, Walter J. McInnis maintained the firm and continued a very active design practice until his retirement in 1976, at age 83. He died nine years later, in 1985.

MISTRESS

(Ex- *Kiddie III;* Ex- *Lark;* Ex- *Janet;* Ex- *Happy Holiday)*

Type: knockabout gaff-Marconi schooner, converted into staysail schooner
Designer: Eldridge-McInnis, Design No. 138
Shipyard: T. H. Soule of South Freeport, Maine
Year of Construction: 1930
Length (sparred): 58'
Length on Deck: 47'6", lengthened to 50'
Length on Waterline: 34'6"
Beam: 11'8"
Draft: 6'8"
Construction: Oregon fir on white oak
Engine: 56-hp Yanmar diesel
Owner: F.W. "Skip" and Kathleen Joest
Home Port: St. Augustine, Florida

The Eastward Schooners

The first Eastward schooner was built in 1928 for the private use of Walter J. McInnis, its designer. The yacht proved so comfortable, so fast and seaworthy that one of the foremost yachting authorities, Sandy Moffat (who later on also commissioned the schooner *Mahdee*) decided that he wanted to have a sister ship built. Also, the specialized press of the time was very favorable about this boat. In an November 1928 article in *The Rudder*, the editors wrote, "Eastward is one of the finest small schooners of the year. Able, fast and seaworthy she is eligible to be ranked with the best." The Eastward schooner attracted so much attention that other yachtsmen requested boats of this same class—as a result there were built six Eastward schooners. The first Eastward schooners had a deck length of 45', with a short stern. However, in subsequent boats that were built, the total length was enlarged to 47'6", probably to give easier access to the full length of the main boom.

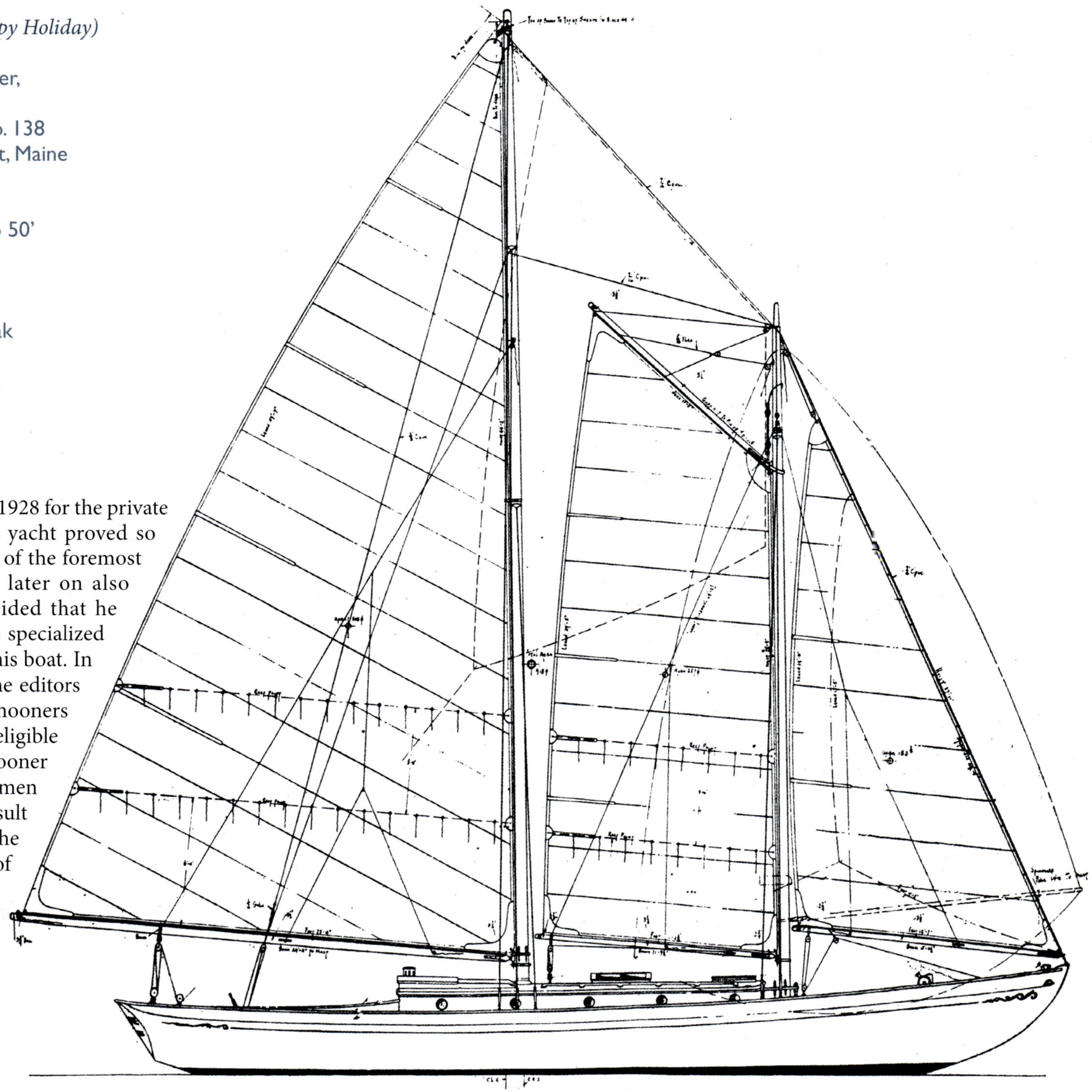

(The Rudder, *November 1928*)

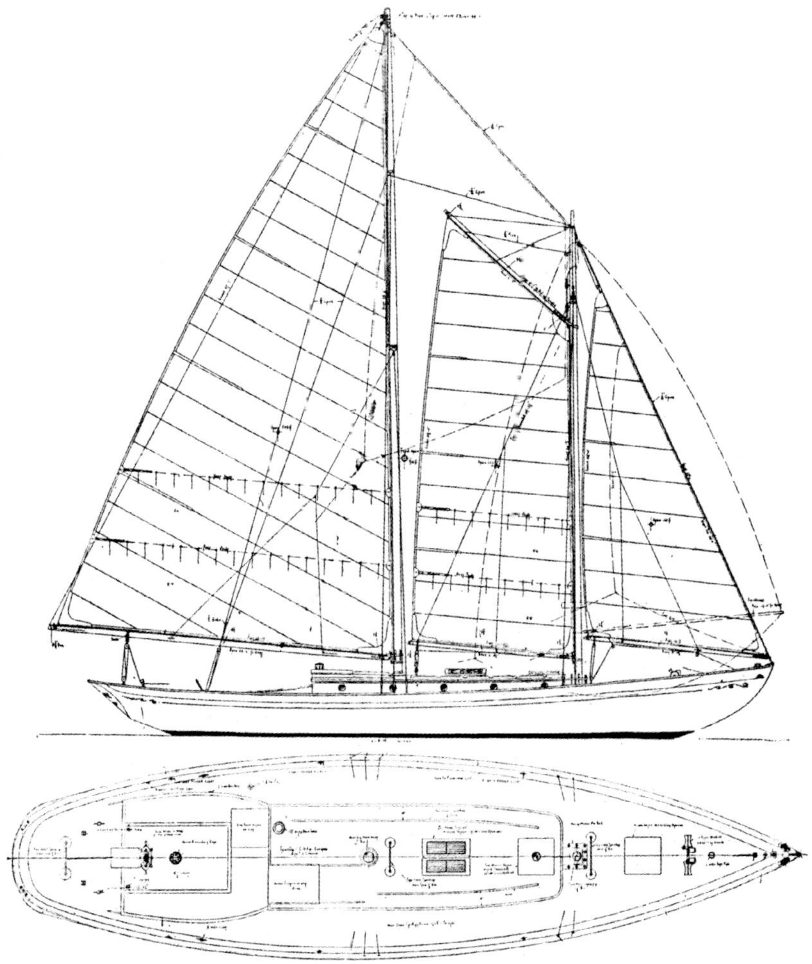

(The Rudder, *November 1928*)

This for sale ad published in *The Rudder* shows *Mistress* when she was new. Note the large Genoa and fisherman sail (The Rudder, *March 1931*).

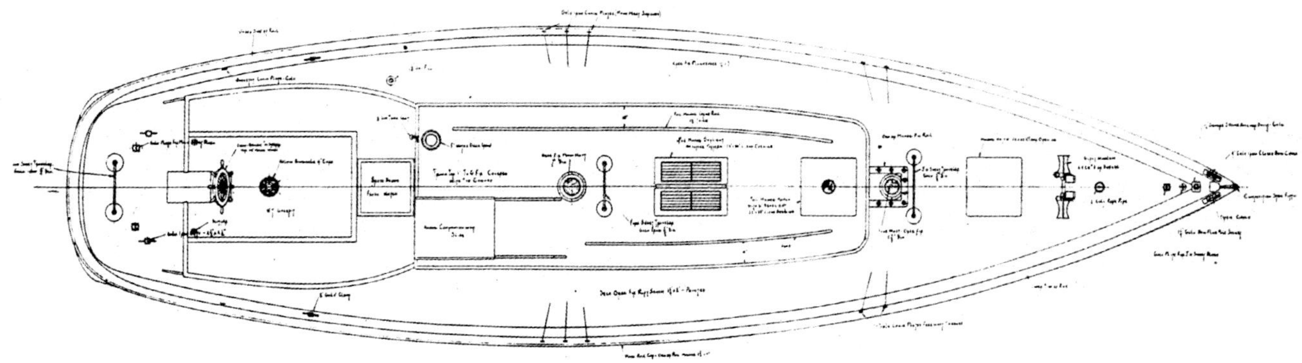

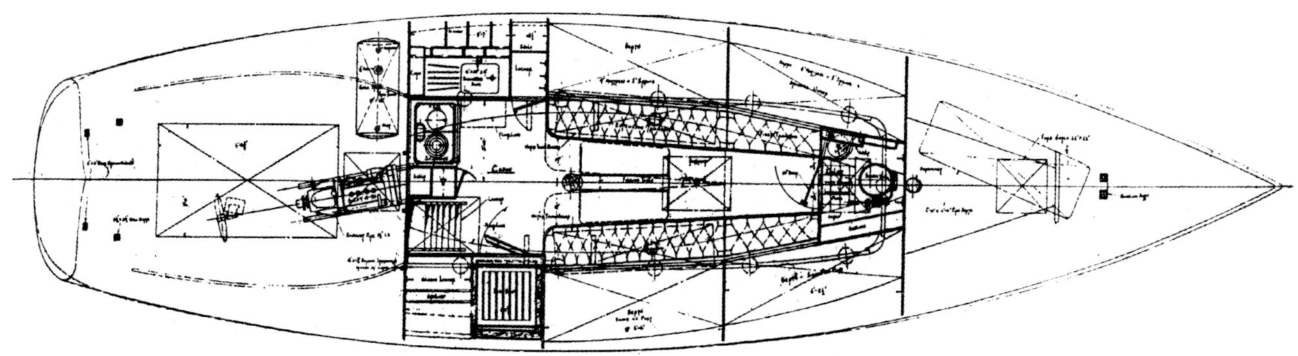

This is the later sail and deck plan of the Eastward schooner, slightly longer in the stern.

Mistress sailing in 1998 in Milwaukee, before her owner died and she was put up for sale. This photo clearly shows her extended stern which was repaired after her engine exploded (*Kathleen Joest Archive*).

Today there still exist, to our knowledge, the Eastward schooners *Ishmael* (Eastward schooner #2), *Wild Goose* (Eastward schooner #4), and *Mistress* (Eastward schooner #6). Furthermore, there are also the original Eastward schooners *Cross Wind* and *Tonga*, but we do not know exactly which numbers they are. These two schooners are sheathed with fiberglass and/or cold molding. It is known that Eastward schooner #3 was lost off the coast of California.

Over the years, several more boats were built to this design, a sign of the success of the Eastward schooner. One noteworthy construction was the *Nyad*, which was built by the Stockwell yard in Detroit in 1948 or 1949, although during construction she was converted to a cutter rig. The yacht had several names; after *Nyad* she was named *Sailbad the Sinner*, *Bonnehomme Richard* (hailing from Cleveland, Ohio), and ultimately, *Prowess*. She sails now in New England waters. As recently as 1991, a well-crafted replica of the Eastward schooner was built, the *Elizabeth Muir*, which is today in pristine condition sailing out of San Francisco.

The Eastward's Design and Construction

The Eastward schooner is equally adapted for racing, coastwise or Southern cruising. It was built to last, with good materials and strong wood.

Up to six people can cruise comfortably in an Eastward schooner. The wide, roomy berths provide good sleeping quarters, and a bulkhead between cabin and engine-room prevents any possibility of fumes and reduces fire hazard, assuring a fresh airy cabin at all times. Separate accommodations and sleeping quarters for one paid hand are located forward. The design provided for a stove, ice-box, sink, and table, all conveniently located in the long cabin.

Although the schooners are more than 47' on deck, and there is over 900 sq. ft. of sail area, two people can easily handle all the miscellaneous work necessary to get her going. As this model is of the knockabout type, the rig is simplicity itself. Under foresail the Eastward takes care of itself indefinitely while the crew eats or sleeps; and underway one hand on the wheel and a maximum of two spokes is all the steering she needs. The design also provided for as few fancy trimmings as possible to assure low maintenance costs.

A powerful marine-type four-cylinder Gray gasoline motor, especially adapted for this type of craft, was installed in the engine room, located under the bridge and cockpit. The engine was capable of maintaining a speed of 7 knots in average weather, by driving a two-blade feathering propeller through a bronze shaft. It was equipped with electric starter and generator, and the controls were located on deck near the wheel box. A copper fuel tank holding 45 gallons of gasoline was installed under the bridge deck.

Eastward schooners were built under the designer's personal direction. The best materials were used to make this craft unusually staunch. Each boat was carefully inspected during construction and after the launch it was put through a series of rigid tests before delivery to the owner.

Mistress: An Original Eastward Schooner

Mistress is an Eldridge-McInnis designed Eastward schooner built in 1930 by T. H. Soule of South Freeport, Maine. Her original name was *Happy Holiday* and she was design number 138, being the sixth and last hull built to this design. She went through several owners her first 15 years and had different names. Thus *Happy Holiday* became *Janet*, *Lark*, and then *Kiddie III*. Her last change of name was into *Mistress*, the name she still bears today.

This was the schooner's hull when Skip started to take out the first rotten planks (*Kathleen Joest Archive*).

This photo shows *Mistress* once the refit was finished (*Kathleen Joest*).

Mistress' interior is being gutted (*Kathleen Joest*).

New frames and buttblocks are being installed (*Kathleen Joest*).

It is believed that she spent the first ten years in New England. It was also rumored that during probation times, she was owned by two brothers who used her for rum running. Although this story has not been confirmed, since she was very fast, this might be possible.

The boat was later transferred to the Great Lakes. *The Chicago Tribune* mentions her in several articles with reference to racing in the 1940s and 1950s. Sometime in the late 1950s to early 1960s she was returning from a race and had a gas engine explosion. This blew off her aft end from the engine hatch back. When she was rebuilt, they extended her three feet. In the early 1960s she arrived in Milwaukee, where she was based at the South Shore Yacht Club.

The owner at the time sailed her until his death. He willed the boat to a sixteen-year old boy, who would grow up on the yacht. When he, in turn, passed away, his widow had a hard time finding someone who would be able to restore the schooner to its former glory. Although others were interested in buying her, no one had given the widow the confidence she needed to let *Mistress* go knowing she would be well taken care of.

When F. W. "Skip" and Kathleen Joest finally bought the boat, there was not a dry eye in the house the day they trucked her away, and they had to make many promises that *Mistress* would see water again.

Skip and Kathleen had seen a small schooner-for-sale-ad and had asked for a video of the haul out. From this they saw that *Mistress* was just what they were looking for in a schooner. Great lines, in need of some work, and an interior they would not mind pulling out because they knew they would be doing a major rebuild on any schooner they bought given their future plans. They flew to Milwaukee to see her and Skip explained their plans and his qualifications as shipwright. She agreed to sell.

Both Skip and Kathleen had grown up in boating families with similar traditional wooden yachts—she on Long Island and he on the Chesapeake. When they celebrated their first anniversary some dozen years ago, she learned of Skip's dream to sail around the world. They began searching for a wooden boat with history, sleek lines, the ability to go fast and the strength to handle tough weather. *Mistress* was just the right choice for them.

Mistress' Rebirth

Mistress went through a six-year-long restoration. In May 2000, *Mistress* was trucked to St. Augustine, Florida, and moved to the owner's backyard. Having her in the backyard helped with the cost of the rebuild because no storage fees were due to a marina. This saved countless dollars over the six years she remained there while Skip worked on the restoration. In addition, it allowed him to work on her day or night. After having her shipped to St. Augustine, the Joests were able to contact Alan McInnis, son of the designer. He was just 5 years old at the time *Mistress* was built, but he gave them some valuable advise on his father's designs.

Skip gets ready to install the interior (*Kathleen Joest*).

Here are the new frames in the engine room (*Kathleen Joest*).

Skip contemplates the finished hull structure with frames, stringers, and deck beams (*Kathleen Joest*).

Mistress' artful chart table shows a wooden, inlaid world map (*Kathleen Joest*).

Besides completely replacing the interior woodwork, Skip took on the challenge of fitting modern conveniences into the classic vessel for the intended voyage without spoiling the traditional appearance.

Overall, the Joests estimate that Skip put 12,500 hours into her during the six-year total restoration. Doing things well was time consuming, but it made sure that she would be strong enough to sail around the world, have the equipment necessary to create all her own power and water, and do it in classic schooner style. She is actually an environmentally friendly blue water boat and it is interesting to see how self-sufficient she is.

In July 2006, the Joests launched *Mistress* and moved aboard the following month. They put up their house for sale and chose the schooner to be their primary home. Since then, they have cruised the East Coast, keeping a blog about their adventures for friends and family to enjoy.

Their participation in the 2007 Great Chesapeake Bay Schooner Race from Baltimore, Maryland, to Norfolk, Virginia, was a great highlight for them and the first opportunity to present their newly restored yacht. They were initially drawn to Beaufort, North Carolina, to help a friend do some deck repairs on an old 28' catboat. At the nearby Moores Marine Center, Skip got then involved in the restoration of a 1939 Trumpy 96' yacht, previously known as *El Presidente*, which served a stint as a patrol boat during World War II and has had every president from Roosevelt to Clinton on board. Once this project was finished, they continued sailing along the coast, getting ready for their planned world cruise.

Mistress sails again. After a multi-year restoration, she is again strong to sail over the oceans. Indeed, her owners plan a circumnavigation (*Kathleen Joest*).

Mistress: A Classic Schooner, or a Modern Cruising Yacht?

Skip has shown that a beautiful classic wooden schooner yacht can offer much more than nostalgic day sailing. Indeed, he has equipped her for long-distance cruising while preserving her classic appearance. On a narrow classic yacht with 50' this is not an easy task. However, the fact that Skip and his wife Kathleen have lived aboard already for five years shows that their yacht has all she needs to live comfortably aboard.

Indeed, many people come to see *Mistress* because of her classic lines. Many walk away amazed by her self-sufficient capabilities. Just before *Mistress* was launched, a new solar power generation system was in development called Solar Stik®. Skip knew the owner of the company and discussed such a system for *Mistress*. Skip also included additional mounts for the GPS, radar, and wind generator. He had the aluminum

A look into the forepeak (*Kathleen Joest*).

The galley is functional and simple. It features a gas stove and a double sink. There is also ample refrigeration space under the cabinets (*Kathleen Joest*).

A look from the companionway forward through the saloon. The combination of white paint and different natural woods creates a clean and welcoming atmosphere (*Kathleen Joest*).

The nav station is functional. It also can be used as an office (*Kathleen Joest*).

The saloon can easily seat up to seven people (*Kathleen Joest*).

Looking aft from forepeak. The Eastward schooners had a narrow cabin house. This can be clearly seen in this photo (*Kathleen Joest*).

sticks powder coated black which did not detract from *Mistress*' good looks. He opted for two, 85-watt panels for the Solar Stik system, one mounted on each stick. The sticks rotate and the panels are mounted on an H-shaped bracket that allow the panels to be tilted and raised and lowered. Because of this, at first light both panels are turned to the east and immediately generate 4 to 6 amperes an hour. By 9 or 10 A.M. they generate 10 to 12 amperes an hour and will continue to do so until 4 to 6 P.M., when again the panels are easily adjusted. In the evening, between 4 and 6 amperes of electricity is generated. This solar system is hooked up to a Blue Sky® controller, which helps increase the amperage input to the batteries and controls overload. Even in high winds (*Mistress* has so far been in winds of more than 75 knots) both panels and all the other equipment attached to the sticks have never suffered or been damaged. Thanks to this efficient system, approximately 95% of all the power used aboard the yacht comes from solar energy.

There is also a Pro-Sign® 2,000-watt inverter to run devices that require AC power, such as the computer, the vacuum cleaner, and the microwave. This also allows them to use all sorts of power tools on board. However, all these electric appliances can only be used as long as the battery capacity is strong enough. Skip opted for four North Star® AGM 8D batteries. Because the footprint for these batteries is half the size of one lead acid 8D, they were able to have twice the capacity in the same space. They have two batteries located under the companionway steps and another two under the chart table seat. *Mistress*' battery bank is capable of holding about 1120 amperes, which allows for considerable electricity consumption while underway. The electric capacity is so strong that they can even run a Simrad® hydraulic linear autopilot.

Another advantage to the North Star is the batteries can be mounted in any direction other than upside down. Therefore, it offers several more mounting possibilities and heels with no problem. The engine battery is separate and *Mistress*' alternator is oversized to allow the engine to boost up the batteries quickly, although they seldom need to run the engine for this purpose.

Skip designed *Mistress* to be his family's primary home for the open seas and therefore she has a few things not usually found on such a classic. An office was built for his wife Kathleen out of cherry wood. There is a writing desk, plenty of cabinet storage, a Ram Mount for the computer, and a printer/fax/scanner/copier. A cell antenna was run to the top of the foremast allowing online capabilities up to 20 miles offshore. A satellite phone can be used in more remote places. A reverse osmosis watermaker produces up to 1.5 gallons per hour, thus further contributing to *Mistress*' independence from shore supplies.

The interior is both elegant and functional with nearly forty different types of hardwoods. The main saloon can be turned into a double-bunk for guests and there is a quarter berth, which is used while underway. The schooner obviously has all necessary safety equipment, such as a four-person offshore life raft and Epirb.

A door in the rear of the saloon leads to the owner's stateroom. Here again, the combination of different types of woods becomes apparent (*Kathleen Joest*).

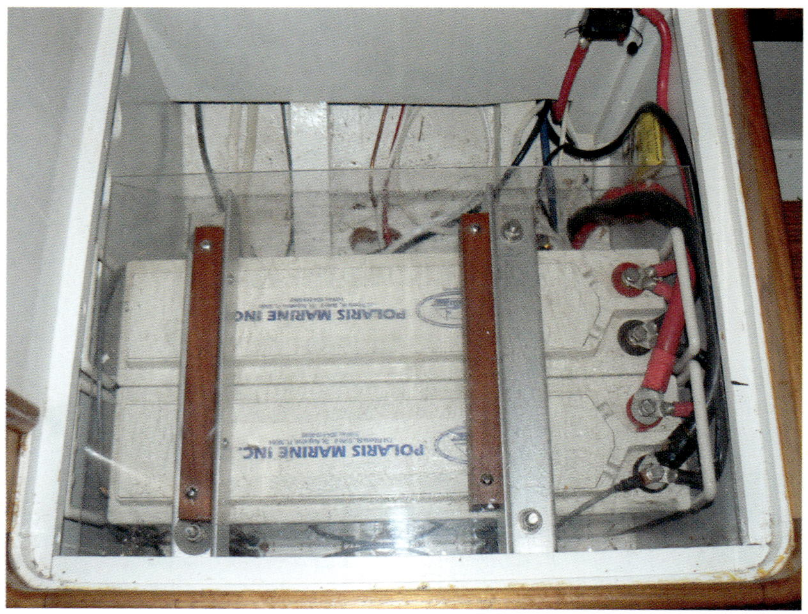

The schooner has four North Star AGM 8D batteries. Because the footprint of these batteries are 1/2 the size of one lead acid 8D, they were able to have twice the capacity. Two batteries are located under the companionway steps and another two under the chart table seat. The total capacity of these four batteries is about 1120 amperes, which allows for considerable electricity consumption while underway (*Kathleen Joest*).

Mistress features Solar Stiks. Skip also included additional mounts for the GPS, radar, and wind generator. He had the aluminum sticks powder coated black so as not to detract from *Mistress*' good looks. He opted for two, 85-watt panels, one mounted on each stick. The sticks rotate and the panels are mounted on an H-shaped bracket that allow them to both tilt and raise and lower the panels (*Kathleen Joest*).

The cockpit was laid out to be very functional and serve as a social area of the yacht. Separated from the cockpit, at its aft end, is the steering station with the wheel, compass, and chart plotter (*Kathleen Joest*).

Mistress makes her way racing against the *Amistad* in the Great Chesapeake Schooner Race (*Kathleen Joest Archive*).

Anchoring between the reefs in Southern Florida. She will soon start a multi-year circumnavigation (*Kathleen Joest*).

Mistress' varnish gleams in the Caribbean sunlight, while the ship's dog Olive Oyl keeps watch (*Kathleen Joest*).

The stern of this schooner is different from all other Eastwards because it was lengthened by three feet after an engine explosion. The result is a very long overhang with a nice little counter stern (*Kathleen Joest*).

Charles D. Mower: Designing Distinctive Racing Yachts

BIOGRAPHY OF CHARLES D. MOWER

Charles Drown Mower was born in 1875 in Lynn, Massachusetts, near the coastal town of Swampscott, and lived in New York, where he became a noted yacht designer and author. At one time he was design editor of *The Rudder* magazine and a contributing author to *Motor Boating* magazine.

He started studying yacht design in 1895 with Arthur Binney and later B. Bowdoin Crowninshield, and then he moved on to a partnership with Thomas D. Bowes in Philadelphia in 1911. In 1903, Mower was the official measurer for the New York Yacht Club. He measured the America's Cup J-Class boat contenders *Shamrock III*, designed by William Fife III, and *Reliance*, a N. G. Herreshoff design. This experience included a trip to the top of *Reliance's* mast, which at 157' was then the tallest in the world. He was also official measurer of the Manhasset Bay Yacht Club and the Cruising Club of America.

After the war, Mower worked either alone or in partnership as Mower and Humphries Ltd. He was also a chief naval architect at Henry B. Nevins, Inc., and in 1937 was associated with the office of Nelson & Reid, Inc. Mower died in 1942 at age sixty-seven.

Some Mower yacht designs that have been well publicized include the A-Cat, the R-Class yachts *Ardette*, *Ace*, *Ardelle*, *Penebscot*, *Nancy*, and *Lady Gay*. He also designed the Fishers Island Design, individual projects such as the Lake Michigan-based 1934 *Tops-o-Cotton* and *Uwhilna*, as well as numerous small dinghies and hydroplanes. He also designed a few large racing schooners for the shallow waters of the Chesapeake and the Great Lakes. He usually designed these yachts with a centerboard. Among these yachts was the centerboard schooner *Windjammer*, launched in 1924, which became well known through competition in ocean races to Bermuda, Havana, and Nassau. Only very few schooners of his design are still existent, and worthy of special mention is the 62' schooner *White Spray*, originally named *Lady Susan*, which recently has been launched after an extensive restoration. The following chapter analyzes this yacht more in detail.

WHITE SPRAY

(Ex- *Narraguagus;* Ex- *Mudlark;* Ex- *Sundance;* Ex- *Poor Richard;* Ex- *Lady Susan)*

Type: centerboard two-mast gaff schooner, converted to fixed keel
Designer: Charles D. Mower
Year of Construction: 1926
Shipyard: Morton Johnson & Co., Bay Head City, New Jersey
Length (sparred): 75'
Length on Deck: 62'
Length on Waterline: 55'
Beam: 16'
Draft: 4'6" (board up, original specification, later added fixed keel with 5' draft)
Displacement: 29 tons
Sail Area: 1,800 sq. ft.
Construction: wood
Engine: Detroit 4-71, 80 hp
Owner: With the Wind, Inc.
Home Port: Brick, New Jersey

The Schooner *White Spray* is an elegant wooden shoal draft schooner designed by Charles D. Mower. Originally built as *Lady Susan* in 1926 by Morton Johnson in Bay Head, New Jersey, she is now being meticulously restored and preserved by With The Wind, Inc, under the attentive command of Joseph Jantzen.

Lady Susan's Early Racing History

The sailing yacht *Lady Susan* was designed as a 62' two-mast centerboard schooner by Charles D. Mower in 1925 for a prominent Philadelphia judge. The boat was built in 1926 by Morton Johnson & Co. in Bay Head City, New Jersey. As it is told, the judge had her built to race against his colleague's schooner, also from Philadelphia. The schooner had subsequently many different owners, and was named *Poor Richard*, *Sundance,* and *Mudlark*, before it was christened *Narraguagus*. She carried this name for many years.

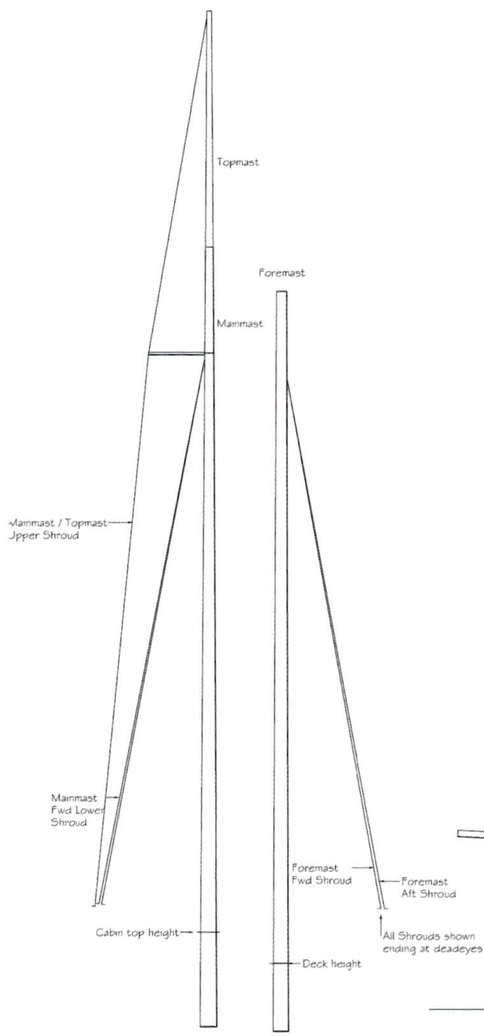

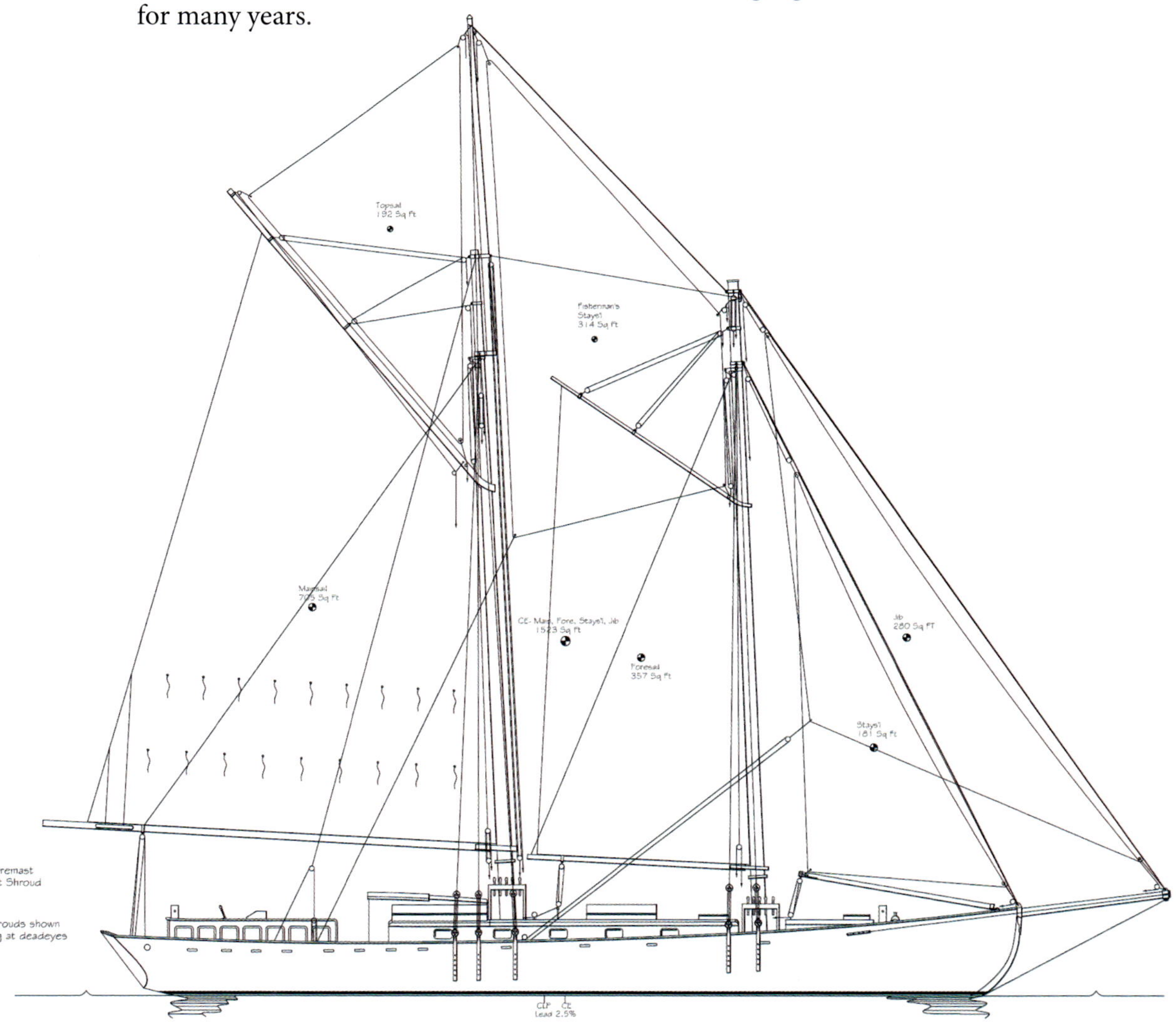

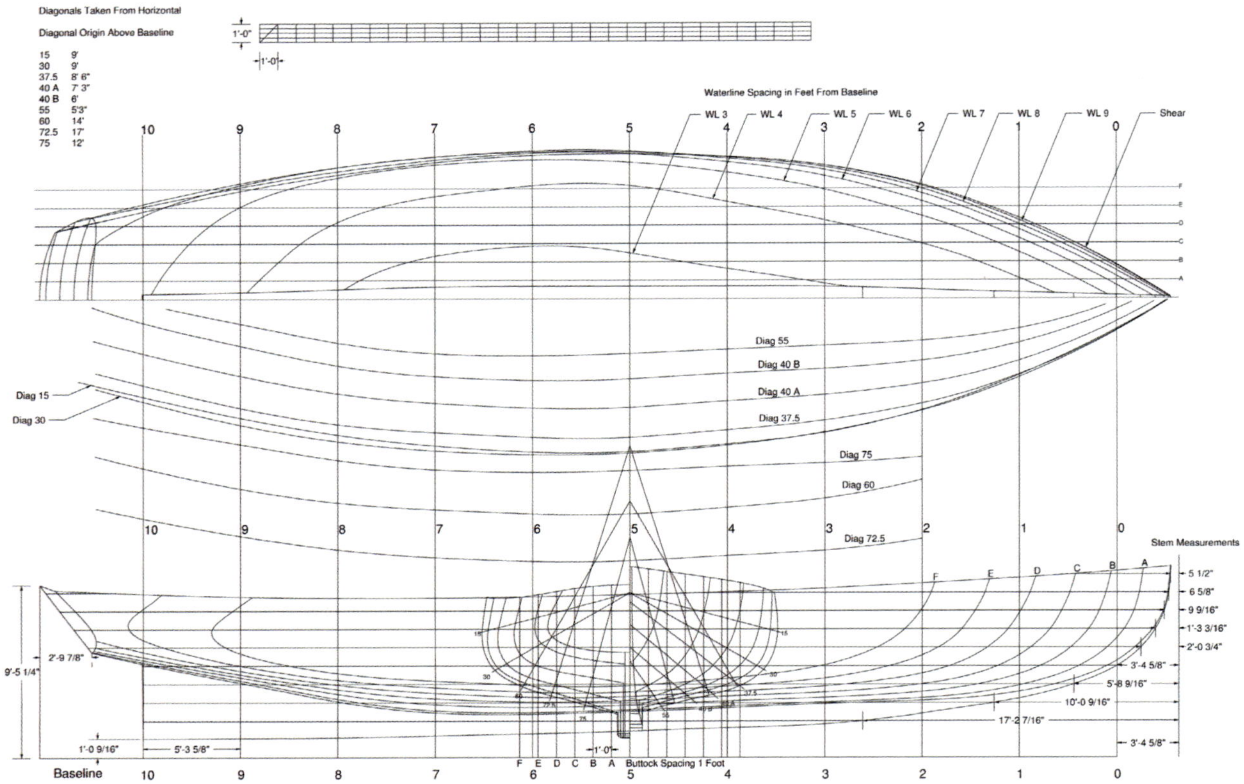
Diagonals Taken From Horizontal
Diagonal Origin Above Baseline
15 9'
30 9'
37.5 8' 6"
40 A 7' 3"
40 B 6'
55 5'3"
60 14'
72.5 17'
75 12'
Waterline Spacing in Feet From Baseline
WL 3
WL 4
WL 5
WL 6
WL 7
WL 8
WL 9
Shear
Diag 55
Diag 40 B
Diag 40 A
Diag 37.5
Diag 15
Diag 30
Diag 75
Diag 60
Diag 72.5
Stem Measurements
5 1/2"
6 5/8"
9 9/16"
1'-3 3/16"
2'-0 3/4"
3'-4 5/8"
5'-8 9/16"
10'-0 9/16"
17'-2 7/16"
3'-4 5/8"
9'-5 1/4"
2'-9 7/8"
1'-0 9/16"
5'-3 5/8"
1'-0"
Buttock Spacing 1 Foot
Baseline

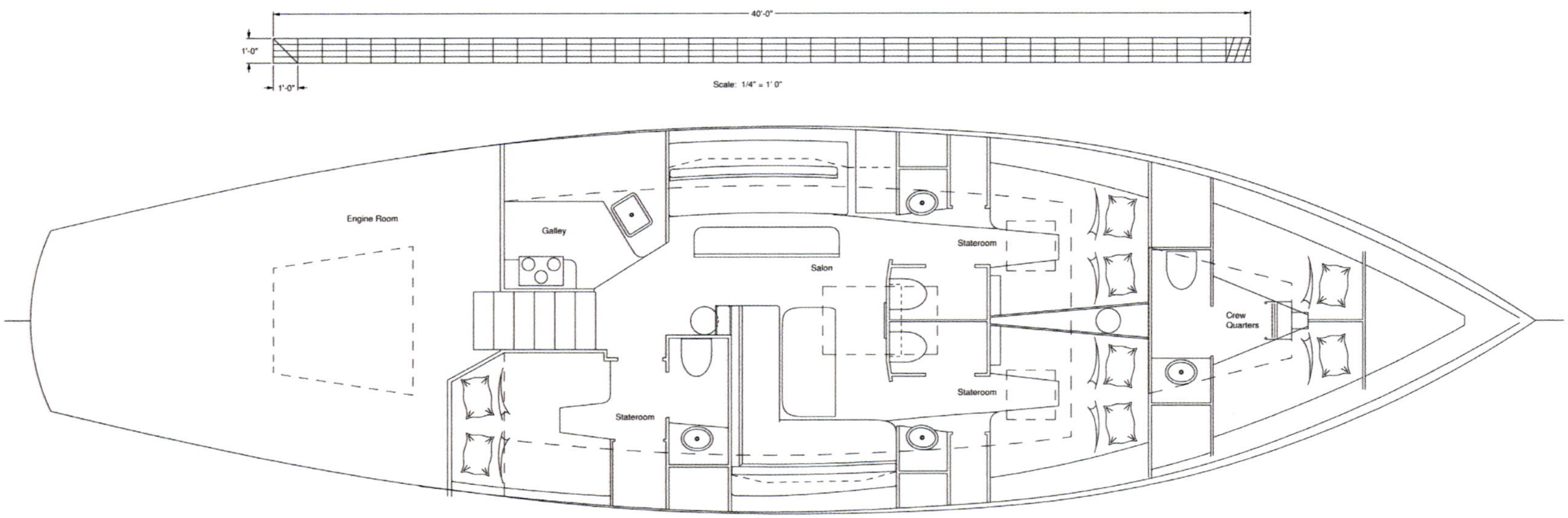
40'-0"
1'-0"
Scale: 1/4" = 1' 0"
Engine Room
Galley
Salon
Stateroom
Stateroom
Stateroom
Crew Quarters

During a refit in 1974, the centerboard was removed, and an additional keel added, bringing the draft to 5'. During this refit the entire hull was cold-molded on top of the original hull planking.

The Discovery of Much Work Needed on *Narraguagus*

The current owners bought the schooner *Narraguagus* in 2001, thinking that they might still be able to sail her. But it turned out that she was in worse shape than they thought. They thus proceeded to repair the cold molded hull and to remove her interior. The project was put into the hands of Joseph A. Jantzen. The Bar Harbor-based company Moose Island Design (MID) redesigned the framing and floors, which were in bad condition. They also made repairs to the keel. MID also completely redesigned the interior per the current owners requirements: to be able to sleep six passengers and three crewmembers. The rig was also reworked and slightly updated.

The centerboard had been removed many years ago, and the current owner did not consider putting it back into the boat. Instead, the fixed-keel depth was increased to improve her sailing characteristics. MID also redesigned the sheer line of the hull to give her a more pleasing line. Since the original drawings were lost in a boatyard fire years ago, and copies that existed have been lost, MID has drawn new plans of the schooner.

In Summer 2011, the schooner was launched again and rechristened *White Spray*. She is intended to cruise widely along the United States' East Coast, and down to the Caribbean.

With a draft of only 5', the *White Spray* is designed to run fast in both inland waters and coastwise. A second set of sails designed for racing will take full advantage of even light winds, making her a worthy competitor on race day. A Detroit diesel auxiliary engine provides a comfortable speed when she needs the power to move in and out of her dock.

Schooner *White Spray*: First view of the Charles Mower schooner in sad condition on jackstands and exposed to the weather in a boatyard in Maine (*Joseph Jantzen*).

Joseph Jantzen climbs aboard for the first time (*Joseph Jantzen*).

Crew Jeanne Sherman works on the first inventory of the schooner, including the park bench cockpit seating (*Joseph Jantzen*).

Much of the original keelson is replaced during the restoration. Here a shipwright installs and planes the new keelson (*Joseph Jantzen*).

The original frames and planking are severely damaged by wood rot spores (*Joseph Jantzen*).

Interior cross braces are built to support the hull while frame and planking restoration is underway. So many of the original frames are removed during the restoration that the hull would loose its original shape without the cross braces (*Joseph Jantzen*).

Schooner *White Spray*—six courses of a new frame member are curing after being steamed and bent to an exact compound curve. Each frame consists of eleven courses and no two frames are alike (*Joseph Jantzen*).

Raising the sheer during the restoration results in a more elegant curve of the sheer line. It also offers more protection from encroaching seas and allows the bowsprit to be raised off the fore deck (*Joseph Jantzen*).

Much of the original keelson is severly damaged by wood rot spores and has to be removed. Here, the seemingly infinite new keelson is being laminated in the workshop (*Joseph Jantzen*).

Each metal fitting, such as these topmast supports, spreaders, boom bales, and anchor brackets, is bead blasted, primed, and epoxy painted (*Joseph Jantzen*).

In the engine compartment, the original frames, planking and rusted nails are removed. The remaining wood is thoroughly cleaned of wood rot spores (*Joseph Jantzen*).

From the port side looking forward, the hull is being faired in preparation for a primer coat. The green splotches indicate high or low areas that need to be sanded or filled (*Joseph Jantzen*).

Close up view of the hull where sanding or filling is needed before the primer coat can be applied. Every inch of the hull is meticulously inspected and reinspected (*Joseph Jantzen*).

As with the interior cross braces erected for restoration, the exterior hull is also thoroughly braced to prevent the hull from collapsing while the frames and keelson are removed and replaced (*Joseph Jantzen*).

From the starboard looking forward, the schooner wears a full primer coat (*Joseph Jantzen*).

Because no surviving original line drawings exist, full-size working mock-ups of the interior are constructed in the workshop. The models, with actual hinges and moving parts, are strong enough to support the weight of actual passengers. A mock-up party with 22 passengers "aboard," is hosted to verify the work flow and assure passenger comforts (*Joseph Jantzen*).

Topside looking aft, the custom teak hatches for the two forward staterooms are fitted to the contour of the house (*Joseph Jantzen*).

Looking forward to the crash bulkhead, new laminated frames and floor are fitted. Interior cross braces are removed (*Joseph Jantzen*).

The hatches are crafted of matched Burmese teak (*Joseph Jantzen*).

Carpet-covered work planks are placed above the frames, allowing the glasswork crew to thoroughly seal every plank and frame with epoxy for preservation (*Joseph Jantzen*).

The schooner emerges from her plastic cocoon with a deep, beautiful cream hull and kelly green boot stripe (*Joseph Jantzen*).

Custom 4' long drill bits are made for drilling through wood and lead. Joseph Jantzen drills holes through the fore mast step for the 3/4" silicone bronze keel bolts (*Joseph Jantzen*).

In the spar workshop, clear, vertical-grain Douglas fir is laminated for the new bowsprit (*Joseph Jantzen*).

In the spar shop, the new bowsprit of clear, vertical-grain Douglas fir is ready for final sanding, stain, and epoxy (*Joseph Jantzen*).

As restoration continues, the painted house and teak bulwark caprail are protected with plastic and foam. The teak skylights above the companionway and salon are fitted to the curve of the house (*Joseph Jantzen*).

At the stern looking forward, the cockpit seating is patterned to surround the wheelbox. High backs and thick seat cushions ensure passenger comfort and safety (*Joseph Jantzen*).

The cabinetry is carefully patterned from the mock-ups and fitted in galley and saloon (*Joseph Jantzen*).

The cockpit seating is designed for both comfort and safety. The bench seating incorporates wide grip rails and rounded edges (*Joseph Jantzen*).

Frank C. Paine: Design for Speed

BIOGRAPHY OF FRANK C. PAINE

Frank Cabot Paine was essentially a yacht racer and sailor. He lacked formal training in yacht design, but he absorbed it during the year when he and L. Francis Herreshoff lived and studied with Wm. Starling Burgess, and through his own intense yacht racing experience. By his early teens, Paine was winning races in the one-design Cataumet Pups designed by Burgess. In 1912, Paine joined Burgess' airplane business in Marblehead, Massachusetts.

The post-World War I years were an important time for yacht design. The Universal and International Rules had stabilized, and Marconi rigs were introduced. It was natural for a team of aircraft pioneers to exploit this new technology. For this reason, in 1921, they founded a firm in their names. Francis Herreshoff and Norman K. Skene were draftsmen. The firm was later renamed Burgess, Swasey, and Paine with the addition of A. Loring Swasey in 1923. The partnership lasted until 1925.

Their offices were a meeting place for New England's great yacht designers. Paine mentored C. Raymond Hunt and contributed to his design of the International 110 in the early years of light-displacement hulls. Francis W. Belknap, Norman L. Skene, and Charles MacGregor also participated in this ongoing exchange of ideas. Also, the vibrant Concordia Company was very near, indeed a few doors down the hallway, so that it was easy to reciprocally influence their works.

Paine was associated with the firm of Paine, Belknap, and Skene from 1925 to 1932. When Skene left the firm, the firm's name was changed to Belknap and Paine. They were in operation until 1937, when Paine established himself as an independent naval architect.

Although Frank Cabot Paine probably considered himself a sailor first and a designer second, his body of work produced many very successful racing yachts. Paine is best remembered for designing the J-Class *Yankee* in 1929, a contender to defend the America's Cup in 1930. In addition, he is famous for the *Highland Light* from 1931, which was a long-time holder of the Bermuda Race record. Paine understood and employed actual and sailing waterline length to increase speed, as illustrated by his R-Class *Gypsy* of 1923. At a time when the average waterline length for this class was 23', Gypsy's was 25'3". Paine's earlier, more prolific work was in the 6- and 8-meter classes and the Q and R Classes. A very successful racing yacht in the 1920s was his Q-Class *Robin*, four-time winner of the Puritan Cup, the annual regatta at Marblehead's Eastern Yacht Club, and his 8-meter *Gypsy*, selected in 1929 to defend the Seawanhaka Cup, an international match-race challenge cup for small yachts. Two of Paine's more recognized vessels, *Yankee* and *Gertrude K. Thebaud*, were designed in 1929. The J-Class *Yankee* competed to defend the America's Cup in 1930. *Thebaud* was the last American fishing schooner to vie for the International Fishermen's Cup, an international challenge series for Grand Banks fishing vessels. Neither vessel achieved its goal that year, although a redesigned *Yankee* nearly won the trials in 1934 and *Thebaud* was the only vessel ever to win a race against her Canadian rival, *Bluenose*. These boats marked a departure for Paine from club to ocean racing designs, and a wider recognition of his talents.

In 1930, Paine acquired a controlling interest in the yacht building concern of the George F. Lawley Corporation, where he served as president until the conclusion of World War II. He continued to maintain a design office, with frequent changes in personnel.

Generally, Paine did not devote much attention to aesthetics when designing yachts; however, the appearance of his boats did not suffer. This is particularly noticeable in his large ocean racing yachts, such as *Kelpie* and *Joan II* (now *Viveka*), both schooners featured in this chapter. Their elegant lines with long overhangs are a stunning testimony of his remarkable design talent.

KELPIE

Type: two-mast staysail schooner
Designer: Frank C. Paine (when working as Paine, Belknap, and Skene)
Year of Construction: 1928
Shipyard: Harvey Gamage, South Bristol, Maine
Length (sparred): 82'
Length on Deck: 65'6"
Length on Waterline: 48'
Beam: 16'6"
Draft: 9'8"
Displacement: 36.8 tons
Ballast: 14 tons
Sail Area: 2,800 sq. ft.
Construction: wood
Engine: Isuzu 6BB1 PW01, 6 cylinders, 120 hp
Owner: Kelpie Charters, Inc.
Home Port: Santa Barbara, California

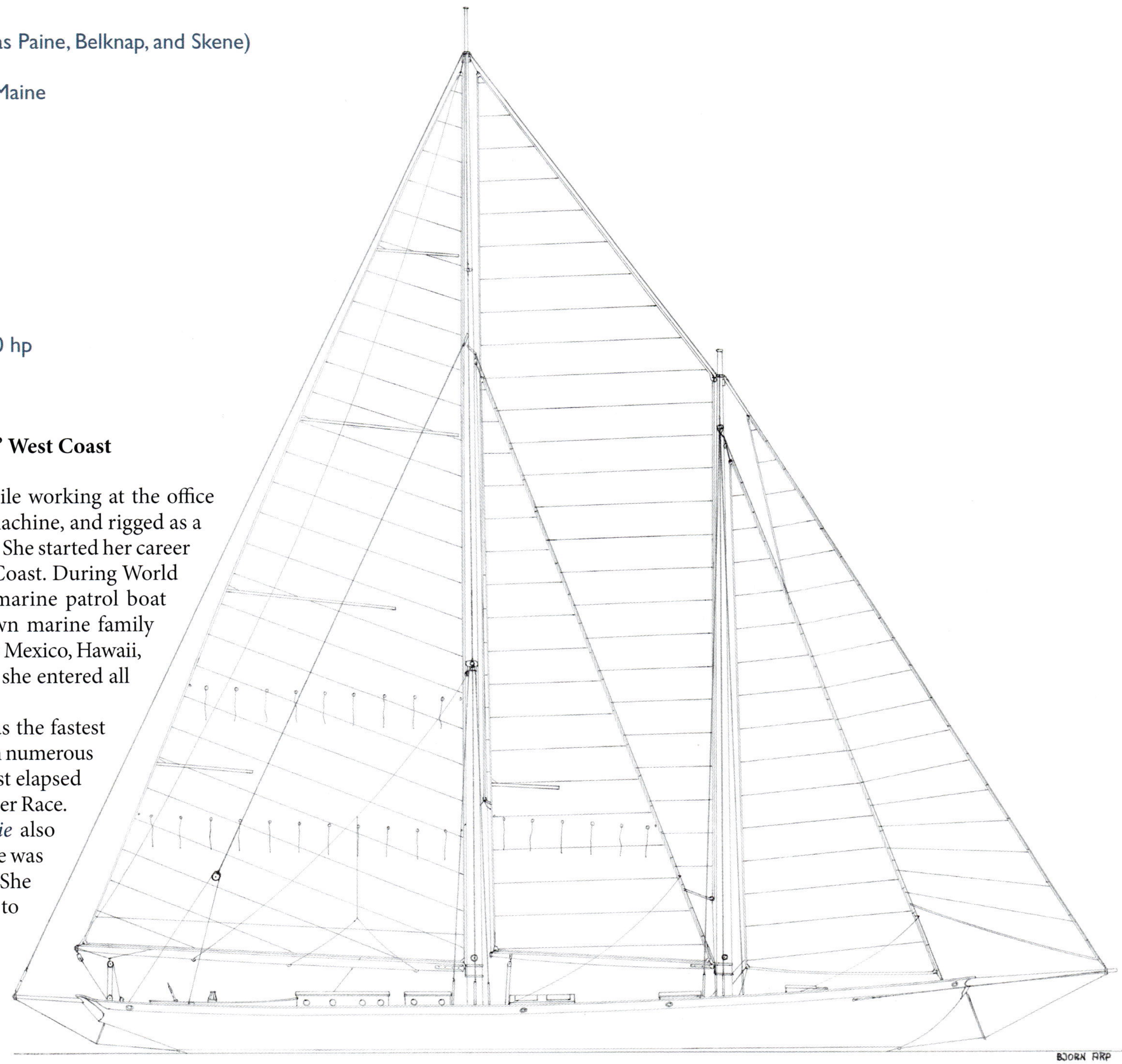

The Fastest Schooner on the United States' West Coast

Kelpie was designed by Frank C. Paine, while working at the office of Paine, Belknap, and Skene, as a pure racing machine, and rigged as a staysail schooner. She had a sparred length of 82'. She started her career as a racing schooner on the United States' East Coast. During World War II, the Navy commissioned her as a submarine patrol boat to survey the New England coast. A well-known marine family purchased the vessel after the war and sailed her to Mexico, Hawaii, and the South Pacific. Once on the West Coast, she entered all the major yacht races that were held there.

Many nautical publications refer to *Kelpie* as the fastest schooner on the West Coast. *Kelpie* finished first in numerous Newport to Ensenada races and in 2000 took first elapsed time and first corrected time in the Ancient Mariner Race. At some point during her earlier history, *Kelpie* also sailed in the New York Yacht Club Cup, where she was the first split rig and the first schooner to finish. She also won four first-place trophies in the Newport to

Kelpie sailing along the California coast in the early 1990s. She is fast even in a light breeze, since she has the capacity to carry an overwhelming amount of sail (*Rudolph Arp Archive*).

At one point the owners tried to bring in sponsors to help maintain the vessel. In exchange for their financial contribution to the boat, they had their trademarks written into her sails (*Rudolph Arp Archive*).

Racing *Kelpie*. Many considered her the fastest schooner on the entire West Coast (*Rudolph Arp Archive*).

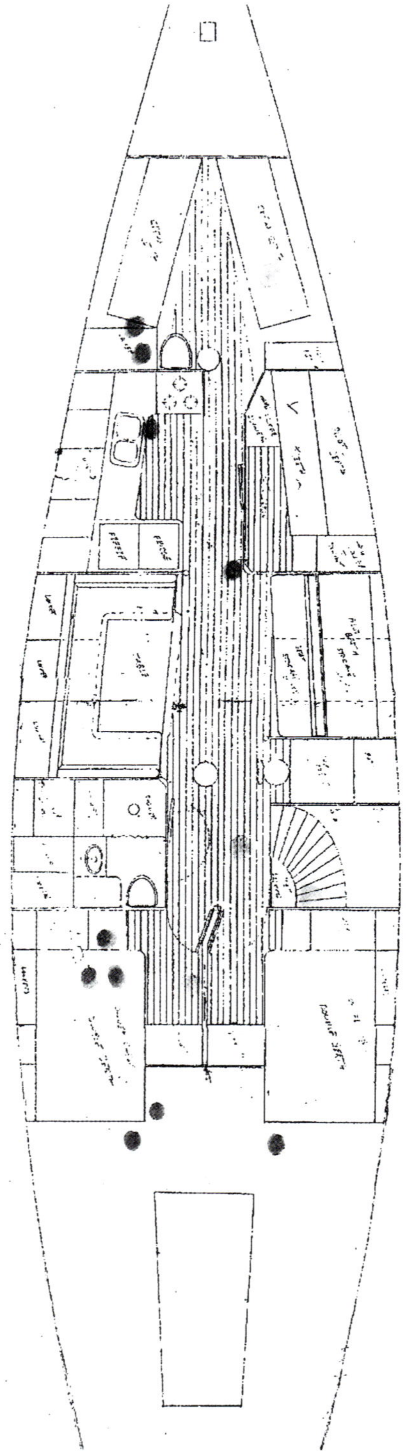

Ensenada Race, which was a first for this race. She has taken the Sarina Race, where she was also the first schooner to finish on several occasions. She has taken first elapsed time and corrected time in the Queens Bay Schooner's Regatta; the Schooners Cup, San Diego; the Heritage Regatta, Newport Beach; and the Richard Henry Dana Cup.

Restorations and Present Use of *Kelpie*

Being engaged so intensely in racing, the vessel needed regular maintenance, both cosmetically and structurally. She was thus substantially refitted in 1985, 1990, and finally in 2001. The 2001 refit included new laminated frames and significant replacement of the framing. Also, the interior was very nicely redone according to the original 1928 design, and painted white, which gives a very light and luminous aspect to *Kelpie's* interior.

The interior is thus very typical of a racing schooner of the early twentieth century. Starting forward, there is a large chain locker and a 2" thick collision bulkhead, followed by a V-berth and a crew head. Aft of this area is the galley to port. The galley is equipped with all sorts of amenities necessary for today's life: a microwave, a LPG gimballed 3-burner stove with oven, top-loading ice-box, double stainless-steel sink, etc. In front of the galley is the captain's or guest cabin to starboard. The saloon is mid-ship with a U-shaped settee and table, and an additional settee opposite. Further aft is a large storage area with a pilot berth above. To starboard of this storage is the navigation station. There is also room for a head with vanity. All the way aft there are two double cabins port and starboard.

The yacht is fitted out with a tank capacity of 100 gallons of fuel, 100 gallons of water, and an appropriate holding tank for black and gray water. She is further equipped with all the necessary electronic equipment for navigation, among them radar, GPS, compass, radio, fathometer, and log.

Kelpie carries a staysail schooner rig since her launch in 1928. She has Sitka spruce fore- and main-masts, while the bowsprit is solid fir, as are also the booms and the boom-kin. The standing rigging is currently stainless steel (originally, it was galvanized steel). In light winds she can add a fisherman sail, a gollywobbler as well as an asymmetrical spinnaker to her sail area.

Kelpie is United States Coast Guard certified to carry 41 passengers for charter excursions under motor, and 24 under sail. She is a proud survivor of the great times of classic yacht racing in the United States, and it can only be hoped and wished that she continues to sail on our coasts and honor her heritage for many years to come.

VIVEKA
(Ex- *Joan II*)

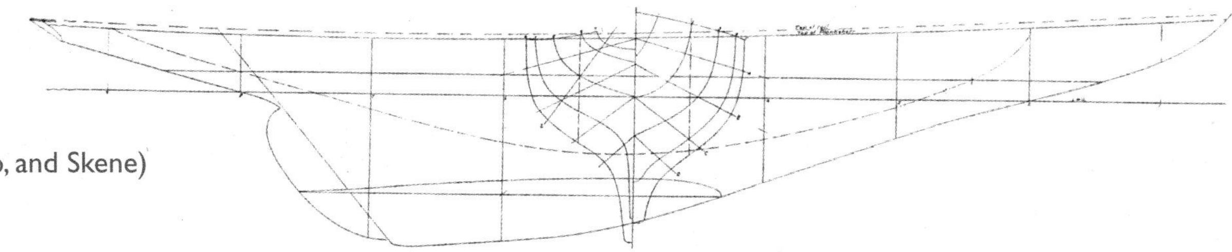

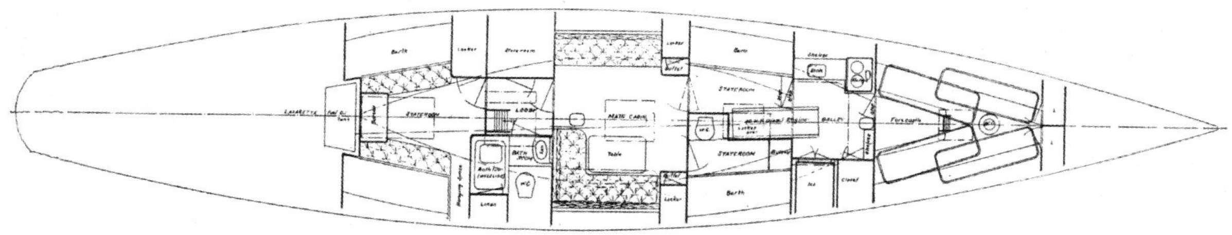

Type: two-mast staysail schooner
Designer: Frank C. Paine (when working as Paine, Belknap, and Skene)
Year of Construction: 1929/30
Shipyard: Fred D. Lawley, Quincy, Massachusetts
Length on Deck: 73'10'
Length on Waterline: 62'
Beam: 14'
Draft: 10'
Displacement: 47 tons
Sail Area: 3,000 sq. ft.
Construction: mahogany on oak
Engine: Perkins diesel 6-354, 130 hp
Owner: Merl Petersen
Home Port: Richmond, California

These are current specs for Joan II *as* Viveka.

Joan II: An Unusual Staysail Schooner

Joan II was designed by Paine, Belknap, and Skene and built by Fred D. Lawley in Quincy, Massachusetts, between the end of 1929 and early 1930. The boat was built of mahogany planking on oak frames. She was designed with a deck length of 72'9", a length on the waterline of 48', a beam of 14', and a draft of 9'1". With these measurements, she displaced, at the time, 34.25 tons. She carried an auxiliary diesel engine with feathering propeller located on the starboard side of sternpost.

The most remarkable feature of this design was the rig. The 2,533 sq. ft. of sail were distributed among the two masts with a staysail schooner rig, with the addition of an inverted leg-o-mutton foresail. This allowed the entire space between the masts to be utilized to the best advantage. The sail hoisted on a track on the mast and set flying on a standing sprit or gaff with sheet leading up to the mainmast, making it self-tending. This concept was tried on this schooner as a possible solution to the difficulties posed by the space between masts above the main staysail. Another option would be the fisherman and yet another option—similar to the one chosen on *Joan II*—the wishbone gaff, which worked similar to a modern surf-sail.

The owner of *Joan II* was J. P. Morgan. He wanted a fast cruiser, putting special emphasis on speed. For this reason, Frank C. Paine designed her to rate at the top of Class G, a 38 rating, and at the same time under the Universal Rules in the 12-meter class. *Joan II* can thus be considered one of the very few schooners that rated in the 12-meter class, typically a realm of sloop and cutter-rigged boats.

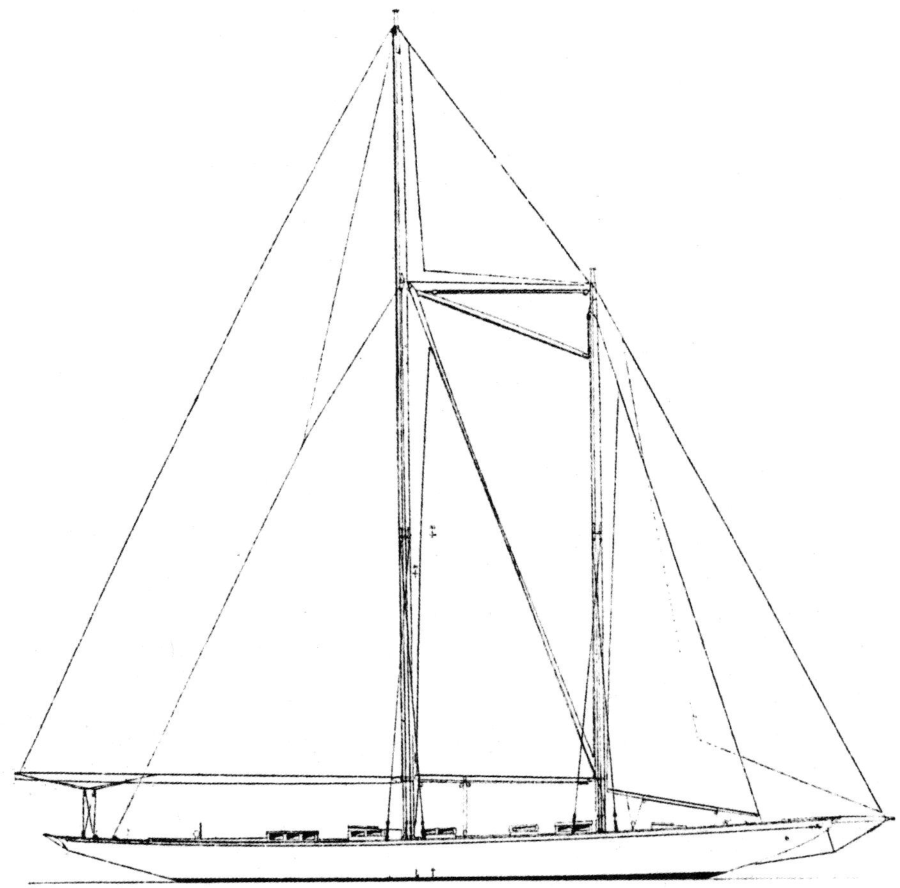

(Yachting, *January 1930*)

Half a Century in the Loving Hands of Merl Peterson

J. P. Morgan sold the schooner to Bob Fraiser, who renamed her *Viveka*. Fraiser sold the schooner to the Silvertooth family, who in turn sold her to Merl Peterson in 1957. He paid $30,000 for the boat at that time, and he sailed her in 1960 to San Francisco, settling in Sausalito. In 1965, Bob Shane of the Kingston Trio talked Merl Peterson into taking her to Hawaii, so they sailed there and settled at Alawai Harbor and raced for some years.

In 1970, Peterson did a major remodeling in Hawaii. He redesigned the interior saloon with new captain's quarters, two double-bunk crew rooms, and a Japanese tub and sauna. He installed a washer and dryer, freezer and refrigeration system, and a propane stove with microwave above. The interior flooring was replaced with teak and holly sole. On the exterior he replaced the teak deck and shortened the long main-boom by 12' so the backstay could be permanent. He added 6' to the fore mast and one foot to the main to get better balance when sailing.

In 1989, he left Hawaii for a circumnavigation, arriving back in San Francisco Bay in 1996. Since then, Merl Petersen has kept *Viveka* in the San Fracisco Bay. She is now located at Marina Bay in Richmond, California. Although Merl Peterson is already 88 years old, he still feels fit and lives aboard the schooner. A few times a year he even gets her out for a sail.

Viveka has recently been measured and now features an overall length of 73'10", a waterline length of 62', a 10' draft, and a 14' beam. Her height is 78' from water to top of the main mast and she displaces 47 tons.

Joan II sailing under full sail along the United States' East Coast. She carried a staysail schooner rig since her launching in 1930 (*The Mariner's Museum, Virginia*).

Viveka is still an impressive vessel, wherever she goes. Here she is racing off Alcatraz Island in the San Francisco Bay (*Merl Peterson*).

Viveka gently sailing in a breeze. Note that she now carries two loose-footed roller-furling staysails (*Merl Peterson*).

Merl Peterson is usually in the company of many good friends when he decides to take *Viveka* out for sail. He is already more than eighty years old, but still sails his schooner (*Merl Peterson*).

Garland Rotch: The Designer-Friend of a Schooner Owner

BIOGRAPHY OF GARLAND ROTCH

Garland Rotch was a practical seaman and did not work in yacht design. He generally worked as a captain or crew on other yachts, but when he entered Tempelton Crocker's services, he worked full-time for him including designing his schooner yacht *Zaca* in 1929. This design was essentially the adaptation of a Grand-Banks fishing schooner as a suitable yacht for Crocker to sail around the world and to cruise for his extensive exploration trips through the Pacific. For this reason, we will focus on the development of the schooner rather than her designer, since his life was very closely related to that of his only large schooner.

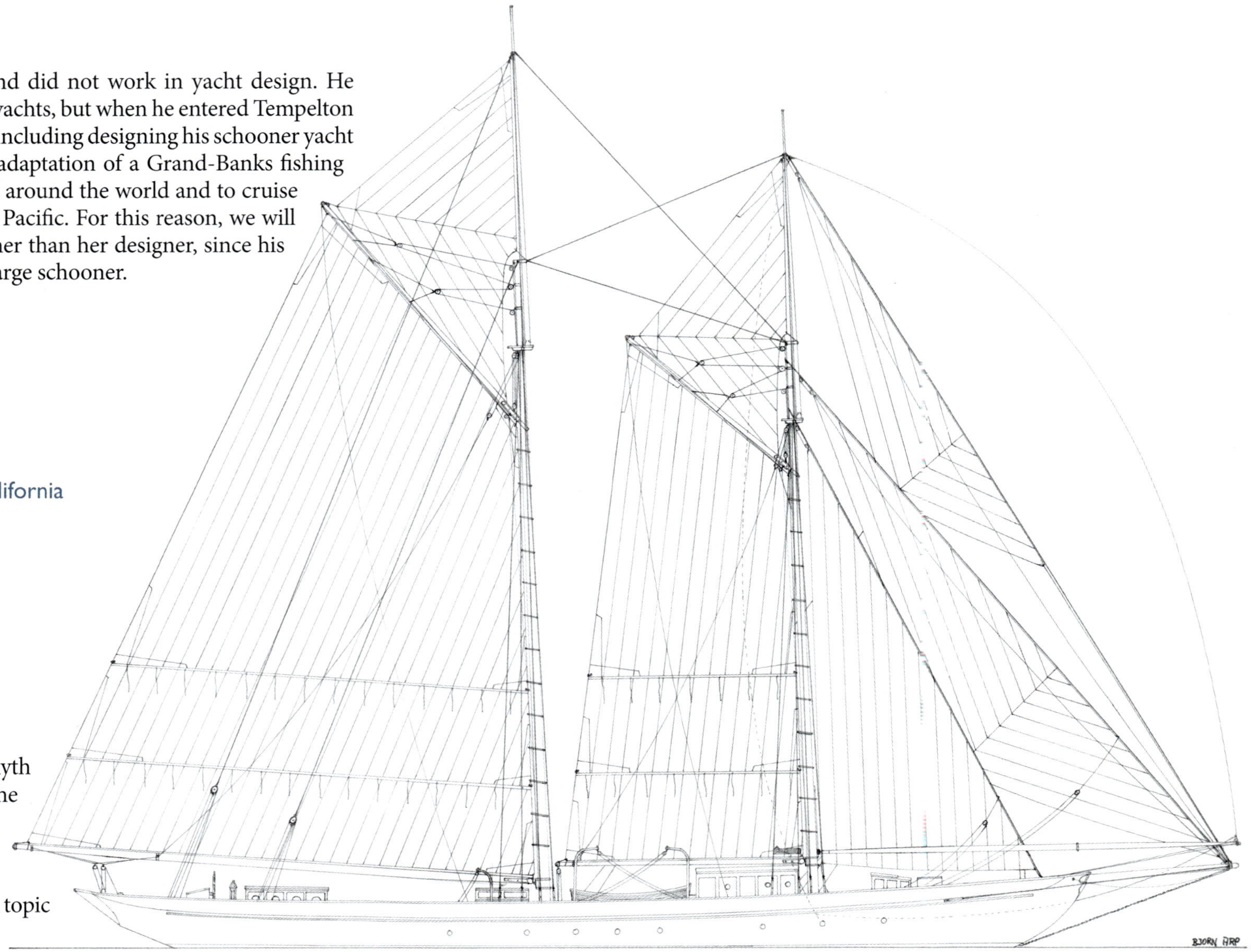

ZACA

(Ex- IX-73; Ex- Zaca)

Type: two-mast gaff schooner
Designer: Garland Rotch
Shipyard: Nunes Brothers, Sausalito, California
Year of Construction: 1930
Length on Deck: 118'
Length on Waterline: 95'11"
Beam: 23'9"
Draft: 14'
Displacement: 122 tons
Construction: Alaskan cedar on teak
Home Port: Monte Carlo, Monaco

Few sailing ships are surrounded by more myth and legend than the yacht *Zaca*. Launched on the eve of the Great Depression, the 118' gaff-rigged schooner has sailed through eighty years of history from one remarkable adventure to the next. Today, berthed in Monaco, *Zaca* remains a topic of fascination in nautical circles.

The First Owner: Templeton Crocker

Hillsborough millionaire Templeton Crocker, a Yale-educated San Francisco banker, socialite, and railroad heir, did things ordinary men could only dream about. By the time he reached his mid-40s in the 1930s, the bespectacled Crocker had seen an opera he composed performed on stage at Monte Carlo, amassed a one-of-a-kind collection of California history, and supervised construction of his lavish, 37-room Peninsula palace the Uplands, modeled after an Italian villa. Everything he undertook, the discerning Crocker did stylishly, without sparing expense.

Among his toys there had always been a boat, which he named *Zaca*. The name *Zaca* means "peace" in a Native American language. The second *Zaca* was an Edson B. Schock-designed schooner with a 62' length over all. This schooner proved to be a very able cruising yacht, with a relatively low rigging profile. Originally built as a gaff-Marconi schooner, Crocker had her transformed into a staysail schooner in the late 1920s. However, when Crocker started thinking of doing a trip around the world he needed a more suitable and larger yacht. In 1929, he envisioned his third *Zaca*, much more luxurious and larger than anything else previously seen in San Francisco. To design such a yacht, Crocker hired Garland Rotch, who most likely already served for him as captain of his second *Zaca*. Rotch borrowed the lines for the third *Zaca* from Canada's famed *Bluenose*, the fastest fishing schooner ever built. Rotch was well known as a "personality of the South Seas," probably influencing Crocker's future interest in those southern waters.

To build a schooner of *Zaca's* size was not an easy proposition. Designer Garland Rotch and owner Templeton Crocker looked across San Francisco Bay to Sausalito-based boat builders Ernie and Antonio Nunes. The 118' vessel was too large to be built in the Nunes Brothers yard, so in August 1929, the keel was laid alongside the shop—in the middle of Sausalito's Main Street. A week later, the stock market crashed. But even as the Great Depression swept the nation, construction of the new *Zaca* went full speed ahead. The yacht was completed in 1930 at a cost of $200,000. Crocker chose to have *Zaca* painted black above the water line, which gave this yacht a sleek yet ominous appearance.

In every aspect *Zaca's* design resembled that of the Newfoundland schooner *Bluenose*. Yet *Zaca's* keel was cut away a little forward and dropped a little aft, giving more of a slanting keel. With a fairly deep keel she could hold the water well when on the wind, while being cut away well forward she would come about better under power. The bow overhang was left the same as in *Bluenose*, though the forward sections were fined down a little to reduce the pounding so disagreeable in a head sea when under power. To prevent her diving, due to the finer bow, her flush deck was raised 16 inches from a point 16' aft of the foremast to within 11' of the stem. This, besides giving more buoyancy forward, raised the flooring of the forward crew quarters, giving additional needed floor space and increasing the space below the crew's quarters used for a chain-locker, frozen-meat refrigerator, and galley stores. The raised deck was not carried entirely forward, but dropped again 11' from the stem to the main deck line to leave a small well for the bowsprit heel and the windlass. This enabled the forestaysail to drop lower, just clearing the forward companionway leading to the forecastle. The after overhang was increased to give a smarter appearance, as the Newfoundland fishermen do not have such a long overhang.

Zaca was very strongly built; stronger than the general practice in yacht construction, but she was built to cruise on any ocean and to stand any weather. While the increased weight of the hull may have slowed her sailing, it offset this by giving a feeling of confidence in a sturdy vessel. Her keel timbers and deadwood are of 16 x 20 inch Oregon pine, with twenty-six tons of cast iron for the keel. The stern post is of iron bark, and the stem of janezero. The frames are double, sawn 4" oak, the beams, shelves, ceiling, decking, and planking being of selected Oregon pine. The design was set up in August 1929, the keel laid in early October, at Nunes Brothers, in Sausalito, California, and she was launched on April 12, 1930. On May 8, 1930 she sailed for Ensenada, Mexico, on her shakedown cruise. This was a short period of time for the construction of a yacht this size.

Zaca was rigged as a two-mast gaff schooner with topsails. The ordinary cruising sails comprised a jib topsail, jib, staysail, foresail, fore topsail, mainsail, and main topsail, giving a sail area of 6,550 sq. ft., in addition to a spinnaker of 3,100 sq. ft. for use when running before the wind. The light-weather sails comprised a balloon jib, balloon fisherman staysail, and club topsails with a combined area of 7,600 sq. ft. The spars, with the exception of the spinnaker pole, were solid Oregon pine manufactured in Portland. The bowsprit had a length of 21' outside. The foremast was 94'6" from deck to truck and the mainmast was 108'5" from deck to truck. The fore boom was 30' long and the main boom was 60' long.

The main engine consisted of two medium-speed Hill diesel engines with a 6-inch bore and 10-inch stroke, each developed 120 hp at 800 revolutions per minute. The propellers were three-bladed bronze, 36" in diameter, and 20" in pitch. To reduce the drag from the propellers when sailing, all shaft bearings were ball bearing. Ball-bearing thrusts were mounted on the inside length of shafting, which enabled the shaft to be uncoupled and the propellers to idle free. With two knots' way on the yacht the propellers would idle.

The yacht was completely wired for electricity. The generating equipment included four, 5-kW, 110 volt DC generators, two were belt-driven from the main engines for use when cruising, and the other two were driven by two, 10-hp, 5 by 7 single-cylinder Hill diesel engines. One of these single-cylinder engines also drove the main air compressor through a clutch, as the main engines were started by compressed air. There was also an electric air-compressor for emergency use in case the main compressor broke down. *Zaca* was bound for long cruises through islands where it would be impossible to have any but the smallest repairs made; her mechanical equipment was duplicated as much as possible.

The auxiliary electrical equipment also included a Frigidaire that maintained a temperature of 22°F in a frozen meat box that was 140 cubic feet, and a temperature of 40°F in a refrigerator that was 200 cubic feet. Another Frigidaire operated a small ice maker capable of making 100 pounds of small ice cubes daily. There was one Northern, gear-type, fire-bilge pump with a capacity of 75 gallons per minute at 90 pounds pressure. From this pump there was a main lead forward and one amidships for two fire hydrants. These were also used for washing decks and pumping bilges. In addition, *Zaca* had an auxiliary bilge and sump pump, the same as the main fire pump, with a capacity of 30 gallons per minute. The shower/baths and sinks, being below the water line, discharged from their drains into a small sump tank that was automatically pumped out by this pump.

The showers and sinks were supplied with hot and cold fresh water under pressure. The showers also had cold salt water. For this service there were three separate pumps which automatically maintained the water pressure. There were also two blower fans, one connected to the living quarters and one to the engine room.

In many out-of-the-way ports the fresh water obtained was going to be unfit for drinking purposes. To cope with this condition, the *Zaca* was equipped with an electric watermaker capable of distilling 50 gallons of water per day.

The radio equipment included one commercial 600-meter set with a range of 250 miles, and one commercial short-wave set, which was used daily in communication with San Francisco up to a range of 11,400 miles. This was considered a very good performance, as the aerial was only 20'. Both radio sets were built by the Radiomarine Corporation of America.

The main cabin had a built-in radio receiver and electric phonograph combined with outlets forward and aft, and on deck for loudspeakers.

The deck equipment included a 7 1/2-hp windlass forward, and two, 1-hp sail hoists, one at the foot of each mast. They were equipped with two drums, and used not only for hoisting sail, but for boats and general utility work. Aft, there was a 2-hp capstan for mooring and at sea for handling the main sheet. With this equipment, three men were all that were required to set the sails.

The ground tackle consisted of two bowers, 700 pounds and 500 pounds, and a 300-pound kedge anchor. There were two, 90-fathom length stud-link chains that were 7/8". Forward of the windlass there were two spring-riding chalks for riding to when at anchor in an open roadstead with a swell running. The chalks were there to take the sudden jerk from the windlass.

The below-deck arrangements, starting from forward, were an 18' forecastle containing six berths, a locker room, and toilet. Below the deck was the chin-locker. Aft of this space on the starboard side were two, two-berth staterooms; on the port side was the galley and the large refrigerator. Below the deck were the cook's stateroom and the freezer. Aft of the galley was the engine room, 11' long, running the entire width of the yacht. Above this space was a sunken deck house used for a radio and breakfast room.

Extending aft of the engine room bulkhead for 14' and across the entire width of the yacht was the main saloon. There was an entrance forward from the deck cabin and one aft from the main passageway leading from the after companionway. Opening off this passageway on the starboard side was the owner's stateroom and study, also a washroom with shower. Along the passageway on this side were small lockers for fishing rods, fishing tackle, guns, ammunition, and steward's supplies. Off the port side of the passageway was a washroom with a shower, and two double staterooms. Aft of the companionway leading to the deck were two single staterooms. This gave the yacht, exclusive of the owner's accommodations, two double and two single staterooms.

A 20' speedboat with a speed of 35 miles per hour, a 20' motor-powered otter boat, a skiff, a dory, and a small collapsible boat comprised the boatage. The otter boat was of the type used by sealing schooners in the Bering Sea for killing seals, and after being equipped with a small gasoline engine proved a very handy boat for work and fishing.

The after deck house was a roomy navigation room with ample drawers for charts and instruments, and lockers for flags and other incidentals for navigating the yacht. Aft of the chart room below decks is the lazarette for the storage of sails, ropes, and gear.

The fuel and water tanks were below the after accommodations, the fuel capacity being 2,000 gallons and the water capacity 2,100 gallons. There were also tanks for 200 gallons of lubricating oil and 200 gallons of kerosene.

On deck there were two 250-gallon gasoline tanks for the powerboats. These tanks were teak-sheathed and formed part of the permanent deck fittings. They had no pipe connections, there being just one opening for filling and drawing off the gasoline. This was done to reduce the risk of leakage through loose connections.

Every possible precaution had been taken to reduce the fire hazard. For this reason, and in addition to the two water-hydrants on deck, the staterooms, galley, engine room, and shaft alleys were equipped with automatic CO_2 fire control.

A shakedown cruise to Mexico was planned for May 1930, but at the christening of the *Zaca* in Sausalito's Hurricane Gulch, observers had some moments of fear that the expensive yacht was jinxed. The champagne bottle, thrown by Marie Dressler, refused to shatter, then the big black hull got stuck in the mud. The day ended when the *Zaca* was towed out to her mooring. When the yacht was taken around the harbor to set her compasses, the port engine stopped, the cause was said to be a "frozen" shaft thrust bearing. Crocker was prepared to sail to Mexico with only one engine, but the skipper refused to go out in this condition and *Zaca* was towed for repairs to the Alameda dry dock. Even after mechanics worked tirelessly on the yacht, more problems arose as a "stuffing box" gave way, allowing water to gush in so fast only hand pumps kept the *Zaca* afloat until she could make it back to dry dock.

Zaca sailing full-and-by in the Mediterranean. No matter what angle you look at her from, she is beautiful (*Guilain Grenier*).

Zaca's Cruise Around the World

To Crocker, most gratifying was the respect he earned sponsoring scientific expeditions to the little-researched exotic South Seas, and helping to rejuvenate the California Historical Society. The maiden voyage started in summer 1930 with Crocker on board for this historic journey. It was the first time a private yacht circumnavigated the globe starting from the West Coast. The crew included about a dozen professional sailors as well as a photographer and, of course, Garland Rotch. It was a good thing Crocker invited Garland along for their year-long trip around the world, because while they were in the South Pacific, Templeton Crocker fired *Zaca's* captain, George Goldrainer. Garland resumed those duties immediately afterward and remained as captain for the rest of their cruise.

Newspapers back in San Francisco reported Crocker's arrival at Pago Pago in Samoa. While at Papeete in Tahiti, Templeton reportedly decorated *Zaca* in bright, colored lights to celebrate the French Revolution and the fall of the Bastille on July 14. An island chief entertained Crocker and his guests with native dances. During this world cruise, Templeton Crocker began to collect batiks and textiles from Java and Bali, known as "the Pearl of the East," and "the last Paradise." On the island of Java, batiks were considered a highly perfected art, a laborious process of dying cloth by applying designs in beeswax. To Crocker's delight, most families in Java performed in their homemade theaters, using carved wooden dolls with elaborate gem-studded headdresses and shadow puppets whose silhouettes were cast against a light colored screen. Other artifacts, including tapas, musical instruments, and boat models were among the treasures making up the collection later loaned by Templeton Crocker to the M.H. deYoung Memorial Museum.

During *Zaca's* stay at Fiji, Crocker met S. M. Lambert, a doctor in tropical medicine for the Rockefeller Foundation. He entertained Crocker with tales of isolated and unexplored regions in the Solomon Islands. There, said Lambert, lived a tribe of Polynesians who, having had no contact with white men, were twenty thousand years behind modern man and the only relics of a prehistoric civilization.

Templeton Crocker wrote a book about this world cruise called *The Cruise of the* Zaca and made other scientific expeditions to the South Seas in the 1930s.

Further Expeditions

There was a voyage to Easter Island, off the coast of Chile, a mysterious place that baffled ethnologists and archaeologists unable to identify the origin of the carved stone remains of houses, towers, and 60-foot statutes. In part to study the unusual version of spoken English, the Crocker expedition visited Pitcairn Island, famed as a final refuge of the mutineers aboard the British ship *Bounty*.

Over time, Crocker's voyages began to take a more serious nature, and one of the early scientific expeditions was to Baja California in 1931. Dr. J. T. Howell, a botanist from the California Academy of Sciences, reported obtaining many rare specimens of plant life on Guadalupe Island, but Crocker the sportsman was ever-present. Templeton hauled in a 300-pound marlin swordfish after a long battle off Cape San Lucas. Reportedly, Crocker brought the "monster" back home on the yacht, frozen in a cake of ice, promising to present the fish to the California Academy of Sciences and Steinhart Aquarium so that the large fish and other "curious trophies" of the expedition could be viewed. The *Zaca* was gaining a reputation as a scientist's floating laboratory, this time sailing under Captain Garland Rotch, on the first of two expeditions to the Galapagos Islands, off the Ecuadorian coast. Made famous by Charles Darwin, the Galapagos Islands were home to the iguana, frigate birds, and elephant seals. Templeton Crocker himself was involved in the serious work of the scientific team, which included a highly esteemed botanist, aquatic zoologist, ornithologist, and ichthyologist from the California Academy of Sciences and Steinhart Aquarium. Also on board was artist Toshio Asaeda, *Zaca's* official photographer.

During the several months-long expedition, the scientists planned to capture specimens of fish from as deep as 250 fathoms, rare birds, plants, sea shells, termites, beetles, and butterflies. Four temperature-controlled tanks with running sea water were placed on the deck to bring back live specimens of 21 varieties of 154 fish such as the golden grouper, a species not seen in aquariums before. In May 1932, a radiogram announced that Crocker, Captain Rotch and other members of the *Zaca's* scientific expedition climbed a 2,690 foot high mountain on Indefatigable Island in the Galapagos. It was a feat never before accomplished, and the mountain was named Mount Crocker in Templeton's honor. On the trip home, the *Zaca* crew and scientists stopped at Acapulco where they brought aboard an ocelot named Castina, which quickly became the ship's pet. Castina later bit a guest at the Sausalito Harbor, causing great embarrassment for Crocker.

On the sixth expedition, a leisurely cruise down the California coast to Mexico and central America in the late 1930s, Templeton was accompanied by author Dr. William Beebe from the New York Zoological Society. Known for his underwater research in a bathysphere, Dr. Beebe intended to collect and observe marine life. A rare find was a tiny sailfish 1 1/4" long and a slightly larger rooster fish. At Culebra Bay, Costa Rica, *Zaca's* seines drew from a tide pool 6,832 fish from 27 species in a single day. The hauls were so great, more collection bottles, vials, and vats were requested.

World War Duty

Templeton Crocker continued to sail *Zaca* until World War II broke out. Due to a lack of available patrol ships, the U.S. Navy seized all privately owned ships over

The restoration of *Zaca* included the rebuild of her original gaff rig. With this rig, she sails reasonably well, although she is heavy; she was built as a sturdy vessel to sail around the world in 1930 (*Guilain Grenier*).

70 feet in length. Crocker had to cede the schooner to the United States Navy for $40,000 on June 12, 1942. The Navy had a strong need for local patrol and rescue craft in the busy waters of the San Francisco area. The Navy had thus good reason to place the schooner in service. This took place on June 19, 1942, when she was painted battleship gray, renamed *IX-73*, and ordered on patrol 500 miles off Eureka, California. She once spotted a Japanese fleet sailing down the coast and her radio report had them turn tail and retreat. *Zaca's* normal duty was as a radio beacon station, although she did carry two 20 mm caliber machine guns "just in case." When she returned to Treasure Island in San Francisco Bay every three weeks, her freezer was reliably full of salmon.

Eventually relieved by the frigates (PFs) of Escort Squadron 41, *Zaca* was placed out of service at Treasure Island October 1944. Turned over to the War Shipping Administration on May 21, 1945, *Zaca* was acquired by speculator Joe Rosenberg for $14,350. He subsequently sold the yacht in 1946 to the famous Australian actor Errol Flynn. He invested $80,000 in a total restoration: new masts, repainting, refurbishing of the interior, etc. The same year, in the company of a pick-up crew, his scientist father, marine biologist Carl Hubbs, and an assortment of actors, relatives, and a documentary film crew, he sailed to Acapulco on a "scientific expedition" that turned into a fiasco. After everyone jumped ship in Acapulco, Flynn trained a Mexican crew and rented *Zaca* to Orson Welles and Rita Hayworth for the filming of *The Lady from Shanghai*.

In 1946, after docking in Kingston, Jamaica, and waiting for repairs to be performed on *Zaca*, Flynn discovered Port Antonio. He returned in 1950 with his third wife, actress Patrice Wymore, and acquired an 1,800-acre cattle ranch and coconut plantation east of town. The Flynns began socializing with Noel Coward and Ian Fleming, among others. And they brought back the fun of leisure rafting down the Rio Grande River.

In 1956 Errol Flynn and Patricia Waymore sailed *Zaca* to Palma de Mallorca in the Mediterranean. They lived on board in the Club Náutico of Palma de Mallorca, partied, and tried to forget problems of debt and court summonses in the United States, usually by drowning them in booze. Eventually they left and Flynn died shortly after, in 1959. An important chapter of *Zaca's* history is that Flynn had used her not only for his pleasure, but also for several films (*Robin Hood*, *Captain Blood*, etc.) made in California, Mexico, Jamaica, and finally in the Mediterranean.

After Flynn's death, *Zaca* stayed at her berth at the Club Náutico, the crew keeping her up with the little money Patrice could get them. The attorneys for Flynn's Estate, in the meanwhile, were plotting to get rid of the costly yacht. Eventually they agreed to consign her to English millionaire playboy Freddie Tinsley, who promised he could sell her in France. Once in France, Tinsley stripped *Zaca* of everything of value and, in 1965, abandoned her in the boatyard of Bernard Voisin in Villefranche. Voisin eventually claimed *Zaca* for non-payment of rent. *Zaca* further deteriorated and turned into a ghost ship. The locals claimed there were emanations of Errol Flynn coming from the vessel and the sound of wild parties at night. This all ceased after a dual Anglican-Catholic exorcism in 1979. In 1987, English electronics mogul Phillip Coussins purchased Voisin's boatyard just to get *Zaca* but the deal ended up in French courts for two years. In 1990, Coussins wound up selling a now sunken *Zaca* to Italian businessman Roberto Memmo. With great financial and organizational effort, Memmo raised *Zaca's* wreck from the bottom of the harbor and restored her at the IMS shipyard in Saint-Mandrier-sur-Mer, near Toulon.

After two years of extensive rebuilding in Toulon, *Zaca* made her grand reappearance at Monaco's classic Regatta in 1993. *Zaca* is today regaled as one of the finest yachts in the world. Skipper Bruno Dal Pias, and a regular crew of four keep *Zaca* busy, visiting such ports as Punta Ala, Gaeta, Capri, Cagliari, and the Aegean. Owner Roberto Memmo has *Zaca* again hosting world leaders, writers, movie stars, and the occasional documentary filmmaker. During the summer, *Zaca* can be seen in person at important classic yacht races in the Mediterranean. In the winter she can be found in her berth in Port de Fontvieille, Monte Carlo.

This stern shot offers a clear view of her raised central deck area. This was done to add space below deck. This was obviously not a typical feature of the Newfoundland schooners (*Guilain Grenier*).

Edson B. Schock: Design Made Simple and Elegant

BIOGRAPHY OF EDSON B. SCHOCK

Edson Burr Schock (1871–1950) began his yacht design career at the age of 28, when he started working as an apprentice draftsman for A. Cary Smith. In 1900, only a year later, Schock opened his own office. In the early years, he supplemented his business with jobs at the Cramp Shipyard in Philadelphia and a shipyard in Groton, Connecticut. Between 1906 and 1910, he was the design editor for *The Rudder* magazine, and he continued to write articles for various publications throughout his life.

At the request of a client in 1910, Schock moved to Vancouver, British Columbia, to supervise construction of a yacht, and he spent the next 40 years at several locations on the West Coast. In 1922, he set up shop in Los Angeles and capitalized on the growth of the movie industry. Many famous and not-so-famous movie makers and actors wanted to have a sailing or motor yacht. During World War II he lived in Stockton, California, where he designed minesweepers and tugs for the war effort. In 1949, he moved to Kingston, Rhode Island, to be near his son, Edson I. Schock.

Schock's design career is characterized by its diversity. He did not specialize in any particular type of boat, but instead designed racing powerboats, motor yachts, racing and cruising sailboats, military and government craft, as well as a variety of commercial vessels, such as freighters, tugs, and fishing boats.

In sailing yachts, he is well known for his preference for simple and fast rigs. He especially liked the staysail schooner rig, which was clearly shown in his design of *Lucky Star*, an elegant and fast 44' racing schooner. Schock was so fascinated by her that he bought her back from her first owner.

Type: two-mast gaff-Marconi schooner
Designer: Edson B. Schock
Shipyard: Preiss and Mitchell, Wilmington, California
Year of Construction: 1937
Length on Deck: 43'8"
Length on Waterline: 31'
Beam: 11'
Draft: 6'4"
Sail Area: 870 sq. ft.
Construction: Douglas fir planking on steam-bent white oak frames and fastened with iron boat nails, rebuilt with double-planked Honduras mahogany on laminated oak frames and bronze fastened
Engine: 40-hp universal diesel
Owner: Craig Downey
Home Port: Paulsbo, Washington

Lucky Star: A Small Staysail Schooner with Good Racing Potential

Lucky Star was designed by Edson Schock for Stephen and Warren Newmark in 1937. At that time Schock worked out of Los Angeles, and built in Wilmington, California. *Lucky Star* was originally framed with white oak and planked in Douglas fir. The deck, cabin trunk, and deck erections were of teak. The spars were of hollow spruce and the standing rigging was galvanized cast steel. Fittings were of bronze. The 870 sq. ft. of sails were made by Ratsey. She was fitted out with a 4-cylinder 3 3/8" by 4" Gray engine, located under the bridge deck, which gave her a speed of 6.5 knots under power. The capacity of the fuel tanks was 50 gallons and the same amount of fresh water could also be carried.

Below decks, the accommodations consisted of a stateroom forward, galley and toilet amidships, and a roomy main cabin aft. Plenty of space was arranged for stowage, including a roomy fore peak.

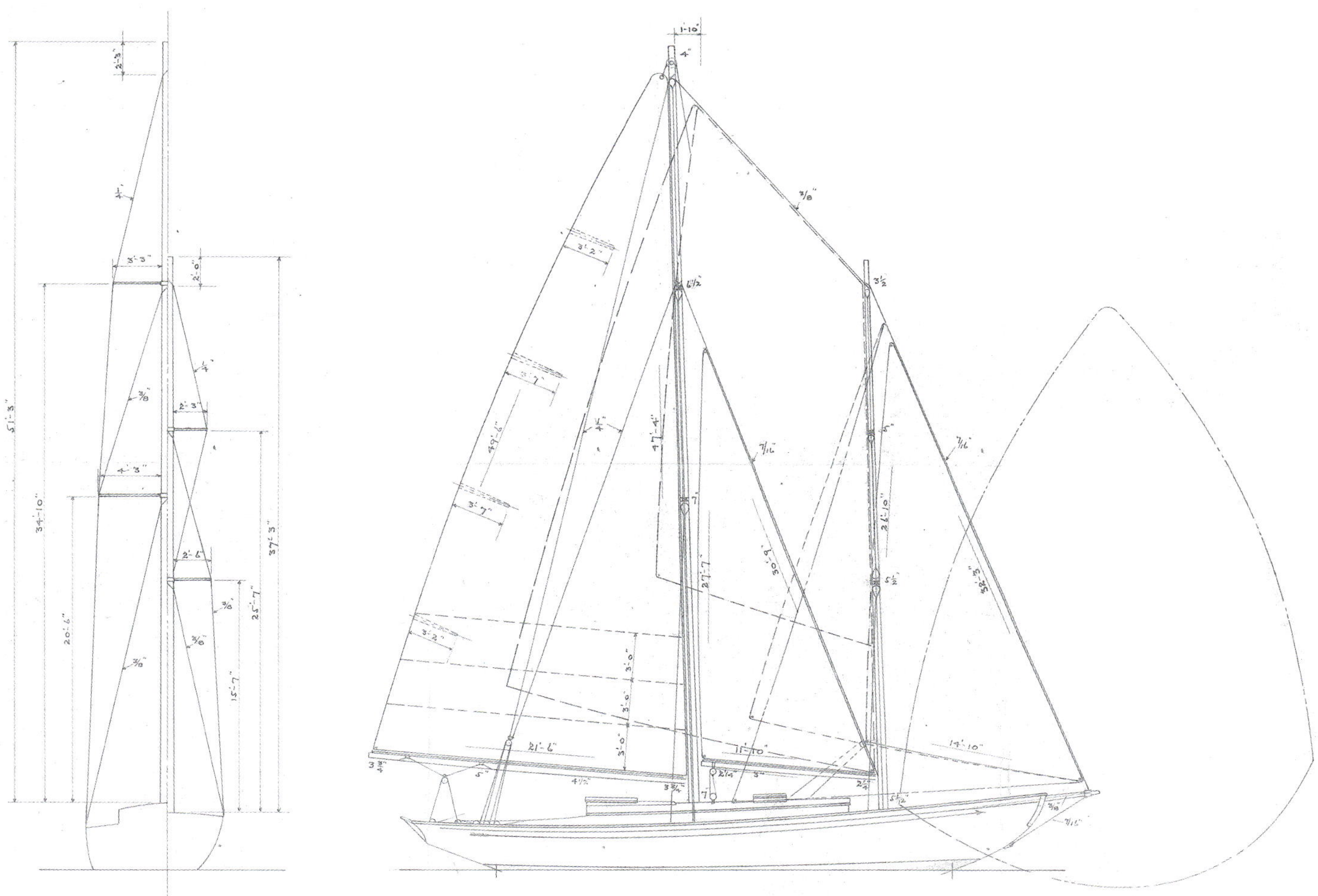

Stephen and Warren Newmark sailed *Lucky Star* for 10 years. Schock was so fond of his design that when *Lucky Star* was put up for sale, he purchased his own boat. But he kept her for only three years. *Lucky Star* then had three different owners, under whom she competed in the Trans Pac and was berthed in Honolulu for five years.

Lucky Star under the Caring Downey Family Ownership

In 1962, Brad Downey purchased her in a very unloved condition. During those years the family built their own sails and campaigned *Lucky Star* nearly every weekend in every available race, winning many and often being the only schooner at the starting line. In 1963, with homemade sails, they won the PHRF Highpoint Series, being the only schooner competing against some 600 newer sloops and divided rigs. *Lucky Star's* design has produced a very close winded schooner, which does extremely well in light air races. She loves to go to weather.

Over the years, *Lucky Star* has been completely rebuilt, with all new double planking in Honduras mahogany, all new glue-laminated oak frames, transom, hatches, and cap rails. The screws used for planking are silicon bronze. In addition, there were many other replacements in a continuous effort to make her sail easier and faster. The schooner still carries her original wooden rig with hollow spruce masts. The external ballast is 4.53 tons of lead. The exterior trim and the interior is still the original varnished teak. Her design already provided for a staysail schooner rig with a Marconi main sail, one main-staysail, and one foresail hoisted from a short bowsprit. The main mast is stayed by running backstays.

Lucky Star is a fast sailing yacht. She has shown that throughout her entire life. She has received more than 65 trophies for wins, including the America's Schooner Cup Races in San Diego in both 1999 and 2000.

The Downey family raised three children in a sailing tradition and has enjoyed many great cruises to all the Channel Islands, races to Ensenada, the San Juan Islands, and a wonderful cruise throughout Southeast Alaska up to Glacier Bay and Skagway with an exciting sail back down the coast to Newport, California.

In 2008, Brad Downey's son, Craig Downey moved the boat to Poulsbo, Washington, where she currently resides and is raced and cruised throughout the Pacific Northwest. The Downey family plans to steep their next generation in the joys of sailing this wonderful schooner.

Lucky Star's hull form can be clearly appreciated in this photo of her sitting on a truck. The star in the center of her underbody is her trademark (*Craig Downey*).

Lucky Star is in a light breeze. However, her gollywobbler enhances her performance and she seems to make good speed (*Craig Downey*).

Here again, going to windward under full sail in a light breeze on the Pacific (*Craig Downey*).

The interior is finely crafted, and fitted out with red velvet cushions. Just like in the 1920s (*Craig Downey*).

Another view of her interior, to the port aft side and the companionway (*Craig Downey*).

Forward part of the interior (*Craig Downey*).

Lucky Star under spinnaker and gollywobbler in a breeze. She seems to enjoy this sailing! (*Craig Downey*).

Lucky Star sailing in Paulsbo, Washington. She serves there well as a racing schooner and a family cruising boat at the same time (*Craig Downey*).

This photo from the front page of the magazine *Dockside* depicts *Lucky Star* from the stern, allowing a sweeping view over her deck. It seems clear that she was designed for racing (*Craig Downey*).

Olin Stephens: Fine Design Applied to Schooner Yachts

BIOGRAPHY OF OLIN STEPHENS

"I was lucky: I had a goal. As far back as I can remember I wanted to design fast boats." The first two sentences of Olin Stephens' autobiography, *All This and Sailing, Too*, summarize the lifetime vocation of the most successful and influential designer of the twentieth century. He was raised near New York City and, as a boy, was introduced to boats on family vacations at Cape Cod. Along with his father, Roderick, and younger brother, Roderick Jr. (called Rod), he learned to sail in a series of family-owned boats.

Stephens enrolled in the Massachusetts Institute of Technology in 1926, only to be forced to drop out during his freshman year due to illness. Throughout his life, although he was a pioneer in scientific yacht design, he would say that he regretted his lack of training in mathematics and engineering. Yet Stephens had aptitudes that suited his calling. "I started my career with the tools of observation and intuition to which quantitative analysis has been gradually added," he wrote in his autobiography. "Whenever possible I studied lines and tried to see the way shape was coupled to performance."

His first published design, a 6-meter, appeared in the January 1928 *Yachting* with these comments by the young designer:

> *In any design the most important factors of speed seem to be long sailing lines and large sail area, with moderate displacement and small wetted surface. Then comes beauty, by which is meant clean, fair, pleasing lines. Though per se beauty is not a factor of speed, the easiest boats to look at seem the easiest to drive.*

To this equation he added stability due to considerable external ballast. Many older designers of offshore boats in the United States placed the lead ballast in the bilge in order to ease the boat's motion through a seaway. Stephens preferred it deep in the keel, where 6-meters and other modern racing boats had it, in order to provide stability and sail-carrying ability for good upwind performance.

After working as a draftsman for Henry J. Gielow and Philip Rhodes, in 1929 Stephens went into partnership with Drake Sparkman, a successful yacht broker, to form Sparkman & Stephens Inc. (S&S). The aggressive Sparkman was the salesman; Stephens, by nature a shy man, ran the design office. Their first project was a 21' keel boat for junior sailing on Long Island Sound called the Sound Junior Class, later renamed the Manhasset Bay One Design. Then came a small cruising boat for his father and several 6-meters.

In 1928, he raced to Bermuda with John Alden in *Malabar IX*. This experience helped him understand the needs of a proper offshore racing yacht. After his grandfather sold the family coal business in 1929, his father commissioned S&S design Number 4, the 52-foot yawl *Dorade*. Her concept was much closer to a 6-meter than a Malabar. She had a tall Bermudian rig, balanced ends, narrow beam, lead ballast deep in the keel, and lightweight, sophisticated construction (with steam-bent rather than sawn frames). *Dorade* was built at the Minneford Yard on City Island, New York, under the supervision of young Rod Stephens, who developed an efficient deck layout and a new type of deck ventilator (the "Dorade" vent) with a baffle that separated incoming air from spray. In 1931 she won the transatlantic race to England against many larger boats by two days on elapsed time and also won a rough Fastnet Race. Thinking *Dorade* too narrow and tender, when Stephens had the opportunity to design another ocean racer in 1934, he increased the beam by two feet and the result was *Stormy Weather*, which he regarded as the better boat. These two boats transformed the design of offshore sailing yachts.

In the meantime, Olin Stephens was playing an important role in the transition of yacht design from an art to a science with artistic disciplines. Scientific yacht design, using experiments and quantification of performance, came about because of his work with Kenneth S. M. Davidson of the Stevens Institute of Technology in Hoboken, New Jersey, to develop a method for evaluating a design by towing models in water tanks.

It was soon used to help design an America's Cup winner. Stephens first became involved with the America's Cup in 1934, when he served in the afterguard of the unsuccessful defense candidate *Weetamoe*, designed by Clinton Crane. In 1936, Harold S. "Mike" Vanderbilt, who had defended the Cup in 1930 and 1934, brought Stephens together with Wm. Starling Burgess as a design team. Out of a series of tests models, some of Burgess' design and some of Stephens', came the great J-Class cutter *Ranger*, which dominated the 1937 America's Cup season.

Throughout the 1930s Stephens continued to design 6-meters and he also designed 12-meters and many cruiser-racers like the New York 32 class and the 72-foot yawl *Baruna*, which after World War II enjoyed famously close racing with another S&S-designed 72-footer, *Bolero*. He saw the future of yachting in sloops and yawls rather than schooners. This may explain why he designed only ten schooners, of which only three have survived: the *Brilliant*, a heavy schooner now owned by the Mystic Seaport Museum; the *So Fong*, another heavy cruising schooner that can be considered a larger version of *Brilliant*; and the *Santana*, a sleeker and smaller schooner yacht adapted for offshore cruising and racing. The following pages will be devoted to the larger *So Fong* and the smaller *Santana* as the most representative examples of Olin Stephens' schooner designs.

After the war, Stephens' work expanded internationally, and S&S-designed ocean racers with different shapes won in Europe and in America. The Royal Ocean Racing Rule in Britain was encouraging relatively narrow, deep-bodied keel boats. The major championships under the Royal Ocean Racing Club rating rule, including the Admiral's Cup and One-Ton Cup, were regularly won by S&S boats. In America, the Cruising Club of America Rule over several years (1955–60) produced beamy centerboarders that also did well in ocean races. While Stephens designed centerboarders, he was not especially enamored of the type because of its relatively low stability. Nevertheless, his name is closely linked with centerboarders because of Carleton Mitchell's 38-foot yawl *Finisterre*, which, beautifully prepared and brilliantly sailed by her owner and his crack crew, won three straight Bermuda Races (1956, 1958, and 1960). In time, the Cruising Club of America Rating Rule was adjusted to encourage narrower boats. In the late 1960s Stephens helped bring about the first international measurement rule, the International Offshore Rule (IOR). He later served as chairman of the rule's International Technical Committee and played an important role in the development of the International Measurement System (IMS).

All this time Stephens was producing successful racing boats, including the winners of a total of eight of the nine America's Cup matches between 1937 and 1980. Other than *Ranger*, the most remarkable of these boats was *Intrepid*, the defender in 1967 and, after alterations by Britton Chance Jr., again in 1970.

While designing America's Cup defenders and ocean racers, Stephens also produced a number of powerboats, motorsailers, cruising boats, and day-racing boats.

After Drake Sparkman's death in 1964, Olin Stephens shouldered the firm's administrative burden. His chief assistants included his brother Rod, who supervised much of the rigging design and construction, and Gil Wyland. Stephens and his wife, Susie, lived in a New York suburb where they raised two sons.

When he retired in 1978, he could look back to a design career where he had designed or supervised the design of more than 2,000 boats and classes. The Stephenses moved then to northern New England, where Stephens continued his varied life into his nineties. He took courses in mathematics at the Dartmouth College and helped teach a course on sailing for engineers. He developed his computer skills, worked with a firm on software for studying aerodynamics, advised America's Cup syndicates, and traveled often and far to technical conferences and meetings of international rating rules committees.

He died at age 100, in September 2008, in his home in Hanover, New Hampshire.

SANTANA

Type: two-mast staysail schooner
Designer: Olin Stephens, design No. 59
Year of Construction: 1935
Shipyard: Wilmington Boat Works, Southern California
Length on Deck: 55'2"
Length on Waterline: 40'6"
Beam: 12'6"
Draft: 7'11"
Displacement: 23 tons
Construction: mahogany on white oak, teak deck
Owner: Paul & Chrissy Kaplan
Home Port: San Francisco, California

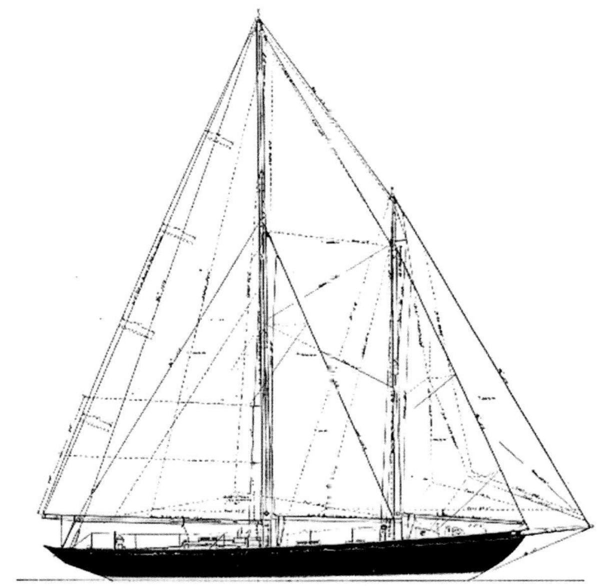

Some yachts are famous because of their racing record. Others, because they have been the venue for film stars and other celebrities. *Santana* can claim fame because of both. Having finished several races in good positions, she became famous in the 1950s as Humphrey Bogart's personal yacht, hosting many Hollywood celebrities. It is currently preserved by a very dedicated owner, sailing out of San Francisco. It seems that time is standing still on this stunning schooner, which is today in the same condition she was when launched in 1935.

Santana's Design and Construction: Yawl or Schooner?

Olin Stephens designed *Santana* for W. L. Stewart, Jr., the son of the founder of the Union Oil Company. Stewart wanted a schooner that could show her heels to the best and brightest on both coasts. Constructed of mahogany planks over white oak frames at Wilmington Boat Works in Southern California, *Santana* was launched on October 24, 1935.

Prior to the start of her construction, Olin Stephens tried to convince Stewart to build a yawl but he resisted; he had always wanted a schooner and that was what *Santana* would be. As it turned out, Stephens' recommendation was correct, and boats like *Baruna* and *Dorade*, both yawls from his drawing board, dominated the racing scene in the late thirties. Nevertheless, *Santana* took part in the 1937 Bermuda Race, and she also sailed successfully in the Pacific races until 1939.

It was Julia Stewart, W. L.'s wife, who persuaded him to build a new boat. She is quoted as saying, "I was the reason he sold *Santana*. I told him, 'You need a bigger boat to accommodate you and your fat friends.'"

Mrs. Stewart thought it would be a shame to rerig *Santana* as a yawl since she was built to be a schooner. W. L. listened to his wife and asked Stephens to design him a 67' yawl, which he named *Chubasco*, Spanish for a small rainstorm, or squall.

Once *Chubasco* was under construction, *Santana* was placed for sale and was

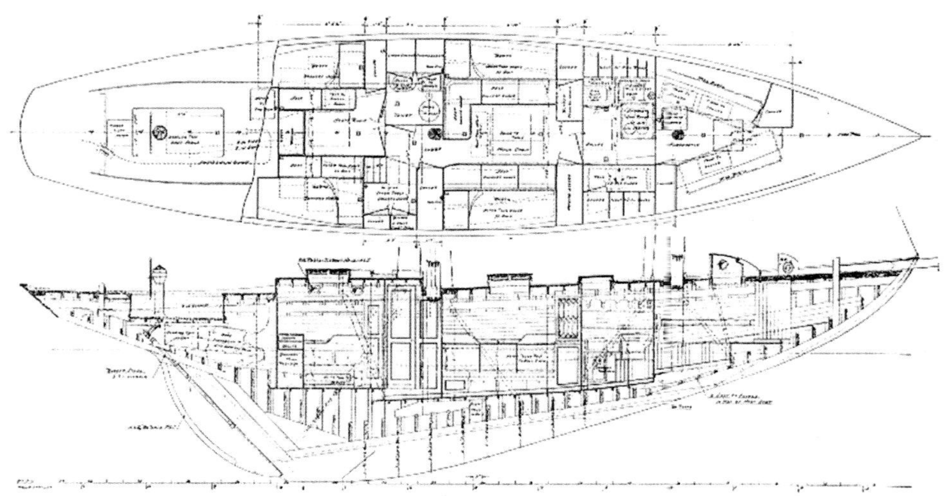

Santana was built as a schooner. Here she is shown shortly after her launch in 1934. Note the particular design of her mainsail, which is loose-footed and cut like a staysail (*Stewart Family Archive*).

To take part in the Bermuda Race, *Santana* was loaded onto one of her owner's merchant ships and brought to the United States' East Coast (*Stewart Family Archive*).

Here she is sitting in a cradle specifically built for her transport to the other side of the United States (*Stewart Family Archive*).

When she sailed east for another race, she sailed all the way on her own keel. In this photo, *Santana* passes through the Panama Canal (*Stewart Family Archive*).

Santana sailing with her schooner rig (*Stewart Family Archive*).

In the early forties *Santana* was converted into a yawl. The result was still a beautiful vessel. She looked very similar to the other famous Stephens' yawls, such as *Baruna* or *Dorade* (*Eden Family Archive*).

soon bought by Charles Isaacs, a businessman from San Diego. Isaacs was married to Eva Gabor, the Hollywood Hungarian who reportedly understood that it is just as easy to love a rich man as a poor one. Isaacs owned *Santana* for two years. Not much more is known about Isaacs or the activities of *Santana* during this period.

Sailing into Hollywood with Style

George Brent was an actor and responsible for introducing *Santana* to movie society, where she became the belle of the Hollywood fleet for the next 16 years. Brent converted *Santana* into a yawl. When he consulted with S&S about the project, they suggested he increase the length of the mast six or eight feet for greater efficiency in light weather. Because of the cost he decided not to build a new mast and the original main mast was moved forward and the mizzen was added. This decision was fortuitous as when the time came 58 years later to convert the boat back into a schooner, it allowed the original main mast to be used.

As an actor, Brent featured in many "women's movies," where most of the time all that could be seen of George was the back of his neck, the screen more focused on whom he was kissing—not bad work if you can get it and it affords you a nice boat. Some of the women kissed by Brent included Kay Francis, Barbara Stanwyck, Myrna Loy, Ann Sheridan, and Bette Davis, with whom he appeared in eleven movies including *Jezebel* (1938) and *Dark Victory* (1939).

Ray Milland owned *Santana* for three months and no one seems to know why he sold her so quickly. It has been speculated that the movie studios played some role in the ownership of the boat, as it was a "photo opportunity" to gain publicity with a handsome yacht and leading man. It was held that Milland was a good sailor; unfortunately, he did not get to enjoy the boat for very long.

Milland played opposite many of the most attractive and talented female stars in Hollywood, ranging from Claudette Colbert, Dorothy Lamour, Frances Farmer, Paulette Goddard, Ginger Rogers, and Marlene Dietrich. One can only guess how many of his co-stars Milland took out for a Sunday sail, but it is known that during *Santana's* Bogart years many of his colleagues, both male and female, sailed on *Santana*.

Much the same as Milland, Dick Powell owned the boat for a very short period of time, lending further credibility to the stories regarding movie studios using *Santana* for publicity purposes. The most notable improvement to *Santana* for which Powell was responsible came at the request of his wife, June Allyson.

The story is that Ms. Allyson required a hiding place to store her jewelry while

Humphrey Bogart and Lauren Bacall aboard *Santana*. The three seemed to have had a love affair…(*Eden Family Archive*)

Humphrey Bogart wasn't the only one to sail the *Santana*. Lauren Bacall also worked with the sails and maneuvered the schooner. In this photo, she steered the boat into the harbor while husband Bogart took in the sails (*Eden Family Archive*).

Bogart felt most happy when he was aboard his *Santana* (*Eden Family Archive*).

Bogart was so connected to *Santana* that at his funeral, *Santana's* model stood right next to his coffin (*Eden Family Archive*).

aboard the boat. She requested a special compartment be built where she could hide her "baubles" and one was built in the owner's stateroom. The drawers in *Santana* became swollen as a result of her sinking years later and it was not until the boat had thoroughly dried that it was possible to remove the drawer. Once removed, it was found to contain a leather money clip. It is not known to whom this belonged, but with the long list of celebrity owners, it is easy to let one's imagination wonder.

Santana and Humphrey Bogart

Regardless of how many owners there have been, or will be, *Santana* will always be known as "Bogie's" boat. Humphrey Bogart wrote this in an article for the *Film Review* in July 1951:

> I started wanting to be sailor when I was ten. I was on vacation with my parents at Seneca Point on Canandaigua Lake in up-state New York. My father gave me a motorboat with a one-cylinder engine, and I used to putt-putt around the lake all day, exploring every watery inch of it. I made up my mind then that I'd have a "real" boat one day. I believe my ideas went way beyond the yacht class. I had something in mind like a private ocean liner!
>
> I never attained the ocean liner; but I have progressed sufficiently from that one-cylinder job to be able to boast (a sailor's privilege) about the *Santana*.

Bogart was so fond of *Santana* that he sailed her between 35 and 45 weekends a year. Most of those weekends were stag, as Bogie felt that "the trouble with having dames on board is you can't pee over the side." In addition to many weekends aboard the boat spent at Catalina, he also did a considerable amount of racing with respectable results. Bogart took first in his class in the San Clemente Island Race of 1950 and first in the 1952 Channel Islands Race.

Bogart and *Santana* played host to many of Hollywood's greatest stars of the time, including Ingrid Bergman, Richard Burton, David Niven, and Frank Sinatra. In David Niven's memoir, *The Moon's a Balloon*, he tells of a weekend when he and his wife Hjordis were aboard *Santana* as guests of the Bogarts. Frank Sinatra and his party were on a chartered motor yacht. In the evening Sinatra's boat tied up next to *Santana*, and accompanied by Jimmy Van Heusen on piano, Sinatra sang, literally, all through the night. "People from other boats rowed over in dinghies and sat in a circle around the two yachts, under a full moon, listening, until the sky began to grow light and the singing ended. Then they rowed quietly away."

During the years that Bogart owned the boat he made only one significant change, that being the addition of the drink holder that is installed around the base of the steering binnacle. Designed to fit a group of large highball glasses, this proved to be a practical and vital improvement for the competitive yachtsman Bogart was. One night after a race in which *Santana* coasted past another yacht, Bogart was asked, "What makes the boat go like that?" Bogie said, "Scotch," and then just walked away. Clearly Bogart put that drink holder to good use both on and off the racecourse.

When Bogart wasn't sailing, he still had *Santana* on his mind. When he formed his own production company in 1947, he called it Santana Productions. Bogie starred with Bacall and Edward G. Robinson in the movie *Key Largo*, and his boat in the film had "*Santana*" on the stern. He also had a complete model of *Santana* on display in his home inside a glass case. Above that case sat his two Academy Awards. If asked what was more important—the Oscars or the boat—no doubt he would have replied, "the Boat." When Bogart died, they eulogized the actor, the husband and the father, but it was the model of *Santana*, his love, that stood alongside the pulpit.

Bogart certainly had a love affair with *Santana*. While some think of her as being special just because she was "Bogie's Boat," in fact quite the opposite was true. Bogart had been a life-long sailor and he knew a good boat when he saw one. It was *Santana's* indescribable virtues that attracted him. It just happened that he was also extraordinarily well known, and this only furthered her notoriety.

After Humphry Bogart…

Following Bogart's death, *Santana* was purchased by Willis Short, a San Diego interior decorator. Short raced the boat locally and made one striking change in her appearance. He removed two cabinet doors of diamond-shaped leaded-glass panels that had flanked the entrance to the galley. Short felt the cabinets made the cabin too dark and he replaced them with translucent panels. These panels evidently were made of fiberglass that had seahorses and seaweed laminated in between, which was then accented with a light behind. Other than this creative contribution to the interior décor, not much more is known about Short and his activities aboard *Santana*.

W. H. (Wally) Nickell was a retired Brigadier General in the United States' Army who became an independent oilman in Sacramento. He was *Santana's* second owner in the oil business. Nickell had owned various boats in the past and Emil "Babe" Lamberdin had been responsible for their upkeep. Once Nickell bought *Santana*, Babe was asked to look after the boat on a full-time basis and accepted the position.

One of Babe's first tasks was to replace the seahorses with something more appropriate in the saloon, and he was more than happy to oblige. While Babe fully appreciated the practical matters with respect to the modern racing yachts, he always talked about how great *Santana* looked when she was a schooner. Knowing full well that Nickell would never change that boat, it was obvious that he too had fallen in love with *Santana*, but as a schooner, not a yawl.

Nevertheless, Babe diligently looked after the boat and she proved to do well on San Francisco Bay, racing as many as 20 times a season. Ultimately, however, Nickell, a competitive fellow, became frustrated with his lack of success on the race course and in 1966 decided to sell the boat.

Mr. Solari, a wealthy attorney, bought *Santana* with the intention of racing her. Babe accepted the job of captain and together they had a wonderful time. Solari once said, "Babe to me is *Santana*." She participated in the St. Francis Yacht Club "Big Boat

Series" and one race to Acapulco and another to Mazatlan. Solari was more interested in sailing than trophies and was once heard to say, "I don't remember where we finished in those races, but we had a marvelous time."

Solari's most ambitious project was entering *Santana* in the 1968 Bermuda Race, 30 years after her triumphant debut there. Babe and his wife Liz sailed the boat around to Newport, Rhode Island, via the Panama Canal. In June, Solari's crew assembled in Newport and set off for Bermuda. Solari said, "We performed very poorly...I zigged when everybody zagged."

With the newer boats being harder to beat, it looked as if *Santana's* racing days were slowing down. The boat was brought back to San Francisco and was sailed for social occasions and less for racing. Eventually the boat stopped sailing and sat in her berth, rarely used. After sitting for a long while, she was put up for sale.

Santana's Trip around the World

Charlie Peet was a Sausalito, California, restaurateur who had adventure in his blood. In 1971, he and his wife, Marty, bought *Santana* to sail around the world. Sailing with them as crew was Jim Leech, now of the sail making firm Leech & Rudiger. Leech recalls that everywhere they went they found people who knew *Santana*. While in Rarotonga, in the Cook Islands, they ran into a photographer whose mother ran a store there and who purportedly lost her virginity on the *Santana* in Avalon (Catalina Island), in 1945.

While *Santana* was built for racing and was constructed out of the best materials of the time, the trip took its toll. She had lost her mizzenmast during a storm with winds to 85 knots. She had sailed 40,000 miles in two years, and it was the last leg from Cabo San Lucas to San Francisco that was the worst. The winds blew so hard that the boat couldn't move to windward. Three times she set out from Cabo and three times *Santana* was beaten back. Finally, Marty Peet flew home in tears, friends say, unable to bear any longer the beating the old boat was taking.

When Peet returned to San Francisco he sold *Santana* to M. Lloyd Carter, a "drama therapist" from Marin County. Carter had it in his head that he, too, was going to sail her around the world.

This never took place, as it most certainly would have destroyed he boat. After many years of hard sailing and little maintenance, the engine room was a pit full of grease and old empty oil cans. Forty-four of her 125 frames or "ribs" were broken. A plank that had popped off near Pitcairn Island had been repaired in a shoddy manner.

In short, the boat was a wreck and needed extensive repairs before she could sail across San Francisco Bay, much less around the world. Fortunately, Tom and Ted Eden persuaded Carter that the smartest thing for him to do would be to sell them the boat, which he did.

Racing under Tom and Ted Eden

Thomas F. and Theodore A. Eden, twin brothers who ran their own successful architectural firm, knew that *Santana* was in need of considerable work and they were prepared for the task. It took them nearly two years with the help of many others to finally get the boat back into sailing condition. Once finished, the boat was used for day sailing, periodic ocean races, and the annual Master Mariner's Regatta.

In 1982, a match race was arranged to settle an old score against *Dorade*, the boat that had beaten *Santana* in the Transpac to Hawaii in 1936. America's Cup skipper Tom Blackaller was at the helm of *Santana*, backed by Ted and Tom Eden and their well-oiled crew. On board *Dorade* was Robert C. Keefe and his well-practiced group. After some hard-fought negotiations, it was agreed that *Santana*, being slightly longer than *Dorade*, would give her 7 seconds per mile. *Santana* beat *Dorade*, by more than six minutes over a 12-mile course, easily saving her time and correcting out to first. Blackaller, in his typically modest manner, proclaimed, "I bet the boat was never this fast when Bogart sailed it!"

After Tom Eden passed away in 1993, the boat did more sitting than sailing. *Santana* was put up for sale in 1994 and then was withdrawn from the market.

The Sinking of *Santana*

Sometime during the night in November of 1997, the automatic bilge pump aboard the boat came on. It started its normal routine of pumping the small amount of water overboard that will accumulate in the bilge of most boats.

Unfortunately, after the pump shut off, the check valve that was connected to the pump discharge line failed to close correctly. This allowed water to siphon into the boat, as the discharge line was located below the waterline. Gradually the bilge began to fill with water from the Bay. It took many hours for the boat to slowly "sink" in her berth. It was not until someone noticed that *Santana's* decks were nearly awash before anything was done to prevent her from going completely to the bottom of the yacht harbor.

In what must have been one of the most painful moments of her celebrated career, the boat was severely damaged—possibly even permanently beyond repair.

After months of deliberation, the owners decided to settle with the insurance company and then elected to sell the boat. *Santana* sat in her berth at the St. Francis Yacht Club in San Francisco, damaged from the sinking, her interior completely torn apart and very much needing someone to come along and embrace the yacht with the enthusiasm needed to bring her back to life.... This was the moment when Paul and Chrissy Kaplan appeared in *Santana's* life. It was in July of 1998. Today they remain the proud owners of this stunning schooner.

Under the Dedicated Ownership of Paul and Chrissy Kaplan

The Kaplans took one peek under *Santana's* boat cover and that was it! While many people cautioned them about such a purchase, intuitively they knew that if they did not buy the boat, it would be something they would regret not doing for the rest of their lives.

Santana underwent a year-long refit that made her the envy of every Concours d'Elegance. And while they were at it, Paul and Chrissy decided to convert her back to a schooner. "We wanted to be as authentic as possible, so we procured copies of the original drawings of the S&S plans from Mystic Seaport."

One third of all the original frames were broken. So new ceilings and new frames had to be installed, and the interior needed to be rebuilt. From the rig to the deck layout and the beveled glass doors of the saloon lockers, *Santana* was restored to Bristol condition with some changes for the sake of practicality. The cockpit features a glass fiber well and was moved aft. The galley was updated and the forward cabin, formerly the crew's quarters, became a lush V-berth. A 75-hp Yanmar turbo diesel replaced the old rustball engine. "They used the original schooner main mast for the yawl conversion," says Kaplan. "This mast was a bit too short for the yawl rig, so that it had been enlarged. To go back to the schooner rig, it was only necessary to take out the enlargement piece. The new bowsprit was carbon fiber with a faux-wood surface."

The *Santana* sails once again, after being lovingly restored to her original configuration as a schooner. Since her restoration, *Santana* has participated in literally all major maritime events on the San Francisco Bay. She has become one of the most photographed and admired yachts in San Francisco's very active classic yacht community.

Designed as a racing schooner, *Santana* has a very clean deck, very suitable for a large crew to work the sails (*Paul Kaplan*).

After Paul Kaplan's extensive restoration between 1998 and 1999, *Santana* again went out into the San Francisco Bay sailing hard. She is an impressive sight on the Bay (*Paul Kaplan*).

Santana sailing under full sail, including fisherman and spinnaker (*Paul Kaplan*).

When converting *Santana* back from yawl to schooner rig, some fittings had to be done new. They were produced in stainless steel, following the original patterns (*Paul Kaplan*).

Santana enjoying a good breeze on the Bay (*Paul Kaplan*).

Santana racing in San Francisco Bay in autumn 2011, just like in 1935 (*Peter Lyons*).

Her large gennaker is a sight to be seen (*Peter Lyons*).

SO FONG

Type: two-mast gaff schooner
Designer: Olin Stephens, design No. 143
Year of Construction: 1937
Shipyard: Ah King Slipway Company in Causeway Bay, Hong Kong
Length on Deck: 89'
Length on Waterline: 76'
Beam: 16'
Draft: 12'
Displacement: 60 tons
Sail Area: 2,691 sq. ft.
Construction: mahogany on white oak, teak deck
Engine: 360-hp diesel
Owner: Vela Clásica de Época, Inc.
Home Port: Palma de Mallorca, Spain

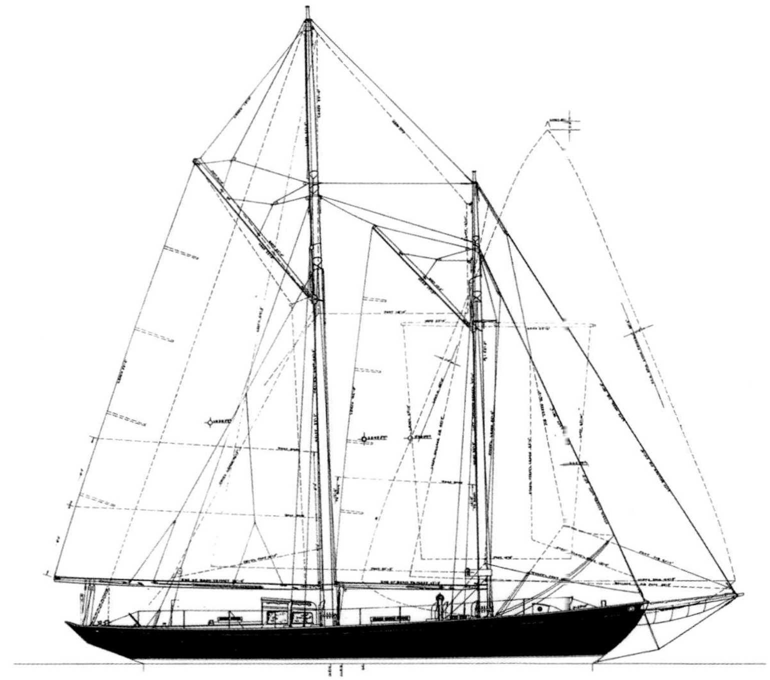

Sparkman & Stephens designed very few schooners. Only *Brilliant*, *Santana,* and *So Fong* remain actively sailing today. Of this very small number of schooners, *So Fong* is a standout, since she is the largest schooner designed by Olin Stephens. Today, just as *Santana* is the flagship of the classic yacht fleet in San Francisco, so too is *So Fong* in Palma de Mallorca, the heart of the Mediterranean.

The Construction and First Circumnavigation

So Fong is a Sparkman & Stephens gaff schooner built in 1937 by Ah King Slipway Company in Causeway Bay, Hong Kong, for Thompson Baker, a New York Stockbroker. *So Fong* is a slightly bigger version of the famous schooner *Brilliant*, which is currently based in Mystic Seaport, Connecticut, where she is kept in immaculate shape.

For *So Fong's* construction, the builder used ironwood for the keelson and floors. Her hull is of the finest Asian teak, her upper sawn frames are teak and yakki (a springy Asian wood), and her deck beams are camphor and teak. The masts and rig were built in the United States and shipped to Hong Kong, as were the blocks, which are lignum vitae with bronze or iron straps.

The name *So Fong* was given to the boat at the time of her launch, as Chinese superstition would not allow a yacht to be put into the water until a name was given. Since the owner had not yet decided on a name for the boat, she was launched as *So Fong*, the nickname for the daughter of Ah King's owner. The name has remained throughout the fascinating history of this stunning and elegant schooner.

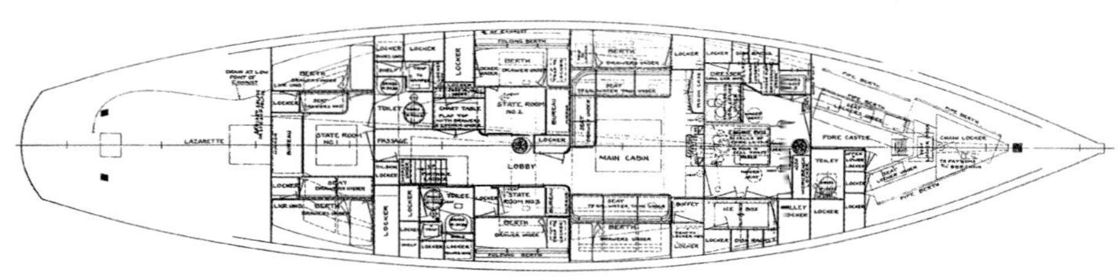

Thompson Baker had commissioned the boat for the purpose of sailing around the world with his son. In the early 1940s, Baker sailed the boat to the United States via the East Indies, Suez, Mediterranean, and the Caribbean. Following this voyage he sold the boat.

The War Years

As so many other large yachts, during World War II, *So Fong* operated as a United States Coast Guard vessel, with a crew of seven. Still today there is a plaque over the head that says "Officers," a reminder of her military service. The Skipper had the spacious aft cabin, two officers had the guest cabins, and four enlisted sailors lived in the forecastle. After the war *So Fong* spent time in the Caribbean and Maine under the ownership of Mr. and Mrs. Henry Becton who raced the boat very competitively for many years in those waters.

Back in Asia

So Fong was bought by Bill Mathers who appears to have been the son of an American senator. The purpose was to use her on a secret mission to try and find a scuttled World War II German submarine that lay somewhere off the coast of North Vietnam. Toward the end of World War II, the Nazis built five super-submarines, one of which was in Hai Phong Harbor toward the end of the war. Rather than have her captured, the German captain took her out and had her scuttled. These submarines were ballasted with quicksilver (mercury), hence the interest. It was reported that there was more than $3 million in quicksilver still in this submarine; they bought the *So Fong* to feign a pleasure trip to see if they could locate the sub. In the process, the *So Fong* and all her crew were captured by the North Vietnamese. The crew was put into prison and remained there for over five months until, through diplomatic channels, the crew was released. The *So Fong* was confiscated and the north Vietnamese thrashed her looking for any evidence that might be used against the crew. Robert Vershoyle negotiated with the North Vietnamese and bought the *So Fong* to restore her. After the close of the deal he and an Australian friend named Sandy jury rigged the *So Fong* and sailed her down to Saigon.

So Fong originally had a black hull. However, in this photo she had already been converted from main-gaff to main Marconi sail (*S&S, Jordi Vidal*).

The Restoration and New Troubles

The refit in Saigon included stripping the boat to bare wood. The masts came out and the decks were taken off. She was refastened, recoppered, and given new deck rails and bulwarks. The masts were original and in good condition, but the main boom was shortened to accommodate a change from the original gaff to a Bermudan rig. All the bronze fittings were recast using old Howitzer shells. Although the region had little in the way of shipwright expertise, at the time, Vershoyle credited the Vietnamese with excellent workmanship, which has lasted to this day.

After a few months, things started to go sour in Vietnam for Robert and the *So Fong*. Their idea was that once *So Fong* had been restored, Robert and his partners were going to charter her out of the Saigon River. To do that Robert had to get a permit from the Vietnamese government. At the time the only way one could do business in Vietnam was doing a joint venture with the government. After months of negotiations and haggling, the owners decided it was not worth working with the Vietnamese and wanted to move the *So Fong* either to Hong Kong or Thailand. But the Vietnamese officers did not give them permission to leave and were trying to get back possession of the schooner. In the meantime, Robert had registered the *So Fong* out of Guernsey, so that she was a foreign flagged vessel being held captive by the Vietnamese government. Robert appealed to the British Consulate in Hanoi, but they were not in any big hurry to help Robert and his plight because they were in the midst of negotiating for oil drilling rights off the Spratley Islands.

The Escape from Vietnam

One of the crew aboard *So Fong* was married to a British lady whose brother was the managing editor with the *Daily Telegraph* in London. The crew member called him and told him that they were being held in Vietnam and were not receiving support from the British consulate. The brother-in-law called the *Daily Telegraph* office in Hong Kong and told their people to look into the matter. They contacted the British consulate and told them they were inquiring about this British registered vessel being held by the Vietnamese. With this pressure, the British officials had no other option than to try to solve this problem quickly and quietly. They approached the Vietnamese and asked if they would release the *So Fong*. The Vietnamese, to save face, told the British consulate they would not release the *So Fong* but would

So Fong has three comfortable staterooms. This stateroom has a double birth (*Jordi Vidal*).

The dining area in the saloon can host up to eight people (*Jordi Vidal*).

This stateroom has two single berths (*Jordi Vidal*).

The doghouse can be used as a shelter in bad weather and as a nav table (*Jordi Vidal*).

A well-equipped chart table serves to do the navigational work. Although it is small, it has all the necessary items for safe navigation at hand (*Jordi Vidal*).

The galley is located in the deckhouse (*Jordi Vidal*).

allow her to escape. Robert knew nothing of this arrangement. A couple of nights later Robert got a visit from the Saigon Port Captain, at two o'clock in the morning. He told Robert that now would be a good time to try out his engines and motor to Vung Tao at the mouth of the Saigon River; he could be there by first light. Robert was scared but went as suggested, started the engines and motored to Vung Tao. Robert said upon arrival there was a motor launch waiting for him and a Vietnamese officer came on board. He thought for sure he and the crew were about to be arrested. However, the officer was very friendly and told Robert that he could anchor at a certain place and buy provisions in the town. He was then informed that at around ten that night there would be an outgoing tide and it would be a good time to leave and head for open ocean. Then the officer left. Robert and his crew went into town as quick as they could, bought provisions, brought them back to boat and waited for nightfall. As soon as it was dark they weighed anchor and set sail on the outgoing tide, all the time waiting to be sunk or boarded and arrested. They initially sailed south until they got out a number of miles, then changed course for Hong Kong. The next day the English version of the *Saigon News* published a front page story of how the *So Fong* and her crew had escaped. The *So Fong* made her way to Hong Kong where some of the owner's friends had their office. There her refit was completed and Robert took her down to Phuket, Thailand, where they charted her for some years. Then they brought her to the Mediterranean to charter her out of Mallorca, Spain.

It might be interesting to note that the Vietnamese never found out why the *So Fong* was off their coast in the first place. Even though they thoroughly thrashed the interior of the *So Fong*, they did not find the most important piece of evidence. Just above the chart table, rolled up in a tight roll, was a set of original drawings of a German Super Submarine. It was still there when Robert Vershoyle sailed out of the Saigon River...

Until recently, *So Fong* was moored in Saint-Tropez under the ownership of a French classic yacht enthusiast who used her for his family and charter.

A New Beginning

The French owner sold the boat to a Canadian who fell in love with the boat after chartering her for a brief period in the spring of 2000. As a sailing and classic yacht enthusiast, he decided to return *So Fong* to her original glory and embarked on an intensive refit, which was completed in 2001. He then sold her to a Spanish businessman in 2006, who continued to honor *So Fong's* charm and class as a sailing yacht. He ultimately went into a business venture with a charter company in Mallorca, offering the vessel to interested parties for charter when he is not using the boat.

Today she is in as pristine a condition as when she was newly built, with her varnished teak neatly gleaming in the warm Mediterranean sun. Her topsides are now painted white, and she has her permanent berth in Palma de Mallorca.

So Fong now sails the Western Mediterranean. Her home port is Palma de Mallorca, in the beautiful Balearic Islands (*Jordi Vidal*).

So Fong sails again with her original gaff sails. As it can be seen in this photo, she needs the gaffs to get enough wind into her sails in a breeze to move fast (*Jordi Vidal*).

So Fong sailing to windward (*Jordi Vidal*).

So Fong under full sail and gennaker heading out of the port of Barcelona, Spain (*Jordi Vidal*).

Her deck layout is the same as in 1937. He white hull combines well with her teak deck and deckhouse. With good reason, she is a leading classic in the Balearic Islands (*Jordi Vidal*).

William F. Stone: Yachts Catering to the San Francisco Sailing Scene

BIOGRAPHY OF WILLIAM F. STONE

William F. Stone was the second out of a family with three generations of boatbuilders and designers. His father, William L. Lidstone, had been a boatbuilder in Dartmouth, England, before moving to San Francisco and changing his name to Stone in 1853. He set up a boatyard upon arrival and over the next forty years he built a variety of boats serving local needs, including about two-dozen yachts. He usually designed these yachts himself. His son was William F. Stone, who took over his father's yard in 1893 and moved it to Tiburon. From there, William subsequently moved his shop several times to different places.

As his father did, William F. Stone designed yachts for his clients, and then he built them in his own facilities. One of his most famous yachts was the racing cutter and later schooner *Yankee*, which is described in more detail in this chapter. William F. Stone's son Lester became a professional yacht designer. Most of his designs, however, were sloop and ketch-rigged.

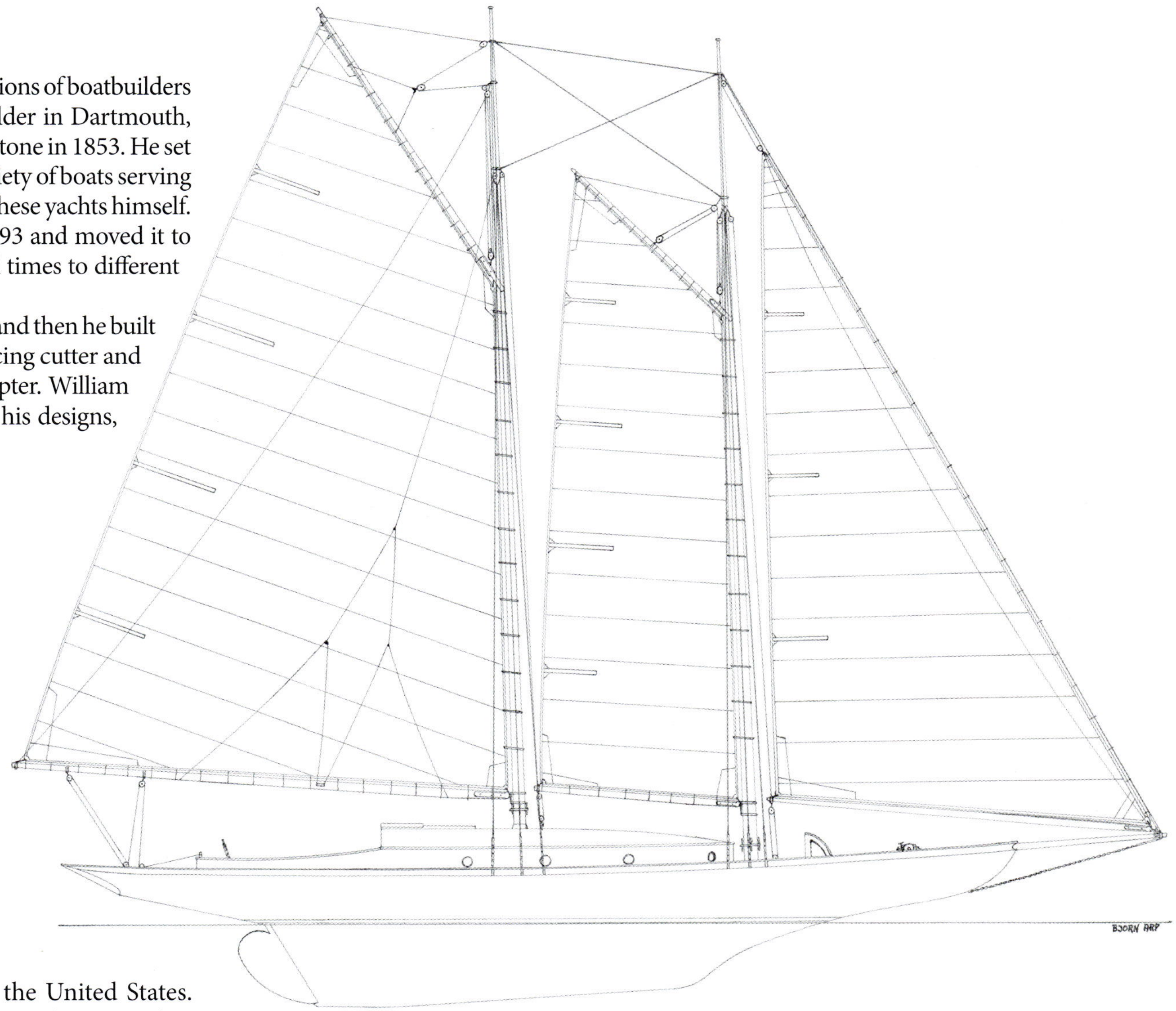

YANKEE

Type: two-mast gaff schooner
Designer: William F. Stone
Year of Construction: 1906
Shipyard: Stone Boatyard, San Francisco, California
Length on Deck: 53'0"
Length on Waterline: 37'3"
Beam: 15'0"
Draft: 5'8"
Construction: wood
Engine: Perkins 4-236, 85 hp
Owner: The Yankee LLC
Home Port: Daly City, California

Yankee is among the oldest schooner yachts still sailing in the United States. Although built as a cutter in the first place, she can be classified as a schooner in her own right, with her distinctive gaff rig and wide beam. She is still sailing today thanks to the work and love of three generations of the same family. She is the type of boat who can proudly wear the name "family cruiser."

Yankee's Premature Launching

On the morning of April 18, 1906, the sleek racing sloop *Yankee* was resting in her cradle in the Stone shipyard, located at the current site of the St. Francis Yacht Club in San Francisco, awaiting her initial launch. But the great San Francisco earthquake rudely launched *Yankee* prematurely! She was hauled back out and completed sometime later that year. In a refit project during the sixties, it was discovered that the counter planking had never been fastened, the disruption likely causing that detail to be overlooked after the premature launching.

Beautiful, finely crafted, and (obviously) smiled upon by fortune, *Yankee* survived her early start. Her current home is the marina directly across from her birthplace.

Custom designed and built by William F. Stone as an engineless gaff sloop, with the mast stepped where the foremast now sits, and a main boom that reached fully eight feet beyond the transom, she sported a very popular rig of the era. A centerboard added four feet to her 5'8" draft when sailing to windward. Winches were not and are not a part of her design, even though R. D. Ford, of the family that now owns her, was an owner and President of Barient Winch Company.

Racing *Yankee* on the Bay

Yankee's first owner was David Abecassis of the Corinthian Yacht Club. Almost immediately after launching, he won *Yankee's* first regatta, the 1906 McDonough Cup with CYC Commodore Carl Westerfield skippering. The following year he raced her in the Farallones race.

Following the tragic earthquake and fire, the Abecassis family determined to relocate east, and *Yankee* was put up for sale in 1907. She was purchased that year by Captain Charles E. Miller, a noted San Francisco yachtsman, who raced and cruised her extensively. He sailed her to Catalina and back almost every winter. During the Bay racing season, he raced her in the Universal Rule—Class N—against such well known yachts as *Nixie*, *Pronto II*, *Presto*, *Fulton G.*, *Alert*, *Mah Pe*, and *Westward*. In the company of this excellent competition, *Yankee* won the inaugural Lipton Trophy, donated for the 1915 Panama Pacific International Exposition. Captain Miller later converted the rig to a schooner, removed the centerboard and added an engine, offset to port to accommodate the trunk and shaft run for the propeller. The *Yankee* has been identified as a schooner since, which justifies her presence among the great American schooner yachts from the beginning of the twentieth century.

During Miller's ownership, *Yankee* was featured in the 1924 silent film *Wild Oranges* directed by King Vidor for Sam Goldwyn. He often took *Yankee* from her home to

This early photograph depicts *Yankee* shortly after her conversion from sloop to schooner, around 1910 (*The Yankee LLC*).

Southern California, and *Yankee's* logs showcased her popularity among celebrities of the day, as she hosted such film notables as Mary Pickford and Theda Bara.

Part of the Ford Family since 1926

In 1925, Robert Davis Ford was riding his bike home from school when he saw *Yankee* docked in San Rafael. The story goes that he told his father, Arthur Waterlow Ford (a.k.a. Skipper), "Dad, I found our boat!" Arthur and his brother Sydney Waterlow

Yankee sailing in the San Francisco Bay in the 1930s. Not much has changed since then in the activity of this family cruising schooner (*The Yankee LLC*).

Lou Cantel steering *Yankee* in 1930 (*The Yankee LLC*).

Arthur Ford, Geoff and Ray Goodwin in the Cockpit, Lou Cantel and Bing Ray on the fantail (*The Yankee LLC*).

Ford purchased *Yankee* and began to race her with gusto under the St. Francis Yacht Club flag. They won a great number of races, and cruised a great deal as well. She won the first race they entered, the Vallejo Race in 1928. She won trophy after trophy through the decades—many of which currently adorn her stateroom.

From the top of the mast in 1937 (*The Yankee LLC*).

In 1942, *Yankee* was conscripted by the United States Navy. The schooner became one of a number of St. Francis Yacht Club yachts enlisted by the Navy for submarine watch duty off the Pacific coast, doing her duty in a persistent shade of Navy gray, some of which remains on the boat below decks today. Her federal registry number, assigned by the Navy, remains her present identity. After the war the Ford family could regain the vessel, thus continuing *Yankee's* family sailing career.

At some point Arthur sold half the boat to his son Robert Davis Ford for $1. After Arthur had passed away, Robert (or RD as he was called) sold half the boat to Richard Fulton Ford, his oldest son, for another $1.

Robert D. and Richard Fulton Ford (or Dick) continued racing and cruising *Yankee* with a crew of wonderful friends and family. In 1933, *Yankee* was stolen from her marina berth, abandoned off Ocean Beach, and washed ashore. She filled with a great deal of sand before being dug out and towed off by a large steam tug. Occasional pockets of sand are still discovered in remote parts of the hull from time to time.

After *Yankee* had been the flagship of three generations of commodores of the St. Francis Yacht Club—Sydney W. Ford (1942–1943), his brother Arthur W. Ford (1951–52), Arthur's son Robert D. Ford (1972), and Bob's son Richard F. Ford (1984), the family decided in 1996 to create The Yankee LLC to establish a durable structure for the continuance of the Ford family's sailing and racing tradition. The founding members of the Yankee LLC were: Richard Fulton Ford, Janet Johnston Ford, Ellen Ford O'Connell, Gerry O'Connell (Ellen's husband), Sophie Julien O'Neal (granddaughter of Robert D. Ford), John R. McNeill (brother-in-law to Richard Fulton Ford, and good friend to the Ford Family).

Coches Prietas Harbor in 1937 (*The Yankee LLC*).

Robert D. Ford, longtime skipper of *Yankee* (*The Yankee LLC*).

Of course, the LLC also had as an objective the conservation and maintenance of the yacht. In 1998, she was hauled out to the KKMI shipyard for a "routine" survey and began an odyssey of more than two years of renovation. Her stem, most ribs, and great sections of her hull were replaced, a herculean labor performed by the master craftsmen of KKMI and the hard-working crew of the LLC.

Yankee proudly returned to the water in 2001, and through the dedicated leadership of skippers Dick Ford and John McNeill, she returned to her racing ways. The boat continues to be a great source of joy for the family's togetherness today. They further count on a reliable and wonderful crew of friends who help work and sail *Yankee*. They, too, are an essential part of the story.

Today, *Yankee* competes in all regattas held for her vintage and class, racing three to four times per year against a well-populated fleet of such yachts on San Francisco Bay. In 2005, at 99 years of age, *Yankee* posted the fastest elapsed time on the course for her division in the Annual Master Mariners Regatta, an event held since 1867. In 2008, at 102, *Yankee* won the gaff division of the Inaugural Great San Francisco Schooner Race with a margin of over forty minutes on the second placed boat. Later, in October 2008, *Yankee*, for the first time ever, won the three-race Jessica Cup Regatta, and was awarded the coveted Yankee Cup, which had been awarded her 75 years earlier. It was a long time between wins.

Helen Ford, Lester Stone, Marie Stone, Sydney, Margie, Norm, Todd at the wheel (*The Yankee LLC*).

On *Yankee*, literally all generations sail and have a hands-on approach, even the youngest family members…(*The Yankee LLC*)

Left column, top to bottom:

Also when it comes to the maintenance, all family members take part and pride in the work (*The Yankee LLC*).

When *Yankee* was hauled out in 1998, significant rot was discovered that required a total restoration. Here is the rotten bow that the family took out at the KKMI shipyard in San Francisco. Almost all the wood needed replacement (*The Yankee LLC*).

Rot was also discovered on the stern in 1998 (*The Yankee LLC*).

Right column, top to bottom:

Replanking progresses at the KKMI shipyard (*The Yankee LLC*).

The finished schooner is hauled out of the shop to get ready for relaunching (*The Yankee LLC*).

An understandably proud family gathers under *Yankee's* stern during her restoration (*The Yankee LLC*).

Since 2001, *Yankee* has been actively sailing in the San Francisco Bay, hopefully for another hundred years (*The Yankee LLC*).

Yankee sailing with her working sails in San Francisco Bay (*The Yankee LLC*).

The boat transpires "family" everywhere. Sailing is the most important social interaction for all of them. Here they are releasing each other on the helm (*The Yankee LLC*).

The round cockpit offers shelter. Because of the large dimensions of this cockpit, it is not even necessary to rig a lifeline on this boat (*The Yankee LLC*).

Reaching in a breeze, which is what *Yankee* needs to come alive (*The Yankee LLC*).

As many classic American yachts from the early twentieth century, *Yankee* is a beamy boat (*The Yankee LLC*).

Cruise of the *Yankee* 1912

One year after being rocked by the earthquake, picked up, and finished, the *Yankee* won the 1907 Farallones Race, the first ocean race ever sailed out of San Francisco Bay. Before it became a St. Francis flagship under the current family of owners, the *Yankee* had only one skipper, the redoubtable Captain Charles E. Miller, who undertook a voyage south in 1912. It was a great adventure for the day. The *Yankee* made stopovers in coastal towns and in the Channel Islands. After a stay in San Diego—and some races proving that the tall-rigged, local boats were indeed faster in light air—Miller headed for home. Here is an excerpt from his account, as the *Yankee* cleared Southern California waters:

> *At nightfall we were ten miles off Point Conception, and it was with fearful hearts that we watched the mercury tumbling again. Jack Brunswick surveyed the horizon. "Looks like it's going to start again," he said. We were in for a battle, and we knew it. The wind started moderately. In an hour or two it had increased in force until it was a gale. It whistled through the rigging and dashed spray over us until we were drenched to the skin. The sea rose fast and soon we were thrashing into it at terrific speed—rail buried—decks awash, and everything straining to the breaking point. All about us was an inky blackness. It was a weird and wonderful sensation—the creaking of ropes, the straining of the hull, and the constant hiss-boom as the* Yankee's *prow crashed through the battering waves. Toward midnight the fury of the sea became so bad that the* Yankee *began to labor and wallow. Smothered under full canvas, she was heeled at such an angle she could no longer rise quickly, and the enormous sea breaking over the bow raked her fore and aft and pored into the cockpit in great streams. "All hands on to reef!" I called. "One or two?" shouted Charles. "Double reef," I yelled back, and we all sprang to our places, tackling the big sail with frenzied energy. The task of reefing at sea is never child's play. It was almost impossible to keep one's footing, and more than once we had to let everything go and throw our arms around the boom to keep from being washed overboard by seas which had us almost entirely submerged. It took us an hour to shorten sail, but immediately the* Yankee *pulled herself together and began to make better way. Although she still buried her nose under an occasional swell, the cockpit was quite dry. We were so tired we could scarcely stand up. Dawn broke at last, and never was the day more welcome. The sky had cleared, but the gale still howled as if it was determined to get us. Whitecaps stretched in every direction. We kept out to sea, and by noon we had no sign of land on any quarter. We took the sun and found we were in latitude 34-36 and longitude 120-43-30, eighty miles at sea and a long way from our destination. The sea calmed considerably in the afternoon, and the angry waves gave way to long, sleek swells. We felt safe in venturing closer to the coast. A few miles in, we encountered a fog that blanketed us on every side and made for cautious going. At the end of the third day, however, we made out Piedras Blancas [some 95 miles north of Point Conception after three days of beating upwind; Ed.], and by nine o'clock that night we were in San Simeon Bay and anchored in smooth water. We spent the night within a stone's throw of the spot where my father and mother were shipwrecked on the clipper "Pioneer" in 1852 after a voyage from New York.*
>
> *–Captain Charles E. Miller*

Theodore D. Wells: Designing Luxury Cruising Yachts

BIOGRAPHY OF THEODORE D. WELLS

Theodore Donald Wells was born in Hudson Falls, New York, on October 22, 1875. Wells went to Europe for his education and obtained a postgraduate degree at the University of Glasgow. He was a naval architect and marine engineer, a member of the Society of Naval Architects and Marine Engineers and also the Institute of Naval Architects in London.

He began his career in 1902 as a member of the firm Herreshoff and Wells, New York City. Working with Herreshoff no doubt had an influence on his designs, which bear similarities to many of the famous Herreshoff-designed yachts of that time. Yet this partnership did not last long, in 1903 he started a new company called Wintringham and Wells. This design company lasted until 1907, when Wells began practicing his profession under his own name for the next ten years.

Wells joined the Navy Department in March 1917 and became Superintending Constructor of the Baltimore District. Notable yachts designed and constructed under his supervision were *Viking*, a 272' steel motor yacht built for George F. Baker in 1929 by Newport News, and *Karina,* a three-mast schooner built for Robert E. Tod in 1932 by Staten Island Shipbuilding. Robert Tod was a well-known offshore yachtsman and the former commodore of the Atlantic Yacht Club in Brooklyn, New York.

Not many yachts from Wells' drawing board have survived over the years until today. Among wooden yachts, only the schooner *Shearwater* is still sailing today. This yacht is beautifully preserved in New York harbor, the original home of her designer.

SHEARWATER
(Ex- *CG67004;* Ex- *Tamarit;* Ex- *Shearwater)*

Type: two-mast gaff-Marconi schooner, later converted to staysail schooner
Designer: Theodore D. Wells
Year of Construction: 1929
Shipyard: Rice Brothers, East Boothbay, Maine
Length (sparred): 81'5"
Length on Deck: 64'6"
Length on Waterline: 48'3"
Beam: 16'6"
Draft: 10'
Displacement: 64 tons
Registered Tonnage: 36 tons
Sail Area: 2,250 sq. ft.
Construction: long leaf yellow pine on white oak, silicon bronze fastened
Engine: Detroit 4-71 diesel
Owner: Manhattan by Sail, Inc.
Home Port: Manhattan, New York

***Shearwater*: Sailing in Luxury in the 1930s**

The shipyard Rice Brothers Corporation in East Boothbay, Maine, built the traditionally rigged cruising-schooner *Shearwater* in 1929. The Rice Brothers Corporation was well known for building luxury pleasure yachts and produced some 4,000 hulls over a period of 64 years. Designed by Theodore D. Wells, the keel was laid on January 4, 1929, and a news clip from the *Boothbay Register* reflects, alongside a photograph, "Tyler Hodgon at the old Tide Mill is getting out timbers for the schooner to be built at Rice's. Vessel to be built of native white oak." East Boothbay was a small coastal town with the only industry being shipbuilding. About forty boatbuilders and carpenters were employed for *Shearwater's* construction.

Shearwater was launched on May 4, 1929, and photographs in the Boothbay Register reflect her graceful and elegant lines. The schooner measured 81'5" in length overall, 64'6" on deck, and 48'3" on the waterline. Her maximum beam was 16'6", and she drew 10', weighting 36 gross tons. The schooner had round bilges, a full keel made of solid oak timbers with external lead ballast, and an attached rudder and transom stern. Her bow was high raking and her freeboard was relatively high, making for a dry and stable cruising yacht rather than a racer. The hull was constructed of carvel-planked long leaf yellow pine over double-sawn oak frames. Her floor timbers are fashioned from oak with bronze plating. The stern was later modified in laminated mahogany. With a total displacement

of 64 tons, she was heavy and needed a lot of canvas to move in light air.

Her first Captain, Leon Esterbrook of Edgarton, Massachusetts, arrived to take charge of the fitting out. Her owner, Charles E. Dunlap, was the president of the Berwind White Coal Mining Co. and the director of the Guaranty Trust Co. of New York. He belonged to the exclusive New York secret society, "the Room," founded by Vincent Astor and other prominent New York powerbrokers and intellectuals, including Winthop W. Aldrich. Regarding his yachting activity, he was a member of the Seawanhaka Corinthian Yacht Club, Oyster Bay, New York, and this became *Shearwater's* first home port after her completion in late September 1929. It was here in Oyster Bay that she first started to thrill those who sailed in luxury aboard her and those who were privileged to crew her on race day.

Since her launching and documentation in *Lloyd's Register of American Yachts* in 1929, she has had a colorful history and has been carefully maintained and restored to standards that few contemporary vessels are able to match; she is truly a piece of American maritime history.

Shearwater was sold around 1939 to Richard E. Danielson of Boston and renamed *Tamarit*, purportedly after the owner's estate in Spain. But Danielson did not own her long. By 1940, the schooner was owned by Maj. Homer B. Millard of the Millard School in Washington, DC. This school prepared young men for West Point and other military careers through a rigorous curriculum of both indoor and outdoor activity.

World War II Service

On November 7, 1942, *Shearwater* was requisitioned by the War Shipping Administration and became a member of the United States Coast Guard's coastal picket patrol during World War II. She was painted gray and bore the numbers CG67004. Based at Little Creek, Virginia, she patrolled the waters east of the Chesapeake Bay entrance and south towards Cape Hatteras. Her skipper during that period reflected on how they used their free time while out on submarine patrol to race against other yachts and in his own words, "sailed in tandem with the schooner *Lord Jim*, racing in and out of port, up and down the East Coast and winning." She was designed and built as a gaff-Marconi schooner but during this period was changed to a staysail schooner rig.

After the war, the schooner was sold to Henry Tenny. He was from Rancho Santa Fe, California. He and his daughter had never sailed, but took part in the delivery cruise from Elizabeth City, North Carolina, to the San Diego Yacht Club in 1946. She would from then on be a very special addition to this club's sailing fleet, until her departure back to the East Coast in 1970.

Tamarit in Marine Research and Charter Trade

In December 1971, Mrs. John B. Thayer of Rosemont, wife of a former trustee and treasurer, donated *Tamarit* to the University of Pennsylvania's Institute of Environmental Medicine. The university used *Tamarit* as a laboratory for research on physiological responses to the stresses of living and working underwater. Captained by James Shearson, she was fitted with compressors, generators, monitoring instruments, and a small decompression chamber.

Then she came again into private hands. She participated in many Ancient Mariner and classic yacht races in the United States as well as racing in the Bay of Islands in New Zealand while on a two and a half-year global circumnavigation in the early 1980s. It is rumored she was once dismasted in the famous Newport to Bermuda race. She was last raced by the previous owners in San Diego in May 1995 in the American Schooner Cup, where she finished second overall.

She entered the yacht charter industry in 1966 while on the West Coast sailing to the Channel Islands and was again used to generate income to keep her shipshape while owned by the University of Pennsylvania. During the chartering industry's infancy in the Caribbean, *Tamarit* was known as the "Queen of the Fleet."

Shearwater Has Become an Iconic Sight of Lower Manhattan

When the company Manhattan by Sail, Inc., led by the dynamic New York entrepreneur Tom Berton, bought *Tamarit*, they changed the name back to her original name *Shearwater*, under which she had become famous along the East Coast. While sailing for this company, she continued chartering and offering the most unique sailing experience to tourists and New Yorkers alike. She regularly passes rigid Coast Guard inspections and can carry up to 48 passengers. *Shearwater* offers an excellent opportunity to experience the ambiance of a vintage sailing vessel while delighting in the splendors of the Manhattan sky-line, the Statute of Liberty, or the beauty of the oceans beyond. The schooner was recognized and registered as a national historic landmark in March 2009.

Shearwater's decks are traditionally laid teak over oak deck beams. The deck houses are made of finished bright teak. The deck layout, fore to aft, consists of a decked pulpit over her bowsprit, an anchor windlass, and the crew's scuttle to the forecastle. Next aft is the spruce foremast followed by a butterfly hatch over the galley. Outboard to port is the life jacket storage deck box. Continuing aft, there is a butterfly hatch over the main saloon followed by the spruce main mast. Next is a deck box followed by a deck-mounted diesel day tank enclosed in teak, outboard of which are skylights to the cabins below with flanking fore-and-aft teak benches above. The deckhouse is next, followed by a depressed cockpit, teak wheel, and after deck.

Shearwater's interior layout is divided into five main spaces: the crew quarters in the forecastle, located just aft of the chain locker and the forward storage area followed by the galley. Next is the main saloon, which has retained its original decorative details and mahogany cabinetry. Aft of the main saloon is a mahogany-paneled passageway that provides access to the head, followed by a double stateroom to port and the guest cabin to starboard. The passageway leads to the deckhouse, which is accessed by a curving stairway to port. Alterations to the interior are minor and restricted to a refitted galley and the introduction of a crash bulkhead aft of the forward storage as required by the Coast Guard in order to carry passengers.

The engine room is located below the deckhouse and is accessed from the port and starboard deckhouse settees and deckhouse floor hatches. Additionally, a door to port of the staircase leading from the passageway to the deckhouse provides entry to the forward end of the engine. The vessel is equipped with a Detroit 4-71 diesel engine.

When originally built, *Shearwater* carried a gaff-Marconi rig, consisting of a Marconi mainsail and a gaff foresail. The current staysail schooner rig is believed to have been introduced during her service in the Coast Guard during World War II. The two laminated spruce masts are stiffed with stainless steel spreaders and shrouds, and the 2,250 sq. ft. sail plan includes a loose-footed jib, forward and main staysails with booms, and a Marconi main sail. The vessel is currently finished with bright caprails, white topsides, and a black bottom with a green boot-stripe.

Shearwater has her permanent berth in the Tidal Basin in downtown Manhattan (*Thomas Berton*).

Shearwater sails mainly in the New York harbor area (*Rudolph Arp*).

The deckhouse features a comfortable chart table and the stairs to the accommodations below to starboard (*Rudolph Arp*).

The master stateroom is in original condition. It features a bed, a dresser, and a desk (*Rudolph Arp*).

A central passageway runs through the entire boat, allowing access to the cabins (*Rudolph Arp*).

The saloon features a beautiful brass furnace. On the wall hangs a photo of *Shearwater* when she was still raced in California (*Rudolph Arp*).

On port in the saloon is the settee with a drop-leaf table. To the side there is a nicely crafted glass cabinet (*Rudolph Arp*).

A close-up of the original saloon cabinet (*Rudolph Arp*).

Looking into the saloon from the galley forward (*Rudolph Arp*).

From the deckhouse there is direct access to the cockpit with binnacle and wheel (*Thomas Berton*).

Among the many activities *Shearwater* offers New Yorkers, one of them is team building activities. Employees from a New York firm are seen here coordinating to set *Shearwater's* sails (*Thomas Berton*).

Also, great weddings can be held aboard *Shearwater*. Such a wedding would certainly be an extraordinary experience (*Thomas Berton*).

The schooner *Shearwater* filling her sails while she passes the Statute of Liberty (*Thomas Berton*).

Shearwater was originally rigged as a gaff-Marconi schooner. However, over the years her rig has been transformed into a staysail schooner. In any case, she has retained her distinctive looks (*Thomas Berton*).

George H. Wayland: A West Coast Designer of Handsome Lines

BIOGRAPHY OF GEORGE H. WAYLAND

George H. Wayland was born in 1885 and formed part of Ted Geary's circle of friends and acquaintances in Seattle. The two grew up together and also designed several yachts together. Wayland went to the University of Washington, and during World War I he worked for the Emergency Fleet Corporation as naval architect and marine engineer. At the end of the war, he had reached as far as the position of assistant superintendent of the Tacoma yard of that Corporation.

In 1920, Wayland joined the firm of Lee and Brinton in Seattle, when the firm changed its name to Lee, Brinton, and Wayland. In addition to their office in Seattle, Wayland opened a new office in San Francisco. Six years later, Wayland decided to start his own design office. From that point he designed many racing and cruising boats that have very much shaped the yachting scene on the West Coast. He died in 1947.

One of his well-known designs was the 56' knockabout schooner *Alotola*, built in 1927 as a sister to *Tamalmar*. She was converted into a sloop in 1949 and began a very successful racing and cruising career on the Puget Sound, where she was even named Boat of the Year in 1950. She later sailed to the Mediterranean, and belonged to a Greek owner for many years, until she went to Denmark. She still actively sails the Baltic waters with her converted sloop rig.

Another famous design, a further development of *Alotola*, was the 56' knockabout schooner *Rejoice*, which was built in 1931. She is featured in this chapter.

Wayland also designed some noteworthy motor yachts. The 50' *Marquita* from 1929, the 47' *Skeeter* from 1930, and the 57' *Graemar* from 1940 are but a few examples of his work. He also designed some working boats.

Although during his time he might not have been a highly celebrated designer, his boats have become more and more appreciated with time, and today his yachts are among the best regarded classic yachts from the West Coast.

REJOICE

Type: knockabout gaff-Marconi schooner, now staysail schooner
Designer: George H. Wayland
Year of Construction: 1931
Shipyard: George Kneas Shipyard, San Francisco
Length on Deck: 56'
Beam: 13'9"
Draft: 9'6"
Mast Height: 75'
Displacement: 32 tons
Sail Area: 1,480 sq. ft.
Construction: fir on oak, teak decks
Owner: La Conner Sea Scouts
Home Port: La Conner, Washington

Rejoice was a custom-designed schooner by George H. Wayland and built in 1931 by the George Kneas Shipyard in San Francisco, California. Rigged as a knockabout schooner, there is no bowsprit. Instead, the spoon-bow has a long and sweeping overhang forward, allowing the foresail to be fitted way before the foremast, while still reachable on deck. This makes the handling of the foresails very easy, especially in rough weather. For light winds the yacht carries a very tall main mast, allowing for a large main to be set, as well as a fisherman sail or gollywobbler. With these sails, this schooner should be able to perform well even in light winds. Although the schooner is large at 56' on deck, Wayland designed the deck to have a cabin trunk. This, in turn, allowed the yacht to have a very low freeboard and thus to have a beautiful and elegant appearance. The downside to this was seen in the interior; with a cabin trunk the headroom available below decks is reduced, compared to a flush deck. However, since *Rejoice* was not designed for long cruises, but rather for racing and weekend cruises, the option to have a cabin trunk was totally adequate.

At some point in her history, the schooner was provided with a teak deck, which adds an elegant feeling to the deck layout, while also increasing the security through its non-skid effect. Another change over time to this vessel has been the substitution of the fore-gaff sail by a staysail. The schooner thus became a staysail schooner, while originally it had been laid out as a gaff-Marconi schooner.

A few years ago the La Conner Sea Scouts club in Washington state received the schooner as a donation. It now sails out of that harbor for training and excursions, taking part in local maritime events. The Sea Scout organization tries to keep up the boat appropriately, and undertakes regular refits and repairs. Among other things, the schooner received a completely new transom, replacing the old one, which was affected by rot. Today *Rejoice* is a popular sight in La Conner, Washington.

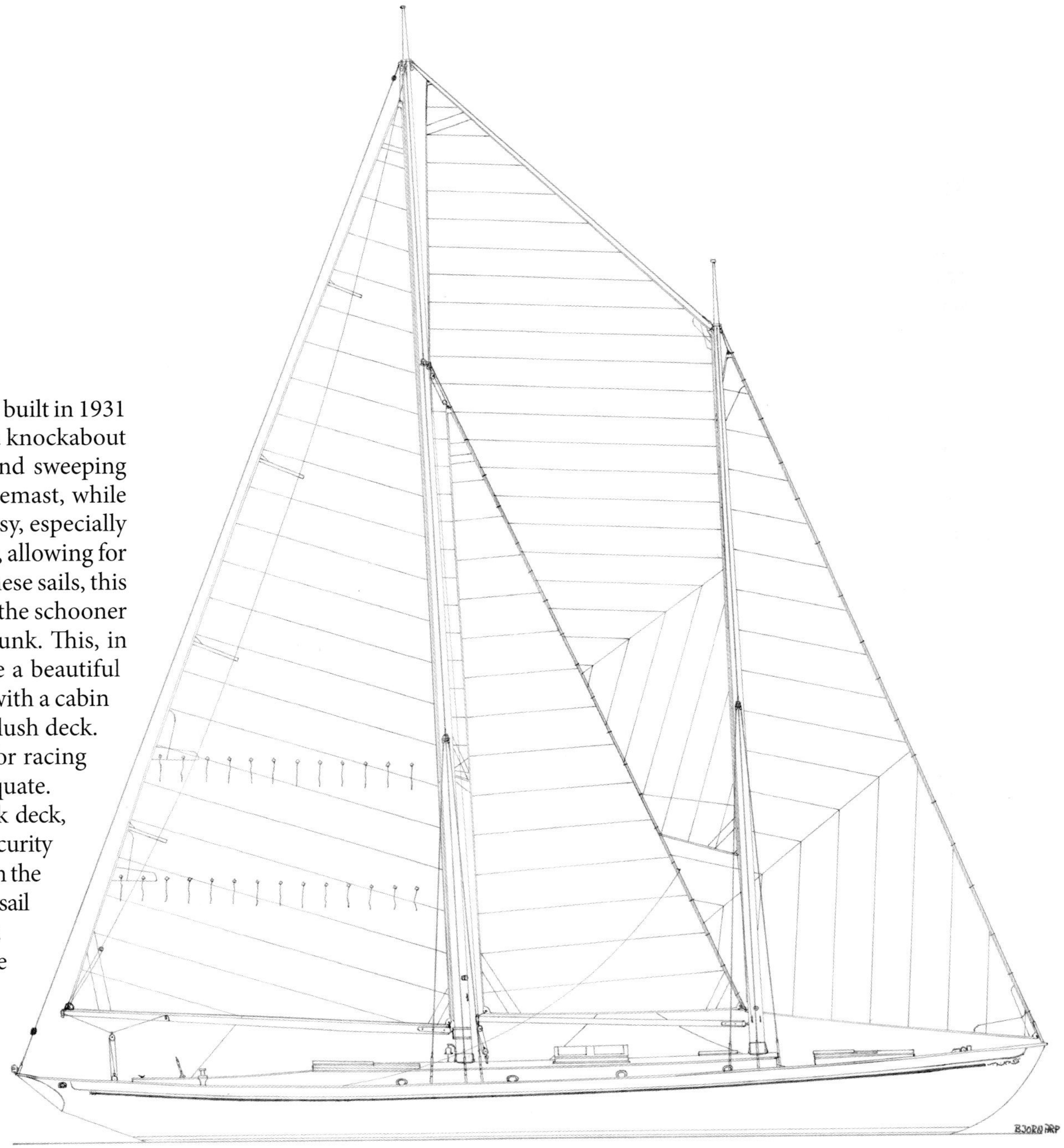

George Wayland probably designed the schooner *Rejoice* as a competitive racing schooner. Her low freeboard and large sail area clearly demonstrate that. However, her interior was comfortable enough to host her owners during longer cruises (*Michael Berman*).

Rejoice sailing to windward in a light breeze. Note the large genoa, which overlaps the foremast and almost reaches the main sail (*Michael Berman*).

Bibliography

[No Author], *The Schooner Book*. Containing the Designs and Plans of Twelve Schooner-Rigged Yachts (Reprinted from *The Rudder*), New York, The Rudder Publishing Company, 1903.

Adams, A. A. *Sea-Quences: Blue Water Sailing Adventures*. (Self-published with Xlibris, 2005).

Arp, B. *Los últimos grandes veleros españoles*. (Agualarga, Madrid, 2004).

Baader, J. *Segelsport – Segeltechnik – Segelyachten*, 2nd edition (Bielefeld/Berlin, Delius Klasing Verlag, 1963, [translation from the original Argentine edition]).

Bray, A. and M. *Designs to Inspire: From* The Rudder, *1897–1942*. (Brooklin, Maine, WoodenBoat Publications, 2000).

Carrick, R. W. and Henderson, R. *John G. Alden and His Yacht Designs*. (Camden, Maine, International Marine Publishing Company, 1983).

Chapelle, H. I. *American Sailing Craft*. (New York, Kennedy Bros., 1936).

Chapelle, H. I. *The American Fishing Schooners, 1825–1935*. (New York, Norton, 1973).

Chapelle, H. I. *The Baltimore Clipper: Its Origin and Development*. (Salem, Massachusetts, The Marine Research Society, 1930).

Compton, N. *The Great Classic Yacht Revival* (New York, Rizzoli International Publications, 2004).

Crocker, S. S. *Sam Crocker's Boats: A Design Catalog*. (Camden, Maine, International Marine Publishing Company, 1958).

Crocker, T. *The Cruise of the Zaca*. (New York and London, Harper & Brothers, 1933).

Crowninshield, B. B. *Fore'n Afters*. (Boston, B. Houghton Mifflin Company, 1940).

Del Sol Knight, L. and MacNaughton, D. B. *The Encyclopedia of Yacht Designers*. (New York / London, W.W. Norton & Company, Inc., 2006).

Fox, U. *Sailing, Seamanship and Yacht Construction*, unabridged republication of the third impression of the work originally published in 1936 by Charles Scribner's Sons. (New York, Dover Publications, 2002).

Henderson, R. *Philip L. Rhodes and His Yacht Designs*. (Camden, Maine, International Marine Publishing, 1981).

Herreshoff, L. F. *Capt. Nat Herreshoff, The Wizard of Bristol: The Life and Achievements of Nathanael Greene Herreshoff, Together with an Account of some of the Yachts He Designed*. (New York, Sheridan House, 1981).

Herreshoff, L. F. *Introduction to Yachting*. With a foreword by Boris Lauer-Leonardi. (New York, Sheridan House, 1963).

Herreshoff, L. F. *Sensible Cruising Designs*. (Camden, Maine, International Marine Publishing Company, 1973).

Herreshoff, L. F. *The Common Sense of Yacht Design*. (New York, Rudder Publishing Company, 1946).

Herreshoff, L. F. *The Compleat Cruiser: The Art, Practice, and Enjoyment of Boating*. (New York, Sheridan House, 1956).

Kaplan, D. *Mine's Bigger. The Extraordinary Tale of the World's Greatest Sailboat and the Silicon Valley Tycoon Who Built It*. (Harper, New York, 2008).

Niven, D. *The Moon's a Balloon*. (New York, Putnam, 1971).

Parker, N. *Wendameen: The Life of an American Schooner from 1912 to the Present*. (Camden, Maine, Down East Books, 2002).

Quemere, E. & Daehn, F.-J., *Die schönsten Segelyachten der Welt*. (Bielefeld, Germany, Delius Klasing Verlag, 1990).

Robinson, B. *The Great American Yacht Designers*. (New York, Alfred Knopf, 1974).

Schoettle, E. J. *Sailing Craft: Mostly Descriptive of Smaller Pleasure Sail Boats of the Day*. (New York, The Macmillan Company, 1937).

Serafini, F. *Veleros, un siglo de vela*. (Madrid, H. Kliczkowski-Onlybook, S.L., 2002).

Skene, N. L. *Elements of Yacht Design*. (New York, The Rudder Publishing Company, 1904).

Snediker, Q. and Jensen, A. *Chesapeake Bay Schooners*. (Centreville, Maryland, Tidewater Publishers, 1992).

Stephens, O. *All This and Sailing, Too: An Autobiography*. (Mystic, CT, Mystic Seaport Museum, 1999).

Taylor, R. C. *Good Boats*. (Camden, Maine, International Marine Publishing Company, 1977).

Taylor, R. C. *More Good Boats*. (Camden, Maine, International Marine Publishing Company, 1979).

Taylor, R. C. *Still More Good Boats*. (Camden, Maine, International Marine Publishing Company, 1981).

Thorndike, V. L. *Windjammer Watching on the Coast of Maine: A Guide to the Famous Windjammer Fleet and Other Traditional Sailing Vessels*, 3rd Ed. (Camden, Maine, Down East Books, 2002).

Yacht and Ship Index

(Featured yachts are marked in bold)

FLENS
BURG